STUDENT STUDY GUIDE TO ACCOMPANY FELDMAN:

SECOND EDITION

ESSENTIALS OF UNDERSTANDING PSYCHOLOGY

ROBERT S. FELDMAN
University of Massachusetts at Amherst

JOHN GRAIFF
University of Massachusetts at Amherst

ERIK J. COATS
University of Massachusetts at Amherst

MARK GARRISON
Kentucky State University

McGraw-Hill, Inc.

New York   St. Louis   San Francisco   Auckland   Bogotá   Caracas   Lisbon
London   Madrid   Mexico City   Milan   Montreal   New Delhi
San Juan   Singapore   Sydney   Tokyo   Toronto

STUDENT STUDY GUIDE TO ACCOMPANY FELDMAN:
ESSENTIALS OF UNDERSTANDING PSYCHOLOGY

 This book is printed on recycled paper containing
10%post consumer waste.

34567890 MAL MAL 90987654

ISBN 0-07-021237-6

The editors were Jane Vaicunas and Laura Lynch;
the production supervisor was Camille Mahadeo.
Malloy Lithographing, Inc., was printer and binder.

CONTENTS

P R E F A C E

This *Student Study Guide* has been prepared with several very important student concerns in mind. First, students need a comprehensive guide to supplement Robert Feldman's *Essentials of Understanding Psychology*, taking advantage of the many features in the book that support effective study habits. Second, students need practice and drill work that focus on the full content of each chapter and present practice questions that are similar to those provided in the instructor's *Test File*. In order to provide a study guide that responds to both of these concerns, the chapter summaries have been organized using the key terms and concepts in the text, and the student learning objectives have page references to the text. In addition, the definitions in the text of the key terms were used to develop the key term drills found throughout the *Study Guide*.

You will also find two practice essay questions for each chapter. These questions are intended to provide you opportunities to practice writing and critical analysis skills. In the answer key at the back of the *Study Guide*, a list of points that should be covered in your answer to each question has been provided. These questions are meant to be difficult and to require you to draw on both conceptual and factual knowledge. Some require that you apply concepts to situations, and others may require that you compare several ideas.

The introduction explains the organization of the *Study Guide* and offers tips on how to use the features of the *Study Guide* to improve your study skills and make your time spent with the text more effective.

USING

ESSENTIALS OF UNDERSTANDING PSYCHOLOGY: STRATEGIES FOR EFFECTIVE STUDY

Essentials of Understanding Psychology has been written with the reader in mind, and it therefore includes a number of unique features that will help you to maximize your learning of the concepts, theories, facts, and other kinds of information that make up the field of psychology. The *Student Study Guide* was designed to help you take full advantage of the features in the textbook, and the steps recommended for the text have been incorporated into this *Study Guide*. By using the *Guide*, you will not only get the most out of *Essentials of Understanding Psychology*, but you will also develop habits that will help you to study other texts more effectively and to think critically about material you are learning.

To take full advantage of *Essentials of Understanding Psychology*, follow these steps:

■ Familiarize yourself with the logic of the book's structure. Begin by reading the Table of Contents. It provides an overview of the topics that will be covered and gives a sense of the way the various topics are interrelated. Next, review the Preface, which describes the book's major features. Note how each chapter is divided into three or four self-contained units; these provide logical starting and stopping points for reading and studying. Also note the major highlights of each chapter: a chapter - opening outline, a Prologue, a Looking Ahead section that includes chapter objectives, Recaps and Reviews of key information following each of the major units, and — at the end of every chapter—a Looking Back section and a list of key terms and concepts. Because every chapter is structured in the same way, you are provided with a set of familiar landmarks as you chart your way through new material, allowing you to organize the chapter's content more readily. This *Study Guide* is designed to lead you through each of these steps.

■ Use a study strategy. Although we are expected to study and ultimately to learn a wide array of material throughout our schooling, we are rarely taught any systematic strategies that permit us to study more effectively. Yet, just as we wouldn't expect a physician to learn human anatomy by trial and error, it is the unusual student who is able to stumble upon a truly effective studying strategy.

Psychologists, however, have devised several excellent (and proven) techniques for improving study skills, two of which are described here. By employing one of these two procedures - known by the initials ''SQ3R'' and ''MURDER'' - you can increase your ability to learn and retain information and to think critically, not just in psychology classes but in all academic subjects. The SQ3R method includes a series of five steps, having the initials S-Q-R-R-R. The first step is to *survey* the material by reading the chapter outlines, chapter headings, figure captions, recaps, and Looking Ahead and Looking Back sections, providing yourself with an overview of the major points of the chapter. The next step — the ''**Q**'' in SQ3R — is to *question*. Formulate questions — either aloud or in writing — prior to actually reading a section of the material. For instance, if you had first surveyed this section of the book, you might jot down in the margin, ''What do ''SQ3R'' and ''MURDER'' stand for?'' The reviews that end each section of the chapter are also a good source of questions. But it is important not to rely on them entirely; making up your own questions is critical. *Essentials of Understanding Psychology* has wide margins in which you can write out your own questions. Such questioning helps you to focus in on the key points of the chapter, while putting you in an inquisitive frame of mind as well.

It is now time for the next, and most crucial, step: to *read* the material. Read carefully and, even more importantly, actively and critically. For instance, while you are reading, answer the questions you have asked yourself. You may find yourself coming up with new questions as you read along; that's fine, since it shows you are reading inquisitively and paying attention to the material. Critically evaluate material by considering the implications of what you are reading, thinking about possible exceptions and contradictions, and examining the assumptions that lie behind the assertions made by the author.

The next step — the second ''**R**'' — is the most unusual. This ''**R**'' stands for *recite*, in which you look up from the book and describe and explain to yourself, or to a friend, the material you have just read and answer the questions you have posed earlier. Do it aloud; this is one time when talking to yourself is nothing to be embarrassed about. The recitation process helps you to identify clearly your degree of understanding of the material you have just read. Moreover, psychological research has shown that communicating material to others (even imaginary others, if you are reciting aloud to yourself and not a friend) aids you in learning it in a different — and deeper — way than material which you do not intend to communicate. Hence, your recitation of the material is a crucial link in the studying process.

The final ''**R**'' refers to *review*. As we will discuss in Chapter 6, reviewing is a prerequisite to learning and remembering fully the material you have studied. Look over the information; reread the Recaps and Looking Back summaries; answer in-text review questions; and use this *Student Study Guide*. Reviewing should be an active process in which you consider how different pieces of information fit together and develop a sense of the overall picture.

An alternative approach to studying — although not altogether dissimilar to SQ3R — is provided by the MURDER system. Despite the unpleasant connotations of its title, the MURDER system is a useful study strategy.

In MURDER, the first step is to establish an appropriate **M**ood for studying by setting goals for a study session and choosing a time and place in which you will not be distracted. Next comes reading for **U**nderstanding, in which careful attention is paid to the meaning of the material being studied. **R**ecall is an immediate attempt to recall the material from memory, without referring to the text. **D**igesting the material comes next; you should correct any recall errors, and attempt to organize and store newly learned material in memory.

You should work next on **E**xpanding (analyzing and evaluating) new material, and try to apply it to situations that go beyond the applications discussed in the text. By incorporating what you have learned into a larger information network in memory, you will be able to recall it more easily in the future. Finally, the last step is **R**eview. Just as with the SQ3R system, MURDER suggests that systematic review of material is a necessary condition for successful studying.

Both the SQ3R and MURDER systems provide a proven means of increasing your study effectiveness. It is not necessary, though, to feel tied to a particular strategy; you might want to combine other elements into your own study system. For example, learning tips and strategies for critical thinking will be presented throughout *Essentials of Understanding Psychology*, such as in Chapter 6 when the use of mnemonics (memory techniques for organizing material to help its recall) are discussed. If these tactics help you to master new material successfully, stick with them.

■ Use the *Study Guide*. The *Study Guide* is designed for use of the SQ3R system. In addition to guidelines providing a systematic way of using the features of the text, the major sections of the *Study Guide* chapters include a check box to the right of the page that will help remind you of the type of activity the section involves. It is a good idea to check each item as you complete the section:

Survey: _____
Question: _____
Read: _____
Recite: _____
Review: _____

■ Study at the best time and in the right place. The last aspect of studying that warrants mention is that *when* and *where* you study are in some ways as important as *how* you study. One of the truisms of the psychological literature is that we learn things better, and are able to recall them longer, when we study material in small chunks over several study sessions, rather than massing our study into one lengthy period. This implies that all-night studying just prior to a test is going to be less effective — and a lot more tiring — than employing a series of steady, regular study sessions.

In addition to carefully timing your studying, you should seek out a special location to study. It doesn't really matter where it is, as long as it has minimal distractions and is a place that you use *only* for studying. Identifying a special ''territory'' allows you to get in the right mood for study as soon as you begin.

A final comment
By using the proven study strategies presented above, as well as by making use of the pedagogical tools integrated in the text, you will maximize your understanding of the material in *Essentials of Understanding Psychology* and you will master techniques that will help you learn and think critically in all your academic endeavors. More importantly, you will optimize your understanding of the field of psychology. It is worth the effort: the excitement, challenge, and promise that psychology holds for you is immense.

C H A P T E R

1

INTRODUCTION TO PSYCHOLOGY

DETAILED OUTLINE

Survey: ____

This detailed outline contains all the headings in Chapter 1: Introduction to Psychology. If you are using the SQ3R method, then an examination of the outline is the best way to begin your survey of the chapter.

Prologue: Flood!
Looking Ahead

The Study of Behavior and Mental Processes: The Common Link among Psychologists

Psychologists at Work
Biopsychologists: The biological foundations of psychology
Experimental psychologists: Sensing, perceiving, learning, and thinking
Developmental and personality psychologists: Understanding change and individual differences
Health, clinical, and counseling psychologists: Physical and mental health
Social, industrial-organizational, consumer, and cross-cultural psychologists: Understanding the social world
Emerging areas
The Cutting Edge Psychology in Space
Psychology's workplace
▪ **Recap and Review I**

A Science Evolves: The Past and the Future
The roots of psychology
Women in psychology: Founding mothers
Contemporary models
  Biological models: Blood, sweat, and fears
  Psychodynamic models: Understanding the inner person
  Cognitive models: Comprehending the roots of understanding
  Behavioral models: Observing the outer person
  Humanistic models: The unique qualities of homo sapiens
Psychology at Work Psychology and the Prevention of AIDS
The Links Between Psychology's Branches and Models
  Psychology's future
▪ **Recap and Review II**

Research in Psychology
  Asking the right quesitions: Theories and hypotheses

1

Finding answers: Psychological research
- **Recap and Review III**

Research Issues
The ethics of research
Threats to experiments: experimenters and subject expectations
The Informed Consumer of Psychology: Critical thinking about research
- **Recap and Review IV**

Looking Back
Key Terms and Concepts

Now that you have surveyed the chapter, read **Looking Ahead**, pages 2-4.
Question: _____
Read: _____

Focus on the questions on page 4.

Note that in this chapter, the introductory remarks continue into the heading **The Study of Behavior and Mental Processes** and the basic format of the book is described in this section which ends with the questions on page 4.

CONCEPTS AND LEARNING OBJECTIVES   *Survey:* _____

These are the concepts and the learning objectives for Chapter 1. Read them carefully as part of your preliminary survey of the chapter.

Concept 1: Psychology is a diversified scientific approach to the understanding of human and animal behavior. Psychologists explore ways of understanding behavior and mental processes as they are manifest in biology, sensation, perception, language, thought, memory, feelings, and many other processes.

1. Define psychology and explain what makes it a science. (pp. 2-4)

2. Name and describe the different branches of psychology. (pp. 4-10)

3. Distinguish the major fields of psychology: biopsychology, experimental psychology, developmental psychology, personality, and others identified in the text. (pp. 4-10)

4. Give examples of the work and workers that illustrate the goals of each field. (pp. 4-10)

Concept 2: Psychology dates its beginning with the foundation of a research laboratory in 1879 by Wilhelm Wundt. The major historical models have been structuralism, functionalism, and gestalt psychology. The five contemporary conceptual models are biological, psychodynamic, cognitive, behavioral, and humanistic.

5. Discuss the early beginnings of the science of psychology and the approaches taken by early psychologists. (pp. 11-14)

6. Define what is meant by the term model, and name each of the five models of psychology. (pp. 14-16)

7. Identify at least one distinguishing feature of each of the five models. (pp. 14-16)

8. Be prepared to distinguish how each model may investigate a particular topic. (pp. 14-16)

Concept 3: The scientific method is crucial to the way psychologists study phenomena of interest to psychology. Psychologists employ a variety of research methods to investigate the relationships between factors, to predict phenomena, and to establish cause-and-effect relationships. These research techniques include archival methods, naturalistic observation, case study, survey, correlational methods, and experiments.

9. Describe the three steps of the scientific method. (pp. 21-22)

10. Define research and distinguish archival, naturalistic observation, survey, and case study research methods. (pp. 22-24)

11. Describe how correlational research shows the relationship between two variables. (pp. 24-26)

12. Discuss the importance of replicating experiments and testing the limits of theories for proving the existence of a causal relationship between variables. (pp. 31-32)

Concept 4: When conducting research, psychologists must remain aware of a number of factors that may influence the outcome or affect the subjects in the study. The ability to evaluate and make critical judgments about research findings is an important one for our society.

13. Describe the ethical concerns involved with the use of deceptive techniques as well as the welfare of human and animal subjects. (pp. 33-34)

14. Identify the possible sources of bias that may undermine the conclusions drawn from an experiment. (pp. 34-36)

CHAPTER SUMMARY

There are several ways you can use this summary as part of your systematic study plan. You may read each concept summary and then read the corresponding pages in the text, or you may read the entire summary and then read the entire chapter in the text. As you finish each section, complete the **Recap and Review** questions that are supplied in the text.

Concept 1:   Prologue and Looking Ahead
               The Study of Behavior and Mental Processes:
                  The Common Link among Psychologists
               Psychologists at Work

Survey: _____
Read: _____

Pages 2-10

Psychology is defined as the study of behavior and mental processes.

Psychologists investigate scientifically what people do as well as their thoughts, feelings, perceptions, reasoning processes, memories, and the biological foundations of these processes. Psychology relies upon scientific method to discover ways of explaining, predicting, modifying, and improving behavior. Studying behavior and mental processes involves examining animal as well as human subjects to find the general laws that govern the behavior of all organisms.

Contrary to the mistaken view held by many people that psychology is interested only in abnormal behavior, psychologists examine a wide array of behaviors and mental processes. The specialty areas are described in the order in which they appear through the text.

Biopsychology explores the relationship between fundamental biological processes and behavior. The study is focused on the brain and the nervous system, and both diseases and healthy functions are examined for contributions to the understanding of behavior.

Experimental psychology is both a specialty and a task undertaken by most psychologists. The scientific work of psychology requires experimental methods to be applied wherever possible. **Cognitive psychology** is a specialty within experimental psychology that focuses on higher mental functions like thought, language, memory, problem solving, reasoning, and decision making, among other processes.

Developmental psychology examines how a person changes and grows throughout life, and **personality psychology** seeks to explain how a person's behavior is consistent through time and why different people respond differently to the same situation.

Several types of psychologists study ways of improving health and assessing and treating mental illness. **Health psychology** explores the relationship between physical and mental health and, especially, the role of stress in health. **Clinical psychology** is primarily involved with the assessment, diagnosis, and treatment of abnormal behavior. **Counseling psychology** focuses on the problems of adjustment to challenges that everyone faces in life. **Educational psychology** examines how educational processes occur, with close examination, for instance, of the student-teacher interaction. **School psychology** is devoted to the assessment and remedy of problems encountered in education, including both learning disabilities and emotional problems.

Social psychology studies the way people's thoughts, feelings, and actions are affected by others. Social psychologists may examine the problem of aggression or the nature of friendship. **Industrial-organizational psychology** applies psychological principles to the workplace and studies topics like job satisfaction and productivity. **Consumer psychology** applies psychological principles to consumer behavior in order to test advertising strategies and to improve products.

Emerging areas of psychology include: **environmental psychology**, the study of how physical environments influence behavior; **forensic psychology**, the study of law and psychology; and **program evaluation**, the application of psychologically based assessment principles to large programs.

About two-thirds of all psychologists are males, but recent trends show a move toward a more equal distribution. Only about 2 percent are black and another two percent are Hispanic, though the percentage for minorities currently in graduate school is higher. Though psychologists are mostly employed in academic settings, they can be found in almost every setting relating to health care and human service.

Concept 2: A Science Evolves: The Past and the Future   *Survey:* ____
                                                                  Read: ____

Pages 11-16

Trephining (drilling holes in the skull to let evil spirits escape), Hippocrates' theory of humors, Gall's ''science'' of phrenology (the association of bumps on the head with traits), and Descartes' concept of animal spirits reflect the psychology of past times. The era of scientific psychology is usually dated from the establishment by Wilhelm Wundt of an experimental psychology laboratory in 1879. Today psychology is based on a number of systems of interrelated ideas and concepts called conceptual **models**. The model associated with Wundt's laboratory is called **structuralism**. Structuralism utilized a technique called **introspection** to examine the basic elements of thought, consciousness, and emotions. Introspection required the subject to report how a stimulus was experienced. A model called **functionalism** replaced structuralism, and instead of focusing on the structure of mental elements, it focused on how the mind works and how people adapt to environments. William James was the leading functionalist in the early 1900s, and one of the leading educators, John Dewey, took a functionalist approach in his development of school psychology. **Gestalt psychology** was another reaction to structuralism that developed in the early 1900s. The gestalt approach is to view phenomena in terms of the whole experience rather than the individual elements, and they are identified with the maxim ''the whole is greater than the sum of the parts.''

Two early female contributors to the field of psychology were Leta Stetter Hollingsworth, known for the term ''gifted'' and for an early focus on women's issues, and June Etta Downey, who studied personality traits in the 1920s.

The field of psychology is now dominated by five major conceptual models. The **biological model** is focused on the study of the relationship between biological processes and behavior. The **psychodynamic model** views behavior as motivated by inner and unconscious forces over which the individual can exert little control. The psychodynamic perspective, developed by Sigmund Freud in the early 1900s, has been a major influence in twentieth-century thinking and continues to have an influence in the treatment of mental disorders. The **cognitive model** has evolved the structuralists' concern with trying to understand the mind into a study of how we internally represent the outside world and how this representation influences behavior. The **behavioral model** began as a reaction to the failure of other early perspectives to base the science of psychology on observable phenomena. John B. Watson developed behaviorism as a study of how environmental forces influence behavior. The newest model, the **humanistic model**, rejects the deterministic views of the other models and instead focuses on the unique ability of humans to seek higher levels of maturity and fulfillment and to express free will. All the major models have active practitioners and continuing research programs.

Concept 3:   The Links Between Psychology's Branches and Models   *Survey:* ____

Read: ____

Pages 16-19

Few psychologists identify exclusively with one model. However, not every branch can utilize any model equally well. Biopsychology is far more focused on the biological model than on others. Social psychologists are more likely to find the cognitive model to be more useful than the biological model.

Major issues and questions form a common ground for psychology. The question of nature versus nurture places models that focus on the environmental influences on behavior against the perspectives that focus on inheritable traits. The model to which a psychologist subscribes determines the view taken concerning this issue. The question of whether behavior is determined by conscious or unconscious forces also separates psychological models. The psychodynamic model interprets behavior as influenced by unconscious forces whereas the cognitive model may attribute abnormal behavior to faulty (conscious) reasoning. The issue of observable behavior versus internal mental processes places the behavioral model against the cognitive model. The very controversial question of free choice versus determinism raises such issues as whether abnormal behavior is a result of intentional choice. Finally, interests in individual differences conflict with the desire to find universal principles. These five key issues should not be viewed in an either-or manner, but instead they should be understood as creating a continuum along which psychologists would place themselves.

In the future, psychology is likely to become more specialized, new models will probably arise, treatment for psychological problems will become more accessible, and psychology's influence over public issues will continue to grow.

The informed consumer of psychology must be able to distinguish the popular conceptions of psychology from rigorous, research-supported claims. To be fully informed, one must know the source of information and advice, realize that complex problems are rarely solved cheaply or quickly, and recognize that there are few universal cures for anything and that even qualified, professional advice is not definitive.

Concept 4:   Research Issues

Survey: ____
Read: ____

Pages 19-36

Issues other than the quality of research are of concern to psychologists. The ethics of certain research practices come into question when the possibility exists of harm to a subject. The use of deception - like that of the Latané and Darley experiment - and similar tactics has led to the need to assure subjects and the scientific community that no harm will come to the subjects. Guidelines have been developed for the treatment of human and animal subjects, and most proposed research is now reviewed by a panel to assure that guidelines are being met. The concept of **informed consent** has become a key ethical principle. Prior to participating in an experiment, subjects must sign a form indicating that they have been told of the basic outlines of the study and what their participation will involve.

The ethical guidelines call for assurance that animals in experiments do not suffer as a consequence of being subjects in the experiment. Not only is physical discomfort avoided, but psychological discomfort is avoided as well. The need for using animals in experiments has become a controversial topic. The advantages of using animals include the fact that they have a shorter life span, that their behavior may be less complex than human behavior, and finally, that circumstances can be manipulated that could not be manipulated with humans.

Another problem that researchers face is **experimental bias**, the factors that distort the experimenter's understanding of the relationship between the independent and dependent variables. **Experimenter expectations** occur when the experimenter unintentionally conveys cues about how the subjects should behave in the experiment. **Subject expectations** are the subject's expectations about the intended goal of the experiment. The subject's guesses about the hypothesis can influence behavior and thus the outcomes. One approach is to disguise the true purpose of the experiment. Another is to use a **placebo** with the control group so that the subjects remain unaware of whether or not they are being exposed to the experimental condition. The **double-blind procedure** guards against these two biases by informing neither the experimenter nor the subject about which treatment group the subject is in.

An informed consumer of psychology must be able to evaluate research by examining the methods used to reach conclusions. Basic questions that an individual may ask include questions concerning whether the research is based in clearly specified theory, how the hypothesis was developed and tested, how well the study was conducted -- including the specific methods used -- and what the assumptions were of the researchers. If the sponsor of the research would benefit from one conclusion or another is also significant in an evaluation of research.

♦ Now that you have surveyed, questioned, and read the chapter and completed the **Recap and Review** questions, review **Looking Back**, page 36.   *Review:* ____

♦ For additional practice through recitation and review, test your knowledge of the chapter material by answering the questions in the **Key Word Drill**, the **Practice Questions**, and the **Essay Questions**.

Key Word Drill   *Recite:* ____

The following **Fill in the Blank** and **Matching Questions** test key words from the text. Check your answers with the Answer Key in the back of the *Study Guide*.

FILL IN THE BLANK

1. _Psychology is_ the scientific study of behavior and mental processes.

2. _Social Psychology_ _____ studies how people's thoughts, feelings, and actions are affected by others.

3. _environmental_ psychology is the branch of psychology that considers the relationship between people and their physical environment.

4. _Models/conceptual_ _modles_ are systems of interrelated ideas and concepts used to explain phenomena.

5. The early approach to psychology, _Structuralism_, focused on the fundamental elements that form the foundation of thinking, consciousness, emotions, and other kinds of mental states and activities.

6. A procedure used by structuralists to study the structure of the mind, _introspection_ required subjects to describe in detail what they were experiencing when they were exposed to a stimulus.

7. Another early approach to psychology, _Functionalism_ concentrated on what the mind does - the functions of mental activity - and the role of behavior in allowing people to adapt to their environments.

8. _Gestal_ _____ psychology is an approach to psychology that focuses on the organization of perception and thinking in a ''whole'' sense, rather than on the individual elements of perception.

9. The human ability to make decisions about one's life is called _Free will_ _determinism_.

10. In order to verify the results of the original experiment, the experiment must undergo _replicatus_.

11. _Experimental bias_ could lead an experimenter to an erroneous conclusion about the effect of the independent variable on the dependent variable.

12. _Experimenter Expection_ are an experimenter's unintentional message to a subject about results expected from the experiment.

13. The _Placebo_ is a biologically ineffective pill used in an experiment to keep subjects, and sometimes experimenters, from knowing whether or not the subjects have received a behavior-altering drug.

MATCHING QUESTIONS

_b_ 14. biopsychology

_a_ 15. experimental psychology

_c_ 16. cognitive psychology

_d_ 17. developmental psychology

a. The branch of psychology that studies the processes of sensing, perceiving, learning, and thinking about the world.

b. The branch of psychology that specializes in the biological basis of behavior.

c. The branch of psychology that focuses on the study of higher mental processes, including thinking, language, memory, problem solving, knowing, reasoning, judging, and decision making.

d. The branch of psychology that studies how people grow and change throughout the course of their lives.

_a_ 18. health psychology

_c_ 19. clinical psychology

_b_ 20. counseling psychology

_d_ 21. personality psychology

a. The branch of psychology that explores the relationship of psychological factors and physical ailments or disease.

b. The branch of psychology that focuses on educational, social, and career adjustment problems.

c. The branch of psychology that deals with the study, diagnosis, and treatment of abnormal behavior.

d. The branch of psychology that studies consistency and change in a person's behavior over time as well as the individual traits that differentiate the behavior of one person from another when each confronts the same situation.

_b_ 22. industrial-organizational psychology

_C_ 23. social psychology

_d_ 24. educational psychology

_a_ 25. school psychology

a. The branch of psychology devoted to assessing children in elementary and secondary schools who have academic or emotional problems and to developing solutions to such problems.

b. The branch of psychology that studies the psychology of the workplace, considering productivity, job satisfaction, and decision making.

c. The branch of psychology that studies how people's thoughts, feelings, and actions are affected by others.

d. The branch of psychology that considers how the educational process affects students.

_C_ 26. biological model

_d_ 27. psychodynamic model

_a_ 28. cognitive model

_b_ 29. behavioral model

_e_ 30. humanistic model

a. The psychological model that focuses on how people know, understand, and think about the world.

b. The psychological model that suggests that observable behavior should be the focus of study.

c. The psychological model that views behavior from the perspective of biological functioning.

d. The psychological model based on the belief that behavior is motivated by inner forces over which the individual has little control.

e. The psychological model that suggests that people are in control of their lives.

_d_ 31. Sigmund Freud   a. The first laboratory

_c_ 32. Hippocrates   b. Giftedness

_e_ 33. Franz Josef Gall   c. The four temperaments

_a_ 34. Wilhelm Wundt   d. Psychoanalysis

_f_ 35. William James   e. Phrenology

_b_ 36. Leta Stetter   f. Functionalism
         Hollingsworth

_____   _____

_d_ 37. experimental   a. The variable that is manipulated in an
         manipulation   experiment.

_c_ 38. variable   b. The experimental group receiving the
                                 treatment, or manipulation.

_e_ 39. treatment
                            c. A behavior or event that can be changed.

_b_ 40. treatment group
                            d. The change deliberately produced in an
_g_ 41. control group   experiment to affect responses or behaviors
                                 in other factors to determine causal
_a_ 42. independent variable   relationships between variables.

_f_ 43. dependent variable e. The manipulation implemented by the
                                 experimenter to influence results in a
                                 segment of the experimental population.

                            f. The variable that is measured and is
                                 expected to change as a result of
                                 experimenter manipulation.

                            g. The experimental group receiving no
                                 treatment.

PRACTICE QUESTIONS   *Recite and Review:* ____

Test your knowledge of the chapter material by answering these **True-False** and **Multiple Choice Questions.** Check your answers with the Answer Key in the back of the *Study Guide.*

TRUE-FALSE QUESTIONS

T (F) 1. A counseling psychologist would be likely to work with someone who is suicidal.

T (F) 2. Clinical psychology focuses for the most part on educational, social, and career adjustment problems.

T (F) 3. Because the psychologists involved in space research are predominantly psychoanalysts, the primary area of research interest is sexual behavior.

T (F) 4. The formal discipline of psychology has been in existence for approximately 200 years.

(T) F 5. Structuralism was the first major approach in psychology.

(T) F 6. According to the text, a model is a system of interrelated ideas and concepts used to explain phenomena.

(T) F 7. A gestalt psychologist working today might be interested in how we experience stereophonic sound.

T (F) 8. Cognitive psychology is based on the belief that behavior is motivated by inner forces over which the individual has little control.

(T) F 9. Psychologists consider one of their contributions to the AIDS crisis to be that of promoting safer sexual behavior.

(T) F 10. In addition to being a medical problem, AIDS is considered to be a behavioral disease.

T (F) 11. The primary purpose of replication in psychological experiments is to be sure that the treatment group did not in any way change, thus upsetting the controls.

T (F) 12. In humans, the best way to investigate the effects of a severe brain injury on learning is through an experiment.

MULTIPLE CHOICE QUESTIONS

1. What kind of psychologist would have a special interest in studying the aspects of Hurricane Andrew people are most likely to recall?
   a. social psychologist
   b. consumer psychologist
   c. educational psychologist
   d. cognitive psychologist

2. A motorist's car stalls on the highway on a cold, windy, and snowy night. Which type of psychologist would be most interested in whether other motorists offered assistance?
   a. a social psychologist
   b. an environmental psychologist
   c. a clinical psychologist
   d. an industrial-organizational psychologist

3. Which of the following techniques distinguishes the kind of inquiry used by scientists from that used by professionals in nonscientific areas like literature, art, and philosophy?
   a. intuitive thought
   b. scientific methods
   c. common sense
   d. construction of new theoretical models

4. According to the text, the definition of psychology must include:
   a. human consciousness and memory.
   b. mental, behavioral, and biological processes.
   c. studying why people think the way they do.
   d. understanding how people will behave in a wide range of circumstances.

5. Biopsychology is the branch of psychology that specializes in:
   a. the biological basis of behavior.
   b. how people grow and change both physically and socially throughout their lives.
   c. studying why people think the way they do.
   d. understanding how people behave in a wide range of circumstances.

6. The relationship of experimental psychology and cognitive psychology might best be described as:
   a. only experimental psychology conducts experiments.
   b. cognitive psychology is not interested in studying learning.
   c. cognitive psychology is a specialty area of experimental psychology.
   d. experimental psychology is a specialty of cognitive psychology.

7. Psychologists often work with several major theoretical models. Which model below does **not** belong among the rest?
   a. cognitive   c. therapeutic
   b. psychodynamic   d. behavioral

8. Professor Greenland has identified a trait he calls persistence, and he has begun to conduct research on the consistency of this trait in various situations. Dr. Greenland is most likely:
   a. a social psychologist.   c. an educational psychologist.
   b. a cross-cultural psychologist. d. a personality psychologist.

9. Health psychology is the branch of psychology that explores:
   a. educational, social, and career adjustment problems.
   b. the relationship between psychological factors and physical ailments.
   c. the diagnosis and treatment of abnormal behavior.
   d. the processes of perceiving, learning, and thinking about the world.

10. Which of the following health-oriented psychologists is involved primarily in administering tests and utilizing evaluative instruments for the assessment of abnormal behavior?
    a. counseling psychologist
    b. health psychologist
    c. personality psychologist
    d. clinical psychologist

11. According to the text, the major distinction between educational and school psychology is that:
    a. educational psychology is devoted to improving the education of students who have special needs, and school psychology is devoted to increasing achievement in all students.
    b. school psychology is devoted to improving the schooling of students who have special needs, and educational psychology is devoted to better understanding of the entire educational system.
    c. school psychology attempts to examine the entire educational process, and educational psychology looks at individual students.
    d. educational psychology attempts to examine the entire educational process, and school psychology is devoted to assessing and correcting academic and school-related problems of students.

12. The ways in which people respond to advertisements is an area of study for:
    a. consumer psychologists.
    b. industrial psychologists.
    c. clinical psychologists.
    d. social psychologists.

13. Questions such as how we are influenced by others and why we form relationships with each other are studied by:
    a. counseling psychologists.
    b. social psychologists.
    c. clinical psychologists.
    d. health psychologists.

14. The effectiveness of government programs such as Head Start and Medicaid would be the focus of psychologists interested in:
    a. experimentation.
    b. evaluation.
    c. forensics.
    d. cognition.

15. Of the following, an environmental psychologist would be most likely to study:
    a. the impact of smoking on health.
    b. experimental ethics.
    c. the effects of crowding on behavior.
    d. program effectiveness.

16. An architect interested in designing an inner-city apartment building that would not be prone to vandalism might consult with:
    a. a clinical psychologist.
    b. a school psychologist.
    c. a forensic psychologist.
    d. an environmental psychologist.

17. According to the discussion in the text, the problem that psychology faces of losing its diversity as a discipline can best be corrected by:
    a. social psychologists becoming more active trainers of psychologists.
    b. more studies in cultural psychology based on demonstrating the importance of diversity.
    c. increasing the ethnic sensitivity of counseling and clinical psychologists.
    d. increasing the number of minorities in the profession.

18. Most psychologists work in:
    a. hospitals.   c. industry.
    b. public schools.   d. universities.

19. Today's scientists believe that the purpose of trephining was to:
    a. enable one person to read another's mind.
    b. allow evil spirits to escape.
    c. increase telekinetic powers.
    d. heal the patient of mental illness.

20. Who established the first psychology laboratory, and when?
    a. William James, 1875
    b. Sigmund Freud, 1899
    c. June Etta Downey, 1884
    d. Wilhelm Wundt, 1879

21. Wilhelm Wundt trained people to describe carefully, in their own words, what they experienced upon being exposed to various stimuli. This procedure for studying the mind is called:
    a. cognition.   c. perception.
    b. mind expansion.   d. introspection.

22. Functionalism shifted the focus of study in psychology from elements to:
    a. cognitions.   c. biological underpinnings.
    b. processes.   d. observable behaviors.

23. Which pair of individuals have been associated with functionalism?
    a. Leta Stetter Hollingsworth and June Etta Downey
    b. Sigmund Freud and Wilhelm Wundt
    c. William James and John Dewey
    d. Wilhelm Wundt and William James

24. ''The whole is greater than the sum of the parts'' is a postulate of:
    a. structuralism.   c. gestalt psychology.
    b. functionalism.   d. behaviorism.

25. Gestalt psychology was developed:
    a. around 1850.   c. during the early 1900s.
    b. in 1879.   d. in the 1950s.

26. Leta Stetter Hollingsworth is known for her contribution of:
    a. the concept of a kindergarten.
    b. the concept of gifted.
    c. the idea that males and females were psychologically different.
    d. the study of personality traits.

27. June Etta Downey is known for her work in:
    a. personality traits.
    b. establishing the first psychology laboratory in 1884.
    c. the concept of the kindergarten.
    d. the psychoanalysis of women.

28. The influence of inherited characteristics on behavior would be studied with the:
    a. cognitive model.   c. behavioral model.
    b. psychodynamic model.   d. biological model.

29. Which of the following sources of evidence would be the least acceptable to behaviorists like John B. Watson?
    a. evidence gathered using introspective
    b. evidence from intelligence tests
    c. evidence regarding emotional growth and development
    d. evidence from perception and sensation experiments

30. The _____ model of psychology places the greatest emphasis on the environment.
    a. biological   c. behavioral
    b. psychodynamic   d. humanistic

31. According to the psychodynamic approach, dreams and slips of the tongue:
    a. represent a distortion of what a person is really feeling.
    b. come from subconscious activity.
    c. become more prevalent as a person grows older.
    d. can be controlled consciously with a little effort.

32. A psychodynamic psychologist would be most interested in:
    a. the learning process.
    b. our perceptions of the world around us.
    c. dreams.
    d. the functioning of the brain.

33. Sigmund Freud believed that behavior is motivated by:
    a. subconscious inner forces.
    b. a desire to achieve personal fulfillment.
    c. the natural tendency to organize data through perception.
    d. inherited characteristics.

34. Which of the following types of psychologist would most likely be involved in the study of the physiological aspects of AIDS?
    a. clinical psychologist   c. health psychologist
    b. biopsychologist   d. social psychologist

35. The humanistic model places an emphasis on:
    a. observable behavior.   c. free will.
    b. inner forces.   d. understanding concepts.

36. More than the others listed below, _____ psychologists frequently employ many, and sometimes all, of the major models of psychology.
    a. experimental   c. clinical
    b. social   d. industrial

37. Which of the following types of psychologists would be most interested in the ''unconscious'' side of the conscious versus unconscious determinants of behavior issue?
    a. a behavioral experimental psychologist
    b. a humanistic psychologist
    c. a psychodynamic clinical psychologist
    d. a structuralist

38. Carrying out research designed to lend support to or to refute an explanation of a phenomenon is a main step in:
    a. scientific method.
    b. developing theories.
    c. naturalistic observation.
    d. statistical analysis of significance.

39. According to the text, identifying questions of interest is one of the steps of:
    a. survey research.   c. scientific method.
    b. case study methods.   d. experimental design.

40. Operationalization requires that:
    a. data always be useful.
    b. procedures are followed exactly.
    c. variables are correctly manipulated.
    d. predictions be made testable.

41. A prospective executive may undergo intensive interviews and extensive psychological testing. The executive may also have to provide references from previous and current occupational and personal sources. This process is most similar to:
    a. a survey.   c. naturalistic observation.
    b. an experimental study.   d. a case study.

42. When the strength of a relationship is represented by a mathematical score ranging from +1.0 to -1.0, we are dealing with a:
    a. dependent variable.   c. correlation.
    b. manipulation.   d. treatment.

43. Which of the following statements is **not** true?
    a. A correlation of 1.0 means that there is a strong positive relationship between two factors.
    b. A correlation of 0.0 means that there is no systematic relationship between two factors.
    c. Correlations tell us that there is a relationship between two factors.
    d. Correlations tell us that one factor is caused by another.

44. Professor Taylor has been studying the effects of light on the tolerance of stress in monkeys for several years. Each experiment varies the conditions slightly, but usually only one factor is altered each time. Dr. Taylor is most likely trying to:
    a. develop a new statistical test.
    b. operationalize her hypothesis.
    c. formulate a new hypothesis.
    d. test the limits of her theory.

45. Informed consent can be dispensed with if a subject:
    a. is assigned to the control group.
    b. has spent time in a mental institution.
    c. is merely given a placebo.
    d. is part of a purely observational study in a public location.

46. Whether a behavioral scientist uses human or animal subjects in an experiment, there are _____ which the scientist must satisfy in order not to violate the rights of the participants.
    a. moral obligations   c. professional standards
    b. religious principles   d. ethical guidelines

47. Deception - disguising the true nature of a study - is sometimes used in experiments in order to:
    a. eliminate subject expectations.
    b. confuse the subject.
    c. eliminate experimenter expectations.
    d. confuse the experimenter.

48. A pill without any significant chemical properties that is used in an experiment is called a(n):
    a. control.   c. dependent variable.
    b. placebo.   d. independent variable.

49. The double-blind procedure is used to:
    a. keep the confederate from influencing other subjects.
    b. eliminate dependent variables.
    c. control the placebo effect.
    d. eliminate subject and experimenter expectations.

ESSAY QUESTIONS   *Recite and Review:* ____

Essay Question 1.1: *Conceptual Models*

Describe the conceptual model that best fits your current understanding of why people behave the way that they do. Be sure to explain why you selected this particular model. Which models do you reject? Why?

_____

_____

_____

_____

_____

_____

_____

_____

_____

_____

_____

_____

_____

_____

_____

_____

_____

_____

_____

Essay Question 1.2: *Deceptive Practices*

Imagine yourself in the Latané and Darley experiment as one of the subjects who hesitates to respond because of the diffusion of responsibility (you thought there were others around to help). Following the experiment, you discover that your behavior has been deceptively manipulated and that the epileptic seizure was staged. What are your reactions to this deception? What are the ethical constraints on the researchers? Can you suggest alternatives to this kind of research? Is it justified?

_____

_____

_____

_____

_____

_____

_____

_____

_____

_____

_____

_____

_____

_____

_____

_____

_____

C H A P T E R
2

THE BIOLOGY UNDERLYING BEHAVIOR

<u>**DETAILED OUTLINE**</u>   *Survey: ____*

This detailed outline contains all the headings in Chapter 2: The Biology Underlying Behavior. If you are using the SQ3R method, then an examination of the outline is the best way to begin your survey of the chapter.

Prologue: Andrea Fyie
Looking Ahead

Neurons: The Elements of Behavior
   The structure of the neuron
   Firing the neuron
 ▪ **Recap and Review I**

Where Neuron Meets Neuron: Bridging the Gap
   Varieties of neurotransmitters

The Nervous System
   Neuronal architecture
   Central and peripheral nervous systems
   Activating the autonomic nervous system
 ▪ **Recap and Review II**

The Brain
   Studying the structure and functions of the brain
   The central core: Our old brain
The Cutting Edge Are Men's and Women's Brains Different?
   The limbic system: Beyond the central core
 ▪ **Recap and Review III**
   The cerebral cortex: Up the evolutionary ladder
        The motor area of the brain
        The sensory area of the brain
        The association area of the brain
   The specialization of the hemispheres: Two brains or one?
Psychology at Work The Commercial Value of the Brain
   The split brain: Exploring the two hemispheres
   Brain modules: The architecture of the brain, revisited

The Endocrine System: Of Chemicals and Glands
The Informed Consumer of Psychology Learning to Control Your Heart - and
   Brain - through Biofeedback

 ▪ **Recap and Review IV**

Looking Back
Key Terms and Concepts

Now that you have surveyed the chapter, read **Looking Ahead**, pages 40-42.
    Question: _____
        Read: _____

Focus on the questions on page 41.

CONCEPTS AND LEARNING OBJECTIVES   *Survey:* _____

These are the concepts and the learning objects for Chapter 2.   Read them
carefully as part of your preliminary survey of the chapter.

Concept 1: The biology of the organism affects its behavior. The brain and its
    basic building blocks, the neurons, are the biological components that have
    the greatest influence on behavior.

1. Understand the importance placed on the biology that underlies behavior
   and identify reasons why psychologists study these biological
   underpinnings - especially the brain and the nervous system. (pp. 40-42)

2. Describe the structure of the neuron and its parts. (pp. 42-45)

3. Describe the action potential and the resting potential of the neuron and
   how the neuron communicates its electrochemical message from initial
   stimulation to transmission across the synapse. (pp. 45-46)

Concept 2: Neurotransmitters are critical to various functions because they are
    the means by which messages are communicated from one neuron to another. The
    main divisions of the nervous system are the central and peripheral division,
    the autonomic and somatic division, and the sympathetic and parasympathetic
    divisions.

4. Name key neurotransmitters and their functions and describe their known
   or suspected roles in behavior as well as in illnesses like Alzheimer's
   and Parkinson's diseases. (pp. 47-52)

5. Describe the major divisions of the nervous system, including the
   central and the peripheral, the parasympathetic and sympathetic, the
   autonomic and motor divisions. (pp. 52-55)

Concept 3: The central core and the limbic system control and monitor basic life
    functions as well as self-preservation needs.

6. Name the techniques used to map and study the brain and describe some of
   the anatomical differences between the brain in males and females that
   have been discovered using these techniques. (pp. 57-59)

7. Name the components of the central core and the limbic system and
   describe the functions of their individual parts. (pp. 59-63)

Concept 4: The higher functions are associated with the cerebral cortex. The role of the endocrine system is to communicate hormones that control growth and behavior through the bloodstream.

8. Name the major areas of the cerebral hemispheres, especially the lobes and the cortex areas, and describe the roles of each area in behavior. (pp. 64-69)

9. Discuss the issues involved with brain specialization, brain lateralization, and the split-brain operation, and what has been learned about the two hemispheres from the procedure. (pp. 69-74)

10. Name the major hormones and describe the function of the endocrine system. (pp. 74-75)

11. Describe how biofeedback can be used to control some of the basic biological processes. (pp. 75-76)

CHAPTER SUMMARY

There are several ways you can use this summary as part of your systematic study plan. You may read each concept summary and then read the corresponding pages in the text, or you may read the entire summary and then read the entire chapter in the text. As you finish each section, complete the Recap and Review questions that are supplied in the text.

Concept 1: Prologue and Looking Ahead
      Neurons: The Elements of Behavior

Survey: ____
Read: ____

Pages 40-47

Advanced brain scanning techniques, like positron emission tomography, can now give extremely detailed and accurate pictures of the brain to aid the diagnosis of disease. This and other techniques have been applied to the study of the brain and the <u>nervous system</u>, and as a result, psychologists' understanding of the brain has increased dramatically in the past few years. **Neuroscientists** examine the biological underpinnings of behavior, and **biopsychologists** explore the ways the biological structures and functions of the body affect behavior.

Specialized cells called **neurons** are the basic component of the nervous system. There are between <u>100 billion</u> and <u>200 billion</u> neurons in the body. Every neuron has a nucleus, a cell body, and special structures for communicating with other neurons. <u>Dendrites</u> are the receiving structures and <u>axons</u> are the sending structures. At the ends of the axons are **terminal buttons** that serve to connect with other neurons. The message is communicated in one direction from the dendrites, through the cell body, and down the axon to the terminal buttons. A fatty substance known as the myelin sheath surrounds the axons of most neurons and serves as an insulator for the electrical signal being transmitted down the axon. It also speeds the signal. In multiple sclerosis, the myelin sheath disintegrates, causing short circuits where electrical messages are communicated to nearby axons of other neurons. Certain substances necessary for the maintenance of the cell body travel up the axon to the cell body in a reverse flow. Amyotrophic lateral sclerosis, or Lou Gehrig's disease, is a failure of the neuron to work in this reverse direction. Epilepsy is thought to result when dendrites in certain areas of the brain ''leak'' information that is supposed to travel to the cell body.

The neuron communicates its message by ''firing,'' which refers to its changing from a **resting state** to an **action potential**. Neurons express the action potential in an all-or-nothing fashion, that is, firing only when a certain level of stimulation is reached. The stimulation involves a reversal of the electrical charge inside the neuron from -70 millivolts to a positive charge. This reversal flows very rapidly through the neuron, and the neuron quickly returns to its resting state. Just after the action potential has passed, the neuron is in an **absolute refractory period**. During this period, the neuron cannot fire again. A relative refractory period follows, during which the neuron can fire if a very strong stimulus is present. The thickness of the myelin sheath and the diameter of the axon determine the speed of the action potential, with action potentials traveling down thicker axons much more rapidly. A neuron can fire as many as 1000 times per second if the stimulus is very strong. However, the communicated message is a matter of how frequently or infrequently the neuron fires, not the intensity of the action potential, since the action potential is always the same strength.

Concept 2:   Where Neuron Meets Neuron: Bridging the Gap   *Survey:* ____
**   The Nervous System   *Read:* ____**

Pages 47-57

The message of a neuron is communicated to the receiving neuron by the release of a **neurotransmitter** across the **synapse**. The synapse is the small space between the terminal button of one neuron and the dendrite of the next. Neurotransmitters can either excite or inhibit the receiving neuron. The exciting neurotransmitter is called an **excitatory message** and the inhibiting neurotransmitter is called an **inhibitory message**. A neuron must summarize the excitatory and inhibitory messages it receives in order to fire. Once the neurotransmitters are released, they lock into special sites on the receiving neurons. They must then be reabsorbed through **reuptake** into the sending neuron or deactivated by enzymes.
      About fifty neurotransmitters have been found. Neurotransmitters can be either exciting or inhibiting depending on where they are released in the brain. One common neurotransmitter is **acetylcholine (ACh)**, which produces contractions of skeletal muscles. **Alzheimer's disease** has been associated with the restricted production of ACh in areas of the brain. **Gamma-amino butyric acid (GABA)** is one of the major inhibiting neurotransmitters. The poison strychnine apparently causes death by restricting the flow of GABA across the synapse so that neurons fire without inhibition, leading to convulsions. Drugs like Valium increase the activity of GABA. **Dopamine (DA)** has both an inhibitory and an excitatory effect, depending on location. A loss of the ability to produce dopamine has been found in Parkinson's disease patients. Some researchers believe that overproduction of dopamine may be responsible for schizophrenia and other disturbances. **Endorphins** are the body's natural morphine, and they interact with sites called **opiate receptors**. Endorphins reduce pain and produce a state of euphoria. This state is often called runner's high when experienced by joggers. Placebos and acupuncture may be effective because they cause endorphins to be released.
      Neurons are linked into **neural networks** which allow the brain to modify information as it travels to and from the brain. Computational neuroscience is devoted to understanding these neural networks. Several circuit patterns have been identified. **Linear circuits** transmit information from one neuron to another. **Multiple-source/convergent circuits** transmit information from many neurons to one neuron. **Single-source/divergent circuits** transmit information from one neuron to many neurons. The total number of connections estimated in the brain is about 1 quadrillion.
      The nervous system is divided into the **central nervous system** - composed of the brain and the spinal cord - and the **peripheral nervous system**. The spinal cord is a bundle of nerves that descend from the brain. The main purpose of the spinal cord is as a pathway for communication between the brain and the body.

Some involuntary behaviors, called **reflexes**, involve messages that do not travel to the brain but instead stay entirely within the spinal cord. **Sensory (afferent) neurons** bring information from the periphery to the brain. **Motor (efferent) neurons** carry messages to the muscles and glands of the body. **Interneurons**, a third type of neuron, connects the sensory and the motor neurons, carrying messages between them. The spinal cord is the major carrier of sensory and motor information. Its importance is evident in injuries that result in **paraplegia**, a condition in which the sufferer cannot move the bottom half of his or her body. While basic reflexes may stay intact, the paraplegic cannot voluntarily control muscles nor can sensations be experienced. The **peripheral nervous system** branches out from the spinal cord. It is divided into the **somatic division**, which controls muscle movement, and the **autonomic division**, which controls basic body functions like heartbeat, breathing, glands, and lungs.

The role of the autonomic nervous system is to activate the body through the **sympathetic division** and then to modulate and calm the body through the **parasympathetic division**. The sympathetic division prepares the organism for stressful situations, and the parasympathetic division returns the body to help the body recover after the emergency has ended.

Concept 3: The Brain

Survey: ____
Read: ____

Pages 57-64

The brain weighs about three pounds and is composed of billions of neurons. Some knowledge of the structure and function of the brain has been gained by studying the results of injuries to the brain, and today, much additional knowledge is being added by using **brain scans**, techniques that picture the brain without having to perform an autopsy. The **electroencephalogram (EEG)** records the electrical activity of the brain by using electrodes placed outside the skull. **Computerized axial tomography (CAT)** utilizes computer imaging to construct an image that is made by combining thousands of separate x-rays taken from different angles. **Magnetic resonance imaging (MRI)** uses powerful magnets to create a picture of the brain. **Positron emission tomography (PET)** scan records the location of radioactive isotopes in the brain during brain activity, thus allowing a picture of the activity.

Because it evolved very early, the **central core** of the brain is referred to as the old brain. It is composed of the **medulla**, which controls functions like breathing and heartbeat, the **pons**, which transmits information helping to coordinate muscle activity on the right and left halves of the body, and the **cerebellum**, which coordinates muscle activity. The reticular formation is a group of nerve cells that serve to alert other parts of the brain to activity. The central core also includes the **thalamus**, which transmits sensory information, and the **hypothalamus** which maintains **homeostasis** of the body's environment. The hypothalamus also plays a role in basic survival behaviors like eating, drinking, sexual behavior, aggression, and child-rearing behavior. The **Cutting Edge** discusses the physical differences between male and female brains. The major difference that has been discovered is that the connecting fibers between the two hemispheres, called the **corpus callosum**, have different shapes in men and women.

The **limbic system** is a set of interrelated structures that includes pleasure centers, structures that control eating, aggression, reproduction, and self-preservation. Intense pleasure is felt through the limbic system, and rats with electrodes implanted in their limbic systems will often stimulate their pleasure centers rather than eat. The limbic system also plays important roles in learning and memory.

Concept 4: The Brain (continued)   *Survey:* ____
          The cerebral cortex: Up the evolutionary ladder   *Read:* ____
          The Endocrine System: Of Chemicals and Glands
                                                                Pages 64-77

The **cerebral cortex** is identified with the functions that allow us to think and
remember. A cortex is a covering, and the cerebral cortex is deeply folded in
order to increase the surface area of the covering. The cortex is divided into
four main sections, or **lobes**. They are the **frontal lobes**, the **parietal lobes**, the
temporal lobes, and the **occipital lobes**. The cortex and its lobes have been
divided into three major areas - the motor area, the sensory area, and the
association area.

The **motor area** of the brain is responsible for the control and direction of
voluntary muscle movements. There are three areas devoted to the **sensory area**,
that of touch, called the **somatosensory area**, that of sight, and that of hearing.
The **association area** takes most of the cortex and is devoted to mental processes
like language, thinking, memory, and speech. The condition called **apraxia** occurs
when a person cannot integrate activities rationally or logically. An **aphasia**
occurs when a person has difficulty with verbal expression. **Broca's aphasia**
refers to difficulty with the production of speech. Wernicke's aphasia refers to
brain damage that involves the loss of the ability to understand the speech of
others.

The two halves of the brain are called **hemispheres**. The left hemisphere
controls the right side of the body, and the right hemisphere controls the left
side. Since each hemisphere appears to have functions that it controls, it is
said that the brain is lateralized. The left hemisphere concentrates on verbally
based skills, like thought and reason. The right half deals with spatial
understanding and pattern recognition. This **lateralization** appears to vary
greatly with individuals, and there may be general differences between the brains
of males and females, as males appear to have language more lateralized. The two
halves of the brain are, however, quite interdependent on each other.

Roger Sperry pioneered the study of the surgical separation of the two
hemispheres for cases of severe epilepsy. Those who have had the procedure are
called **split-brain patients**.

Brain modules refers to a current way of understanding how the brain works.
Brain modules are units of the brain that carry out specific tasks. These modules
incorporate components of different brain areas and parts and specialize in the
tasks. They also appear to operate relatively independently of each other.

The **endocrine system** is a chemical communication network that delivers
hormones into the bloodstream which, in turn, influence growth and behavior.
Sometimes called the ''master gland,'' the **pituitary gland** is the major gland of
the endocrine system. The hypothalamus regulates the pituitary gland.

The informed consumer of psychology discusses the use of **biofeedback** to
control a variety of body functions. It has been successfully applied to the
control of headaches, blood pressure, and other medical and physical problems.

♦ Now that you have surveyed, questioned, and read the chapter and completed the
   Recap and Review questions, review **Looking Back**, pages 77-78. *Review:* ____

♦ For additional practice through recitation and review, test your knowledge of
   the chapter material by answering the questions in the **Key Word Drill**, the
   Practice Questions, and the **Essay Questions**.

KEY WORD DRILL

The following **Fill in the Blank** and **Matching Questions** test key words from the text. Check your answers with the Answer Key in the back of the *Study Guide*.

FILL IN THE BLANK

1. The psychologists and researchers who study the nervous system are called _____, while the psychologists who study the ways biological structures and body functions affect behavior are known as _____.

2. _____ _____ follows the triggering of a neuron, and during this period, the neuron cannot fire again, no matter how much stimulation it receives.

3. _____ _____ is an electric nerve impulse that travels through a neuron when it is set off by a ''trigger,'' changing the cell's charge from negative to positive.

4. The type of neuron called _____ _____ acts to reduce the experience of pain.

5. _____ usually results from an injury to the spinal cord and refers to the inability to voluntarily move any muscles in the lower half of the body.

6. An organism tries to maintain an internal biological balance or steady state through the process called _____.

7. The _____ _____ _____ scan produces a powerful magnetic field in order to provide a detailed, computer generated image of brain structure or any other biological structure.

8. The _____ records the electrical signals being transmitted inside the brain.

9. When one hemisphere of the brain controls a specific function, the function is considered _____.

10. The term _____ _____ refers to the separate units of the brain that carry out specific tasks.

MATCHING QUESTIONS

_a_ 11. neurons

_e_ 12. dendrites

_c_ 13. axon

_b_ 14. terminal buttons

_d_ 15. myelin sheath

a. Specialized cells that are the basic elements of the nervous system that carry messages.

b. Small branches at the end of an axon that relay messages to other cells.

c. A long extension from the end of a neuron that carries messages to other cells through the neuron.

d. An axon's protective coating, made of fat and protein.

e. Clusters of fibers at one end of a neuron that receive messages from other neurons.

_____ 16. neurotransmitter

_____ 17. excitatory message

_____ 18. inhibitory message

_____ 19. neural networks

_____ 20. linear circuits

_____ 21. multiple-source/ convergent circuits

_____ 22. single-source/divergent circuits

a. A chemical secretion that makes it more likely that a receiving neuron will fire and an action potential will travel down its axons.

b. A hierarchical network of neurons into a potentially vast number of recipients.

c. A network of neurons in which a single neuron transmits messages to a potentially vast number of recipients

d. A chemical secretion that prevents a receiving neuron from firing.

e. A chemical that carries the message from one neuron to another when secreted as the result of a nerve impulse.

f. Groups of organized communication links between cells.

g. Neurons joined in a single line, receiving and transmitting messages only to the next neuronal link.

_____23. peripheral nervous system

_____24. somatic division

_____25. autonomic division

_____26. sympathetic division

_____27. parasympathetic division

a. The part of the autonomic division of the peripheral nervous system that calms the body, bringing functions back to normal after an emergency has passed.

b. All parts of the nervous system except the brain and the spinal cord (includes somatic and autonomic divisions).

c. The part of the nervous system that controls involuntary movement (the actions of the heart, glands, lungs, and other organs).

d. The part of the autonomic division of the peripheral nervous system that prepares the body to respond in stressful emergency situations.

e. The part of the nervous system that controls voluntary movements of the skeletal muscles.

_____

_____28. central core

_____29. medulla

_____30. pons

_____31. cerebellum

_____32. reticular formation

_____33. thalamus

_____34. hypothalamus

_____35. corpus callosu

_____

a. The part of the brain that joins the halves of the cerebellum, transmitting motor information to coordinate muscles and integrate movement between the right and left sides of the body.

b. A bundle of fibers that connects one half of the brain to the other.

c. The part of the brain's central core that transmits messages from the sense organs to the cerebral cortex and from the cerebral cortex to the cerebellum and medulla.

d. The part of the central core of the brain that controls many important body functions, such as breathing and heartbeat.

e. The part of the brain that controls bodily balance.

f. The ''old brain,'' which controls such basic functions as eating and sleeping and is common to all vertebrates.

g. A group of nerve cells in the brain that arouses the body to prepare it for appropriate action and screens out background stimuli.

h. Located below the thalamus of the brain, its major function is to maintain homeostasis.

_____36. limbic system

_____37. cerebral cortex

_____38. frontal lobes

_____39. temporal lobes

_____40. occipital lobes

_____41. motor area

_____42. somatosensory area

_____43. association area

a. The brain structure located at the front center of the cortex, containing major motor and speech and reasoning centers.

b. The structures of the brain lying behind the temporal lobes; includes the visual sensory area.

c. The area within the cortex corresponding to the sense of touch.

d. One of the major areas of the brain, the site of the higher mental processes, such as thought, language, memory, and speech.

e. The ''new brain,'' responsible for the most sophisticated information processing in the brain; contains the lobes.

f. The portion of the brain located beneath the frontal and parietal lobes; includes the auditory sensory areas.

g. One of the major areas of the brain, responsible for voluntary movement of particular parts of the body.

h. The part of the brain located outside the ''new brain'' that controls eating, aggression, and reproduction.

PRACTICE QUESTIONS   *Recite and Review:* _____

Test your knowledge of the chapter material by answering these **True-False** and **Multiple Choice Questions**. Check your answers with the Answer Key in the back of the *Study Guide*.

TRUE-FALSE QUESTIONS

T   F   1. The all-or-nothing law states that neurons are either firing or in a resting state, but nothing in between.

T   F   2. Generally speaking, the autonomic nervous system operates without conscious effort of the individual.

T   F   3. Sexual arousal is mainly controlled by the parasympathetic nervous system.

T   F   4. Research has been unable to show differences in the functional organization of the brain between human males and human females.

T   F   5.   The two cerebral hemispheres work interdependently to produce the full range and richness of human thought.

T   F   6.   Broca's aphasia is a language disorder in which the afflicted individual has difficulty comprehending what others say.

T   F   7.   The motor area of the cerebral cortex is responsible for planning and coordinating a sequence of behavior, such as putting a suitcase in the trunk of a car.

T   F   8.   The chemical messengers of the endocrine system are called hormones.

T   F   9.   As an electroencephalogram records brain activity over time, electrical impulses are emitted and recorded on paper.

T   F   10. The diameter of an neuron influences how quickly an impulse travels from the dendrites to the axon.

T   F   11. Parkinson's disease is caused by decreased production of dopamine in the adrenal glands.

T   F   12. A neuroscientist might investigate how personality is influenced by muscle and bone changes associated with aging.

MULTIPLE CHOICE QUESTIONS

1. Which of the following specializes in investigating the role of the central nervous system in behavior?
    a. neurologists   c. physiologists
    b. biopsychologists   d. zoologists

2. Dendrites, cell body, axon, and terminal buttons are parts of the:
    a. neurotransmitter.   c. muscle spindle.
    b. spinal cord.   d. neuron.

3. Neurons communicate with each other through specialized structures known as:
    a. glial cells.   c. somas.
    b. myelin sheaths.   d. dendrites and axons.

4. The myelin sheath surrounds:
    a. a dendrite.   c. a cell body.
    b. an axon.   d. a terminal button.

5. In multiple sclerosis, the _____ deteriorates, exposing parts of the _____. The result is a short circuit between the nervous system and muscle, which leads to difficulties with walking, vision, and general muscle coordination.
    a. cell body; nucleus   c. terminal button; nucleus
    b. dendrite; terminal button   d. myelin sheath; axon

6. Epilepsy is associated with all of the following except:
    a. misfiring electrical discharges from the dendrites.
    b. seizures and convulsions.
    c. a leak of information to nearby neurons.
    d. reverse flow.

7. Which of the following determines the rate at which a neuron can fire?
   a. presence of ions   c. resting state
   b. reverse flow mechanism   d. refractory period

8. The gap between neurons is called the:
   a. terminal button.   c. synapse.
   b. cell body.   d. refractory period.

9. The purpose of reverse flow of some substances from the axon to the cell body
   is to:
   a. release neurotransmitters.
   b. clear metabolites from the cell.
   c. bring nourishment to the cell.
   d. regenerate an action potential after firing.

10. Immediately after firing, the neuron cannot fire again. This is called the:
    a. action potential.   c. relative refractory period.
    b. all-or-nothing law.   d. absolute refractory period.

11. Neural impulses travel:
    a. electrically between and within each neuron.
    b. chemically between and within each neuron.
    c. electrically between neurons and chemically within each neuron.
    d. chemically between neurons and electrically within each neuron.

12. A chemical that is released from the terminal button upon the arrival of an
    action potential is called:
    a. a neurotransmitter.   c. a synapse.
    b. an enzyme.   d. a stimulator.

13. In most cases, after neurotransmitters have sent their message to the
    receiving neuron, they are:
    a. deactivated by enzymes.
    b. reabsorbed by the terminal buttons.
    c. absorbed into the body and filtered through the kidneys.
    d. absorbed into the receiving neuron.

14. A deficiency of acetylcholine is associated with:
    a. depression.   c. Parkinson's disease.
    b. Alzheimer's disease.   d. Huntington's chorea.

15. Morphine and other opiates are most like which of the following
    neurotransmitters?
    a. acetylcholine   c. endorphins
    b. dopamine   d. norepinephrine

16. According to the text, the main function of the endorphins is:
    a. contraction of muscle tissue.
    b. reduction of pain in the body.
    c. smooth and coordinated motor movements.
    d. alertness and emotional expression.

17. The portion of the nervous system that is particularly important for
    reflexive behavior is the:
    a. brain.   c. sensory nerve.
    b. spinal cord.   d. motor nerve.

18. Afferent is to _____ as efferent is to _____.
    a. sensory; association   c. motor; association
    b. sensory; motor   d. motor; sensory

19. Reflexes:
    a. are learned from infancy.
    b. involve the peripheral nervous system.
    c. involve both the peripheral and central nervous systems.
    d. do not involve the brain at all.

20. Which of the following, taken together, constitute the peripheral nervous system?
    a. somatic nervous system and autonomic nervous system
    b. brain and spinal cord
    c. sympathetic nervous system and brain
    d. spinal cord and parasympathetic nervous system

21. The autonomic nervous system controls:
    a. habitual, automatic movements such as applying the brakes of an automobile.
    b. the functions of the spinal cord.
    c. the body's response to an emergency or crisis.
    d. most of the spinal reflexes.

22. Sympathetic division is to parasympathetic division as:
    a. fight is to flight.   c. arousing is to calming.
    b. central is to peripheral.   d. helpful is to hurtful.

23. Which of the following is not likely to happen during activation of the sympathetic division of the nervous system?
    a. increase in digestion   c. increase in sweating
    b. increase in heart rate   d. increase in pupil sizes

24. The technique that measures the activity of the brain by sensing a radioactive tracer in the person being studied is:
    a. positron emission tomography (PET) scan.
    b. the electroencephalogram (EEG).
    c. nuclear magnetic resonance (NMR) scan.
    d. computerized axial tomography (CAT) scan.

25. Which of the following structures is not part of the ''central core'' of the old brain?
    a. medulla   c. hypothalamus
    b. pituitary   d. reticular formation

26. The word most closely associated with the function of the limbic system is:
    a. thinking.   c. emergency.
    b. survival.   d. emotion.

27. According to the text, which of the following may be the most critical structure for maintaining homeostasis, a steady internal state of the body?
    a. hippocampus   c. hypothalamus
    b. cerebral cortex   d. cerebellum

28. Which of the following structures is not directly involved in the control of motor function?
    a. cerebellum   c. pons

(b) medulla   d. spinal cord

29. Which of the following controls important bodily functions such as heartbeat
    and breathing?
    (a) medulla   c. thalamus
    b. cerebellum   d. hypothalamus

30. Damage to or lesions in which of the following brain structures would be most
    likely to cause dramatic changes in emotionality and behavior?
    a. pons   c. cerebellum
    b. medulla   (d) limbic system

31. The capacities to think and remember probably best distinguish humans from
    other animals. These qualities are most closely associated with the function
    of the:
    (a) cerebral cortex.   c. cerebellum.
    b. medulla.   d. limbic system.

32. _____ in the cerebral cortex create(s) the most sophisticated
    integration of neural information by providing for much greater surface area
    and complex interconnections among neurons.
    (a) Convolutions   c. Lateralization
    b. Mapping   d. Hemispheric dominance

33. Which of the following is true of both the sensory and motor areas of the
    cortex?
    a. They both contain pleasure centers.
    (b) More cortical tissue is devoted to the most important structures.
    c. Electrical stimulation produces involuntary movement.
    d. Destruction of any one area affects all the senses.

34. The diagram with parts of the ''little man'' on the surface of the motor
    cortex of a cerebral hemisphere shows that:
    (a) body structures requiring fine motor movements are controlled by large
        amounts of neural tissue.
    b. major motor functions are controlled by the right hemisphere.
    c. large body parts on the diagram (e.g., fingers on a hand) receive little
       motor input.
    d. certain areas of the body are more responsive to touch, temperature, and
       other stimulation.

35. The area of the brain associated with thinking, language, memory, and speech
    is called the:
    a. sensory area.   c. motor area.
    b. somatosensory area.   (d) association area.

36. Which area has the largest portion of the cortex?
    a. motor area   c. sensory area
    b. somatosensory area   (d) association area

37. Phineas Gage was a shrewd, energetic business executive who persistently
    carried out all his plans of operation. The dramatic changes in him
    following his accident suggest which area of his cerebral cortex was injured?
    a. neuromuscular   c. sensory-somatosensory
    (b) association   d. motor

38. When a person is unable to carry out purposeful, sequential behaviors, the

condition is known as:
a. dyslexia.
b. aphasia.

(c) apraxia.
d. paraplegia.

39. Which of the following is characterized by difficulty understanding the speech of others and producing coherent speech?
(a). Wernicke's aphasia
b. Lou Gehrig's disease

c. Broca's aphasia
d. Phineas Gage's disease

40. Left hemisphere is to _____ function as right hemisphere is to _____ function.
a. sequential; successive
(b). sequential; global

c. successive; sequential
d. global; sequential

41. Wernicke's aphasia is to _____ as Broca's aphasia is to _____.
a. spasticity; flaccidity
b. motor cortex; sensory cortex
c. overeating; irregular gait
d. difficulty in comprehending words; searching for the correct word.

42. Appreciation of music, art, and dance, and understanding of spatial relationships are more likely to be processed in the:
a. right side of the brain.
b. left side of the brain.

c. occipital lobes.
d. temporal lobe.

43. According to the text, in right-handed people, which of the following is usually responsible for logical thought processes and reasoning?
a. occipital lobes
b. temporal lobes

c. left hemisphere
d. right hemisphere

44. Damage to which of the following areas is most likely to cause people to have difficulty with pattern recognition tasks and spatial memory?
a. frontal lobe
b. left hemisphere

c. right hemisphere
d. temporal lobe

45. Which statement about the cerebral hemispheres does not apply to most right-handed people?
a. The left hemisphere processes information sequentially.
b. The right hemisphere processes information globally.
c. The right hemisphere is associated with language and reasoning.
d. Women display less hemispheric dominance than men, particularly with skills such as language.

46. One primary difference in the organization of male and female brains is that:
a. logical abilities are on the opposite sides in males and females.
b. language abilities are more evenly divided between the two hemispheres in females.
c. the right hemisphere is almost always dominant in females.
d. spatial abilities are on the opposite sides in males and females.

47. A split-brain patient has had:
a. a stroke.
b. the nerves between the hemispheres cut.
c. damage to one of the hemispheres.
d. epilepsy.

48. Which part of the brain is most closely linked to the function of the

endocrine system?
a. hypothalamus   c. limbic system
b. pons   d. cerebellum

49. Which response listed below is least likely to be treated with biofeedback?
a. impotence
b. headaches
c. high blood pressure
d. problems with maintaining optimal skin temperature

50. Which of the following is primarily intended to be a procedure by which we
can come to control our internal physiological processes?
a. biofeedback   c. electrical stimulation
b. hypnosis   d. hypothalamic regulation

ESSAY QUESTIONS   *Recite and Review:* ____

Essay Question 2.1: *The Benefits of Knowledge about the Brain*

Describe the specific benefits of our knowledge of brain function and the effect of injury on the brain. What are some of the possible consequences of research in neurotransmitters, biofeedback, and even sex differences in the brain?

_____

_____

_____

_____

_____

_____

_____

_____

_____

_____

_____

_____

_____

_____

_____

_____

_____

_____

_____

_____

_____

_____

Essay Question 2.2: *Ethics and Brain Research*

Recent developments raise important questions for ethical consideration. What are some of the problems that arise when surgery separates the two hemispheres? What are the potential dangers of transplanting tissue into the brain? Discuss these ethical and moral issues. Are there other issues?

_____

_____

_____

_____

_____

_____

_____

_____

_____

_____

_____

_____

_____

_____

_____

_____

_____

_____

_____

_____

ACTIVITIES AND PROJECTS

1.   Fill in the labels that are missing from the
     following diagram of a neuron.

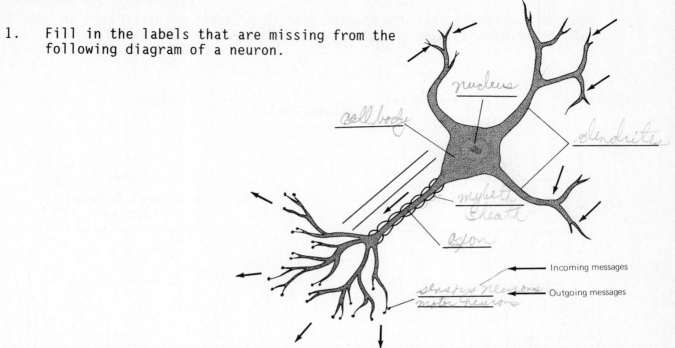

2.   Fill in the labels that are missing from the diagram of the brain.

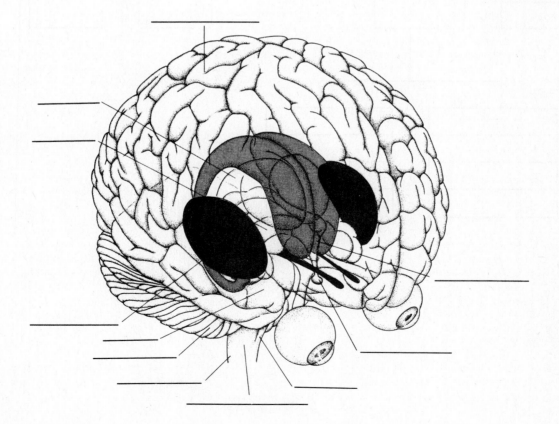

3. Fill in the labels that are missing from this flowchart describing the parts
    of the nervous system.

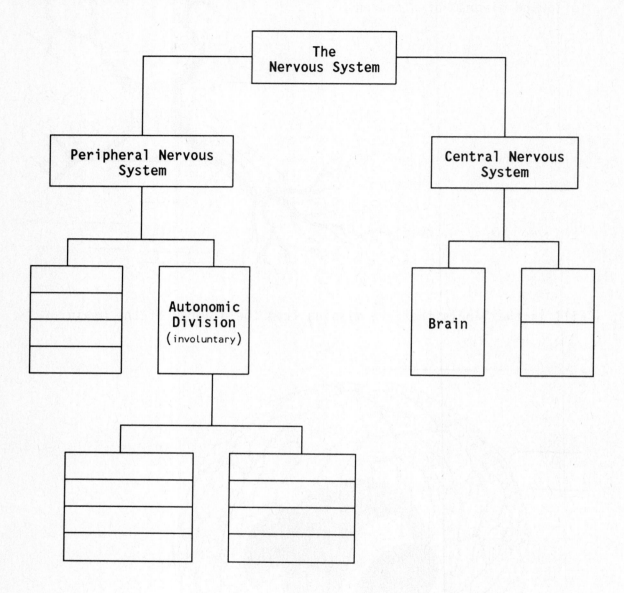

3

SENSATION AND PERCEPTION

DETAILED OUTLINE   *Survey:* _____

This detailed outline contains all the headings in Chapter 4: Sensation and Perception. If you are using the SQ3R method, then an examination of the outline is the best way to begin your survey of the chapter.

Prologue: Pete Townshend
Looking Ahead

Sensing the World Around Us
    Absolute thresholds
    Signal detection theory
    Just noticeable differences
    Sensory adaptation
▪ **Recap and Review I**

The Five+ Senses
    Vision: The eyes have it
▪ **Recap and Review II**
    The sense of sound and balance
Psychology at Work Improving the Senses with Technology
    Smell, taste, and the skin senses
The Cutting Edge Discovering the Origins of Food Preferences
▪ **Recap and Review III**

Making Sense of the World: Perception
    The Gestalt laws of organization
    Feature analysis: From whole to parts
    Top-down and bottom-up processing
    Perceptual constancy
    Depth perception: Translating 2-D to 3-D
    Motion perception: As the world turns
    Selective attention: Sorting out the world
▪ **Recap and Review IV**

Perceptual Illusions
    Visual illusions: Misperceptions of the eye
The Informed Consumer of Psychology Discovering and Treating Dyslexia
▪ **Recap and Review V**

Looking Back
Key Terms and Concepts

Now that you have surveyed the chapter, read **Looking Ahead**, pages 82-83.
>   *Question:* _____
>   *Read:* _____

Focus on the questions on page 83.

CONCEPTS AND LEARNING OBJECTIVES   *Survey:* _____

These are the concepts and the learning objects for Chapter 3. Read them
carefully as part of your preliminary survey of the chapter.

Concept 1:   Sensation is the means by which information from the world around
us is conveyed to the brain. The study of sensation requires examining the
nature of physical stimuli and its relationship to the kinds of sensory
responses they can evoke.

1. Define sensation and physical stimulus. (pp. 82-84)

2. Distinguish the concept of absolute threshold from the role of signal
   detection theory of stimuli. (pp. 85-86)

3. Describe the concept of just noticeable differences, Weber's law, and
   sensory adaptation. (pp. 86-88)

Concept 2:   Vision is the most studied of the five plus senses, and the details
of the transfer of a light image from its entrance into the eye, through its
transformation into a neural message to its destination in the visual cortex,
illustrates the complexity of sensation.
     The ear is responsible for detecting sound, body position, as well
as movement. Smell and taste are detected through chemical contact. The
skin senses include touch, pressure, temperature, and pain.

4. Discuss how the image is conveyed from the eye to the brain and the role
   of feature detection in processing visual information, and describe how
   we adapt to different light levels. (pp. 88-95)

5. Distinguish the two theories of color vision, and discuss how they
   describe complementary processes. (pp. 95-98)

6. Describe the structure of the ear and the role of each part in detecting
   sound. (pp. 99-104)

7. Describe the mechanisms that produce the senses of smell and taste. (pp.
   104-105)

8. Describe the skin senses of touch, pressure, and temperature and discuss
   the gate-control theory of pain. (pp. 105-107)

Concept 3:   Perception is the means of organizing and giving meaning to sensory
information. The gestalt approach starts out with perceptual organization
founded on basic principles of organization. Feature analysis identifies the
components of sensory information and combines them into complex perception.
     The characteristics of perception include perceptual constancy, the
ability to perceive depth even though the retinal image is two-dimensional,
and the selective nature of attention.

9. Define perception and distinguish it from sensation. (pp. 108-113)

10. Describe the types of perceptual constancy and how it affects perception, and contrast constructive and ecological theories of perceptual constancy. (pp. 113-116)

11. Discuss the role of selective attention in perception and the possibility of perception occurring beyond our awareness through subliminal perception. (pp. 116-119)

Concept 4: Visual illusions are misperceptions that arise as a result of the nature of some physical stimuli. Like an illusion, dyslexia reverses many features of written letters, creating a reading disability.

12. Describe and illustrate the major illusions, especially the Müller-Lyer and the Poggendorf illusions. (pp. 120-123)

CHAPTER SUMMARY

There are several ways you can use this summary as part of your systematic study plan. You may read each concept summary and then read the corresponding pages in the text, or you may read the entire summary and then read the entire chapter in the text. As you finish each section, complete the **Recap and Review** questions that are supplied in the text.

**Concept 1: Prologue and Looking Ahead
Sensing the World Around Us**

Survey: ____
Read: ____

Pages 82-88

The loss of hearing experienced by Pete Townshend illustrates how valuable our senses are to us. His illness, called tinnitus, is the result of frequent exposure to loud sound — in his case, loud music. To a musician, this kind of loss is devastating.

We detect the world around us through our senses. A **stimulus** is any physical energy that can be detected by a sense organ. A **sensation** is the activity of the sense organ when it detects a stimulus. Stimuli vary in type and intensity. **Intensity** refers to the physical strength of the stimulus. Psychophysics studies the relationship between the strength of a stimulus and the nature of the sensory response it creates.

Absolute threshold refers to the smallest amount of energy, the smallest intensity, needed to detect a stimulus. The absolute threshold for sight is illustrated by a candle burning at 30 miles on a dark night; for hearing, the ticking of a watch 20 feet away in a quiet room; for taste, one teaspoon of sugar in two gallons of water; for smell, one drop of perfume in three rooms; and for touch, a bee's wing falling one centimeter onto a cheek. **Noise** refers to the background stimulation for any of the senses.

The ability to detect a stimulus is influenced not only by the stimulus but also by conditions like expectations and experience. **Signal detection theory** attempts to explain the role of psychological factors in detecting stimuli. Two miscalculations are made: one, that a stimuli is present when it is not, and the other, that the stimuli is not present when it actually is. Signal detection theory has great practical importance, ranging from helping people who must distinguish various items on radar screens to improving how witnesses identify suspects in a police lineup.

The smallest noticeable difference between two stimuli is called the **difference threshold**, or the **just noticeable difference**. The amount of stimulus required for the just noticeable difference depends upon the level of the initial stimulus. **Weber's law** states that the just noticeable difference is a constant proportion for each sense. Weber's law is not very accurate at extreme high or low intensities.

After prolonged exposure to a sensory stimulus, the capacity of the sensory organ adjusts to the stimulus in a process called **adaptation**. The receptor cells are most responsive to changes in stimuli, because constant stimulation produces adaptation. Context also affects judgments about sensory stimuli. People's reactions to sensory stimuli do not always accurately represent the physical stimuli that cause them.

Concept 2:   The Five+ Senses   *Survey:* ____
           Vision: The eyes have it   *Read:* ____
           The sense of sound and balance

Pages 88-107

Most psychological research has focused on vision and hearing. The stimulus that produces vision is **light**. Light is the electromagnetic radiation that our visual apparatus is capable of detecting. The range of visible light is called the **visual spectrum**.

Light enters the eye through the **cornea**, a transparent, protective window. It then passes through the **pupil**, the opening in the **iris**. The iris is the pigmented muscle that opens and closes the pupil depending on how much light is in the environment. The narrower the pupil is, the greater is the focal distance for the eye. After the pupil, the light passes through the **lens**, which then bends and focuses the light on the back of the eye by changing its thickness, a process called **accommodation**. The light then strikes the **retina**, a thin layer of nerve cells at the back of the eyeball. The retina is composed of light-sensitive cells called rods, which are long and cylindrical, and cones, which are shorter and conical in shape. The greatest concentration of cones is in the **fovea**, an area that is extremely sensitive. Cones are responsible for color vision, and rods are insensitive to color and play a role in **peripheral vision**, the ability to see objects to our side, and in night vision.

Rods contain **rhodopsin**, a complex substance that changes chemically when struck by light. This chemical change sets off a reaction. The response is then transmitted to two other kinds of cells, first to the **bipolar cells** and then to **ganglion cells**. The ganglion cells organize and summarize the information and then convey it to the **optic nerve**. Where the optic nerve goes from the retina back through the eyeball there are no rods or cones, which results in the blind spot. The optic nerves from both eyes meet behind the eyes at the **optic chiasm** where each optic nerve splits. Nerve impulses from the right half of each eye go to the right side of the brain, and nerve impulses from the left half of each eye go to the left half of the brain. The disease called **glaucoma** is a restriction of the nerve impulses across the optic nerve. The restriction is caused by buildup of fluid in the eye, and as the pressure increases, the vision becomes more restricted, resulting in **tunnel vision**.

The visual message is processed from the beginning by ganglion cells, and continues to the visual cortex, where many neurons are highly specialized. Their roles are specialized to detect certain visual features, and the process is called **feature detection**.

When a person goes into a dark room from a well-lit space, **light adaptation** is experienced. **Light adaptation** is the temporary insensitivity to light dimmer than that to which the eye has most recently been exposed. After time, the person becomes accustomed to the dark and experiences **dark adaptation**, the adjustment to low levels of light. The changes that make this adjustment are chemical changes in the rods and cones.

A person with normal color vision can distinguish about seven million different colors. Color vision involves two processes. The first of these processes is called the **trichromatic theory of color vision**. The trichromatic theory says that there are three types of cones: one sensitive to blue-violet colors, another sensitive to green, and another sensitive to red-yellow. This theory does not explain how two colors mix to make gray, and it does not explain afterimages. **Opponent-process theory** explains afterimages as the result of the opposing color of linked pairs of cones continuing to compensate for the stimulation of the first color. Apparently, the trichromatic process is at work at the level of the retina, and the opponent processes are at work at the retina level and at later stages in the processing of visual information. The processing of visual information takes place in all parts of the visual system.

The **outer ear** collects sounds and guides them to the internal portions of the ear. **Sound** is the movement of air that results from the vibration of objects. Sounds are funneled into the **auditory canal** toward the **eardrum**. Sound waves hit the eardrum, which in turn transmits its vibrations into the **middle ear**. The middle ear contains three small bones, the **hammer**, the **anvil**, and the **stirrup**. These three bones transmit the vibrations to the **oval window**. Each step of the way amplifies the sound waves that reach the ear. The **inner ear** contains the organs for transmitting the sound waves into nerve impulses as well as the organs for balance and position. The **cochlea** is a coiled tube that contains the **basilar membrane**. The basilar membrane is covered with **hair cells** that vibrate. Sound may also enter the cochlea through the bones that surround the ear.

Sound is characterized by **frequency**, or the number of waves per second, and **pitch** is our experience of this number as high or low. **Intensity** may be thought of as the size of the waves — how strong it is. Intensity is measured in **decibels**. The **place theory of hearing** is based on the fact that parts of the basilar membrane are sensitive to different pitches. The **frequency theory of hearing** suggests that the entire basilar membrane vibrates in response to any sound, and the nerves send signals that are more frequent for higher pitches and less frequent for lower pitches. Both of these theories appear to have merit. The auditory cortex appears to be like a map of frequencies, with cells that respond to similar frequencies close to each other.

The inner ear is also responsible for the sense of balance. The structures responsible for balance are the **semicircular canals**, three tubes filled with fluid that moves around in the tubes when the head moves. The fluid affects **otoliths**, small motion-sensitive crystals in the semicircular canals.

We are able to detect about 10,000 different smells, and women have a better sense of smell than do men. Some animals can communicate using odor. **Pheromones** are chemicals that can produce a reaction in members of a species. These chemicals have a role in sexual activity and identification. Odor is detected by molecules of a substance coming into contact with the **olfactory cells** in the nasal passages. Each olfactory cell responds to a narrow band of odors. Taste is detected by **taste buds** on the tongue. Taste buds detect sweet, sour, salty, or bitter flavors. The experience of taste also includes the odor and appearance of food.

The **skin senses** include touch, pressure, temperature, and pain. Receptor cells for each of these senses are distributed all over the body, though each sense is distributed in varying concentrations. The major theory of pain is called the **gate-control theory of pain**. This theory states that nerve receptors send messages to the brain areas related to pain, and whenever they are activated, a ''gate'' to the brain is opened and pain is experienced. The gate can be shut by overwhelming the nerve pathways with non-painful messages. It can also be closed by the brain producing messages to reduce or eliminate the experience of pain. **Acupuncture** may be explained by the first option in which the needles shut off the messages going to the brain. Endorphins may also close the gate.

A number of methods for dealing with pain have been developed. They include drug therapy, hypnosis, biofeedback, relaxation techniques, surgery (cutting the nerve fiber that carries the pain message), nerve and brain stimulation, and psychological counseling.

Concept 3:   Making Sense of the World: Perception
Perceptual constancy

Survey: ____
Read: ____

Pages 108-119

Human perceptual errors have played a central role in many airline and other transportation fatalities. Errors in perception occur because **perception** is an *interpretation* of sensory information. The difference between perception and sensation is that sensation involves the organism's first encounter with physical stimuli, and perception is the process of interpreting, analyzing, and integrating sensations.

Through perception we try to simplify complex stimuli in the environment. This tendency toward simplicity and organization into meaningful wholes follows basic principles called the **gestalt laws of organization**. **Gestalt** refers to a ''pattern.'' Basic patterns identified by the gestalt psychologists are: (1) *closure*, groupings tend to be in complete or enclosed figures; (2) *proximity*, elements close together tend to be grouped together; (3) *similarity*, elements that are similar tend to be grouped together; and (4) *simplicity*, the tendency to organize patterns in a basic, straightforward manner.

The distinction between **figure** and **ground** is crucial to perceptual organization. The tendency is to form an object in contrast to its ground, or background. This is illustrated by the two faces versus a single vase. Because we must actively organize this figure, we cannot see both the faces and the vase at the same time. The gestalt psychologists argued that perception goes beyond combining individual elements and that when we organize the elements, we actively make the result more than the parts.

In contrast to the gestalt view that we perceive by putting elements into an organized whole, the recent approach called **feature analysis** suggests that we perceive first the individual components and then formulate an understanding of the overall picture. Specific neurons respond to highly specific components of stimuli, suggesting that each stimuli is composed of a series of component features. In this view, our perception involves matching new stimuli to components in memory. The three steps of feature analysis are: (1) identify component features; (2) combine the features; and (3) compare the combined features to existing memories.

Perception proceeds in two ways, though top-down or through bottom-up processing. In **top-down processing** perception is controlled by higher-level knowledge, experience, expectations, and motivation. Top-down processing helps sort through ambiguous stimuli or missing elements. Context is critical for filling in missing information. Isolated stimuli illustrate how context is important for top-down processing. **Bottom-up processing** consists of recognizing and processing information about individual components. If we cannot recognize individual components, recognizing the complete picture would be very difficult. Both processes are at work simultaneously in perception.

One phenomenon that contributes to our perception of the world is that of **perceptual constancy**, the tendency for objects to be perceived as unvarying and consistent even as we see them from different views and distances. The rising moon is one example of how perceptual constancy works. The moon illusion is explained as resulting from the intervening cues of landscape and horizon which give it context. When it rises, there are no context cues. Perceptual constancies occur with size, shape, and color. Perceptual constancy depends upon experience, as cross-cultural studies have illustrated. Two theories have been offered to account for perceptual constancy. The **constructive theory** states that prior experience and expectations are used to make judgments about location of objects that have a known size. We then infer location because of our prior experience of size. Ecological theory states that relationships between different objects provide clues about size and location. The appearance of the surface textures of distant objects will be different, thus allowing a direct judgment about location.

The ability to view the world in three dimensions is very important to our ability to get around in it. This ability is called **depth perception**. Depth perception is primarily a result of our having two eyes. The main aspect of having two eyes is that the two slightly different positions of the eyes give rise to minute differences in the visual representation in the brain, a phenomenon called **binocular disparity**. Discrepancy between the two images from the retinas gives clues to the distance of the object or the distance between two objects. The larger the disparity, the larger the distance. Two ears develop the same kind of disparity that helps us locate the sources of sounds. Other cues for visual depth perception can be seen with only one eye, and so they are called **monocular cues**. **Motion parallax** is a monocular cue in which the position of distant objects moves on the retina slower than does the position of closer objects when the head moves. **Relative size** depends on the distant object having a smaller retinal image. **Linear perspective** is the phenomenon where railroad tracks appear to join together.

Motion perception judges the movement of objects relevant to stable objects. However, our perception compensates for head and eye movements. When objects move too fast for the eye to follow, we tend to anticipate the direction and speed of movement.

Selective attention refers to the process by which we choose which stimulus we will focus upon. We attend to the bright, large, loud, novel, or contrasting stimulus. Meaning and interest also attract our attention to stimuli. The **Stroop task** illustrates a situation during which our attention can be divided between two kinds of stimuli. The task requires the subject to attend to both the color and the meaning of a word, and the word ''red'' may be colored blue or green (see Figure 3-18). Selective attention in the auditory system is tested using the **dichotic listening** procedure, in which a person hears a different message in each ear. The person is asked to repeat, called **shadowing**, the message that is coming to one ear. The individual is then asked about the message heard in the other ear. People are able to recall whether the voice was male or female and whether their name was mentioned. The importance of the message in the shadowed ear is also important, and if the message shifts to the other ear, the listener will switch ears also. Selective attention can have negative consequences if people fail to attend to important information that then leads to accidents. Research has developed principles for designing instruments to prevent errors. They include minimizing the number of sources of information, simplifying the display, and keeping the sources close together.

Section 4: Perceptual Illusions

Survey: ____
Read: ____

Pages 120-123

The importance of our knowledge about perception has been evident since the time of the ancient Greeks. The Parthenon in Athens is built with an intentional illusion to give the building a greater appearance of straightness and stability. **Visual illusions** are physical stimuli that produce errors in perception. **The Poggendorf illusion** and the **Müller-Lyer illusion** are two of the more well-known illusions. Explanations of the Müller-Lyer illusion focus on the apparatus of the eye and the interpretations made by the brain. The eye-based explanation suggests that the eyes are more active where the arrow tips point inward, giving the illusion of greater length. The brain-base explanation suggests that we interpret the lines with the inward arrows as interior spaces and the outward pointing lines as close exterior spaces. In comparison the inside corner then seems larger.

The suspected cause of **dyslexia** is a brain malfunction related to vision. Dyslexics tend to reverse letters, have difficulty distinguishing left from right, make unusual spelling errors, and appear more clumsy than their peers. Treatment techniques include sounding out words, repetitive practice with making the sound of a letter, writing it, and viewing it. Self-esteem and self-confidence are also very important.

♦ Now that you have surveyed, questioned, and read the chapter and completed the **Recap and Review** questions, review **Looking Back**, pages 124-126. *Review:* ____

♦ For additional practice through recitation and review, test your knowledge of the chapter material by answering the questions in the **Key Word Drill**, the **Practice Questions**, and the **Essay Questions**.

KEY WORD DRILL

Recite: ____

The following **Fill in the Blank** and **Matching Questions** test key words from the text. Check your answers with the Answer Key in the back of the *Study Guide*.

FILL IN THE BLANK

1. A _____ can be any source of physical energy that produces a response in a sense organ.

2. _____ _____ _____ theory acknowledges that observers may miscalculate in one of two ways, either by reporting that a physical stimulus is present when it is not or by failing to report when it is, and the theory uses data about these miscalculations to address the role of psychological factors in our ability to identify stimuli.

3. The ability of the lens to vary its shape in order to focus incoming images on the retina is called _____ and _____ refers to an adjustment in sensory capacity following prolonged exposure to stimuli.

4. The _____ - _____ theory of color vision suggests that receptor cells are linked in pairs, working in opposition to each other.

5. At least 1000 separate _____ _____ have
   been identified so far, and each of these responds to a very small band of
   different odors.

6. _____ is the sorting out, interpretation, analysis, and
   integration of sensations from our sensory organs.

7. A series of principles, the _____
   of organization, describe how we organize pieces of information into
   meaningful wholes.

8. Psychologists describe perception guided by knowledge, experience,
   expectations, and motivations as _____ -_____
   processing; and recognition and processing of information about the
   individual components of a stimulus is considered _____ -
   _____ processing.

9. _____ theory suggests that prior experience and
   expectations about the size of an object are used to make inferences about
   its location.

10. In the _____ - _____ illusion, two lines
    of the same length appear to be of different lengths because of the direction
    of the arrows at the ends of each line; the line with arrows pointing out
    appears shorter than the line with arrows pointing in.

MATCHING QUESTIONS

___c___ 11. sensation

___a___ 12. intensity

___d___ 13. absolute threshold

___e___ 14. noise

___b___ 15. difference threshold

a. The strength of a stimulus.

b. The smallest detectable difference between
   two stimuli.

c. The process of responding to a stimulus.

d. The smallest amount of physical intensity
   by which a stimulus can be detected.

e. Background stimulation that interferes with
   the perception of other stimuli.

_d_ 16. rods

_c_ 17. bipolar cells

_a_ 18. cones

_b_ 19. ganglion cells

_e_ 20. optic nerve

a. Light-sensitive receptors that are responsible for sharp focus and color perception, particularly in bright light.

b. Nerve cells that collect and summarize information from rods and carry it to the brain.

c. Nerve cells leading to the brain that are triggered by nerve cells in the eye.

d. Light-sensitive receptors that perform well in poor light but are largely insensitive to color and small details.

e. A bundle of ganglion axons in the back of the eyeball that carry visual information to the brain.

_____

_b_ 21. outer ear

_f_ 22. auditory canal

_d_ 23. eardrum

_c_ 24. middle ear

_g_ 25. hammer

_h_ 26. anvil

_a_ 27. stirrup

_e_ 28. oval window

a. A small bone in the middle ear that transfers vibrations to the oval window.

b. The visible part of the ear that acts as a collector to bring sounds into the internal portions of the ear.

c. A tiny chamber containing three bones - the hammer, the anvil, and the stirrup - which transmit vibrations to the oval window.

d. The part of the ear that vibrates when sound waves hit it.

e. A thin membrane between the middle ear and the inner ear that transmits vibrations while increasing their strength.

f. A tubelike passage in the ear through which sound moves to the eardrum.

g. A tiny bone in the middle ear that transfers vibrations to the anvil.

h. A minute bone in the middle ear that transfers vibrations to the stirrup.

_b_ 29. gestalts

_g_ 30. closure

_d_ 31. proximity

_a_ 32. similarity

_c_ 33. simplicity

_f_ 34. figure/ground

a. The tendency to group together those elements that are similar in appearance.

b. Patterns studied by the gestalt psychologists.

c. The tendency to perceive a pattern in the most basic, straightforward, organized manner possible - the overriding gestalt principle.

d. The tendency to group together those elements that are close together.

f. Figure refers to the object being perceived, whereas ground refers to the background or spaces within the object.

g. The tendency to group according to enclosed or complete figures rather than open or incomplete ones.

_b_ 35. perceptual constancy

_c_ 36. binocular disparity

_a_ 37. motion parallax

_f_ 38. linear perspective

_e_ 39. Stroop task

_d_ 40. visual illusion

a. The change in position of the image of an object on the retina as the head moves, providing a monocular cue to distance.

b. The phenomenon by which physical objects are perceived as unvarying despite changes in their appearance or in the physical environment.

c. The difference between the images that reach the retina of each eye; this disparity allows the brain to estimate distance.

d. A physical stimulus that consistently produces errors in perception (often called an optical illusion).

e. An exercise requiring the division of our attention between two competing stimuli - the meaning of words and the colors in which they are written.

f. The phenomenon by which distant objects appear to be closer together than nearer objects, a monocular cue.

PRACTICE QUESTIONS   *Recite and Review:* ____

Test your knowledge of the chapter material by answering these **True-False** and **Multiple Choice Questions**. Check your answers with the Answer Key in the back of the *Study Guide*.

TRUE-FALSE QUESTIONS

(T)   F   1. The study of the relationship between the physical nature of stimuli and a person's sensory responses to them is called psychophysics.

T   (F)   2. A candle flame can be seen 45 miles away on a dark, clear night.

T   (F)   3. Glaucoma, a disorder that may result in loss of vision, is most common in adults between 20 and 35 years of age.

(T)   F   4. The outer ear contains no neural receptors that communicate vibrations to the brain.

T   (F)   5. According to the text, pheromones play a significant role in human sexual responses.

T   (F)   6. Perception is generally considered to involve simpler and more fundamental processes than sensation.

(T)   F   7. Learning and experience play an important role in perception.

T   (F)   8. Ecological theory and constructive theory are sometimes used to explain figure/ground phenomena.

(T)   F   9. According to the theory of selective attention, if you are considering buying a certain model of car, you are more likely to notice a car of this model when it passes on the road.

(T)   F   10. Visual illusions can occur because of cultural factors.

MULTIPLE CHOICE QUESTIONS

1. The physical energy that activates a sense organ is called a:
   a. sensation.   c. transmitter.
   b. stimulus.   d. threshold.

2. The study of the relationship between the physical nature of stimuli and a person's sensory responses to them is called:
   a. introspection.   c. psychophysics.
   b. operationalization.   d. perception.

3. Psychophysicists define absolute threshold as the:
   a. minimum amount of change in stimulation which is detectable.
   b. range of stimulation to which each sensory channel is sensitive.
   c. maximum intensity which is detectable to the senses.
   d. minimum magnitude of stimulus which is detectable.

4. An absolute threshold:
    a. is similar for a given sense (e.g., vision) in humans and in various animals.
    b. demonstrates that the amount of energy required to stimulate the eye, ear, skin, and other receptors is very similar.
    c. is the minimum physical energy required to produce a response to sensory stimulation in a sense receptor.
    d. is the degree of change required in sensory stimulation in order for the stimulus to be detected as different.

5. Your text defines noise as:
    a. background stimulation that interferes with other stimuli.
    b. sounds that the individual finds distasteful.
    c. stimuli that interfere with healthy bodily functioning.
    d. the relative amount of auditory stimulation in urban versus rural areas.

6. An antiaircraft operator watching a radar scope may fail to identify the blips signaling the presence of an aircraft because they occur so infrequently. This suggests that:
    a. expectations about the frequency of events influence detection.
    b. detection of a stimulus depends only upon sensory factors.
    c. radar operators are highly atypical in their sensitivity to stimulation.
    d. past exposure is relatively unimportant in stimulus detection.

7. The objective of signal detection theory in psychophysics is to:
    a. determine absolute thresholds.
    b. explain the role of psychological factors.
    c. explain magnitude estimation.
    d. determine the nature of the stimulus.

8. When you first visit a farm you notice noxious odors. After only one week you no longer notice them. This example illustrates the value of:
    a. sensory adaptation.   c. Weber's law.
    b. the just noticeable difference.   d. signal detection theory.

9. Sensory adaptation is the same as:
    a. getting used to a stimulus.
    b. first being aware of a stimulus.
    c. noticing a slight increase in a stimulus.
    d. sensing a stimulus that is not there.

10. Sam rented an apartment just across the street from the fire station. At first, he woke up every time the siren went off at night. After a few weeks, however, Sam failed to notice the siren and slept right through it. This example illustrates:
    a. signal detection theory.   c. a just noticeable difference.
    b. Weber's law.   d. absolute thresholds.

11. The function of the retina is to:
    a. turn the image of the object upside down.
    b. redistribute the light energy in the image.
    c. convert the light energy into neural impulses.
    d. control the size of the pupil.

12. Which type of receptor is used in peripheral vision?
    a. cone   c. fovea
    b. rod   d. rhodopsin

13. The blind spot is located:
    a. at the center of the iris.
    b. in the fovea.
    c. at the opening for the optic nerve.
    d. at the corner of the lens.

14. One of the most frequent causes of blindness is:
    a. an underproduction of rhodopsin.
    b. a restriction of impulses across the optic nerve.
    c. tunnel vision.
    d. an inability of the pupil to expand.

15. Glaucoma may lead to blindness through:
    a. deterioration of the cones.
    b. deterioration of the rods.
    c. buildup of the myelin sheaths around the optic nerve.
    d. buildup of pressure within the eye.

16. Feature detection is best described as the process by which specialized
    neurons in the cortex:
    a. identify fine details in a larger pattern.
    b. see things clearly that are far away.
    c. discriminate one face from another.
    d. recognize particular shapes or patterns.

17. The trichromatic theory is based on the assumption that:
    a. there are three different kinds of cones in the retina.
    b. each cone can respond to only three different colors.
    c. the retina is divided into three areas which have different densities
       of rods versus cones.
    d. light passes through three tiny filters as it is detected in the cone.

18. According to the text, afterimages can best be explained by the:
    a. opponent-process theory of color vision.
    b. trichromatic theory of color vision.
    c. place theory of color vision.
    d. receptive-field theory of color vision.

19. The primary function of the hammer, anvil, and stirrup in the middle ear is
    to:
    a. protect the inner ear from infection.
    b. suppress interference from the visual system.
    c. transmit vibrations to the oval window.
    d. conduct sound toward the eardrum.

20. A neural message is sent to the brain through the auditory nerve when the:
    a. hair cells on the basilar membrane are bent.
    b. oval window is activated by the ossicle.
    c. eardrum is stimulated.
    d. auditory cortex is activated by the eardrum.

21. On a piano keyboard, the keys for the lower-frequency sounds are on the left side; the keys for the higher-frequency sounds are on the right. If you first pressed a key on the left side of the keyboard, and then a key on the right side, you might expect that:
    a. pitch would depend on how hard the keys were struck.
    b. the pitch would be lower for the first key that was played.
    c. the pitch would be lower for the second key that was played.
    d. the pitch would be identical for each.

22. Intensity is to _____ as frequency is to _____.
    a. resonance; loudness
    b. loudness; pitch
    c. acoustic nerve; auditory canal
    d. external ear; consonance

23. Loudness is to _____ as frequency is to _____.
    a. decibels; cycles per second
    b. millimicrometers; loudness
    c. cycles per second; wavelength
    d. cochlea; auditory nerve

24. The _____ theory of hearing states that different sound frequencies stimulate different areas of the basilar membrane.
    a. place
    b. opponent-process
    c. frequency
    d. volley

25. Which sensory structure below is **not** associated with the function that follows it?
    a. otoliths; balance
    b. eardrum; hearing
    c. anvil; taste
    d. rod; vision

26. Which statement about smell is **not** correct?
    a. Some animals have lower olfactory thresholds than humans.
    b. People over 60 years of age do not sense odors as well as younger people.
    c. The olfactory sensitivities do not differ between men and women.
    d. A small number of people have no olfactory sensitivity at all.

27. According to the text, which factor does not influence the sense of smell in humans?
    a. illness
    b. smoking
    c. age
    d. weight

28. Chemical molecules that promote communication between members of a species are called:
    a. pheromones.
    b. neurotransmitters.
    c. hormones.
    d. odorants.

29. The receptors in the nose are called:
    a. pheromones.
    b. olfactory cells.
    c. rhodopsin.
    d. opponent processes.

30. The sense of taste and the sense of smell are alike in that they both:
    a. have four basic qualities of sensation.
    b. depend on chemical molecules as stimuli.
    c. use the same area of the cortex.
    d. utilize opponent processes.

31. Which alternative below is **not** one of the four basic tastes?
    a. sweet
    b. tangy
    c. sour
    d. salty

32. Which of the following theories holds that certain nerve receptors lead to specific areas of the brain that sense pain?
    a. endorphin   c. opponent process
    b. opiate   d. gate control

33. The gate control theory relates to the sensation of:
    a. pain.   c. smell.
    b. taste.   d. ticklishness.

34. The most common treatment for recducing pain is:
    a. surgery   c. drug therapy
    b. biofeedback   d. relaxation

35. Perception differs from sensation in that:
    a. perception is less dependent upon prior learning and experience.
    b. perception considers only information from the receptors, without the need for higher mental processing while sensation requires higher mental processing.
    c. perception is less dependent upon the organism's developmental history.
    d. perception involves interpretation, analysis, and integration of sensory information while sensation provides sensory information.

36. According to your text, one of the principal functions served by perception is to:
    a. stabilize figure/ground relationships.
    b. simplify the complexity of environmental stimuli.
    c. code stimuli into neural messages.
    d. transfer sensations directly into memory.

37. Objects are perceived as unvarying despite changes in their appearance or the surrounding environment because of:
    a. similarity.   c. closure.
    b. simplicity.   d. constancy.

38. We can judge the size of a large rock by viewing a person standing in front of it. This illustrates:
    a. feature analysis.
    b. ecological theory.
    c. the gestalt laws of organization.
    d. constructive theory.

39. Which of the following suggests that the relationships among different objects in a scene give us clues about their sizes?
    a. perceptual constancy
    b. ecological theory
    c. the gestalt laws of organization
    d. constructive theory

40. The idea that perceptual constancy is brought about by direct perception of all the stimuli in a scene is the basis of:
    a. constructive theory.
    b. the overriding gestalt principle of simplicity.
    c. ecological theory.
    d. the law of proximity.

41. According to the text, which of the following processes is most important
     in order for major-league baseball players to be able to hit the ball when
     it reaches the plate?
     a. tracking   c. anticipation
     b. focusing   d. eye coordination

42. Selective attention refers to:
     (a) choosing which stimulus to monitor.
     b. listening to two messages at once.
     c. repeating aloud a message that is heard in only one ear.
     d. determining whether an enlarging retinal images means the object is
         getting closer or growing in size.

42. Dichotic listening and shadowing are procedures for studying:
     a. binocular disparity.   c. motion parallax.
     b. selective attention.   d. linear perspective.

43. Which factor is least likely to increase the audience's attention to TV
     advertising for a product?
     a. a printed description at the bottom of the TV screen stating the
         advertisement's message
     b. the meaningfulness of the advertisement's message
     c. running the advertisement at times of the day when its message is most
         relevant
     d. bright contrast and higher volume

44. The reason small children who have very little interest in television will
     stop what they are doing and watch a commercial illustrates how we are
     especially attentive to all of the features of a commercial except:
     a. loudness.
     b. novelty.
     (c) contrast with the video images that precede it.
     d. content.

45. Which kind of stimulus is least likely to attract or hold a person's
     attention?
     a. novel   c. loud
     b. large   d. continuous

46. As a part of a listening task, a subject is fitted with earphones and hears
     a different message played simultaneously in each ear. The subject is asked
     to repeat aloud one of the two messages while it is being played into the
     subject's ear. This technique is called:
     a. selective attention.   c. dichotic listening.
     b. perceptual screening.   d. shadowing.

47. The Parthenon in Athens looks as if it:
     a. is leaning backward from the viewer.
     b. is completely upright with its columns formed of straight lines.
     c. has bulges in the middle of the columns.
     d. is ready to fall over.

48. Architects and engineers sometimes use perceptual devices to cause certain behaviors to occur. Which alternative is not mentioned in your text as an application for such objectives?
    a. getting people to slow down before a toll booth by painting perpendicular lines on the highway.
    b. encouraging people to interact at social functions by using colors and shapes associated with kindness and affection in childhood relationships.
    c. using lines and angles to make tall buildings look perfectly vertical when, in fact, they slant inward.
    d. using different colors in the seating section of a stadium so that it always looks full.

49. Of the following alternatives, visual illusions are most likely due to:
    a. errors in interpretation of sensations.
    c. distortions of visual memory.
    b. distorted retinal images.
    d. architectural errors.

50. According to the text, which alternative below is not an important factor that influences illusions?
    a. amount of formal education
    b. cultural experiences
    c. structural characteristics of the eye
    d. interpretive errors of the brain

ESSAY QUESTIONS

Recite and Review: ____

Essay Question 3.1: *The Problem of Extra Senses*

Consider what it would be like if our senses were not within their present limits. What visual problems might we face? If our hearing had a different range, what would we hear? What if we were more sensitive to smell? What about the other senses?

_____

_____

_____

_____

_____

_____

_____

_____

_____

_____

_____

_____

_____

_____

_____

_____

_____

_____

_____

_____

_____

_____

Essay Question 3.2:   *The Importance of Perceptual Constancy*

Describe the advantages of perceptual constancy and illustrate examples of each form of constancy. What would perception be like if we did not have priciples like perceptual constancy?

_____

_____

_____

_____

_____

_____

_____

_____

_____

_____

_____

_____

_____

_____

_____

_____

_____

_____

_____

_____

_____

ACTIVITIES AND PROJECTS

1. Fill in the labels that are missing from this diagram of the ear.

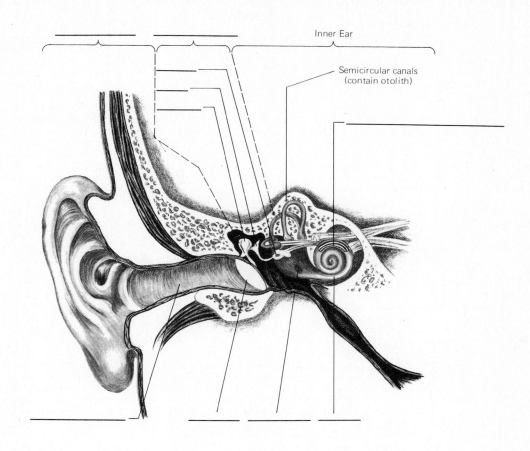

Inner Ear

Semicircular canals
(contain otolith)

2. Look at the Necker cube below. Stare at it until it reverses. What makes
    this illusion work?

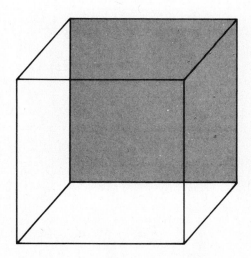

4

STATES OF CONSCIOUSNESS

DETAILED OUTLINE   *Survey:* ____

This detailed outline contains all the headings in Chapter 4: States of Consciousness. If you are using the SQ3R method, then an examination of the outline is the best way to begin your survey of the chapter.

Prologue: Ryan Shafer
Looking Ahead

Sleep and Dreams
  The cycles of sleep
    REM sleep: The paradox of sleep
  Is sleep necessary?
  Circadian rhythms: Life cycles
The Cutting Edge Illuminating Circadian Rhythms
  The function and meaning of dreaming
  Daydreams: Dreams without sleep
  Sleep disturbances: Slumbering problems
The Informed Consumer of Psychology Sleeping Better
▪ **Recap and Review I**

Hypnosis and Meditation: Altered States of Consciousness
  Hypnosis
  A different state of consciousness?
  Meditation: Regulating your own state of consciousness
▪ **Recap and Review II**

Drug Use: The Highs and Lows of Consciousness
  Stimulants: Drug highs
      Cocaine
      Amphetamines
  Depressants: Drug lows
      Barbiturates
Psychology at Work The Sound of Intoxication
  Narcotics: Relieving pain and anxiety
  Hallucinogens: Psychedelic drugs
The Informed Consumer of Psychology Identifying Drug and Alcohol Problems
▪ **Recap and Review III**

Looking Back
Key Terms and Concepts

Now that you have surveyed the chapter, read **Looking Ahead**, pages 128-130.
  Question: ____
      Read: ____

Focus on the questions on page 130.

CONCEPTS AND LEARNING OBJECTIVES   *Survey:* ____

These are the concepts and the learning objects for Chapter 4. Read them carefully as part of your preliminary survey of the chapter.

Concept 1: Consciousness is a person's awareness of sensations, thoughts, and feelings that are experienced at any given moment. Other than full alertness, sleep is one of the most important states of consciousness we experience.

1. Define consciousness and altered states of consciousness. (pp. 128-130)

2. List and define the cycles of sleep and discuss the roles of circadian rhythms in our lives. (pp. 130-136)

3. Distinguish the various theories concerning the function of and meaning of dreaming and daydreaming. (pp. 136-142)

4. Describe the sleep disturbances identified in the text and discuss ways of improving sleep. (pp. 142-143)

Concept 2: Hypnosis and meditation are two altered states of consciousness that are achieved without the aid of any drugs or other substances. They are two important, and sometimes controversial, areas of research into altered states of consciousness.

5. Describe hypnosis, the controversy regarding whether it is an altered state, and the therapeutic values it has. (pp. 144-147)

6. Describe how meditation works and the changes that can occur during meditation. (pp. 147-148)

Concept 3: Psychoactive drugs represent a major social problem. Psychologists study addiction, consequences of drug abuse, and how to help people overcome drug dependency. Some psychoactive drugs, like caffeine and alcohol, have socially accepted uses.

7. Describe the characteristics, addictive properties, and psychological reactions to stimulants and depressants. (pp. 149-157)

8. Describe the characteristics, addictive properties, and psychological reactions to narcotics and hallucinogens. (pp. 157-159)

9. Discuss the symptoms of drug abuse. (pp. 159-160)

CHAPTER SUMMARY

There are several ways you can use this summary as part of your systematic study plan. You may read each concept summary and then read the corresponding pages in the text, or you may read the entire summary and then read the entire chapter in the text. As you finish each section, complete the **Recap and Review** questions that are supplied in the text.

Concept 1: Prologue and Looking Ahead
Sleep and Dreams

Survey: ____
Read: ____

Pages 128-143

The story of Ryan Shafer illustrates the tragic consequences of extreme drug abuse.   Drug use is one of many ways to alter the experience we call consciousness. **Consciousness** is our awareness of the sensations, thoughts, and feelings being experienced at any given moment. Consciousness can range from the perceptions during wakefulness to dreams.   The variation in how we experience stimuli can be wide as well, and consciousness varies from active to passive states.   Because of its personal nature, the use of introspection made early psychological approaches appear unscientific.   Today the study of consciousness depends on several approaches that have measurable, scientific bases, like the use of electrical recording, studying the effects of drugs, and other approaches. **Altered states of consciousness** refers to conscious states that differ from a normal waking state. Altered states of consciousness share common characteristics.   Thinking may be disturbed, the sense of time becomes distorted, perceptions may be changed, we may lose our sense of self-control, and we may not be able to understand rationally the experience when we are in an altered state of consciousness.

The example of Donald Dorff's sleep-walking condition illustrates the range of sleep experiences.   Much of our knowledge of sleep itself comes from the use of the **electroencephalogram (EEG)** to record brain activity throughout the cycles of sleep.   The amplitude and frequency of the wavelike patterns formed by the EEG during sleep show regular and systematic patterns of sleep.   These patterns identify four stages of sleep.   The first stage, called **stage 1 sleep**, is the stage of transition to sleep, and the brain waves are rapid, low-voltage waves. **Stage 2 sleep** is characterized by slower, more regular waves and by occasional sharply pointed waves called spindles. **Stage 3 sleep** brain waves become even slower with higher peaks and lower valleys. **Stage 4 sleep** has even slower wave patterns.   Stage 4 is experienced soon after falling to sleep, and through the night sleep becomes lighter and is characterized by more dreams.

The period of sleep associated with most of our dreaming is identified by the rapid back and forth movement of the eyes called **rapid eye movement**, or **REM sleep**.   REM sleep, which occupies about 20 percent of the total sleep time, is also called paradoxical sleep because the body is in a state of paralysis even as the eyes are moving about rapidly.   People who are deprived of REM sleep by being awakened whenever it begins to occur experience a rebound effect that is marked by a significant increase in the amount of REM sleep during subsequent sleep.

Sleep requirements vary from person to person; and over time, individual sleep patterns change.   Some people need very little sleep, others need much more. People deprived of sleep over long periods of time, up to 200 hours in some experiments, do not experience any long-term effects, but they do experience weariness, loss of concentration, decline in creativity, irritability, and tremors while they remain awake in the studies.

Circadian rhythms refer to the daily rhythms of the body, including the sleep and waking cycle, as well as the cycles of sleepiness throughout the day. People who work on night shifts experience difficulty in changing their basic rhythms. Sleep researchers have found that exposure to bright lights helps reset the circadian rhythms, and this technique was used to prepare a space shuttle crew for night shift on the *Columbia*.

Nightmares are unusually frightening dreams. They appear to occur frequently, perhaps about 24 times a year on average. **Night terrors** are even more frightening than nightmares, and the emotion can be so intense that the dreamer awakens screaming. Most dreams, however, involve daily, mundane events. Freud believed that dreams were a guide into the unconscious and that they expressed **unconscious wish fulfillment**. The true meaning of these wishes was disguised, and Freud used the label of **latent content of dreams**, because the meanings were too threatening. Freud called the story line of the dream the **manifest content of dreams**. Freud sought to uncover the latent content by interpreting the symbols of the dream. Many psychologists reject this theory of dreams, instead preferring to interpret the content in terms of its more obvious references to everyday concerns. Another theory of dreams is called the **reverse learning theory**. This theory suggests that dreams flush away unnecessary information accumulated through the day. Dreams then have little meaning. Another theory is the **dreams-for-survival theory** which suggests that dreams involve a reconsideration and reprocessing of critical information from the day. Dreams in this theory have meaning as they represent important concerns having roots in daily experiences. The most influential theory is the **activation-synthesis theory** which claims that dreams are by-products of biological processes. These processes are random firings related to changes in neurotransmitter production. Because these activities activate memories that have importance, what begins randomly becomes meaningful.

Another form of **dreaming** is daydreams - fantasies produced while awake. Daydreams are under the control of individuals, and thus their content is relevant to current concerns and immediate events. Evidence suggests that people may daydream for about 10 percent of the time. There is little relationship between daydreaming and psychological disturbances.

The most common sleep disturbance is **insomnia**, the experience of difficulty in falling asleep. As many as one-quarter of the people in the United States experience insomnia. Affecting about 20 million people, **sleep apnea** is another sleep disturbance. In sleep apnea, a person has difficulty breathing and sleeping at the same time. In extreme cases a person may awaken as many as 500 times a night. **Sudden infant death syndrome**, a syndrome in which apparently healthy infants die in their sleep, may be related to sleep apnea. Although the causes of **narcolepsy** are unknown, the uncontrollable urge to fall asleep, afflicts many people. In narcolepsy, the sleeper falls directly into REM sleep. Sleepwalking and sleeptalking are two usually harmless disturbances.

The Informed Consumer of Psychology section recommends tips for dealing with insomnia. These include exercising before bed, choosing a regular bedtime, using bed for sleep and not for watching TV or studying, avoiding caffeine drinks after lunch, drinking a glass of warm milk, avoiding sleeping pills, and if all fails, trying not to go to sleep. Research suggests that people with insomnia may actually sleep more than they think, but may also be aware of events around them even when they are asleep, thus having the impression of being awake.

Concept 2:   Hypnosis and Meditation: Altered States   *Survey:* _____
**   of Consciousness**   *Read:* _____

Pages 144-148

Hypnosis is a state of heightened susceptibility to the suggestion of others. When people are hypnotized, they will not perform antisocial behaviors, they will not carry out self-destructive acts, they will not reveal hidden truths about themselves, and they are capable of lying. Between 5 and 20 percent of the population cannot be hypnotized at all, and about 15 percent are highly susceptible. Hilgard has argued that hypnosis does represent a state of consciousness that is significantly different from other states. The increased suggestibility, greater ability to recall and construct images, increased memories from childhood, lack of initiative, and ability to accept suggestions that contradict reality suggest that hypnotic states are different from other

states. Some researchers have established that some people do pretend to be
hypnotized. Moreover, adults do not have a special ability to recall childhood
events while hypnotized. Hypnotism has been used successfully to control pain,
to end tobacco addiction, in psychotherapy, for law enforcement, and in
professional sports.

Meditation is another altered state. Meditation is a learned technique for
refocusing attention that brings about the altered state. Transcendental
meditation (TM), brought to the United States by the Maharishi Mahesh Yogi, is
perhaps the best-known form of meditation. TM uses a **mantra**, a sound, word, or
syllable, that is said over and over. In other forms, the meditator focuses on
a picture, flame, or body part. In all forms the key is to concentrate
intensely. Following meditation, people are relaxed, they may have new insights,
and in the long term, they may have improved health. The physiological changes
that accompany meditation are similar to relaxation: heart rate declines, oxygen
intake declines, and brain-wave patterns change.   The simple procedures of
sitting in a quiet room, breathing deeply and rhythmically, and repeating a word
will achieve the same effects as trained meditation techniques.

Concept 3: Drug Use: The Highs and Lows of Consciousness

Survey: ____
Read: ____

Pages 149-160

Psychoactive drugs are drugs that affect consciousness by influencing a person's
emotions, perceptions, and behavior. Drug use among high school students has
declined, as today about half of the seniors have used an illegal drug in their
lives, where the figure had been as much as 20 to 25 percent higher in the past.
The most dangerous drugs are those that are addictive. **Addictive drugs** produce
psychological or biological dependence in the user, and the withdrawal of the
drug leads to cravings for it. The reasons for taking drugs range from seeking
altered spiritual states, to taking them simply for the experience, to escaping
the pressures of life, to the thrill of doing something illegal.

Drugs that affect the central nervous system by increasing its activity and
by increasing heart rate, blood pressure, and muscle tension are called
stimulants.   The stimulant **caffeine** is found in coffee, soft drinks, and
chocolate. Caffeine increases attentiveness and decreases reaction time. Too
much caffeine leads to nervousness and insomnia. Stopping caffeine can cause
headaches and depression. **Nicotine** is the stimulant found in tobacco products.
Cocaine and its derivative crack are illegal stimulants. Cocaine produces
feelings of well-being, confidence, and alertness when taken in small quantities.
(See Table 4-3 in the text for a listing of illegal drugs and their effects.)
Cocaine blocks the reuptake of excess dopamine, which in turn produces
pleasurable sensations. Cocaine abuse makes the abusers crave the drug and go
on binges of use.   The withdrawal from cocaine has three stages: first a
''crash''; then a withdrawal marked by boredom and lack of motivation, and in
spite of the decrease in cravings, the users are highly sensitive to cues related
to cocaine; and then a third stage in which the cravings are further reduced and
moods are more normal.

Amphetamines are a group of very strong stimulants that bring about a sense
of energy and alertness, talkativeness, confidence, and a mood ''high.'' The
amphetamine Benzedrine is commonly known as speed, and excessive amounts of the
drug can lead to overstimulation of the central nervous system, convulsions, and
death.

Drugs that slow the central nervous system are called **depressants**. Feelings
of **intoxication** come from taking small doses. **Alcohol** is the most common
depressant. The average person drinks about 200 alcoholic drinks a year (based

on liquor sales). People's reactions to alcohol vary widely. The relaxation, feelings of happiness, and loss of inhibitions make people perceive the effects of alcohol as increasing sociability and well-being (the opposite of depression). **Alcoholics** are people who abuse alcohol, rely upon it, and continue to use it when they have serious problems. Alcoholism requires some people to drink just to be able to function normally. In some cases, alcoholics have sporadic binges and drink excessive quantities. The reasons for the tolerance to alcohol that leads to alcoholism are not clear, though there is evidence that there may be genetic factors. Environmental stressors are thought to play a role as well.

Barbiturates are a form of depressant drug used to induce sleep and reduce stress. They are addictive and can be deadly when combined with alcohol. Quaalude is an illegal drug similar to barbiturates.

Narcotics increase relaxation and relieve pain and anxiety. **Morphine** and **heroin** are two powerful narcotics. Morphine is used to reduce pain, but heroin is illegal. Heroin effects include an initial rush followed by a sense of well-being. When the sense of well-being ends, the heroin user feels anxiety and the desire to use the drug again. With each use, more heroin is needed to have any effect. A successful treatment for heroin addiction is the use of **methadone**, a drug that satisfies the cravings but does not produce the high. Methadone is biologically addicting.

Drugs that produce hallucinations are called **hallucinogens**. The most common hallucinogen is **marijuana**, and its active ingredient is tetrahydrocannabinol. The effects of marijuana include euphoria and well-being, and sensory experiences can be more intense. There is no scientific evidence for marijuana being addictive, and the short-term effects appear to be minor. However, the long-term effects of heavy use include temporary decreases in the male sex hormone, decreased activity of the immune system, and damage to the lungs.

Vivid hallucinations are produced by **lysergic acid diethylamide**, or **LSD**. Perceptions of colors, sounds, and shapes are altered, time perception is distorted, or the user may have a terrifying experience. After use, people can also experience flashbacks during which they hallucinate. **Phencyclidine**, or **PCP**, is similar to LSD, but can be more dangerous with side effects that include paranoid and destructive behavior.

The text lists a number of signs that could indicate drug abuse problems. Individuals with these symptoms should be encouraged to seek professional help.

♦ Now that you have surveyed, questioned, and read the chapter and completed the **Recap and Review** questions, review **Looking Back**, pages 160-162. *Review:* ____

♦ For additional practice through recitation and review, test your knowledge of the chapter material by answering the questions in the **Key Word Drill**, the **Practice Questions**, and the **Essay Questions**.

KEY WORD DRILL   *Recite:* ____

The following **Fill in the Blank** and **Matching Questions** test key words from the text. Check your answers with the Answer Key in the back of the *Study Guide*.

FILL IN THE BLANK

1. The term _____ refers to a person's awareness of the sensations, thoughts, and feelings that he or she is experiencing at a given moment.

2. Experiences of sensations or thought that differ from a normal waking consciousness are said to be _____ _____ of _____.

3. The biological processes that occur repeatedly and on approximately a twenty-four-hour cycle are _____ _____ .

4. Sigmund Freud proposed that dreams result from _____ _____ _____ , in other words, that dreams represent unconscious wishes that a dreamer wants to fulfill.

5. _____ is the state of heightened susceptibility to the suggestions of others.

6. Virtually every religion has some form of _____ , a learned technique for refocusing attention that brings about an altered state of consciousness, and many forms use a _____ , a sound, word, or syllable repeated over and over to take one into the altered state.

7. Drugs that influence a person's emotions, perceptions, and behavior are called _____ drugs.

8. Psychologists have named drugs that produce a physical or psychological dependence in the user _____ drugs.

9. Drugs that affect the central nervous system, causing increased heart rate, blood pressure, and muscle tension are called _____ ; and drugs that slow down the nervous system are called _____ .

10. _____ refers to the class of drugs that increase relaxation and relieve pain and anxiety.

MATCHING QUESTIONS

_a_ 11. stage 1 sleep

_e_ 12. stage 2 sleep

_c_ 13. stage 3 sleep

_b_ 14. stage 4 sleep

_d_ 15. rapid eye movement (REM) sleep

a. The deepest stage of sleep, during which we are least responsive to outside stimulation.

b. Sleep characterized by increased heart rate, blood pressure, and breathing rate; erections; and the experience of dreaming.

c. A sleep deeper than that of stage 1, characterized by sleep spindles.

d. The state of transition between wakefulness and sleep, characterized by relatively rapid, low-voltage brain waves.

e. A sleep characterized by slow brain waves, with greater peaks and valleys in the wave pattern.

_a_ 16. latent content of dreams

_e_ 17. manifest content of dreams

_c_ 18. reverse learning theory

_d_ 19. dreams-for-survival theory

_b_ 20. activation-synthesis theory

a. According to Freud, the ''disguised'' meanings of dreams, hidden by more obvious subjects.

b. Hobson's view that dreams are a result of random electrical energy stimulating memories lodged in various portions of the brain, which the brain then weaves into a logical story line.

c. The view that dreams have no meaning in themselves, but instead function to rid us of unnecessary information that we have accumulated during the day.

d. The proposal that dreams permit information critical for our daily survival to be reconsidered and reprocessed during sleep.

e. According to Freud, the overt story line of dreams.

_e_ 21. rebound effect

_c_ 22. nightmares

_f_ 23. night terrors

_g_ 24. daydreams

_a_ 25. insomnia

_h_ 26. sleep apnea

_b_ 27. sudden infant death syndrome

_d_ 28. narcolepsy

a. An inability to get to sleep or stay asleep.

b. A disorder in which seemingly healthy infants die in their sleep.

c. Unusually frightening dreams.

d. An uncontrollable need to sleep for short periods during the day.

e. An increase in REM sleep after one has been deprived of it.

f. Profoundly frightening nightmares which wake up the dreamer.

g. Fantasies people construct while awake.

h. A sleep disorder characterized by difficulty in breathing and sleeping simultaneously.

_e_ 29. caffeine

_a_ 30. nicotine

_c_ 31. cocaine

_b_ 32. amphetamines

_d_ 33. alcohol

_f_ 34. intoxication

a. An addictive stimulant present in cigarettes.

b. Strong stimulants that cause a temporary feeling of confidence and alertness but may increase anxiety and appetite loss and, taken over a period of time, suspiciousness and feelings of persecution.

c. An addictive stimulant that when taken in small doses, initially creates feelings of confidence, alertness, and well-being, but eventually causes mental and physical deterioration.

d. The most common depressant, which in small doses causes release of tension and feelings of happiness, but in larger amounts can cause emotional and physical instability, memory impairment, and stupor.

e. An addictive stimulant found most abundantly in coffee, tea, soda, and chocolate.

f. A state of drunkenness.

_b_ 35. barbiturates

_h_ 36. morphine

_a_ 37. heroin

_d_ 38. methadone

_f_ 39. hallucinogen

_g_ 40. marijuana

_e_ 41. lysergic acid diethylamide (LSD)

_c_ 42. phencyclidine (PCP)

a. A powerful depressant, usually injected, that gives an initial rush of good feeling but leads eventually to anxiety and depression; extremely addictive.

b. Addictive depressants used to induce sleep and reduce stress; abuse, especially when combined with alcohol, can be deadly.

c. A powerful hallucinogen that alters brain-cell activity and can cause paranoid and destructive behavior.

d. A chemical used to detoxify heroin addicts.

e. One of the most powerful hallucinogens, affecting the operation of neuro-transmitters in the brain and causing brain cell activity to be altered.

f. A drug that is capable of producing changes in the perceptual process, or hallucinations.

g. A common hallucinogen, usually smoked.

h. Derived from the poppy flower, a powerful depressant that reduces pain and induces sleep.

PRACTICE QUESTIONS   *Recite and Review:* _____

Test your knowledge of the chapter material by answering these **True-False** and **Multiple Choice Questions.** Check your answers with the Answer Key in the back of the *Study Guide*.

TRUE-FALSE QUESTIONS

(T)   F   1. The body and brain are active, rather than dormant, during the night.

T   (F)   2. Stage 4 sleep is characterized by rapid brain waves with high peaks and valleys.

T   (F)   3. Dreams are not experienced by everyone during a night's sleep.

(T)   F   4. If a person is deprived of rapid eye movement (REM) sleep, normal mental functioning becomes impaired.

T   (F)   5. Sleep deprivation has lasting effects on the performance of cognitive tasks.

(T)   F   6. Experiments with the neurotransmitter acetylcholine caused sleepers to enter rapid eye movement (REM) sleep quickly and to report dream activity similar to that occurring during normal sleep.

T   (F)   7. Daydreaming is a common sign of psychological disturbance.

(T)   F   8. A psychological addiction is characterized by a person believing that he or she needs a substance in order to deal with the stress of the day.

(T)   F   9. Although most people perceive alcohol as a stimulant, its actual effects are those of a depressant.

(T)   F 10. Tetrahydrocannabinol is the active ingredient in marijuana.

MULTIPLE CHOICE QUESTIONS

1. Most psychologists today agree that the study of consciousness is:
    a. better left to philosophers.
    b. improper for scientific study.
    c. not highly personal.
    (d.) a legitimate area of study for psychologists.

2. Which of the following is not characteristic of altered states of consciousness?
    (a.) undisturbed thought processes   c. changed image of the world
    b. disturbed sense of time   d. loss of self-control

3. Sleep involves four different stages. What is the basis for differentiating these stages of sleep?
   a. They are defined according to the electrical properties recorded by an electroencephalogram (EEG) attached to the sleeper.
   b. They are defined by the amount of time elapsed from the onset of sleep.
   c. They are based on the mental experiences described when sleepers are awakened and asked what they are thinking.
   d. They are characterized by patterns of overt body movements recorded with a videocamera that is positioned over the sleeper.

4. During the course of a night's sleep, we tend to _____ as morning approaches.
   a. sleep less deeply
   b. dream less
   c. be less responsive to outside stimulation
   d. sleepwalk more often

5. Which stage represents the transition from wakefulness to sleep?
   a. stage 1   c. stage 3
   b. stage 2   d. rapid eye movement (REM)

6. Stage 1 sleep is characterized by:
   a. slow, low-voltage brain waves.
   b. rapid, low-voltage brain waves.
   c. slow, high-voltage brain waves.
   d. rapid, high-voltage brain waves.

7. As we progress through the stages of sleep toward deepest sleep, within a single sleep cycle the EEG pattern gets:
   a. faster and more regular.   c. slower and lower in amplitude.
   b. faster and more irregular.   d. slower and more regular.

8. Which sleep stage is characterized by electrical signals with the slowest frequency, by waveforms that are very regular, and by a sleeper who is very unresponsive to external stimuli?
   a. rapid eye movement (REM)   c. stage 3
   b. stage 2   d. stage 4

9. Which of the following stages of sleep is characterized by irregular breathing, increased blood pressure, and increased respiration?
   a. stage 1   c. rapid eye movement (REM)
   b. stage 2   d. non-rapid eye movement (NREM)

10. REM sleep is referred to as paradoxical because:
    a. brain activity is low but eye movement is high.
    b. brain activity is low, but muscle activity is high.
    c. eye movement becomes rapid and brain activity is high.
    d. the brain is very active, but body muscles are paralyzed.

11. The major muscles of the body act as if they are paralyzed during:
    a. stage 1 sleep.   c. stage 4 sleep.
    b. stage 3 sleep.   d. rapid eye movement (REM).

12. The increase in REM sleep during periods after a person has been deprived of it is called:
    a. paradoxical sleep.   c. latent dreaming.
    b. the rebound effect.   d. somnambulism.

13. A friend comes to you concerned about his health after having stayed up for thirty-six hours straight studying without sleep. The most valid thing you could tell him is that:
    a. if he is going to stay up for so long, he should see a doctor regularly.
    b. if he continues to stay up for so long, he will probably get sick.
    c. there will most likely be rather severe long-term consequences of not sleeping for that amount of time.
    d. research has demonstrated that lack of sleep will affect his ability to study.

14. The effects of sleep deprivation:
    a. are long-term and debilitating.
    b. are not known at the present time.
    c. are short-term, with no enduring effects.
    d. show how important sleep is to survival.

15. According to Freud, dreams:
    a. are reflections of day-to-day activities.
    b. are reflections of conscious activity.
    c. are reflections of unconscious wish fulfillment.
    d. are remnants of our evolutionary heritage.

16. Freud referred to the story line of a dream as its:
    a. libidinal content.   c. manifest content.
    b. unconscious content.   d. latent content.

17. Freud called the disguised meaning of dreams the:
    a. latent content.   c. manifest content.
    b. sexual fantasy.   d. image fantasy.

18. Sharon dreams that Jim climbs a stairway and meets her at the top. According to Freudian dream symbols described in the text, this would probably suggest:
    a. that Sharon would like to start a friendship with Jim.
    b. that Sharon is really afraid to talk to Jim, though she would like to start a friendship.
    c. that Jim and Sharon probably work together in a building where there are stairs.
    d. that Sharon is dreaming of sexual intercourse with Jim.

19. If you had a dream about carrying grapefruits down a long tunnel, Freud would interpret the grapefruit as a dream symbol suggesting a wish to:
    a. take a trip to the tropics.   c. caress a man's genitals.
    b. caress a woman's body.   d. return to the womb.

20. When injected into people, drugs similar to which of the following are most likely to induce rapid eye movement (REM) stage of sleep and active dreaming?
    a. noradrenalin   c. tryptophan
    b. acetylcholine   d. serotonin

21. While in calculus class, Rob fantasized about sailing to Tahiti. He was experiencing a:
    a. nervous breakdown.   c. diurnal emission.
    b. daydream.   d. mantra.

22. Which of the following does not describe a common characteristic of daydreams?
    a. fantastic and creative
    b. mundane, ordinary topics
    c. a part of normal consciousness
    d. a prevalence of sexual imagery

23. According to studies, the average person daydreams about:
    a. 10 percent of the time.
    b. 20 percent of the time.
    c. 30 percent of the time.
    d. 40 percent of the time.

24. People pass directly from a conscious, wakeful state to REM sleep if they suffer from:
    a. narcolepsy
    b. insomnia
    c. somnambulism
    d. rapid eye movement showers

25. Insomnia is a condition in which a person:
    a. uncontrollably falls asleep.
    b. sleeps more than twelve hours per night on a routine basis.
    c. has difficulty sleeping.
    d. exhibits abnormal brain wave patterns during rapid eye movement (REM) sleep.

26. The uncontrollable need to sleep for short periods that can happen at any time during the day is called:
    a. narcolepsy.
    b. sleep apnea.
    c. hypersomnia.
    d. insomnia.

27. Having difficulty sleeping and breathing simultaneously is called:
    a. narcolepsy.
    b. sleep apnea.
    c. hypersomnia.
    d. insomnia.

28. According to research discussed in the text, which of the following may account for sudden infant death syndrome?
    a. narcolepsy
    b. sleep apnea
    c. somnambulism
    d. insomnia

29. Which of the following statements about sleep difficulties is not correct?
    a. Insomnia is the most common sleep disorder.
    b. Sleep apnea sometimes causes people to have inadequate oxygen in their blood while they sleep.
    c. Narcolepsy is an uncontrollable need to sleep for short periods during the day.
    d. Sudden infant death syndrome kills infants who have unusually irregular sleep patterns.

30. Which of the following statements about sleepwalking is not true?
    a. Sleepwalkers should not be awakened.
    b. Sleepwalking occurs in stage 4 sleep.
    c. Sleepwalkers are somewhat aware of their surroundings.
    d. Sleepwalking occurs most frequently in children.

31. Generalizing from the text, all of the following are typical suggestions for overcoming insomnia except:
    a. Choose regular bedtimes.
    b. Don't try to go to sleep.
    c. Avoid drinks with caffeine.
    d. Watch TV in bed.

32. Which of the following is true regarding a person under hypnosis?
    a. The person can be induced to perform antisocial behaviors.
    b. The person cannot be hypnotized against his or her will.
    c. The person can commit self-destructive acts.
    d. The person's ability to draw on memories decreases.

33. The procedure, introduced in the United States by Maharishi Mahesh Yogi, in which a person focuses on a mantra to reach a different state of consciousness is called:
    a. transactional analysis.   c. exorcism.
    b. Zen Buddhism.   d. transcendental meditation.

34. During transcendental meditation, a person repeats a(n) _____ over and over again.
    a. mantra   c. banta
    b. allegory   d. analogy

35. In what way is meditation and hypnosis similar?
    a. They are both accompanied by changes in brain activity.
    b. They both result in a decrease in blood pressure.
    c. They are both based on Eastern religious practices.
    d. They both result in total relaxation.

36. _____ drugs are considered most dangerous to physical and mental well-being.
    a. Sleep-inducing   c. Birth-control
    b. Over-the-counter   d. Addictive

37. A psychoactive drug:
    a. affects a person's behavior only if he or she is receptive to ''mind expanding'' experiences.
    b. influences thoughts and perceptions and is usually physically addictive.
    c. affects a person's emotions, perceptions, and behavior.
    d. acts primarily on biological functions such as heart rate and intestinal mobility.

38. Which of the following statements about addiction to drugs is not true?
    a. Addiction may be biologically based.
    b. Addictions are primarily caused by an inherited biological liability.
    c. All people, with few exceptions, have used one or more ''addictive'' drugs in their lifetime.
    d. Addictions may be psychological.

39. Caffeine, nicotine, cocaine, and amphetamines are considered:
    a. anesthetic agents.   c. anti-anxiety drugs.
    b. central nervous system stimulants.   d. hallucinogens.

40. The most common central nervous system depressant is:
    a. phenobarbital.   c. Valium.
    b. alcohol.   d. Quaalude.

41. Which alternative below does not belong with the others?
    a. coffee   c. nicotine
    b. alcohol   d. amphetamines

42. Nembutal, Seconal, and phenobarbital are all depressants and forms of:
    a. opiates.   c. hallucinogens.
    b. barbiturates.   d. hypnotics.

43. The most common hallucinogen in use in the United States is:
    a. PCP.   c. cocaine.
    b. LSD.   d. marijuana.

44. Which of the following is a hallucinogen?
    a. heroin   c. marijuana
    b. cocaine   d. morphine

45. Which of the following appears to be nonaddictive with minimal withdrawal symptoms?
    a. alcohol   c. marijuana
    b. nicotine   d. morphine

ESSAY QUESTIONS   *Recite and Review:* ____

Essay Question 4.1: *Hypnotism*

Discuss the competing theories of hypnotism. Is it a real phenomenon? Do
you consider it to be an altered state? Defend your answer.

_____

_____

_____

_____

_____

_____

_____

_____

_____

_____

_____

_____

_____

_____

_____

_____

_____

_____

Essay Question 4.2: *Decriminalizing Psychoactive Drugs*

Debates regarding the legalization of drugs, especially marijuana, seem to come and go. If that debate were to be revitalized today, what do you think psychology should contribute? What are your feelings? Should some drugs be legalized or given through prescription? Defend your answer.

_____

_____

_____

_____

_____

_____

_____

_____

_____

_____

_____

_____

_____

_____

_____

_____

_____

_____

_____

ACTIVITIES AND PROJECTS

1. Prepare a dream journal. Some people are able to record their dreams in the morning when they awaken, while others will place a notepad and pencil next to their bed at night and record their dreams throughout the night by waking and writing a few notes immediately after the dream occurs. Use this second method, before you fall asleep give yourself the suggestion to awaken after each dream (you may wish to include in your suggestion that you will be able to record your dream and fall back to sleep without any problem). After one week of keeping a journal, you should examine it for patterns or recurring themes (recurrent dreams will be very noticeable without keeping a journal). If other students in the class are doing this activity, you may desire to share a few of your dreams and discuss their possible meanings.

2. Go to a local drug store or to the section of the campus bookstore that has cold remedies, sleep aids, and other over-the-counter medications. Record the active ingredients and the names of the products. Then go with the list to any medical reference and find the description of the active ingredient. This drug should also be classified according to what type of psychoactive drug it is. Is it a depressant or a stimulant? Is it related to a narcotic or hallucinogen? Is it classed as antianxiety or antidepressant? (Check Chapter 13 for a description of these two drug classes.)

3. Your library should have a relaxation tape that you can check out. If not, ask your psychology instructor or someone in the campus counseling center. After locating a tape, find a quiet spot where you will not be disturbed and you can play the tape. Before playing the tape, take a pulse rate and count the number of breaths you take in a minute. Now play the tape. After the tape has ended, wait a few moments and take your pulse and breathing rates again. How do you feel? In what way is this like meditation? In what way is it different?

5

LEARNING

DETAILED OUTLINE   *Survey:* _____

This detailed outline contains all the headings in Chapter 5: Learning. If you are using the SQ3R method, then an examination of the outline is the best way to begin your survey of the chapter.

Prologue: Brad Gabrielson and Bo
Looking Ahead

Classical Conditioning
   The basics of conditioning
   Applying conditioning principles to human behavior
   Extinction: Unlearning what you have learned
   Spontaneous recovery: Return of the conditioned response
   Generalization and discrimination
   Higher-order conditioning
   Beyond traditional classical conditioning: Challenging basic assumptions
      The interval between the CS and the UCS
▪ **Recap and Review I**

Operant Conditioning
   Thorndike's law of effect
   The basics of operant conditioning
      Reinforcing desired behavior
Psychology at Work Saving Lives with Operant Conditioning: Dolphin
      Defenses and Pigeon Posses
   Positive reinforcers, negative reinforcers, and punishment
   The pros and cons of punishment: Why reinforcement beats punishment
▪ **Recap and Review II**
   Schedules of reinforcement: Timing life's rewards
      Fixed- and variable-ratio schedules
      Fixed- and variable-interval schedules: The passage of time
   Discrimination and generalization in operant conditioning
   Superstitious behavior
   Shaping: Reinforcing what doesn't come naturally
   Using programmed instruction in college classes: Programs as professors
The Cutting Edge Learning Like Humans: Building Neural Networks via
      Computer
   Discriminating between classical and operant conditioning
   Biological constraints on learning: You can't teach an old dog just any
      trick
▪ **Recap and Review III**

Cognitive Approaches to Learning
   Rule-learning in animals

Observational learning: Learning through copying
Learned helplessness: Accepting the unacceptable
The unresolved controversy of cognitive learning theory
The Informed Consumer of Psychology Behavior Analysis and Behavior
      Modification
• **Recap and Review IV**

Looking Back
Key Terms and Concepts

Now that you have surveyed the chapter, read **Looking Ahead**, pages 164-165.
      Question: _____
            Read: _____

Focus on the questions on page 165.

CONCEPTS AND LEARNING OBJECTIVES   *Survey:* _____

These are the concepts and the learning objects for Chapter 5. Read them
carefully as part of your preliminary survey of the chapter.

Concept 1: Learning is the relatively permanent change in behavior that results
      from experience. Classical conditioning, the learning theory pioneered by
      Ivan Pavlov, understands learning to be the substitution of a new stimulus
      for a preexisting stimulus in a stimulus-response association.

  1. Define learning and describe the basic concepts and application of
      classical conditioning. (pp. 164-169)

  2. Define and describe the major principles of classical conditioning,
      including extinction, spontaneous recovery, stimulus generalization,
      stimulus discrimination, and higher-order conditioning. (pp. 169-172)

  3. Identify the challenges that have been made to the traditional views of
      classical conditioning. (pp. 172-174)

Concept 2: Operant conditioning, utilizes the consequences of behavior to shape
      behavior. Reinforcement is the principle that accounts for the increase of
      particular behaviors.

  4. Describe the basic procedures of operant conditioning. (pp. 175-177)

  5. Define positive and negative reinforcement, types of reinforcers, and
      punishment. (pp. 177-181)

Concept 3: Most reinforcement of behavior follows schedules that provide partial
      reinforcement, and often leads to greater resistance to extinction. Operant
      conditioning has a number of applications, including computerized programmed
      instruction.

  6. Outline the schedules of reinforcement and define the operant view of
      generalization and discrimination, superstitious behavior, and shaping.
      (pp. 182-187)

  7. Describe applications of operant conditioning, especially programmed
      instruction. (pp. 187-188)

8. Discuss the distinction between classical and operant conditioning and the limits to conditioning like biological constraints. (pp. 188-191)

Concept 4: Cognitive approaches to learning focus on the role of cognitive processes, especially observation, in the learning of new behaviors.

9. Describe the cognitive learning aspects of latent learning, rule-learning behavior and observational learning. (pp. 191-195)

10. Describe Seligman's concept of learned helplessness. (pp. 196-197)

11. Outline the methods of behavior modification discussed in the text. (pp. 197-199)

CHAPTER SUMMARY

There are several ways you can use this summary as part of your systematic study plan. You may read each concept summary and then read the corresponding pages in the text, or you may read the entire summary and then read the entire chapter in the text. As you finish each section, complete the **Recap and Review** questions that are supplied in the text.

Concept 1:   Prologue and Looking Ahead   *Survey:* _____
Classical Conditioning   *Read:* _____

Pages 164-174

The Prologue illustrates how effectively learning principles can be applied to animal behavior by describing the behavior of Bo, Brad Gabrielson's dog. Bo was able to go and find a neighbor to help Brad back into his wheelchair, and though it appears incredible, this was a result of Bo's training.
   Learning is distinguished from **maturation** on the basis of whether the resulting change in behavior is a consequence of the environment (learning) or of growth (maturation). Short-term changes in performance, the key measure of learning, can also result from fatigue, tension, and other factors that are not reflections of learning. According to some, learning can only be inferred indirectly from performance, and performance does not always indicate learning.
   Ivan Pavlov's studies concerning the physiology of digestive processes led him to discover the basic principles of classical conditioning. In **classical conditioning**, an organism learns to respond to a stimulus that did not bring about the response earlier. An original study involved Pavlov's training a dog to salivate when a tuning fork was sounded. In this process, the tuning fork's sound is considered the **neutral stimulus** because it does not bring about the response of interest. The meat powder, which does cause salivation, is called the **unconditioned stimulus (UCS)**. The salivation, when it occurs due to the presence of the meat powder (UCS), is called the **unconditioned response (UCR)**. The conditioning process requires repeated pairing of the UCS and the neutral stimulus. After training is complete, the neutral stimulus - now called the **conditioned stimulus (CS)** - will now bring about the UCR, now called the **conditioned response (CR)**. Pavlov noted that the neutral stimulus had to precede the UCS by no more than several seconds for the conditioning to be the most effective.
   One of the more famous applications of classical conditioning techniques to humans is the case of the 11-month-old infant, Albert. Albert was taught a fear of a white rat, to which he had shown no fear initially, by striking a bar behind

him whenever he approached the rat. Whenever we associate one stimulus with another and then behave differently as a result of the association, we are experiencing classical conditioning.

The process of ending the association of the UCS and the CS is called **extinction**, which occurs when a previously learned response decreases and disappears. If the tuning fork is repeatedly sounded without the meat powder being presented, the dog will eventually stop salivating. Extinction is the basis for the treatment principle called **systematic desensitization**, which is used to treat phobias. Systematic desensitization requires that the repeated presentation of the frightening stimulus (a CS) without the presentation of the occurrence of the negative consequences.

When a CS has been extinguished, and a period of time has passed without the presentation of the CS, a phenomenon called **spontaneous recovery** can occur. The CS is presented and the previously extinguished response recurs, though it is usually weaker than in the original training and can be extinguished again more easily.

Stimulus generalization occurs when a conditioned response occurs in the presence of a stimulus that is similar to the original conditioned stimulus. In the case of baby Albert, the fear response was generalized to white furry things, including a white Santa Claus mask. The generalized response is not usually as intense as the original, though the more the new stimulus resembles the original, the more similar the response will be. **Stimulus discrimination** occurs when an organism learns to differentiate (discriminate) one stimulus from another and responds only to one stimulus and not the others.

When a conditioned stimulus has been established and is then repeatedly paired with another neutral stimulus until the conditioned response becomes conditioned to the new stimulus, then **higher-order conditioning** has occurred. Some investigators have used the concept of higher-order conditioning to explain how people develop and maintain prejudices against members of racial and ethnic groups.

Many of the fundamental assumptions of classical conditioning have been challenged. The cognitive learning theorists argue that the learner develops an expectancy concerning which UCSs are matched to CSs. Leon Kamin's study of **blocking**, a process in which the learning of one CS-UCS connection blocks the learning of another response to a second stimulus, is an example. If the first CS causes sufficient expectations regarding the response, the animal is likely to ignore a second stimulus. The notion that learners tend to ignore a stimulus suggests the presence of cognitive processes. Another challenge has been to question the length of the interval between the neutral stimulus and the unconditioned stimulus. Garcia found that nausea caused by radiation, a state that occurred hours after exposure, could be associated with water drunk that has unusual characteristics or with water drunk in a particular place. Garcia's findings that the association could be made with delays as long as eight hours is a direct challenge to the idea that the pairing must be made within several seconds to be effective.

Concept 2: Operant Conditioning   *Survey:* ____
                                                                    Read: ____

                                                                    Pages175-181

Operant conditioning is learning in which the response is strengthened or weakened according to whether it has positive or negative consequences. The term ''operant'' suggests that the organism operates on the environment in a deliberate manner to gain a desired result.

Edward L. Thorndike found that a cat would learn to escape from a cage by performing specific actions in order to open a door that allows it access to food, a positive consequence of the behavior. Thorndike formulated the **law of effect**, stating that responses with satisfying results would be repeated, those with less satisfying results would be less likely to be repeated.

B. F. Skinner took Thorndike's law of effect and suggested that chance behaviors that lead to desirable consequences are then repeated. Pigeons will accidentally peck a key that releases food pellets, and then begin to peck until satisfied, learning the contingency between the pecking and the food.

The food released by the pecking is called a **reinforcer**, which is any stimulus that increases the probability that a preceding behavior will be repeated. A **primary reinforcer** satisfies a biological need without regard to prior experience. A **secondary reinforcer** is a stimulus that reinforces because of its association with a primary reinforcer.

Operant conditioning has been used to train animals to help in rescue missions. Dolphins can locate and tag divers in the Navy's Marine Mammal Program, and pigeons have been trained to locate missing sailors in the ocean by pecking a series of keys when they sight the orange color of the life jacket.

Reinforcers are also distinguished as positive or negative. **Positive reinforcers** bring about an increase in the preceding response. **Negative reinforcers**, however, lead to an increase in a desired response when they are removed. Negative reinforcement requires that an individual take an action to remove an undesirable condition. Negative reinforcement is used in **escape conditioning**, where an organism learns to escape from an aversive situation, and in **avoidance conditioning**, where the organism learns to act to avoid the aversive situation. **Punishment** refers to the use of an **aversive stimulus**, by adding it to the environment, in order to decrease the probability that a behavior will be repeated. Punishment includes the removal of something positive, such as the loss of a privilege.

The effectiveness of punishment depends greatly on how it is used. The use of punishment is usually an opportunity for reinforcing an alternate, preferred behavior. Also, in rare cases, such as autism, quick and intense physical punishment may be used to prevent or end self-destructive behavior. The disadvantages of punishment make its use questionable. It must be delivered shortly after the behavior or it will be ineffective. Physical punishment may convey the idea that physical aggression is an appropriate behavior. Punishment does not convey information about alternative behaviors.

Concept 3: Operant Conditioning (Continued)   *Survey:* ____
                                                                          Read: ____

                                                                          Pages 182-191

The frequency and timing of reinforcement depends upon the use of **schedules of reinforcement**. With continuous reinforcement, the behavior is reinforced every time it occurs. **Partial reinforcement** describes the technique of using reinforcement some of the time but not for every response. Partial reinforcement schedules maintain behavior longer than continuous reinforcement before extinction occurs. A **cumulative recorder** automatically records the number of responses and the amount of time between responses. It also notes the number of times a reinforcement is given (see Figure 5-5).

A **fixed-ratio schedule** delivers a reinforcement after a certain number of responses. A **variable-ratio schedule** delivers reinforcement on the basis of a varying number of responses. The number of responses often remains close to an average. The fixed- and variable-ratio schedules depend upon a number of responses, and the fixed- and variable-interval schedules depend upon an *amount of time*. **Fixed-interval schedules** deliver reinforcements to the first behavior occurring after a set interval, or period, of time. **Variable-interval schedules** deliver reinforcement after a varying interval of time. Fixed intervals are like weekly paychecks, variable intervals are like pop quizzes.

Discrimination and generalization are achieved in operant conditioning through **stimulus control training**. In stimulus control training, a behavior is reinforced only in the presence of specific stimuli. The specific stimulus is called a **discriminative stimulus**, a stimulus that signals the likelihood of a particular behavior being reinforced. Stimulus generalization occurs when an organism responds in situations similar to the original and expects reinforcement in the new situation just as the original was reinforced.

Superstitious behavior refers to a behavior that involves the repetition of elaborate rituals. Learning theory accounts for superstitious behavior as behavior that occurs prior to a reinforcement but is coincidental to the behavior that leads to the reinforcement. Also, these behaviors are strengthened because they are only partially reinforced.

When a complex behavior is desired, a trainer may shape the desired behavior by rewarding closer and closer approximations of the behavior. Initially, any similar behaviors are reinforced, and gradually the reinforcement is restricted to ever closer approximations. Many complex human and animal skills are acquired through **shaping**.

The most common application of shaping in human learning is in the use of programmed instruction, now mostly relying on computers, though developed sixty years ago. In **programmed instruction**, correct responses to questions are immediately reinforced and errors are used to direct the user to review previous material. The use of computers has allowed the development of sophisticated programs that can be highly individualized and can move quickly between kinds of information and activities. Critics of programmed instruction feel that it may distract from real laboratory work and that students are limited by the program's ability to answer specific questions. In contrast, computers are now beginning to learn the way humans learn, and the computer is being used to imitate human neural networks.

Classical and operant conditioning can be distinguished on several grounds even though it is important to remember that they have similarities, like the processes of generalization and discrimination. Most of our behavior is probably learned through a mixture of both processes. The key distinction between them, however, is that in classical conditioning, the unconditioned stimulus precedes the response, and the response is elicited by the unconditioned stimulus. In operant conditioning, the response is emitted prior to the reinforcement and is therefore intentionally done.

Sometimes learning is constrained by behaviors that are biologically innate, or inborn. Not all behaviors can be taught to all animals equally well because of these **biological constraints**. Pigs might root a disk around their cages and raccoons might hoard and then clean similar disks.

Concept 4: Cognitive Approaches to Learning   *Survey:* ____
                 The Informed Consumer of Psychology Behavior   *Read:* ____
                 Analysis and Behavior Modification

                                                                   Pages 191-199

The approach that views learning in terms of thought processes is called **cognitive learning theory**. This approach does not deny the importance of classical and operant conditioning. They include the consideration of unseen mental processes as well. **Latent learning** is behavior that is learned but not demonstrated until reinforcement is provided for demonstrating the behavior. Latent learning occurs when rats are allowed to wander about a maze without any reward at the end, but once they learn that a reinforcement is available, they will quickly find their way through the maze even though they had not been reinforced for doing so in the past. The wandering around apparently leads them to develop a cognitive map of the maze. Humans apparently develop **cognitive maps** of their surroundings based on landmarks.

Experiments with pigeons have led cognitive learning psychologists to conclude that pigeons can learn to respond according to rules, such as whether or not a tree is present in a picture, and the rule can be made of several components, such as the presence of leaves or branches or a particular size. Animals can also learn elaborate sequences of numbers. This evidence suggests that animals act upon a thoughtful, internal representation of the world.

Albert Bandura has proposed that observational learning accounts for a large portion of learning in humans. **Observational learning** is learning that occurs by observing the behavior of another person, called the **model**. The classic experiment involved children observing a model strike a Bobo doll, and then later those who had seen the behavior were more prone to act aggressively. Four processes are necessary for observational learning: (1) paying attention to critical features; (2) remembering the behavior; (3) reproducing the action; and (4) being motivated to repeat the behavior. We also observe the kinds of reinforcement that the model receives for the behavior.

Martin Seligman has proposed that **learned helplessness**, the learned belief that no control can be exerted over the environment, can be used to understand why people give up or fail to try to eliminate an aversive stimulus. After repeated exposure to stimuli over which animals and humans have no control, they will fail to try later, even when they do have control. Learned helplessness has been used to explain why battered children will not seek relief when they have the opportunity and also to explain depression. One view of the difference between cognitive theory - that depends on internal factors - and classical and operant conditioning - that depends on external factors - is to argue that neither of these approaches is sufficient to account for behavior but instead must be taken as complementary approaches.

Behavior modification refers to the formalized use of basic principles of learning theory to change behavior by eliminating undesirable behaviors and encouraging desirable ones. Behavior modification can be used to train mentally retarded individuals, help people lose weight, quit smoking, or teach people to behave safely. The steps of a typical behavior program include: (1) identifying goals and target behaviors; (2) designing a data recording system and recording preliminary data; (3) selecting a behavior change strategy; (4) implementing the program; (5) keeping careful records after the program has been implemented; and (6) evaluating and altering the ongoing program.

♦ Now that you have surveyed, questioned, and read the chapter and completed the **Recap and Review** questions, review **Looking Back**, pages 200-201. *Review:* ____

♦ For additional practice through recitation and review, test your knowledge of the chapter material by answering the questions in the **Key Word Drill**, the **Practice Questions**, and the **Essay Questions**.

KEY WORD DRILL   *Recite:* ____

The following **Fill in the Blank** and **Matching Questions** test key words from the text. Check your answers with the Answer Key in the back of the *Study Guide*.

FILL IN THE BLANK

1. When a relatively permanent change in behavior is brought about by experience, ___learning___ is said to have occurred.

2. In contrast to learning, ___maturation___ is the unfolding of biologically predetermined patterns of behavior due to aging.

3. When the association of one conditioned stimulus with an unconditioned stimulus obstructs the learning of a response to a second stimulus, conditioning has been ___Blocked___ .

4. Edward Thorndike proposed the ___Law of effect___ that says that responses that satisfy are more likely to be repeated, whereas those that don't satisfy are less likely to be repeated.

5. When learning is based on the coincidental association between the idea, object, or behavior and subsequent reinforcement, the mistaken belief that particular ideas, objects, or behavior will cause certain events to occur is called ___Superstitous behavior___ .

6. ___Shaping___ is the process of teaching a complex behavior by rewarding closer and closer approximations of the desired behavior.

7. The development of learning by using _____ _____ requires building gradually on basic knowledge, with review and reinforcement when appropriate.

8. _____ _____ are built-in limitations in an organism's ability to learn particular behaviors.

9. A _____ _____ is a mental representation of spatial locations and directions.

10. _____ _____ occurs when a belief that one has no control of the environment is learned.

MATCHING QUESTIONS

_C___ 11. classical conditioning

_e___ 12. operant conditioning

_13__ 13. escape conditioning

_F___ 14. avoidance conditioning

_a___ 15. cognitive learning theory

_d___ 16. latent learning

_b___ 17. observational learning

a. The study of the thought processes that underlie learning.

b. Learning that involves the imitation of a model.

c. A previously neutral stimulus comes to elicit a response through its association with a stimulus that naturally brings about the response.

d. A new behavior is acquired but not readily demonstrated until reinforcement is provided.

e. A voluntary response is strengthened or weakened, depending on its positive or negative consequences.

f. A response to a signal of an impending unpleasant event in a way that permits its evasion.

g. A response which brings about an end to an aversive situation.

_b___ 18. neutral stimulus

_a___ 19. unconditioned stimulus (UCS)

_e___ 20. unconditioned response (UCR)

_c___ 21. conditioned stimulus (CS)

_d___ 22. conditioned response (CR)

a. A stimulus that brings about a response without having been learned.

b. A stimulus that, before conditioning, has no effect on the desired response.

c. A once-neutral stimulus that has been paired with an unconditioned stimulus to bring about a response formerly caused only by the unconditioned stimulus.

d. A response that, after conditioning, follows a previously neutral stimulus (e.g., salivation at the sound of a tuning fork).

e. A response that is natural and needs no training (e.g., salivation at the smell of food).

_a_ 23. extinction

_f_ 24. systematic desensitization

_b_ 25. spontaneous recovery

_d_ 26. stimulus generalization

_e_ 27. stimulus discrimination

_c_ 28. higher-order conditioning

a. The weakening and eventual disappearance of a conditioned response.

b. The reappearance of a previously extinguished response after a period of time during which the conditioned stimulus has been absent.

c. Occurs when an already conditioned stimulus is paired with a neutral stimulus until the neutral stimulus evokes the same response as the conditioned stimulus.

d. Response to a stimulus that is similar to but different from a conditioned stimulus; the more similar the two stimuli, the more likely generalization is to occur.

e. The process by which an organism learns to differentiate among stimuli, restricting its response to one in particular.

f. A form of therapy in which fears are minimized through gradual exposure to the source of fear.

_____

_c_ 29. primary reinforcer

_e_ 30. secondary reinforcer

_d_ 31. positive reinforcer

_f_ 32. negative reinforcer

_a_ 33. punishment

_b_ 34. aversive stimuli

a. An unpleasant or painful stimulus that is added to the environment after a certain behavior occurs, decreasing the likelihood that the behavior will occur again.

b. Unpleasant or painful stimuli.

c. A reward that satisfies a biological need (e.g., hunger or thirst) and works naturally.

d. A stimulus added to the environment that brings about an increase in the response that preceded it.

e. A stimulus that becomes reinforcing by its association with a primary reinforcer (e.g., money, which allows us to obtain food, a primary reinforcer).

f. A stimulus whose removal is reinforcing, leading to a greater probability that the response bringing about this removal will occur again.

_b_ 35. continuous reinforcement schedule

_e_ 36. partial reinforcement schedule

_c_ 37. cumulative recorder

_g_ 38. fixed-ratio schedule

_a_ 39. variable-ratio schedule

_f_ 40. fixed-interval schedule

_d_ 41. variable-interval schedule

a. Reinforcement occurs after a varying number of responses rather than after a fixed number.

b. Reinforcing of a behavior every time it occurs.

c. A device that records and graphs the pattern of responses.

d. Reinforcement is given at various times, usually causing a behavior to be maintained more consistently.

e. Reinforcing of a behavior some, but not all, of the time.

f. Reinforcement is given at established time intervals.

g. Reinforcement is given only after a certain number of responses is made.

_c_ 42. reinforcer

_e_ 43. schedules of reinforcement

_f_ 44. stimulus control training

_d_ 45. discriminative stimulus

_b_ 46. model

_a_ 47. behavior modification

a. A formalized technique for promoting the frequency of desirable behaviors and decreasing the incidence of unwanted ones.

b. A person serving as an example to an observer; the observer may imitate that person's behavior.

c. Any stimulus that increases the probability that a preceding behavior will be repeated.

d. A stimulus to which an organism learns to respond as part of stimulus control training.

e. The frequency and timing of reinforcement following desired behavior.

f. Training in which an organism is reinforced in the presence of a certain specific stimulus, but not in its absence.

PRACTICE QUESTIONS   *Recite and Review:* ____

Test your knowledge of the chapter material by answering these **True-False** and **Multiple Choice Questions**. Check your answers with the Answer Key in the back of the *Study Guide*.

TRUE-FALSE QUESTIONS

(T)   F   1.   Learning cannot be observed directly; it must be inferred.

T   **(F)**   2.   Something that naturally causes a response without previous learning is called a conditioned stimulus.

(T)   F   3.   When a response recurs after extinction, spontaneous recovery has taken place.

T   **(F)**   4.   Watson's experiments with Baby Albert involved conditioning trials with a white rat. Yet Baby Albert also became fearful of other white, furry objects. This is an example of stimulus discrimination.

T   **(F)**   5.   In his experiments with rats that avoided water in the radiation chamber, Garcia showed that conditioning will not occur if there is a long delay between the presentation of the conditioned stimulus and the unconditioned stimulus.

(T)   F   6.   Sue wrote an exceptional term paper for psychology class; when her instructor graded it, he wrote many comments of praise on it. This behavioral sequence illustrates operant conditioning.

(T)   F   7.   Running away from a situation which you find noxious illustrates negative reinforcement.

T   **(F)**   8.   Punishing a child for misbehavior illustrates negative reinforcement.

T   **(F)**   9.   Behavior acquired under a continuous reinforcement schedule is learned faster and is maintained longer than behavior learned under a partial reinforcement schedule.

(T)   F   10. Behaviors learned on a partial reinforcement schedule are more resistant to extinction than those learned on a continuous reinforcement schedule.

MULTIPLE CHOICE QUESTIONS

1. Your text describes the story of Brad Gabrielson and Bo, his helper. The story illustrates:
   a. the complete devotion of the dog at all costs.
   b. another handicapped person with lesser liabilities.
   c. a person who was highly trained to care for Gabrielson's handicap because of participation in a special experimental government training program.
   d. how specially trained animals can improve the lives of handicapped individuals.

2. All performance improvements that result from simply getting older are considered:
   a. maturation.   c. modeling.
   b. learning.   d. imitation.

3. Learning is best defined as:
   a. a change in behavior brought about by growth and maturity of the nervous system.
   b. a measurable change in behavior brought about by conditions such as drugs, sleep, and fatigue.
   c. a behavioral response that occurs each time a critical stimulus is presented.
   d. a relatively permanent change in behavior brought about by experience.

4. The changes in behavior brought about by learning:
   a. are hard to measure.   c. must be measured indirectly.
   b. are easily extinguished.   d. are generally maturational.

5. In classical conditioning, the stimulus that comes to elicit a response that it would not previously have elicited is called the:
   a. classical stimulus.   c. conditioned stimulus.
   b. unconditioned stimulus.   d. discriminative stimulus.

6. Through conditioning, a dog learns to salivate at the sound of a bell because the bell signals that food is coming. In subsequent learning trials, a buzzer is sounded just prior to the bell. Soon the dog salivates at the sound of the buzzer. In this case, the bell acts as the:
   a. unconditioned stimulus.   c. unconditioned response.
   b. conditioned stimulus.   d. conditioned response.

7. In classical conditioning, the unconditioned stimulus automatically produces the:
   a. unconditioned response.   c. conditioned stimulus.
   b. neutral stimulus.   d. generalized response.

8. In preparing food for her daughter, Joanna uses a juicer. Soon the baby knows that the sound of the juicer signals that food is on the way. In this case, the food acts as:
   a. an unconditioned stimulus.   c. an unconditioned response.
   b. a conditioned stimulus.   d. a conditioned response.

9. In preparing food for his young son, Ron uses a blender. Soon the baby
    knows that the sound of the blender signals that food is on the way. In
    this case, the blender acts as:
    a. an unconditioned stimulus.   c. an unconditioned response.
    b. a conditioned stimulus.   d. a conditioned response.

10. The primary result of classical conditioning is that:
    a. the conditioned stimulus produces a conditioned response, signifying
        that learning has occurred.
    b. voluntary responses become associated with the unconditioned stimulus.
    c. the unconditioned response is elicited by the conditioned stimulus
        whenever it is presented.
    d. it has been demonstrated in a variety of animal species.

11. The child who stands fearfully in line while waiting to be inoculated is
    exhibiting:
    a. an unconditioned response.   c. systematic desensitization.
    b. an innate, involuntary response.   d. a conditioned response.

12. Prior to the conditioning trials in which Watson planned to condition fear
    of a rat in Baby Albert, the rat - which Albert was known not to fear -
    would have been considered:
    a. an unconditioned stimulus.   c. a discriminative stimulus.
    b. an adaptive stimulus.   d. a neutral stimulus.

13. Which of the following takes place after conditioning, when the conditioned
    stimulus is presented repeatedly without being paired with the unconditioned
    stimulus?
    a. learning   c. systematic desensitization
    b. perception   d. extinction

14. Systematic desensitization is achieved by:
    a. no longer allowing the conditioned stimulus and the unconditioned
        stimulus to be paired in real-life situations.
    b. constructing a hierarchy of situations that produce fear and then
        gradually pairing less stressful situations with strategies to relax.
    c. identifying the situations that produce fear in order to modify or
        eliminate them.
    d. gaining exposure to the most fearful situations so that the unpleasant
        reactions can be extinguished quickly.

15. Systematic desensitization is most closely associated with:
    a. operant conditioning.   c. spontaneous recovery.
    b. token economy.   d. extinction.

16. A previously conditioned response becomes weaker and eventually disappears
    through:
    a. operant conditioning.   c. spontaneous recovery.
    b. token economy.   d. extinction.

17. A classically conditioned response can be extinguished by:
    a. adding another conditioned stimulus to the pairing.
    b. no longer presenting the unconditioned stimulus after the conditioned
        response.
    c. using stimulus substitution.
    d. reintroducing the unconditioned stimulus.

18. Victor participates in aversive conditioning in order to stop smoking. Now
     he dislikes cigarettes and has also linked his dislike to the store where
     he used to buy them. This reaction illustrates:
     a. operant conditioning.   c. higher-order conditioning.
     b. stimulus discrimination.   d. systematic desensitization.

19. You can distinguish a certain make of automobiles by the design of the
     grillwork. This ability is an example of:
     a. stimulus discrimination.   c. spontaneous recovery.
     b. higher-order conditioning.   d. instrumental conditioning.

20. The U.S. Customs Service uses dogs at airports and docks to stop illegal
     drug shipments. Typically, the dogs are trained to sniff out a specific
     drug, such as cocaine, and to ignore all other drugs. The ability of the
     dogs to respond only to the specific drug they were trained to detect is an
     example of:
     a. stimulus discrimination.   c. partial reinforcement.
     b. response generalization.   d. spontaneous recovery.

21. Pavlov's assumption that stimuli and responses were linked in a mechanistic,
     unthinking way has been challenged by:
     a. cognitive learning theorists.
     b. the animal trainers, the Brelands.
     c. Edward Thorndike's law of effect.
     d. operant conditioning.

22. Garcia's behavioral investigations of rats which were treated with doses of
     radiation illustrate that:
     a. rats obey slightly different principles of classical conditioning than
         humans do.
     b. some research findings involving classical conditioning do not appear
         to obey Pavlov's conditioning principles.
     c. classical conditioning is a very robust form of learning, since it is
         not weakened even by large doses of medication.
     d. changes in classical conditioning are highly sensitive indicators of
         radiation effects.

23. Operant conditioning is to _____ as classical conditioning is to
     _____.
     a. voluntary response; involuntary response.
     b. observational learning; cognitive map
     c. volitional behavior; free will.
     d. negative reinforcer; positive reinforcer.

24. Brushing your teeth is an example of behavior that is learned through:
     a. cognitive learning.   c. maturation.
     b. spatial conditioning.   d. operant conditioning.

25. Which alternative below is not an example of operant conditioning?
     a. A cat pushes against a lever to open a door on its cage.
     b. A student drives within the speed limit to avoid getting another parking
         ticket.
     c. A dog rolls over for a dog biscuit.
     d. A student's blood pressure increases when she anticipates speaking with
         her chemistry professor.

26. When we continue to act in a manner that will lead to pleasing consequences, we behave according to the:
   a. law of frequency.   c. law of effect.
   b. principle of similarity.   d. principle of contiguity.

27. Which name below is not associated with classical conditioning or operant conditioning?
   a. Pavlov   c. Wertheimer
   b. Skinner   d. Thorndike

28. The distinction between primary reinforcers and secondary reinforcers is that:
   a. primary reinforcers satisfy some biological need; secondary reinforcers are effective because of their association with primary reinforcers.
   b. organisms prefer primary reinforcers to secondary reinforcers.
   c. primary reinforcers are not effective with all organisms.
   d. primary reinforcers depend upon the past conditioning of the organism; secondary reinforcers have a biological basis.

29. Typically, food is a _____, whereas money is a _____
   a. discriminative stimulus; conditioned reinforcer
   b. need; motive
   c. primary reinforcer; secondary reinforcer
   d. drive reducer; natural reinforcer

30. Any stimulus that increases the likelihood that a preceding behavior be repeated is called:
   a. a punisher.   c. a response.
   b. a reinforcer.   d. an operant.

31. According to the definition given in the text, which of the following is most likely to be considered a primary reinforcer?
   a. money   c. good grades
   b. water   d. a hammer

32. Negative reinforcement:
   a. is a special form of punishment.
   b. is a phenomenon that results when reward is withheld.
   c. involves the decrease or removal of an aversive stimulus.
   d. occurs in both classical and instrumental conditioning.

33. According to the text, in which of the following situations would the use of punishment be most effective in reducing the undesired behavior?
   a. An employee is demoted for misfiling a report.
   b. A child is spanked for hitting her sister.
   c. A teenager is denied the opportunity to attend the Friday dance for staying out late on Monday.
   d. A child is spanked for running into the street.

34. Under variable schedules of reinforcement, the response rate is:
   a. always high.
   b. always constant and low.
   c. easily extinguished.
   d. highly resistant to extinction.

35. Piecework in a factory, where a worker is paid for three pieces made, is an example of a:
    a. fixed-interval schedule of reinforcement.
    b. variable-interval schedule of reinforcement.
    c. variable-ratio schedule of reinforcement.
    d. fixed-ratio schedule of reinforcement.

36. Because the number of responses made by a door-to-door salesperson before reinforcement in the form of a sale is not certain, he or she is working on a:
    a. variable-ratio schedule.   c. variable-interval schedule.
    b. fixed-ratio schedule.   d. fixed-interval schedule.

37. With a fixed-interval schedule, especially in the period just after reinforcement, response rates are:
    a. speeded up.   c. relatively unchanged
    b. extinguished.   d. relatively low.

38. The typical study pattern of a college student that ''crams'' right before the examinations looks most like the response rate that is observed in a:
    a. fixed-interval schedule of reinforcement.
    b. variable-interval schedule of reinforcement.
    c. variable-ratio schedule of reinforcement.
    d. fixed-ratio schedule of reinforcement.

39. Superstitious behavior is thought to arise because of:
    a. continuously reinforced patterns of behavior that have led to results related to the behavior.
    b. universal biological constraints that guide specific kinds of behavior.
    c. religious dogma.
    d. partial reinforcement of the connection of incidental events to a specific consequence.

40. Rewarding each step toward a desired behavior _____ the new response pattern.
    a. inhibits   c. disrupts
    b. shapes   d. eliminates

41. Which alternative below is probably not good advice in selecting materials for computer-assisted programmed instruction?
    a. Determine if the materials use shaping procedures when incorrect answers are given.
    b. Establish that the programs provide appropriate reinforcement for correct answers.
    c. Determine whether the materials have been field-tested.
    d. Ensure that the developers of the materials have taken courses in learning and memory.

42. Which of the following is a limitation of programmed instruction?
    a. The user cannot ask questions beyond those programmed into the computer.
    b. There is no provision for error analysis.
    c. Reinforcement is routinely delayed.
    d. Computers are not generally available.

43. A new generation of computers can teach themselves to learn through the technology of:

    a. programmed instruction.   c. partial reinforcement.
    b. neural networks.   d. multiaxial connections.

44. _____ constitute built-in hereditary limitations to conditioning.

    a. Fixed action patterns   c. Cognitive maps
    b. Biofeedback mechanisms   d. Biological constraints

45. Psychologists who emphasize unseen mental processes that intervene in learning are would be called:

    a. personality psychologists.   c. cognitive psychologists.
    b. sensory psychologists.   d. biopsychologists.

46. Which of the following is especially effective in situations where shaping may be inappropriate or unethical (like neurosurgery, race car driving, and parenting)?

    a. classical conditioning   c. observational learning
    b. learned helplessness   d. insight

47. People who exhibit learned helplessness feel that they:

    a. are unable to learn anything new.
    b. have no control over their environment.
    c. can learn only if new behaviors are shaped.
    d. have no control over their behavior.

ESSAY QUESTIONS

Recite and Review: ____

Essay Question 5.1: *Using Physical Punishment*

The use of physical punishment has become quite controversial. Most school systems now outlaw its use, and many parents try to find alternatives to it. Define the issues related to the use of punishment, and answer the question, ''Is it wrong to use physical punishment to discipline children?'' As you answer, consider whether there are circumstances that may require routine use, or whether its use should be rare. Describe alternatives for use in normal disciplining of children.

_____

_____

_____

_____

_____

_____

_____

_____

_____

_____

_____

_____

_____

_____

_____

_____

_____

_____

_____

_____

_____

Essay Question 5.2: Which Approach Is Correct?

Three approaches to learning are described in the text. Both classical and operant conditioning rely on external determinants of behavior, cognitive learning depends in part on internal, mental activity. How can differences between these three approaches be reconciled?

_____

_____

_____

_____

_____

_____

_____

_____

_____

_____

_____

_____

_____

_____

_____

_____

_____

_____

_____

ACTIVITIES AND PROJECTS

1. Either write about or discuss with a friend a fear that you have - a fear
    of cats, mice, dogs, insects, spiders, flying, heights, being home alone,
    or any other fear. How did you acquire the fear? Is there any connection
    between acquiring the fear and the principles of classical conditioning?
    How might the fear be explained through conditioning? Has the fear extended
    to other stimuli as the result of higher-order conditioning? Or was it
    through stimulus generalization? Why has your fear not been extinguished?

2. Keep a record for several days of the activities that you undertake and the
    kinds of rewards and other reinforcements you give yourself or receive from
    others. In your notes, include the time you do the activity and if anyone
    was with you. After several days, review the list and all of the related
    reinforcement. Are there any patterns? Do you tend to accept offers to do
    things that distract you from study (like going for pizza, going to the game
    room, or watching television) more easily than offers that distract you from
    other activities? What other patterns do you find? Do you reinforce your
    study time with food or with some other form of relaxation?

C H A P T E R
6
MEMORY

DETAILED OUTLINE

Survey: ____

This detailed outline contains all the headings in Chapter 6: Memory. If you are using the SQ3R method, then an examination of the outline is the best way to begin your survey of the chapter.

Prologue: Pamilla Smith
Looking Ahead

Encoding, Storage, and Retrieval of Memory
    The three stages of memory: The storehouses of memory
        Sensory memory
        Short-term memory: Our working memory
        Rehearsal
        Long-term memory: The final storehouse
        Episodic and semantic memories
The Cutting Edge Implicit Memory: Retention without Remembering
        Storage in long-term memory
    Levels of processing
- **Recap and Review I**

Recalling Long-Term Memories
    Flashbulb memories
    Constructive processes in memory: Rebuilding the past
Psychology at Work Memory on Trial: The Fallibility of Witnesses
    Autobiographical memory: Where past meets present
    Everyday memory: Different in the laboratory?
- **Recap and Review II**

Forgetting: When Memory Fails
    Proactive and retroactive interference: The before and after of
      forgetting
    The biological bases of memory: The search for the engram
    Memory dysfunctions: Afflictions of forgetting
The Informed Consumer of Psychology Improving Your Memory
- **Recap and Review III**

Looking Back
Key Terms and Concepts

Now that you have surveyed the chapter, read **Looking Ahead**, pages 204-205.
    Question: ____
       Read: ____

Focus on the questions on pages 204-205.

CONCEPTS AND LEARNING OBJECTIVES   *Survey:* ____

These are the concepts and the learning objects for Chapter 6.   Read them carefully as part of your preliminary survey of the chapter.

Concept 1:   The role of memory in human behavior is to aid in the management of information. Memory involves three main processes: encoding, storage, and retrieval. There are also three main types of memory: sensory, short-term, and long-term, and these types are distinguished according to how long the information stays in them (storage), how they are acquired (encoded), and how they are recalled (retrieval).

1. Define memory and the basic processes of encoding, storing, and retrieving information. (pp. 204-206)

2. Describe the three stages of memory, and discuss sensory memory. (pp. 206-208)

3. Describe the characteristics and limitations of short-term memory. (pp. 208-211)

4. Describe the characteristics of long-term memory and the way information is stored in and retrieved from long-term memory, and distinguish implicit and explicit memory. (pp. 211-214)

5. Distinguish the levels of processing theory from the three stages of sensory, short-term, and long-term memory. (pp. 214-215)

Concept 2:   Recollection from long-term memory presents a number of issues that revolve around the accuracy of the memory, the way it was stored, and its specific nature.

6. Define the means of recalling information from long-term memory and the characteristics of memory that improve recall. (pp. 216-219)

7. Define constructive processes and discuss how schemas, serial production, and the soap opera effect construct memories as well as issues regarding the accuracy of constructed memory. (pp. 219-222)

8. Describe autobiographical and everyday memory. (pp. 222-224)

Concept 3:   Forgetting is a normal process of memory, and it is required in order to make memory more efficient. The major forms of forgetting include decay theory and the concept of interference. Memory dysfunctions may be rooted in biological and psychological causes.

9. Discuss how memories are forgotten, especially the role of proactive and retroactive interference. (pp. 224-227)

10. Describe the biological basis of memory processes. (pp. 227-228)

11. Discuss the common memory dysfunctions. (pp. 228-229)

12. Describe techniques for improving memory skills. (pp. 230-232)

CHAPTER SUMMARY

There are several ways you can use this summary as part of your systematic study plan. You may read each concept summary and then read the corresponding pages in the text, or you may read the entire summary and then read the entire chapter in the text. As you finish each section, complete the **Recap and Review** questions that are supplied in the text.

Concept 1: Prologue and Looking Ahead   *Survey:* ____
**   Encoding, Storage, and Retrieval of Memory**   *Read:* ____

Pages 204-215

The case of Pamilla Smith described in the Prologue illustrates the importance of memory to daily life. Her loss of the ability to form new memories also illustrates the close connection between the biological foundation of memory and its proper function.

Three processes comprise memory. **Encoding** is the process of placing information in a form that can be used by memory. **Storage** is the process of retaining information for later use. **Retrieval** is the process of recovering information from storage. By definition, then, **memory** is the sum of these three processes. Forgetting is an important part of memory because it allows us to make generalizations and abstractions from daily life.

The memory system is typically divided into three storage components or stages. The initial stage is that of **sensory memory**, where momentary storage of sensory information occurs. **Short-term memory** includes information that has been given some form of meaning, and it lasts for fifteen to twenty-five seconds. **Long-term memory** is the relatively permanent storage of memory. While there are no locations in the brain of these memory stages, they are considered abstract memory systems with different characteristics.

Sensory memories are considered to differ according to the kind of sensory information, and the sensory memory is thought of as several types of sensory memories based on the source of the sensory messages. Visual sensory memory is called **iconic memory**, and its source is the visual sensory system; and auditory sensory memory is called **echoic memory**, and its source is the auditory sensory system. Sensory memory stores information for a very short time. Iconic memory may last no more than a second, and echoic memory may last for three to four seconds. The duration of iconic memory was established by George Sperling's classic experiment in which subjects were unable to recall an entire array of letters but could, on a cue after the array was shown for one-twentieth of a second, recall any part of the array. Unless the information taken into the sensory memories is somehow transferred to another memory system, they are quickly lost.

Sensory memories are raw information without meaning. In order to be transferred to the long-term memory, these sensory memories must be given meaning and placed in short-term memory. One view of this process suggests that the short-term memory is composed of verbal representations that have a very short duration. George Miller has identified the capacity of short-term memory as seven plus or minus two **chunks**, or meaningful groups of stimuli that are stored as a unit in the short-term memory. Chunks can be several letters or numbers or can be complicated patterns, like the patterns of pieces on a chessboard. However, to be placed in a chunk, the board must represent a real or possible game even for chess masters to be able to make a chunk.

Memory can be held in short-term memory longer by **rehearsal**, the repetition of information already in the short-term memory. Rehearsal is also the beginning of transferring memory into long-term memory. The kind of rehearsal influences the effectiveness of the transfer to long-term memory. Elaborative rehearsal occurs whenever the material is associated with other information through placement in a logical framework, connection with another memory, the formation of an image, or some other transformation. The strategies for organizing memories are called **mnemonics**. Mnemonics are formal techniques for organizing information so that recall is more likely.

The evidence for the existence of a separate long-term memory system comes from cases like that of Pamilla Smith and others who have damage that allows short-term memories but not the creation of new long-term memories. Experiments have demonstrated that if new information is not allowed to be processed, then after a period of time, the information is lost.

Two kinds of long-term memory have been identified. **Episodic memories** are memories of specific events related to individual experiences. **Semantic memories** are those that consist of abstract knowledge and facts about the world. Psychologists use the **associative model** to suggest that semantic memories represent the associations between mental representations of various pieces of information. When we think about a particular thing, related ideas are activated because of the association. **Priming** refers to the activation of one item, thereby making recall of related items easier. **Explicit memory** refers to intentional or conscious effort to recall memory, and **implicit memory** refers to memories of which people are not consciously aware but nevertheless affect later performance and behavior. Implicit memory is illustrated by a tendency for surgical patients to use words in an association test that were spoken during the surgery when they were under anaesthesia.

One of the main ways memories are stored in long-term memory is through the **linguistic code**, that is, language. We also store information in an **imaginal code**, or visual images, and a third way is through the motor code, or physical activity.

An alternative to the three-stage view of memory is the **levels-of-processing theory**. This theory suggests that the difference in memories depends on the depth to which particular information is processed, that is, the degree to which information is analyzed and considered. The more attention information is given, the deeper it is stored and the less likely it is to be forgotten. Superficial aspects of information are given shallow processing, and when meaning is given, the processing is at its deepest level. The levels-of-processing approach suggests that memory requires more active mental processing than does the three-stage approach.

Concept 2: Recalling Long-Term Memories

Survey: ____
Read: ____

Pages 216-224

Retrieving information from long-term memory may be influenced by many factors. The **tip-of-the-tongue** phenomenon, where one is certain of knowing something but cannot recall it, represents one difficulty. The simple number of items of information that has been stored may influence recall. We sort through this quantity with the help of **retrieval cues**. These are stimuli that allow recall from long-term memory. **Recall** consists of a series of processes - a search through memory, retrieval of potentially relevant information, then a decision whether the information is accurate, and a continuation of these steps until the right information is found. In contrast, **recognition** involves determining whether a stimulus that has been presented is correct, such as the selection of the stimulus from a list or determining whether the stimulus has been seen before.

In particularly intense events, we may develop **flashbulb memories**, where due to a specific, important or surprising event memories are so vivid that they appear as if a snapshot of the event. Research regarding flashbulb memories concerning President Kennedy's assassination has revealed common details, such as where the person was, who told the person, the person's own emotions, and some personal detail of the event. Harsh and Neisser asked students the day after the *Challenger* accident how they had heard about it, and then asked the same question three years later. One-third were wrong, a result suggesting that flashbulb memories may be inaccurate. Memories that are exceptional may be more easily retrieved than commonplace information. The **von Restorff effect** refers to the increase in likelihood of recall with the increase in distinctiveness of information.

Our memories reflect **constructive processes**, processes in which memories are influenced by the meaning we have attached to them. Guesses and inferences thus influence memory. Sir Frederic Bartlett first suggested that people remember in terms of schemas, which are general themes without specific details, and that these schemas were based on understanding of the event, expectations, and an understanding of the motivation of others. The process of serial reproduction, a process that requires people to pass information from one to another in a sequence, has shown the effect of schemas. The final story is much changed in comparison to the original version, and it reflects the expectations of those retelling the story. Apparently, prior knowledge and expectations influence how we initially store the information. How we understand peoples' motivation also influences memory. In the **soap opera effect**, knowledge about a person's motivation leads to an elaboration of past events involving that person.

The imperfection of memory has led to research into the accuracy of eye-witness testimony. The mistaken identification of individuals can lead to imprisonment. When a weapon is involved, the weapon draws attention away from other details. In research involving staged crimes, witnesses vary significantly in their judgment of the height of the perpetrator, with judgments differing by as much as two feet. The wording of questions can influence testimony. Children are especially prone to unreliable recollections.

Autobiographical memories are our collections of information about our lives. People tend to forget information about the past that is incongruent with the way they currently see themselves. Depressed people tend to recall sad events more readily than happy ones from their past. More recent information also appears to be more affected than recollections from earlier times.

Everyday memory differs from memories studied in a laboratory. In one study, a researcher and a companion took a bicycle tour of Europe, and the researcher recorded daily details. After the trip, the companion was able to recall the frequency of events with accuracy. Critics of this naturalistic study argue that it is difficult to generalize results from this kind of study. The middle ground is to suggest that research depends upon the care taken, not where it is done.

Concept 3: Forgetting: When Memory Fails   *Survey:* _____
                                                              Read: _____

                                                             Pages224-232

Herman Ebbinghaus studied forgetting by learning a list of nonsense syllables and then timing how long it took him, at a later trial, to relearn the list. The most rapid forgetting occurs in the first nine hours. Two views concerning the forgetting of information have been developed. One theory explains forgetting by **decay**, or the loss of information through nonuse. When a memory is formed, a **memory trace**, or **engram**, occurs. An engram is an actual physical change in the brain. The decay theory assumes that memories become more decayed with time, but the evidence does not support this happening, though there is support for the existence of decay. The other theory proposes that **interference** between bits of information leads to forgetting.   In interference, information blocks or displaces other information, preventing recall. Most forgetting appears to be the result of interference.

There are two kinds of interference. One is called **proactive interference,** which occurs when previously learned information blocks the recall of newer information. **Retroactive interference** is when new information blocks the recall of old information.   Most research suggests that information that has been blocked by interference can eventually be recalled if appropriate stimuli are used.

It was originally thought that memories were evenly distributed throughout the brain. However, the current view suggests that the areas of the brain that are responsible for processing information about the world also store that information. The appearance of the even distribution of information is probably the result of the fact that every memory is composed of a variety of information about particular events or skills; thus several areas of the brain must be involved in every memory. Evidence also suggests that the hippocampus plays a central role in the formation of memories by transforming sensory information into the form that eventually becomes the long-term memory. Neurotransmitters and glucose in the blood also have an influence on memory.

Alzheimer's disease has severe memory problems as one of its many symptoms. Initially, the symptoms appear as simple forgetfulness, progressing to more profound loss of memory, even failure to recognize one's own name and the loss of language abilities. The protein beta amyloid, important for maintaining neural connections, has been implicated in the progress of the disease. **Amnesia** is another memory problem. Amnesia is a loss of memory occurring without apparent loss of mental function. **Retrograde amnesia** is memory loss for memories that preceded a traumatic event. **Anterograde amnesia** is a loss for memories that follow a traumatic event. Long-term alcoholics who develop **Korsakoff's syndrome** also have amnesia. Korsakoff's syndrome is related to thiamine deficiency. A perfect memory, one with total recall, might actually be very discomforting. A case studied by Luria of a man with total recall reveals that the inability to forget becomes debilitating.

The Informed Consumer of Psychology section outlines several mnemonic techniques and how they can be applied to taking tests. They include the **keyword technique**, in which one pairs a word with a mental image, or in the case of learning a foreign language, the foreign word with a similar sounding English word. The **method of loci** requires that one imagine items to be remembered as being placed in particular locations. Another phenomenon that affects memory is called **encoding specificity**. Recall is best when it is attempted in conditions that are similar to the conditions under which the information was originally learned. The organization of text and lecture material may enhance memory of it. Practice and rehearsal also improve long-term recall. Rehearsal to the point of mastery is called **overlearning**. It should be noted that cramming for exams is an ineffective technique, and the better approach is to distribute practice over many sessions.

♦ Now that you have surveyed, questioned, and read the chapter and completed the **Recap and Review** questions, review **Looking Back**, pages 233-234. *Review:* ____

♦ For additional practice through recitation and review, test your knowledge of the chapter material by answering the questions in the **Key Word Drill**, the **Practice Questions**, and the **Essay Questions**.

KEY WORD DRILL
Recite: ____

The following **Fill in the Blank** and **Matching Questions** test key words from the text. Check your answers with the Answer Key in the back of the *Study Guide*.

FILL IN THE BLANK

1. _Memory_ is defined as the capacity to record, retain, and retrieve information.

2. In short term-memory, a meaningful grouping of stimuli would be stored as a _chunk_ .

3. _mnemonics_ refers to the formal techniques for organizing material to increase the likelihood of its being remembered.

4. Intentional or conscious recollection of information is called _explicit_ memory and memories of which people are not consciously aware, but which can improve subsequent performance and behavior is called _implicit_ memory.

5. The _level_ -of- _processing theory_ theory suggests that the way information is initially perceived and learned determines how difficult it is to recall.

6. Whenever you experience an inability to recall information, but you realize that you know it, the _Tip_ -of-the- _tongue phenomenon_ has probably resulted because of the difficulty of retrieving information from long-term memory.

7. _Constructive processes_ result when memories are influenced by the interpretation and meaning we give to events. Book 219

8. When we remember situations in terms of general themes, we are using _Schemas_ .

9. Information is lost through _decay_ when it is not used.

10. The phenomenon called _interference_ refers to occasions when recall is hindered because of other information in memory which displaces or blocks it out.

MATCHING QUESTIONS

✓ d 11. encoding

F 12. storage

a 13. retrieval

C 14. sensory memory

e 15. short-term memory

b 16. long-term memory

a. Locating and using information stored in memory.

b. Relatively permanent memory.

c. Information recorded as a meaningless stimulus.

d. Recording information in a form usable to memory.

e. Working memory that lasts about fifteen to twenty-five seconds.

f. The location where information is saved.

_e_ 17. iconic memory

_d_ 18. echoic memory

_b_ 19. episodic memories

_c_ 20. semantic memories

_a_ 21. motor code

a. Memory storage based on physical activities.

b. Stored information relating to personal experiences.

c. Stored, organized facts about the world (e.g., mathematical and historical data).

d. The storage of information obtained from the sense of hearing.

e. The storage of visual information.

_f_ 22. retrieval cue

_a_ 23. recall

_e_ 24. recognition

_d_ 25. flashbulb memories

_b_ 26. von Restorff effect

_g_ 27. serial reproduction

_c_ 28. soap opera effect

a. Drawing from memory a specific piece of information for a specific purpose.

b. The phenomenon by which distinctive stimuli are recalled more readily than less distinctive ones.

c. The phenomenon by which memory of a prior event involving a person is more reliable when we understand that person's motivations.

d. Memories of a specific event that are so clear they seem like ''snapshots'' of the event.

e. Acknowledging prior exposure to a given stimulus, rather than recalling the information from memory.

f. A stimulus such as a word, smell, or sound that aids recall of information located in long-term memory.

g. The passage of interpretive information from person to person, often resulting in inaccuracy through personal bias and misinterpretation.

___b___ 29. memory trace

___g___ 30. proactive interference

___c___ 31. retroactive interference

___a___ 32. keyword technique

___e___ 33. method of loci

___f___ 34. encoding specificity

___d___ 35. overlearning

a. The pairing of a foreign word with a common, similar sounding English word to aid in remembering the new word.

b. A physical change in the brain corresponding to the memory of material.

c. New information interferes with the recall of information learned earlier.

d. Rehearsing material beyond the point of mastery to improve long-term recall.

e. Assigning words or ideas to places, thereby improving recall of the words by envisioning those places.

f. Memory of information is enhanced when re-called under the same conditions as when it was learned.

g. Information stored in memory interferes with recall of material learned later.

_____   _____

___c___ 36. rehearsal

___g___ 37. associative models

___a___ 38. priming

___d___ 39. linguistic code

___b___ 40. imaginal code

___e___ 41. autobiographical memory

___f___ 42. engram

a. A technique of recalling information by having been exposed to related information at an earlier time.

b. Memory storage based on visual images.

c. The transfer of material from short- to long-term memory by repetition.

d. Memory storage relying on language.

e. Recollections of the facts about our own lives.

f. A physical change in the brain corresponding to the memory of material.

g. A technique of recalling information by thinking about related information.

_a_ 43. Alzheimer's disease

_c_ 44. amnesia

_e_ 45. retrograde amnesia

_d_ 46. anterograde amnesia

_b_ 47. Korsakoff's syndrome

a. An illness associated with aging that includes severe memory loss and loss of language abilities.

b. A memory impairment disease among alcoholics.

c. Memory loss unaccompanied by other mental difficulties.

d. Memory loss of the events following an injury.

e. Memory loss of occurrences prior to some event.

PRACTICE QUESTIONS

Recite and Review: ____

Test your knowledge of the chapter material by answering these **True-False** and **Multiple Choice Questions**. Check your answers with the Answer Key in the back of the *Study Guide*.

TRUE-FALSE QUESTIONS

(T)   F   1. It is probably difficult for the average person to store phone numbers of ten digits or more in short-term memory.

(T)   F   2. In order for information to reach long-term memory, it must first be transferred from sensory memory to short-term memory.

T   (F)   3. A psychology student's understanding of the concept of semantic memory is likely to be stored in memory as an imaginal code.

(T)   F   4. Flashbulb memories are memories that are centered around a specific, important event.

T   (F)   5. Heather is having difficulty recalling the name of a favorite restaurant in a nearby city. As she drives into that town, however, the name suddenly comes to mind. This phenomenon is called serial reproduction.

T   (F)   6. Using the process of serial reproduction, memory researchers have noted that people are remarkably accurate in their descriptions of incidents.

T   (F)   7. We fail to remember events mainly because of the passage of time between our first exposure and recall.

T   (F)   8. Most of forgetting is due to decay of the memory trace.

T   (F)   9. It would be very advantageous to have a type of memory in which nothing is ever forgotten.

T   (F)   10. Korsakoff's syndrome is a disease of unknown cause, resulting in memory loss and confusion.

MULTIPLE CHOICE QUESTIONS

1. The process of recording information in a form that can be recalled is:
    a. encoding.   c. decoding.
    b. storage.   d. retrieval.

2. Recording information in the memory system is referred to as:
    a. encoding.   c. decoding.
    b. storage.   d. retrieval.

3. The process of identifying and using information stored in memory is referred to as:
    a. storage.   c. recording.
    b. retrieval.   d. learning.

4. The stage of momentary storage of information, lasting only an instant and consisting only of raw stimuli, is called:
    a. sensory memory.   c. episodic memory.
    b. short-term memory.   d. long-term memory.

5. _____ stores information for approximately fifteen to twenty seconds.
    a. Sensory memory   c. Iconic memory
    b. Short-term memory   d. Long-term memory

6. As Mark listened to the television news, his young son talked excitedly about the new puppy next door. Somewhat frustrated, the boy exclaimed, ''You're not paying attention to me!'' At this point, Mark diverted his attention to his son and recited the last few things the boy had said. Which memory system is responsible for this ability?
    a. episodic memory   c. iconic memory
    b. echoic memory   d. short-term memory

7. Which of the following statements about sensory memory is true?
    a. The information is held until it is replaced by new information.
    b. The information is an accurate representation of the stimulus.
    c. The information is an incomplete representation of the stimulus.
    d. The information is lost if it is not meaningful.

8. Information in short-term memory is stored according to its:
    a. meaning.   c. length.
    b. intensity.   d. sense.

9. Short-term memory can hold approximately:
    a. five items.   c. ten items.
    b. seven items.   d. eighteen items.

10. The process of grouping information into units for storage in short-term memory is called:
    a. similarity.   c. chunking.
    b. priming.   d. closure.

11. One purpose of rehearsal is:
    a. to attach linguistic codes to echoic memory.
    b. to maintain information in short-term memory.
    c. to transfer information from sensory to short-term memory.
    d. to organize material for chunking.

12. In order to enhance transferral to long-term memory, _____ may be necessary while information is in the short-term stage.
    a. massed practice   c. interpolation
    b. elaborative rehearsal   d. interference

13. Which is not a characteristic of long-term memory?
    a. It has almost unlimited storage capacity.
    b. Memories recalled are highly accurate, faithful, and almost verbatim reproductions of the original information.
    c. It is nonexistent in some patients with brain injury.
    d. It retains memories for years.

14. Recalling what we have done and the kinds of experiences we have had best illustrates:
    a. periodic memory.   c. semantic memory.
    b. episodic memory.   d. serial production memory.

15. Knowledge about grammar, spelling, historical dates, and other knowledge about the world best illustrates:
    a. periodic memory.   c. semantic memory.
    b. episodic memory.   d. serial production memory.

16. Episodic memories are different from semantic memories in that:
    a. episodic memories deal with personal experiences.
    b. episodic memories deal with thought and language.
    c. episodic memories exist in long-term memory, whereas semantic memories exist only in short-term memory.
    d. the number of episodic memories is restricted.

17. Which codes would most likely be used to establish a cognitive map?
    a. semantic codes   c. linguistic codes
    b. imaginal codes   d. mnemonic codes

18. Your memory of how to skate is probably based on:
    a. a motor code.   c. elaborative rehearsal.
    b. semantic memory.   d. an imaginal code.

19. Memory storage based on mental, visual representation is called:
    a. a linguistic code.   c. an imaginal code.
    b. a semantic code.   d. a motor code.

20. Storage of verbal material in long-term memory without visual imagery is accomplished through:
    a. an imaginal code.   c. a sensory code.
    b. a motor code.   d. a linguistic code.

21. Linguistic, imaginal, and motor codes are ways that information is:
    a. introduced to short-term memory.
    b. shifted from long-term to short-term memory.
    c. stored in long-term memory.
    d. transferred from sensory to long-term memory.

22. According to the levels-of-processing model, what determines how well specific information is remembered?
    a. the stage attained   c. the quality of information
    b. the meaning of the information   d. the depth of processing

23. Which alternative below is not a distinguishing feature of the levels-of-processing approach?
   a. It maintains the distinction between short-term and long-term memory stages.
   b. It suggests that the way information is processed initially greatly influences how well that information is remembered.
   c. It suggests that relating initial information to other memories will improve recall.
   d. It suggests that examination of various strategies for how initial information is processed (such as shape or meaning) will provide a useful understanding of memory.

24. Information from long-term memory is easier to access with the aid of:
   a. a retrieval cue.   c. interpolated material.
   b. distractors.   d. a sensory code.

25. Finding the correct answer on a multiple choice test depends on:
   a. serial search.   c. mnemonics.
   b. recall.   d. recognition.

26. The tip-of-the-tongue phenomenon exemplifies difficulties in:
   a. encoding.   c. storage.
   b. decoding.   d. retrieval.

27. The detailed, vivid account of what you were doing when you learned of the *Challenger* disaster represents a:
   a. cognitive map.   c. flashbulb memory.
   b. schema.   d. seizure.

28. Constructive processes are associated with all of the following except:
   a. memorization.   c. expectation.
   b. motivation.   d. organization.

29. Which of the following experiences would be least influenced by the von Restorff effect?
   a. You recall almost word for word what your psychology professor said to you and your class of over 100 peers about your exceptional term paper on neuropsychology.
   b. During a memory experiment, you remember the random number 6701 from a list of four-digit numbers.
   c. You remember to stop at the cleaners after buying groceries because your roommate included the word ''cleaners'' on your grocery list with a smiling face beside it.
   d. You remember the shape of the customized tail fins on your 1957 Chevy because you designed them and did the body work yourself.

30. After memorizing a series of nonsense syllables, Ebbinghaus discovered that forgetting was most dramatic _____ following learning.
   a. two days   c. ten days
   b. an hour   d. one day

31. Which explanation has not been offered to account for how we forget information that was learned?
   a. decay
   b. interference
   c. spontaneous inhibition
   d. inadequate processing during learning

32. You are asked to write a definition of psychology that is based on text and
     lecture materials in your course. Instead, you write a definition based on
     materials learned prior to the course. You are experiencing:
     a.   retroactive interference.   c.   amnesia.
     b.   fugue.   d.   proactive interference.

33. John learns the word-processing program ''Easy Word'' on his personal
     computer. Then he learns a second program, ''Perfect Word,'' at work. He
     now finds it difficult to remember some of the commands when he uses his
     word processor at home. This is an example of:
     a.   work-induced interference.   c.   proactive interference.
     b.   retroactive interference.   d.   spontaneous interference.

34. Susan first learned to drive an automobile with a manual transmission and
     clutch. Now she has a car with an automatic transmission. From time to
     time, she finds herself trying to ''push in the clutch'' on the new car.
     This is an example of:
     a.   proactive interference.   c.   spontaneous interference.
     b.   work-induced interference.   d.   retroactive interference.

35. Current research indicates that:
     a.   most neural traces are located in the left hemisphere.
     b.   most neural traces are located in the right hemisphere.
     c.   the location of the neural trace depends on the nature of the material
          being learned.
     d.   there does not appear to be any physical area where traces are located.

36. All of the following have been associated with the biological basis of
     memory except:
     a.   the hippocampus.   c.   protein synthesis.
     b.   carrots.   d.   highly sweetened lemonade.

37. Which of the following statements about Alzheimer's disease is not correct?
     a.   Initially, the afflicted individual simply appears to be forgetful.
     b.   Alzheimer's disease affects primarily older people.
     c.   The disease usually results in marked impairments in memory.
     d.   The disease usually can be effectively treated with medication.

38. Alzheimer's disease is associated with deterioration of:
     a.   the neurological connection between the spinal cord and muscles.
     b.   the connection between the hemispheres.
     c.   the manufacture of beta amyloid.
     d.   the basal ganglia and lower brain structures.

39. Which statement about memory is not true?
     a.   Recent studies of memory have substantiated Ebbinghaus's curve of
          forgetting.
     b.   Women appear to be superior to men in their ability to learn a variety
          of information.
     c.   After something is forgotten, it is easier to learn it the second time
          than it was initially.
     d.   The savings associated with the relearning of forgotten information
          apply to memories as diverse as motor skills and academic information.

40. Which situation below is characteristic of anterograde amnesia?
    a. A person has loss of memory for events prior to some critical event.
    b. A person receives a physical trauma to the head and has difficulty
        remembering things after the accident.
    c. A person forgets simple skills such as how to dial a telephone.
    d. A person begins to experience difficulties in remembering
        appointments and relevant dates such as birthdays.

41. Which of the following syndromes is the least common?
    a. retrograde amnesia   c. Alzheimer's disease
    b. anterograde amnesia   d. Korsakoff's syndrome

42. Which situation below is most characteristic of retrograde amnesia?
    a. A person begins to experience difficulties in remembering
        appointments and relevant dates such as birthdays.
    b. A person receives a physical trauma to the head and has difficulty
        remembering things after the accident.
    c. A person forgets simple skills such as how to dial a telephone.
    d. A person has loss of memory for events prior to some critical event.

43. The keyword technique is a memory aid that can be helpful in learning a
    foreign language. The first step is to identify:
    a. a word that has similar meaning in a familiar language and pair it
        with the foreign word to be learned.
    b. a word that has a similar sound in a familiar language to at least
        part of the foreign word and pair it with the foreign word to be
        learned.
    c. a word that suggests similar imagery in a familiar language and pair
        it with the foreign word to be learned.
    d. the first word to come to mind in a familiar language and pair it
        with the foreign word to be learned.

44. Kevin is preparing a long speech. He associates the main body of the
    speech with walking into his living room. This technique is called:
    a. the method of loci.   c. the keyword technique.
    b. serial production memory.   d. retroactive interference.

45. Which alternative below is least likely to help you do well on your next
    psychology quiz?
    a. Use a prioritized strategy by studying the material only the day
        before the quiz and avoiding any other subjects which might
        interfere.
    b. Overlearn the material.
    c. Take brief lecture notes that focus on major points and that
        emphasize organization.
    d. Ask yourself questions about the material as you study.

ESSAY QUESTIONS   *Recite and Review:* ____

Essay Question 6.1: *Writing about Eyewitness Testimony*

What role should psychologists play in helping the courts deal with witness fallibility? Consider both the advantages and disadvantages of the answer you give.

_____

_____

_____

_____

_____

_____

_____

_____

_____

_____

_____

_____

_____

_____

_____

_____

_____

_____

_____

_____

_____

_____

Essay Question 6.2: *Comparing the Laboratory and Real Life*

Compare memory research that takes place in the laboratory with research that takes place in natural surroundings. What are the advantages and disadvantages of each? How would the ''middle ground'' between these two approaches be able to have the advantages of each but not the disadvantages?

_____

_____

_____

_____

_____

_____

_____

_____

_____

_____

_____

_____

_____

_____

_____

_____

_____

_____

_____

_____

_____

ACTIVITIES AND PROJECTS

1. If you are currently studying a foreign language, use the keyword technique to memorize ten words in the language. Learn an additional ten words using the methods you normally use. Either test yourself, or try this prior to a vocabulary test in your language class. Which method is more effective? Does the key word make the foreign term easier to recall? Which set of words did you remember better on the test? Remember, in the keyword system, to combine the foreign word with a common, similar sounding English word to enhance your memory of the foreign word.

2. Try to remember what you were doing one year ago from this date. At first this may seem impossible, but as you begin thinking about it, you will more than likely be able to reconstruct the memory. Out loud, try to verbalize the methods that you are using to remember what you were doing that day. This verbalization should help you understand the steps you are taking as you reconstruct the memory. Ask a friend to try the same.

3. With members of your psychology class, construct lists of nonsense syllables in order to replicate the research done by Ebbinghaus. The lists should be fourteen to twenty-one ''words'' long. Now each person should rehearse a list until it is comfortably memorized. Test each other through the day and record the number of forgotten items and how many hours since the list was memorized. Do not review the list. The forgetting curve can be charted based on the gradual decline in the number of ''words'' recalled correctly. Several variations of this can be attempted - be creative!

7

COGNITION AND LANGUAGE

DETAILED OUTLINE   *Survey:* ____

This detailed outline contains all the headings in Chapter 7: Cognition and Language. If you are using the SQ3R method, then an examination of the outline is the best way to begin your survey of the chapter.

Prologue: Rescue in Space
Looking Ahead

Thinking and Reasoning
   Thinking
   Concepts: Categorizing the world
   Decision making
      Deductive and inductive reasoning
      Algorithms and heuristics
The Cutting Edge Thinking Too Much? When Thought Leads to Poor Decisions
▪ **Recap and Review I**

Problem Solving
   Preparation: Understanding and diagnosing problems
      Kinds of problems
      Representing and organizing the problem
   Production: Generating solutions
      Subgoals
      Insight
   Judgment: Evaluating the solutions
   Impediments to problem solving
      Functional fixedness and mental set
      Inaccurate evaluation of solutions
   Creativity and problem solving
The Informed Consumer of Psychology Thinking Critically and Creatively
▪ **Recap and Review II**

Language
   Grammar: Language's language
   Language development: Developing a way with words
   Understanding language acquisition: Identifying the roots of language
   Do animals use language?
   Does thought determine language - or does language determine thought?
Psychology at Work Classrooms of Babel: Bilingual Education
▪ **Recap and Review III**

Looking Back
Key Terms and Concepts

Now that you have surveyed the chapter, read **Looking Ahead**, pages 236-237.
Question: ____
Read: ____

Focus on the questions on page 237.

CONCEPTS AND LEARNING OBJECTIVES   *Survey:* ____

These are the concepts and the learning objects for Chapter 7. Read them carefully as part of your preliminary survey of the chapter.

Concept 1: Cognitive psychology is focused on the study of processes we usually identify with thinking. Most central to our ability to think is the process of forming concepts, the placing of concepts in categories, and the processes of decision making.

1. Define cognition and the processes of thinking, reasoning, and conceptualizing. (pp. 236-238)

2. Describe the processes that are involved in decision making, including deductive reasoning and syllogistic logic. (pp. 238-241)

3. Discuss how algorithms and heuristics influence our judgments and decision making. (pp. 241-243)

Concept 2: Problem solving is also a central process related to thinking. We have both systematic and nonsystematic ways of approaching and understanding problems.

4. Explain the importance of understanding and diagnosing problems as the first step in effective problem solving. (pp. 244-247)

5. Describe the heuristic at work in generating possible solutions to problems and how solutions should be evaluated. (pp. 247-251)

6. Illustrate how efforts to develop solutions can be blocked by functional fixedness, mental set, and confirmation bias. (pp. 251-252)

7. Describe the factors that contribute to creativity and the role of creativity in problem solving and critical thinking. (pp. 252-254)

Concept 3: Language is the means by which thoughts can be represented to others and by which objects and events that surround us can be processed mentally and stored for later use. The key relationship between thought and language continues to be of concern for psychology.

8. Define the basic components of language, grammar, and syntax. (pp. 255-257)

9. Discuss the developmental processes of language and the theories of language acquisition. (pp. 257-259)

10. Identify the issues that arise with animal language, the linguistic relativity hypothesis, and bilingual education. (pp. 259-262)

CHAPTER SUMMARY

There are several ways you can use this summary as part of your systematic study plan. You may read each concept summary and then read the corresponding pages in the text, or you may read the entire summary and then read the entire chapter in the text. As you finish each section, complete the **Recap and Review** questions that are supplied in the text.

Concept 1: Prologue and Looking Ahead	*Survey:* ____
Thinking and Reasoning	*Read:* ____

Pages 236-243

The branch of psychology that studies problem solving and other aspects of thinking is called **cognitive psychology**. The term **cognition** brings together the higher mental processes of humans, including understanding the world, processing information, making judgments and decisions, and describing knowledge. **Thinking** is the manipulation of mental representations - words, images, sounds, or data in any other modality - of information. Thinking transforms the representation in order to achieve some goal or solve some problem. **Concepts** are categorizations of objects, events, or people that share common properties. Because we have concepts, we are able to classify newly encountered material on the basis of our past experiences. **Artificial concepts** are those that are defined by a clear set of properties and features. **Natural concepts** represent common objects which share characteristic features; however, they have features that vary and are not necessarily universal. **Natural concepts** are usually represented by **prototypes** which are typical, highly representative examples of a concept. Concepts provide an efficient way of understanding events and objects as they occur in the complex world.

Decision making is one of the most complex forms of thinking. Formal reasoning procedures have been studied as a way of understanding decision making. Deductive and inductive reasoning are the two major forms of formal reasoning. **Deductive reasoning** involves the application of inferences and implications from a set of assumptions to specific cases. The technique for studying deductive reasoning is called the syllogism. The **syllogism** presents two assumptions and a conclusion derived from them. If the assumptions are true, then the conclusion must be true. It is possible to have logically valid conclusions even if the premises are untrue. The use of formal deductive reasoning may not succeed because of inaccurate assumptions, erroneous conclusions, or the failure to apply formal logic. **Inductive reasoning** infers general rules from specific cases. The problem with inductive reasoning is that conclusions may be biased by insufficient or invalid evidence.

An **algorithm** is a rule that guarantees a solution if it is properly followed. Applying mathematical rules to equations will give us the answer even when we do not know why it works. A **heuristic** is a rule of thumb or some other shortcut that may lead to a solution. Heuristics can help, but they often lead to erroneous solutions. People often use a **representativeness heuristic** to determine whether something belongs to a category or not. The decision is based on whether an observed characteristic belongs in the category. The availability heuristic judges the probability of an event on how easily the event can be recalled from memory. We assume that events that are easier to remember must have happened more often and that similar events are more likely to recur. When heuristics are misapplied, they can become hindrances to decision making.

Concept 2: Problem Solving   *Survey:* _____
                                                                    Read: _____

Pages 244-254

Problem solving typically involves three major steps: preparation, production of solutions, and evaluation of solutions. Problems are distinguished as either well-defined or ill-defined. In a **well-defined problem** the problem itself is clearly understood and the information needed to solve it is clearly understood. The appropriate solution is thus easily identified. In an **ill-defined problem**, both the problem and what information is needed may be unclear.

There are three categories of problem types. **Arrangement problems** require the recombination or reorganization of a group of elements in order to solve the problem. Jigsaw puzzles are a common example. With **problems of inducing structure**, the problem solver must identify a relationship between elements and then construct a new relationship among them. A common example is number sequence problems where a test taker may be asked to supply the next number in the sequence. The third kind of problem is **transformation problems**. Transformation problems have a desired goal and require a series of steps or changes to take place in order to reach the goal. The Tower of Hanoi problem described in the text is a transformation problem. Once the category of problem is understood, it becomes easier to determine how to represent the problem and how to organize it.

The creation of solutions may proceed at the simplest level as trial and error, but this approach may be inadequate for problems that have a large number of possible configurations. The use of heuristics aids in the simplification of problems. The heuristic of **means-ends analysis** proceeds by testing the difference between the current status and the desired outcome, and with each test it tries to reduce the difference. This strategy is effective only if there is a direct solution. In cases where indirect approaches are necessary, the means-ends analysis would require avoiding these indirect paths and so become a hindrance. Another heuristic divides the goal into intermediate steps, or **subgoals**, and works on each one individually. The problem here is that sometimes problems cannot be subdivided, and this approach may make the problem bigger than it was. The use of **insight** takes a slightly different approach to problem solving, requiring a reorganization of the entire problem in order to achieve a solution. The reorganization of existing elements requires prior experience with the elements.

The final step of problem solving is to evaluate the adequacy of a solution. If the solution is not clear, criteria to judge the solution must be made clear.

In the progress toward a solution, there are several obstacles that can be met. **Functional fixedness** refers to the tendency to think of an object according to its given function or typical use. Such a block may prevent us from realizing new uses for an object. Functional fixedness is an example of a large phenomenon called mental set. **Mental set** is the tendency for old patterns of solutions to persist. The Luchin's jar problem is an example of mental set. In the first trials, a set of combinations is required to solve the problem of filling a jar. The final problem is straightforward, but the problem solver usually attempts to use the solutions applied to the previous trials. Sometimes people inaccurately evaluate solutions and act on the wrong solution because they ignore contradictory evidence. This tendency to ignore contradictory evidence is called the **confirmation bias**, where an initial hypothesis is favored and alternatives are ignored.

Problems often require creative solutions. Cognitive psychologists have tried to identify the factors that constitute creativity for a long time. **Creativity** is usually defined as the combining of responses or ideas in novel ways. One of the factors thought to be related to creativity is divergent thinking. **Divergent thinking** refers to the ability to generate unusual yet appropriate responses to problems. **Convergent thinking** produces responses that are based primarily on knowledge or logic. Cognitive complexity is another factor in creativity. Cognitive complexity is the use of elaborate, intricate, and complex stimuli and thinking patterns. Humor can increase creative output as well. Apparently intelligence is not related to creativity, perhaps because the tests for intelligence test convergent thinking rather than divergent thinking.

Creativity and problem solving can be improved by engaging in one or more of the following: redefine problems, use fractionation (breaking a concept into its parts), adopt a critical perspective, use analogies, think divergently, take the perspective of others, use heuristics, and experiment with different solutions.

Concept 3: Language

Survey: ____
Read: ____

Pages 255-262

Language is the systematic, meaningful arrangement of symbols. It is important for cognition and for communication with others. The basic structure of language is **grammar**, the framework of rules that determine how thoughts are expressed. The three components of grammar are: **phonology**, the smallest units of sound, called **phonemes**, that affect the meaning of speech and how words are formed; **syntax**, the rules that govern how words and phrases are combined to form sentences; and **semantics**, the rules governing meaning of words and sentences.

Language develops through set stages. At first children **babble**, producing speechlike but meaningless sounds. Babbling gradually sounds like actual speech, and by one year, sounds that are not part of the language disappear. After the first year, children produce short, two-word combinations followed by short sentences. **Telegraphic speech** refers to the short sentences that contain a critical message but sound as if written as a telegram, with noncritical words left out. As children begin to learn speech rules, they will apply them without flexibility, a phenomenon known as **overregularization**, where an ''ed'' might be applied to every past tense construction. Adults speak to children slowly, using primitive vocabulary, substituting nouns for pronouns, and with simpler sentence structure. By the age of 5, most children have acquired the rules of language.

The **learning-theory approach** to language acquisition suggests that the reinforcement and conditioning principles are responsible for language development. Praise for saying a word like ''mama'' reinforces the word and increases the likelihood of its being repeated. Shaping then makes child language become more adultlike. This approach has difficulty explaining the acquisition of language rules, because children are also reinforced when their language is incorrect. An alternative proposed by Noam Chomsky suggests that there exist **innate mechanisms** responsible for the acquisition of language. All human languages have a similar underlying structure he calls **universal grammar**, and a neural system in the brain, the **language-acquisition device**, is responsible for the development of language.

Whether animals use language depends on demonstrating whether they can create unique meanings that use a grammar system. Many animals as well as insects have communication systems, but they do not qualify as language. Psychologists have taught chimps to use language at the level of 2-year-old humans. Critics suggest that the language is not sophisticated enough to be considered language. In either case, humans are much better equipped for language.

Psychologists are also concerned whether the structure of language influences the structure of thought or whether thought influences language. The **linguistic-relativity hypothesis** suggests that language shapes thought, determining how people of a particular culture perceive and understand the world. In an alternative view, language may reflect the different ways we have of thinking about the world, essentially that thought produces language. A study by Eleanor Rosch concerning color perception of the Dani of New Guinea found that even though the Dani have only two color words, they could distinguish colors as well as English-speaking people who have hundreds of color words. In this respect, the linguistic-relativity hypothesis is considered to be unsupported. However, language does influence how we store memories and form categories.

Children who enter school as nonnative speakers of English face a number of hardships. The debate over whether to take a bilingual approach or whether all instruction should be in English is a major controversy. Evidence suggests that bilingual children have cognitive advantages, being more flexible, more aware of the rules of language, and higher scores on verbal and nonverbal intelligence tests. Evidence also suggests that initial instruction in the native language may enhance the acquisition of the second language.

♦ Now that you have surveyed, questioned, and read the chapter and completed the **Recap and Review** questions, review **Looking Back**, pages 263-264. *Review:* ____

♦ For additional practice through recitation and review, test your knowledge of the chapter material by answering the questions in the **Key Word Drill**, the **Practice Questions**, and the **Essay Questions**.

KEY WORD DRILL   *Recite:* ____

The following **Fill in the Blank** and **Matching Questions** test key words from the text. Check your answers with the Answer Key in the back of the *Study Guide*.

FILL IN THE BLANK

1. _Cognition_ encompasses the higher mental processes by which we understand the world, process information, make judgments and decisions, and communicate knowledge to others.

2. The manipulation of mental representations of information refers to _thought_

3. _Concepts_ are categorizations of objects, events, or people that share common properties.

4. The reasoning process whereby inferences and implications are drawn from a set of assumptions and applied to specific cases is called _deductive_ reasoning, and the reasoning process whereby a general rule is inferred from specific cases, using observation, knowledge, and experience is called _i) deductive_ reasoning.

5. A problem whose nature is clear - with the information needed to solve it available - is considered a _well_ - _defined_ problem, while a problem whose specific nature is unclear - with the information required to solve it not obvious - is called an _ill_ - _defined_ problem.

6. _functional_ _fixedness_ refers to the tendency to think of an object in terms of its most typical use.

7. _language_ is both essential for communication and reflects the way we think about and understand the world because of its close link with thought.

8. According to the ___learning___ - ~~theory~~ *theory* ___ approach, language acquisition follows the principles of reinforcement and conditioning.

9. The ___linguistic___ - ___relativity___ *hypothesis* claims that language shapes and may even determine the way people perceive and understand the world.

10. The use of and preference for elaborate, intricate, and complex stimuli and thinking patterns is a sign of ___Congitive___ *Complexity* and is closely related to creativity.

MATCHING QUESTIONS

_e_ 11. syllogism

_b_ 12. algorithm

_d_ 13. heuristic

_a_ 14. representativeness heuristic

_c_ 15. availability heuristic

a. A rule in which people and things are judged by the degree to which they represent a certain category.

b. A set of rules that, if followed, guarantee a solution, though the reason they work may not be understood by the person using them.

c. A rule for judging the probability that an event will occur by the ease with which it can be recalled from memory.

d. A rule of thumb that may bring about a solution to a problem but is not guaranteed to do so.

e. A major technique for studying deductive reasoning, in which a series of two assumptions are used to derive a conclusion.

_d_ 16. arrangement problems

_c_ 17. problems of inducing structure

_a_ 18. transformation problems

_e_ 19. means-ends analysis

_b_ 20. subgoals

a. Problems to be solved using a series of methods to change an initial state into a goal state.

b. A commonly used heuristic to divide a problem into intermediate steps and to solve each one of them.

c. Problems whose solution requires the identification of existing relationships among elements presented so as to construct a new relationship among them.

d. Problems whose solution requires the rear-rangement of a group of elements in order to satisfy a certain criterion.

e. Repeated testing to determine and reduce the distance between the desired outcome and what currently exists in problem solving.

_____

_____

_b_ 21. insight

_a_ 22. mental set

_e_ 23. confirmation bias

_f_ 24. creativity

_d_ 25. divergent thinking

_c_ 26. convergent thinking

a. The tendency for patterns of problem solving to persist.

b. Sudden awareness of the relationships among various elements that had previously appeared to be independent of one another.

c. A type of thinking which produces responses based on knowledge and logic.

d. The ability to generate unusual but appropriate responses to problems or questions.

e. A bias favoring an initial hypothesis and disregarding contradictory information suggesting alternative solutions.

f. The combining of responses or ideas in novel ways.

_____

_____

_a_ 27. grammar

_d_ 28. phonology

_e_ 29. phonemes

_c_ 30. syntax

_b_ 31. semantics

a. The framework of rules that determine how our thoughts can be expressed.

b. The rules governing the meaning of words and sentences.

c. The rules that indicate how words are joined to form sentences.

d. The study of how we use those sounds to produce meaning by forming them into words.

e. The smallest units of sound used to form words.

_____

_____

_b_ 32. telegraphic speech

_c_ 33. overregularization

_e_ 34. innate mechanism

_d_ 35. universal grammar

_a_ 36. language-acquisition device

a. A neural system of the brain hypothesized to permit understanding of language.

b. Sentences containing only the most essential words.

c. Applying rules of speech in instances in which they are inappropriate.

d. An underlying structure shared by all languages, according to Chomsky's theory that certain language characteristics are based in the brain's structure and are therefore common to all people.

e. According to Chomsky, the innate linguistic capability in humans that emerges as a function of maturation.

_d_ 37. cognitive psychology

_b_ 38. artificial concepts

_a_ 39. natural concepts

_c_ 40. prototypes

a. Concepts that are defined by a set of general, relatively loose characteristic features, such as prototypes.

b. Concepts that are clearly defined by a unique set of properties or features.

c. Typical, highly representative examples of a concept.

d. The branch of psychology that specializes in the study of cognition.

PRACTICE QUESTIONS   *Recite and Review:* ____

Test your knowledge of the chapter material by answering these **True-False** and **Multiple Choice Questions**. Check your answers with the Answer Key in the back of the *Study Guide*.

TRUE-FALSE QUESTIONS

T   *(F)*   1. Algorithms and heuristics rarely lead to the wrong solutions to problems.

(T)   F   2. An algorithm always guarantees a solution to a problem, but the solution may be wrong if the algorithm is misapplied.

(T)   F   3. The representativeness heuristic is based on the principle of overgeneralization.

(T)   F   4.   The organization and representation of a problem are crucial in determining whether the problem will be solved.

(T)   F   5.   Insight depends on previous experience with the elements involved in a problem.

(T)   F   6.   Unfortunately, the person who evaluates the quality of a solution to a problem may not be making as objective and valid an evaluation as he or she thinks.

(T)   F   7.   Sometimes, there are a number of identifiable factors in problem solving which limit the development of creative, appropriate, and accurate solutions.

T   (F)   (8.   Bill is considering voting for a particular candidate. He then learns additional information that supports his decision. This illustrates confirmation bias.

T   (F)   9.   Intelligence tests provide good measures of a person's ability to think creatively.

(T)   F   10.   Creative problem solvers tend to rely on heuristics and unusual strategies rather than on algorithms and established rules.

T   (F)   11.   According to the text, language production precedes language comprehension.

T   (F)   12.   Saying ''I falled down'' instead of ''I fell down'' is an example of telegraphic speech.

MULTIPLE CHOICE QUESTIONS

1.   Which alternative below does not fit within your text's definition of cognition?
   a.   the higher mental processes of humans
   b.   how people know and understand the world
   c.   how people communicate their knowledge and understanding to others
   d.   how people's eyes and ears process the information they receive

2.   The study of higher mental processes in humans is called:
   a.   perception.   c.   linguistics.
   b.   cognition.   d.   semantics.

3.   Cognitive psychologists study all of the following except:
   a.   how the sensory system takes in information.
   b.   how people understand the world.
   c.   how people process information.
   d.   how people make judgments.

4.   A concept is defined as:
   a.   an idea or thought about a new procedure or product.
   b.   a group of attitudes which define an object, event, or person.
   c.   a categorization of people, objects, or events that share certain properties.
   d.   one of many facts which collectively define the subject matter for a specific area of knowledge (such as psychology).

5.   Prototypes of concepts are:
     a.   new concepts to describe newly emerging phenomena.
     b.   new concepts that suddenly emerge within a language and then are
          retained or discarded.
     c.   representative examples of concepts.
     d.   concepts from other languages which are incorporated into a native
          language if they appear useful.

6.   Concepts are similar to perceptual processes in that:
     a.   concepts, like visual illusions, produce errors in interpretation.
     b.   concepts allow us to simplify and manage our world.
     c.   concepts are to language what figure-ground relationships are to
          perception.
     d.   some concepts and perceptual processes are innate.

7.   Drawing inferences and implications from a set of assumptions and then
     applying them to specific cases is the definition of:
     a.   decision making.   c.   heuristic.
     b.   algorithms.   d.   deductive reasoning.

8.   A syllogism is defined as:
     a.   a reasoning error made when the decision makers fail to use
          systematic techniques.
     b.   any time a representativeness heuristic is used in a humorous
          manner.
     c.   a series of two assumptions that is used to derive a conclusion.
     d.   an analogy concerning the relationship between two sets of paired
          items, like ''A is to B as C is to D.''

9.   The use of inaccurate premises, coming to erroneous conclusions, and simply
     failing to use formal reasoning are all errors related specifically to the
     use of:
     a.   deductive reasoning.   c.   availability heuristics.
     b.   inductive reasoning.   d.   algorithms.

10. If you fail to solve a problem because you misapply a category or set of
     categories, you have relied on:
     a.   an availability heuristic.   c.   functional fixedness.
     b.   a mental set.   d.   representativeness heuristic.

11. You have had a number of troublesome, time-consuming, expensive, and
     emotionally trying experiences with people who sell used cars. Then you
     find out that your roommate for next term is a part-time used-car dealer.
     You are convinced, even without meeting your future roommate, that you
     should not be paired with this person. You have used the _____
     heuristic to arrive at your conclusion.
     a.   means-ends   c.   availability
     b.   representativeness   d.   personality

12. Which alternative below is not a major step in problem solving?
     a.   evaluation of solutions generated
     b.   preparation for the creation of solutions
     c.   documentation of all solutions
     d.   production of solutions

13. According to your text, problems fall into one of three categories. Which
    of the following is not one of them?
    a.   arrangement   c.   structure
    b.   affability   d.   transformation

14. According to the text, an ill-defined problem is one that:
    a.   has many solutions.
    b.   has no solution.
    c.   depends on unavailable information for its solution.
    d.   is vague in nature.

15. Identifying existing relationships among elements and constructing a new
    relationship is an example of:
    a.   an inducing-structure problem.   c.   an arrangement problem.
    b.   an organization problem.   d.   a transformation problem.

16. According to the text, which of the following is perhaps the most frequently
    used heuristic technique for solving problems?
    a.   availability heuristic   c.   representativeness heuristic
    b.   categorical processing   d.   means-ends analysis

17. According to the text, the elements of the problem undergo changes in state
    in:
    a.   problems of inducing structure.   c.   arrangement problems.
    b.   representation problems.   d.   transformation problems.

18. According to the text, which of the following is not associated with
    defining and understanding a problem?
    a.   dropping inessential information   c.   dividing the problem in half
    b.   simplifying essential information d.   clarifying the solution

19. Breaking down a complex issue into a sequence of steps illustrates the
    heuristic called:
    a.   insight.   c.   availability heuristic.
    b.   subgoal analysis.   d.   means-ends analysis.

20. Insight is a:
    a.   sudden awareness of the relationships among various elements in a
         problem that previously appeared to be independent of one another.
    b.   sudden awareness of the solution to a problem with which one has had
         no prior involvement or experience.
    c.   sudden awareness of a particular algorithm that can be used to solve
         a problem.
    d.   spontaneous procedure for generating a variety of possible solutions
         to a problem.

21. Which of the following statements about insight is true?
    a.   It is an unexplained discovery of a solution without prior
         experience with any elements of the problem.
    b.   It often results from a methodical trial-and-error process.
    c.   It is a sudden realization of relationships among seemingly
         independent elements.
    d.   It is a solution that is independent of trial, error and experience.

22. The tendency for old patterns of problem solving to persist is called:
    a.   both functional fixedness and convergent thinking.
    b.   both mental set and divergent thinking.

c.   both convergent thinking and divergent thinking.
d.   both mental set and functional fixedness.

23. An obstacle to problem solving that is based on the tendency to think of an object in terms of its typical use is called:
a.   functional fixedness.   c.   mental set.
b.   means-ends analysis.   d.   subgoal analysis.

24. Thinking of a wrench in conventional terms may handicap your efforts to solve a problem when a possible solution involves using the wrench for a novel use. This phenomenon is called:
a.   functional fixedness.   c.   awareness.
b.   insight.   d.   preparation.

25. Which kind of thinking is exemplified by logic and knowledge?
a.   creative   c.   divergent
b.   convergent   d.   imaginal

26. Which of the following is characteristic of a creative thinker?
a.   convergent thought   c.   high intelligence
b.   divergent thought   d.   recurrent thought

27. The ability to conceive and implement alternate, unique solutions to a problem is called:
a.   deductive reasoning.   c.   divergent thinking.
b.   cognitive reflection.   d.   retroactive diversity.

28. The order of the words forming a sentence is generated by:
a.   synthetics.   c.   syntax.
b.   semantics.   d.   systematics.

29. The syntax of a language is the framework of rules that determine:
a.   the meaning of words and phrases.
b.   how words and phrases are combined to form sentences.
c.   the sounds of letters, phrases, and words.
d.   how thoughts can be translated into words.

30. The slight difference in meaning between the sentences ''The truck hit the pole'' and ''The pole was hit by the truck'' is determined by the rules of:
a.   grammar.   c.   syntax.
b.   phonology.   d.   semantics.

31. It is not true that babbling:
a.   occurs from 3 to 6 months of age.
b.   includes words such as ''dada'' and ''mama.''
c.   is speechlike.
d.   produces sounds found in all languages.

32. Of the following, which is the first refinement in the infant's learning of language?
a.   production of short words that begin with a consonant.
b.   disappearance of sounds that are not in the native language.
c.   emergence of sounds that resemble words.
d.   production of two-word combinations.

33. Telegraphic speech in young children refers to the fact that:
    a.   speech is very rapid.
    b.   seemingly nonessential words are omitted from phrases and sentences.
    c.   the tonal quality of speech is limited.
    d.   speech may speed up, slow down, or contain pauses.

34. In the English language, the fact that ''mama'' and ''dada'' are among the first words spoken:
    a.   is unusual, since these words do not contain the first sounds a child can make.
    b.   suggests that they are responses the child is born with.
    c.   is not surprising, since these words are easy to pronounce, and the sound capabilities of the young child are limited.
    d.   demonstrates that the sounds heard most frequently are the sounds spoken first.

35. Generalizing from information presented in the text, which of the following two-word combinations is least likely to be spoken by a 2-year-old?
    a.   Daddy up.   c.   I'm big.
    b.   Mommy cookie.   d.   More, more.

36. A child exhibits a speech pattern characterized by short sentences, with many noncritical words missing. Which of the following is not true?
    a.   The child is between 2 and 3 years old.
    b.   The child is exhibiting telegraphic speech.
    c.   The child is building complexity of speech.
    d.   The child is using overregularization.

37. According to the text, a child acquires most of the basic rules of grammar by:
    a.   2 years of age.   c.   4 years of age.
    b.   3 years of age.   d.   5 years of age.

38. According to Noam Chomsky, the brain contains a neural system designed for understanding and learning language called the:
    a.   linguistic relativity system.   c.   limbic system.
    b.   language acquisition device.   d.   phonologic linguistic device.

39. Which alternative below is not associated with current ideas about how language is acquired?
    a.   consonant drift   c.   innate processes
    b.   shaping   d.   reinforcement

40. Which of the following statements does not reflect Chomsky's view of language acquisition?
    a.   All languages share universal grammar.
    b.   The main determinant of language is reinforcement.
    c.   The brain has a language acquisition device.
    d.   Language is a uniquely human phenomenon.

41. Learning theorists view the learning of language as a process of:
    a.   classical conditioning.   c.   shaping.
    b.   stimulus generalization.   d.   chaining.

42. Psychologists who argue that the language of the child depends on exposure to the language of the parents would say that language is acquired through:
    a. classical conditioning.   c. universal grammar.
    b. shaping.   d. biological unfolding.

43. Which statement below is not true about the language skills of humans and apes?
    a. Many critics feel that the language skills acquired by chimps and gorillas are no different from a dog learning to sit on command.
    b. The language skills of chimps and gorillas are about equal to those of a 5-year-old human child.
    c. Sign language and response panels with different-shaped symbols have been used to teach chimps and gorillas language skills.
    d. Humans are probably better equipped than apes to produce and organize language into meaningful sentences.

44. Eskimos have several verbal expressions to identify snow. This fact has been used to support:
    a. the theory that language determines thought.
    b. the theory that thought determines language.
    c. the existence of the language acquisition device.
    d. development of the nativistic position.

45. Rosch's study with the Dani tribe of New Guinea showed that:
    a. English speakers perceived colors differently from the Dani.
    b. the number of categories in a language depends on perception.
    c. language does not limit the way that colors are perceived.
    d. a specific number of color names available determines the perception of color.

46. The linguistic relativity hypothesis might be paraphrased as:
    a. ''Without thought there is no language.''
    b. ''Thought creates language.''
    c. ''Language and thought are synonymous.''
    d. ''Language determines thought.''

47. The notion that language shapes the way that people of a particular culture perceive and think about the world is called the:
    a. semantic-reasoning theory.   c. prototypical hypothesis.
    b. cultural-language law.   d. linguistic-relativity theory.

<u>**ESSAY QUESTIONS**</u>   *Recite and Review:* ____

Essay Question 7.1: *Problem Solving*

Identify a major challenge that you anticipate facing in the next several years. It can involve getting married, selecting a major, choosing a career or one of many others. Describe the problem or challenge briefly, and then describe how you would apply the problem-solving steps presented in the text to the problem to generate solutions that you might try.

_____

_____

_____

_____

_____

_____

_____

_____

_____

_____

_____

_____

_____

_____

_____

_____

_____

_____

_____

_____

_____

Essay Question 7.2: *Is Language Uniquely Human?*

Some consider language to be the capability that uniquely distinguishes us as human. Weigh the arguments for the language skills of specially trained chimpanzees and develop your position on this issue. Is language unique to humans? If so, how would you characterize the communication abilities of chimpanzees? If not, then what capability does distinguish us from other animals?

_____

_____

_____

_____

_____

_____

_____

_____

_____

_____

_____

_____

_____

_____

_____

_____

_____

_____

_____

_____

_____

_____

ACTIVITIES AND PROJECTS

1. To counteract functional fixedness and to foster creativity, record as many uses as you can for a paper clip. Limit yourself to three minutes. Repeat the exercise with a brick and a coat hanger. Ask a friend to do the same thing and then compare the number of unique items each of you have. Consider the extent to which this exercise reflects intelligence (and what kind of intelligence) and creativity. Are the types of uses you identified specific to one or two of Gardner's types of intelligence? If you have a high number of uses, is this an indication of strength in practical intelligence? Does the exercise dependent on linguistic or cultural skills? (One particularly interesting variation is to ask a friend who is from another culture or ethnic group to do the exercise and then determine whether some of the uses are unique as a result of cultural experience.)

2. Select several common nouns like ''house,'' ''tree,'' and ''dog.'' Then ask people in the following age groups to give you a definition:

    Child, age 3 to 4 years old
    Child, age 9 to 10 years old
    Teenager
    Adult

    To vary the activity, you may want to ask a young child to describe the size or some other feature of one or more of the common objects. The descriptions will reflect the child's conception of the object (''a star is about twenty feet bigger than a house''). Be sure to ask the adult and teenager for a description of the same object.

3. Try to observe and record (with a tape recorder or on a note pad) examples of the language production in one or more children between the ages of six months and four years. Then compare the examples with those given in the text. Which of the basic concepts of language acquisition were you able to observe?

8

INTELLIGENCE

DETAILED OUTLINE

Survey: ____

This detailed outline contains all the headings in Chapter 8: Intelligence. If you are using the SQ3R method, then an examination of the outline is the best way to begin your survey of the chapter.

Prologue: Leslie Lemke
Looking Ahead

Defining Intelligent Behavior
   Measuring intelligence
   Measuring IQ
   Achievement and aptitude tests
   Alternative formulations of intelligence
The Cutting Edge Emotional Intelligence: Getting Smart about Emotions
   Is information processing intelligence? Contemporary approaches
Psychology at Work Is Practical Intelligence Different from School
   Intelligence?
The Informed Consumer of Psychology Can You Do Better on Standardized
   Tests?
▪ **Recap and Review I**

Variations in Intellectual Ability
   Mental retardation
   The intellectually gifted
▪ **Recap and Review II**

Individual Differences in Intelligence: Heredity, Environment – or Both?
   The basic controversy: The relative influence of heredity and of
     environment
   Placing the heredity/environment question in perspective
▪ **Recap and Review III**

Looking Back
Key Terms and Concepts

Now that you have surveyed the chapter, read **Looking Ahead**, pages 268-269.
   Question: ____
     Read: ____

Focus on the questions on page 269.

CONCEPTS AND LEARNING OBJECTIVES   *Survey:* ____

These are the concepts and the learning objects for Chapter 8. Read them carefully as part of your preliminary survey of the chapter.

Concept 1: Intelligence is understood as a predictor of school success, and is also viewed as a limited expression of the cognitive capacity of individuals. Alternative views of intelligence include the view that there exist numerous intelligences, including practical intelligence, which is made up of skills needed to survive in cultural and social settings.

1. Define intelligence and the issues related to its definition. (pp. 268-271)

2. Discuss how intelligence is measured, define intelligence quotient, and describe how achievement and aptitude differ from intelligence. (pp. 271-274)

3. Describe the alternative views of intelligence. (pp. 274-276)

4. Explain how cognitive psychology uses information processing to define intelligence. (pp. 276-277)

5. Describe the concept of practical intelligence and discuss whether performance on achievement tests can be improved with training. (pp. 278-280)

Concept 2: The extremes in intellectual function lead to distinctions of mental retardation and giftedness. The basic challenge for identifying these groups is to identify and utilize educational resources in order to best serve the two populations.

6. Define and describe mental retardation and its causes. (pp. 281-283)

7. Define and describe intellectual giftedness. (pp. 283-284)

Concept 3: The major debate in intelligence is over the relative influence on intelligence of heredity and environment, and the extent to which these two influences can be understood in order to improve intellectual potential.

8. Analyze the issues related to the heredity versus environment debate, and discuss the problem of cultural bias in intelligence tests. (pp. 285-289)

CHAPTER SUMMARY

There are several ways you can use this summary as part of your systematic study plan. You may read each concept summary and then read the corresponding pages in the text, or you may read the entire summary and then read the entire chapter in the text. As you finish each section, complete the **Recap and Review** questions that are supplied in the text.

Concept 1: Prologue and Looking Ahead   *Survey:* ____
            Defining Intelligent Behavior   *Read:* ____

Pages 268-281

The Prologue describes Leslie Lemke, a blind, crippled, and mentally retarded individual with an exceptional musical talent. Leslie Lemke's condition is called the ''savant syndrome,'' a condition in which an otherwise handicapped individual has an exceptional talent in a very specific area, like Lemke's ability to play the piano.

Intelligence has many different meanings, depending upon whether it is applied to behavior in a Pacific culture like that of the Trukese who can navigate in open sea without any equipment or to someone who can get around the New York subway system. In the examples in the text, the common theme is that intelligent people can use their resources more effectively than others in accomplishing whatever task is at hand. In a survey of laypersons, three major components of intelligence were identified: (1) problem-solving ability, (2) verbal ability, and (3) social competence. Psychologists have defined **Intelligence** as the capacity to understand the world, think rationally, and use resources effectively. Intelligence remains difficult to determine, though intelligence tests have been successful in identifying individuals who need help in school, who have cognitive difficulties, and who need help making choices about school.

Alfred Binet developed the first formal intelligence test to identify the ''dullest'' students in the Parisian school system. His test was able to distinguish the ''bright'' from the ''dull'' and eventually made distinctions between age groups. The original test became the **Stanford-Binet test**, and it is based on items that vary according to the age of the subject. An IQ score is determined by the level at which a person performs on the test in relation to others of the same age. Other IQ tests given in America are the **Weschler Adult Intelligence Scale-Revised**, the **WAIS-R**, and the **Weschler Intelligence Scale for Children-III**, the **WISC-III**. The WAIS-R and the WISC-III have verbal and performance scales. The two scales allow a more accurate picture of the person's abilities. The Stanford-Binet, the WAIS-R, and WISC-III require individual administration. A number of ''paper and pencil'' tests have been developed, but they sacrifice flexibility and fail to motivate the test taker. Also, they are not easily given to children or to people with low IQs.

The **achievement test** is a test meant to determine the level of achievement of an individual, that is, what the person has actually learned. An **aptitude test** measures and predicts an individual's ability in a particular area. The SAT is an exam that predicts how well a student will do in college. There is quite a bit of overlap among the IQ, achievement, and aptitude tests.

In the two dominant tests, the score is considered to be a reflection of the intelligence of the person. It remains unclear whether intelligence is a single factor or a combination of factors. The single-factor view suggests that there is a general factor for mental ability called **g**, or **g-factor**. Recently, two factors have been accepted by most. They are **fluid intelligence**, the ability to deal with new problems and situations, and **crystallized intelligence**, the store of information, skills, and strategies acquired through experience. Fluid intelligence is thought to decline in the elderly. In an alternate formulation, Howard Gardner has proposed the existence of seven multiple intelligences: (1) musical intelligence, (2) bodily-kinesthetic intelligence, (3) logical-mathematical intelligence, (4) linguistic intelligence, (5) spatial intelligence, (6) interpersonal intelligence, and (7) intrapersonal intelligence. Gardner suggests that these separate intelligences do not operate in isolation. Results from Gardner's work include the acceptance of more than one answer as correct on a test. Other kinds of intelligence include emotional intelligence, the set of skills that underlie the accurate assessment, evaluation, expression, and regulation of emotions. Emotional intelligence allows people to use emotions to achieve goals.

The information-processing approach to intelligence views intelligence as the ability to process information. Effective problem solvers have traditionally been those who also score high on intelligence tests. In solving an analogy problem, a bright student will go through a series of steps, first encoding the information in a useful way, then making inferences about the analogy relationship, then mapping the relationship from the first half of the analogy to the second half, then applying the relationship to test answers, then responding with a solution. People with higher intelligence levels tends to get the right answer and to have qualitatively different methods for solving problems. High scorers spend more of their time on the initial stage of encoding, identifying parts of the problems, and retrieval from memory.

Robert Sternberg has proposed a **triarchic theory of intelligence**. The three components are: the componential aspect that focuses on rational behavior, the experiential aspect that focuses on how prior experience is applied, and the contextual aspect that focuses on how successful people respond to the demands of the everyday environment. **Practical intelligence** grows from Sternberg's attention to the practical demands of everyday life. One of the problems is that though IQ tests predict performance in school, they do not correlate with career success. Several tests have been designed that measure practical intelligence in the business world.

There are many coaching services that claim to help students improve their scores on the Scholastic Aptitude Test. Though the service that produces the test originally argued that these were not helpful, it now has accepted that some coaching may help. One must determine what is sought from the coaching in selecting a type of coaching. Hints for improving testing include: previewing the section of the test as soon as you begin, timing yourself carefully, checking the scoring to see if you will be penalized for wrong answers (if so, then do not guess), and completing the answer sheets accurately.

Concept 2: Variations in Intellectual Ability   *Survey:* ____
                                                                    Read: ____

                                                                    Pages 281-285

About 6.5 million people in the United States are classified as mentally retarded, and the populations that comprise the mentally retarded and the exceptionally gifted require special attention in order to reach their potential. **Mental retardation** is defined by the American Association on Mental Deficiency as when there is ''significantly subaverage general intellectual functioning existing concurrently with deficits in adaptive behavior and manifested during the developmental period.'' This definition includes mild to severe retardation. **Mild retardation** includes individuals whose IQ scores fall in the 55 to 69 range. This comprises about 90 percent of the people with mental retardation. **Moderate retardation**, with scores ranging from 40 to 54, **severe retardation**, with scores from 25 to 39, and **profound retardation**, with scores below 25, present problems that become more pronounced as the IQ becomes lower. The moderately retarded require some supervision during their entire lives, and the severe and profound groups require institutionalization. One-third of the people classified as retarded suffer from biological causes of retardation, mostly from **Down syndrome**, a genetic disorder caused by an extra chromosome. **Familial retardation** occurs in cases when there is no biological cause but instead may be linked with a family history of retardation. This may be caused by environmental factors like severe poverty, malnutrition, and possibly a genetic factor that cannot be determined. In 1975, Congress passed a law that entitles mentally retarded individuals to a full education and to education and training in the **least-restrictive environment**. This law leads to a process of returning individuals to regular classrooms, a process called **mainstreaming**. The view is that by mainstreaming individuals, they interact with nonretarded individuals and benefit from the interaction.

The **intellectually gifted** comprise about 2 to 4 percent of the population. This group is generally identified as those individuals with IQ scores higher than 130. Contrary to the stereotype, these individuals are usually outgoing, well-adjusted, popular people who do most things better than the average person. Lewis Terman conducted a well-known longitudinal study following 1500 gifted children (with IQs above 140). They have an impressive record of accomplishments, though being gifted does not guarantee success.

Concept 3:   Individual Differences in Intelligence: *Survey:* ____
Heredity, Environment - or Both?   *Read:* ____

Pages 285-290

In the determination of the causes of individual differences, cultural differences in the framing of questions on the test can play an important role. Adrian Dove has developed a test that illustrates how foreign culture-specific tests can be by asking questions drawn from the experience of inner-city black populations. On standard intelligence tests, some culture and ethnic groups score lower than others, as with blacks, who tend to score fifteen points lower than whites. Because of the possibility of bias and discrimination, some states have banned the use of traditional intelligence tests.

Attempts to develop a **culture-fair IQ test** that does not discriminate have led in some cases to even greater disparities in scores. The controversy based on ethnic and minority differences in intelligence tests reflects a greater concern of whether intelligence is predominantly a result of heredity or of environmental forces.   On the heredity side, the explanation for lower performance by a population would be that it is less intelligent as a result of genetics. The debate reached a major peak when Arthur Jensen argued that the difference between white and black IQ scores could not be explained by environmental differences - because even when socioeconomic factors were considered the difference did not disappear. Intelligence does show a high degree of **heritability**, the measure of the extent to which a characteristic is related to genetic, inherited factors. The closer two people are linked genetically, the closer their IQ scores are likely to be. Jensen argued that 75 to 80 percent of the variability in IQ scores was a result of genetics. Critics of Jensen have argued, with the support of most of the psychological community, that such a factor as socioeconomic status is itself a highly variable factor, with wide variations from one household to another. Other research has demonstrated that blacks raised in enriched environments similar to whites do not have lower IQ scores. The real differences between IQ scores cannot be between the means of groups but must be understood as the difference between individuals.

The issue of heredity and environment is one in which experimental research that might establish causal relationships cannot be devised because of ethical issues. A question that should be of concern is how can we maximize the potential intellectual development of individuals.

♦ Now that you have surveyed, questioned, and read the chapter and completed the **Recap and Review** questions, review **Looking Back**, pages 290-291. *Review:* ____

♦ For additional practice through recitation and review, test your knowledge of the chapter material by answering the questions in the **Key Word Drill**, the **Practice Questions**, and the **Essay Questions**.

Key Word Drill   *Recite:* ____

The following **Fill in the Blank** and **Matching Questions** test key words from the text. Check your answers with the Answer Key in the back of the *Study Guide*.

FILL IN THE BLANK

1. When we speak of _____, we are referring to our capacity to understand the world, think rationally, and use resources effectively when faced with challenges.

2. In order to compare a person's performance on an IQ test to the performance of others, a means of calculating the IQ score called the _____ _____ _____ is used.

3. An _____ test is intended to determine a person's level of knowledge in a given subject, while an _____ test is designed to predict a person's ability in a particular line of work.

4. Early psychologists assumed the existence of a _____-_____, a theoretical single general factor accounting for mental ability and thought to underlie performance on every aspect of intelligence.

5. The _____ theory of intelligence suggests the existence of three major aspects of intelligence: the componential, the experiential, and the contextual.

6. _____ is defined by a significantly subaverage level of intellectual functioning that is also accompanied by deficits in adaptive behavior.

7. The official phrase from PL94-142, _____-_____- _____, refers to the guarantee of the right of full education for retarded people in an environment that is most similar to the educational environment of typical children.

8. The integration of retarded people into regular classroom situations has been called _____.

9. Psychologists have tried to devise tests that assess experiences common to all cultures; these _____-_____ IQ tests are designed to avoid discrimination against members of any minority culture group.

10. _____ is a measure of the degree to which a characteristic is related to genetic, inherited factors as opposed to environmental factors.

MATCHING QUESTIONS

_c_ 11. intelligence tests

_b_ 12. Stanford-Binet test

_a_ 13. Wechsler Adult Intelligence Scale-Revised (WAIS-R)

_d_ 14. Wechsler Intelligence Scale for Children-III (WISC-III)

a. A test of intelligence consisting of verbal and nonverbal performance sections, providing a relatively precise picture of a person's specific abilities.

b. A test of intelligence that includes a series of items varying in nature according to the age of the person being tested.

c. A battery of measures to determine a person's level of intelligence.

d. An intelligence test for children; see Wechsler Adult Intelligence Scale-Revised.

_f_ 15. mild retardation

_g_ 16. moderate retardation

_a_ 17. severe retardation

_e_ 18. profound retardation

_d_ 19. Down syndrome

_b_ 20. familial retardation

_c_ 21. intellectually gifted

a. Characterized by an IQ between 25 and 39 and difficulty in functioning independently.

b. Mental retardation in which there is a history of retardation in a family but no evidence of biological causes.

c. Characterized by higher-than-average intelligence, with IQ scores above 130.

d. A common cause of mental retardation, brought about by the presence of an extra chromosome.

e. Characterized by an IQ below 25 and an inability to function independently.

f. Characterized by an IQ between 55 and 69 and the ability to function independently.

g. Characterized by an IQ between 40 and 54.

_d_ 22. mental age

_f_ 23. chronological age

_b_ 24. intelligence quotient (IQ) score

_e_ 25. fluid intelligence

_c_ 26. crystallized intelligence

_a_ 27. practical intelligence

a. Intelligence related to overall success in living, rather than to intellectual and academic performance.

b. A measure of intelligence that takes into account an individual's mental and chronological ages.

c. The store of specific information, skills, and strategies that people have acquired through experience.

d. The typical intelligence level found for people at a given chronological age.

e. The ability to deal with new problems and encounters.

f. A person's physical age.

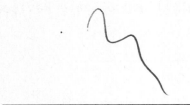

_____   _____

PRACTICE QUESTIONS   _Recite and Review:_ ____

Test your knowledge of the chapter material by answering these **True-False** and **Multiple Choice Questions**. Check your answers with the Answer Key in the back of the _Study Guide_.

TRUE-FALSE QUESTIONS

(T)   F   1. A 16-year-old adolescent with a mental age of 15 would have an IQ score under 100.

(T)   F   2. The majority of people who take intelligence tests fall within 15 IQ points of the average score.

T   (F)   3. The Stanford-Binet and the Wechsler intelligence tests can be administered to a group of people.

T   (F)   4. An aptitude test measures what a person has actually learned.

T   (F)   5. The Stanford-Binet intelligence test is administered as a paper-and-pencil test.

(T)   F   6. Some psychologists feel that tests such as the Stanford-Binet and the Wechsler (WAIS-R or WISC-R) give little information about the nature of intelligence.

(T)   F   7. Cognitive psychologists use an information-processing model to understand intelligence.

T   (F)   8. Traditional measures of intelligence are very good predictors of career success.

T   (F)   9. The process of mainstreaming usually places children of normal
            intelligence among mentally retarded children in special education
            classrooms.

(T)   F 10. Some culture-fair intelligence tests produce larger differences in
            average scores between the majority and minority groups.

MULTIPLE CHOICE QUESTIONS

1. A person who is diagnosed as having _____ may exhibit extraordinary
    talents yet be mentally retarded.
    a.   Down syndrome
    b.   the symptoms of Alzheimer's disease
    c.   Kleinfelter's syndrome
    (d). savant syndrome

2. The feature or ability common to virtually all definitions of intelligence
    is:
    a.   high score on a written test.
    b.   verbal proficiency.
    c.   mastery of logical thought.
    (d). effective use of environmental resources.

3. Your textbook defines intelligence as:
    a.   the ability to understand subject matters from different disciplines
         in an academic setting.
    b.   a complex capability in humans and animals that allows them to think,
         act, and function adaptively.
    (c). the capacity to understand the world, think rationally, and use
         resources effectively when faced with challenges.
    d.   a multidimensional human capability which is determined by a person's
         heredity and environment.

4. In order to distinguish more intelligent from less intelligent people,
    psychologists generally have relied on:
    (a). intelligence tests.   c. achievement tests.
    b.   genealogy.   d. projective tests.

5. According to Binet, a retarded person's mental age would be _____ the
    person's chronological age.
    (a). lower than   c. the same as
    b.   higher than   d. unrelated to

6. The measure of intelligence that takes into consideration both mental and
    chronological age is called the:
    a.   achievement scale.   (c.) intelligence quotient.
    b.   aptitude level.   d. g-factor.

7. The intelligence quotient was developed to:
    a.   increase the reliability of the early intelligence tests.
    b.   provide a way to compare the performance of French and American
         children on intelligence tests.
    (c). allow meaningful comparisons of intelligence among people of
         different ages.
    d.   correct a systematic scoring error in the first American
         intelligence tests.

8. If an 8-year-old child receives a score on an IQ test that is usually achieved by a typical 10-year-old, the child's IQ is:
    a. 80.   c. 125.
    b. 100.   d. 180.

9. Using standard testing procedures and the IQ formula, which of the following will have the highest IQ?
    a. a 12-year-old with a mental age of 10
    b. a 10-year-old with a mental age of 12
    c. a 25-year-old with a mental age of 23
    d. a 23-year-old with a mental age of 25

10. If a 12-year-old child receives a score on an IQ test that is usually achieved by a typical 9-year-old, the child's mental age is:
    a. 9.
    b. 12.
    c. 10 and a half.
    d. not determined without further investigation.

11. The formula _____ is used to calculate ratio IQ.
    a. CA ÷ MA x 100 = IQ.   c. MA + CA x 100 = IQ.
    b. CA ÷ MA x .01 = IQ.   d   (MA - CA) ÷ 100 = IQ.

12. The first intelligence test was designed and used by:
    a. Alfred Binet.   c. Howard Gardner.
    b. David Wechsler.   d. Sigmund Freud.

13. Which alternative about the first intelligence test is not correct?
    a. It was designed to identify ''gifted'' children in the school system.
    b. It was developed by Alfred Binet in France.
    c. It assumed that performance on certain items and tasks improved with age.
    d. Many items were selected for the test when ''bright'' and ''dull'' students scored differently on them.

14. About two-thirds of all people have IQ scores of:
    a. 95-105.   c. 85-115.
    b. 90-110.   d. 70-110.

15. The two major categories of the Wechsler intelligence tests are:
    a. visual and conceptual.   c. performance and verbal.
    b. spatial and verbal.   d. performance and spatial.

16. Of the following, which IQ range has the lowest percentage of individuals in it?
    a. 55-70   c. 85-100
    b. 70-85   d. 100-115

17. The administration of the Stanford-Binet test is ended when:
    a. all items have been administered.
    b. the person misses a total of five items.
    c. the person misses a total of ten items.
    d. the person cannot answer any more questions.

18. Which of the following is not one of the verbal subtests on the Wechsler intelligence scale?
    a. information   (c) block design
    b. similarities   d. vocabulary

19. Which of the following is not one of the performance subtests on the Wechsler intelligence scale?
    (a) comprehension   c. picture arrangement
    b. picture completion   d. digit symbol

20. Which of the following types of tests was designed to measure a person's level of knowledge in a given subject area?
    a. motor skills tests   c. aptitude tests
    b. personality tests   (d) achievement tests

21. Aptitude tests are designed to:
    (a) predict future performance.
    b. measure achievement in a certain area.
    c. measure intelligence.
    d. calculate the g-factor.

22. Crystallized intelligence is dependent on _____ for its development.
    a. heredity   (c) fluid intelligence
    b. nutrition and diet   d. native intelligence

23. If you were asked to solve a problem using your own experience as a basis for the solution, you would be using:
    a. availability heuristics.   c. fluid intelligence.
    (b) crystallized intelligence.   d. g-factors.

24. _____ is the most detailed perspective of intelligence to date.
    a. Spearman's g-factor
    b. Thurstone's primary abilities
    c. Cattell's fluid and crystallized intelligence
    (d) Gardner's multiple intelligences

25. Gardner suggested that we have seven types of intelligence. Which of the following is not among them?
    (a) general information intelligence   c. spatial intelligence
    b. musical intelligence   d. interpersonal intelligence

26. Gardner asserts that there are seven types of intelligence. Which alternative below is not one of them?
    (a) technical   c. linguistic
    b. interpersonal   d. logical-mathematical

27. Among Gardner's suggested intelligences, which intelligence is described as ''skill in interacting with others such as sensitivity to moods''?
    a. linguistic   (c) interpersonal
    b. bodily-kinesthetic   d. intrapersonal

28. Cognitive psychologists use the _____ approach to understand intelligence.
    a. structure-of-intellect   c. aptitude-testing
    b. deviation IQ   (d) information-processing

29. The _____ approach to understanding intelligence emphasizes processes.
    a. cognitive   c. environmental
    b. learning   d. physiological

30. To find out if you are particularly well suited to a career in business, you would be best advised to take the intelligence test devised by:
    a. Alfred Binet.   c. Raymond Cattell.
    b. Robert Sternberg.   d. Seymour Epstein.

31. According to Sternberg, intelligence and success in business:
    a. are strongly correlated.   c. cannot be correlated.
    b. are minimally correlated.   d. are inversely correlated.

32. Mental retardation is primarily defined by:
    a. ability to get along in the world and with other people.
    b. deficits in intellectual functioning and adaptive behavior.
    c. ability to perform in school.
    d. ability to perform on intelligence tests.

33. A significantly subaverage level of intellectual functioning accompanied by deficits in adaptive behavior defines:
    a. savant syndrome.   c. mental retardation.
    b. profound retardation.   d. severe retardation.

34. IQ scores falling below _____ fit the criterion for mental retardation.
    a. 80   c. 60
    b. 70   d. 50

35. The most common form of mental retardation that is clearly biologically based is:
    a. profoundly disabled.   c. savant syndrome.
    b. familial.   d. Down syndrome.

36. Which of the following statements about mental retardation is not true?
    a. Retardation often runs in families.
    b. Retardation is often caused by genetic defects.
    c. Retarded children are mainstreamed whenever possible.
    d. Profoundly retarded children are placed in special-education classes.

37. Most cases of mental retardation are classified as being caused by:
    a. Down syndrome.   c. Kleinfelter's syndrome.
    b. familial retardation.   d. traumatic injury.

38. Familial retardation:
    a. results from hereditary factors.
    b. results from environmental factors.
    c. is a paradox, since there are no known hereditary or environmental causes.
    d. may result from either hereditary or environmental factors, although there are no known biological causes.

39. According to the terminology used in the text, people with unusually low IQs
    (such as 42) are referred to as _____, whereas people with unusually
    high IQs (such as 164) are referred to as _____.
    a.   mental defectives; geniuses
    b.   the mentally retarded; the intellectually gifted
    c.   the slow; the gifted
    d.   the congenitally retarded; the intellectually superior

40. For the retarded youngster, mainstreaming means:
    a.   more opportunities to relate to other retarded students.
    b.   increased opportunities for education and socialization.
    c.   the exclusion of other retarded students from the classroom.
    d.   separating retarded and normal students.

41. Legislation designed to protect the rights of the mentally retarded,
    including providing a ''least restrictive environment,'' has led to:
    a.   mainstreaming.
    b.   special-education classrooms.
    c.   resource classrooms.
    d.   mandatory IQ testing for all students with suspected deficits.

42. An intellectually gifted person:
    a.   has an IQ higher than 130.   c.   is antisocial.
    b.   is very shy.   d.   is successful in everything.

43. Youngsters with very high IQs:
    a.   are gifted in every academic subject.
    b.   have adjustment problems later in life.
    c.   should not be mainstreamed.
    d.   show better social adjustment in school than others.

44. A culture-unfair intelligence test is one in which the information being
    tested:
    a.   is strictly academic.
    b.   is cultural in nature.
    c.   is easier for members of a particular culture.
    d.   ignores all aspects of culture.

45. A _____ measure of intelligence does not favor any particular cultural
    group over another.
    a.   quantitative   c.   verbal
    b.   conventional   d.   culture-fair

46. What percentage of the variation in intelligence from one person to another
    did Arthur Jensen argue was inherited?
    a.   25   c.   75
    b.   50   d.   100

ESSAY QUESTIONS   *Recite and Review:* ____

Essay Question 8.1: *Defining Intelligence*

Describe and outline the definitions of intelligence offered in the text. Which of these do you find most acceptable? Support your view with examples or other evidence. What additional evidence would be required to strengthen the validity of the definition you have chosen?

_____

_____

_____

_____

_____

_____

_____

_____

_____

_____

_____

_____

_____

_____

_____

_____

_____

_____

_____

_____

Essay Question 8.2: *The Heredity/Environment Question*

Outline the basic issues involved in the heredity versus environment debate. The text suggests that the more important concern is how to intelligences is to be maximized. Considering the concepts introduced so far in the text, what methods ought to be considered in our efforts to reach our fullest intelligence potential?

_____

_____

_____

_____

_____

_____

_____

_____

_____

_____

_____

_____

_____

_____

_____

_____

_____

_____

_____

ACTVITIES AND PROJECTS

1. Survey your friends and classmates regarding their views of what makes a
    person intelligent. Your questions may include items regarding whether
    intelligence necessarily correlates with success in school or work; items
    concerning the existence of emotional and practical intelligence, as well
    as the seven types of intelligence defined by Howard Gardner (page 275 in
    the text). Your objective should be to determine the preconceived, commonly
    held attitudes about intelligence. For instance, you may also include
    questions regarding the social skills of very bright and gifted people, and
    the view that many intelligent people lack common sense.

2. It is also interesting to explore the views and attitudes concerning the
    role of genetic inheritance on intelligence and related factors like
    personality. Do intelligent people view themselves as having their
    intelligence as a result of their genetic make-up? Do they expect their
    children to be as intelligent as they are? (This could be a sign of their
    tacitly holding the view that intelligence is inherited to a large extent.)

C H A P T E R

9

MOTIVATION AND EMOTION

<u>**DETAILED OUTLINE**</u>   *Survey:* ____

This detailed outline contains all the headings in Chapter 9: Motivation and
Emotion. If you are using the SQ3R method, then an examination of the outline
is the best way to begin your survey of the chapter.

    Prologue: Peter Potterfield
    Looking Ahead

    Explanations of Motivation
      Instincts: Born to be motivated
      Drive-reduction theories of motivation
      Arousal theory: The search for stimulation
      Incentive theory: The pull of motivation
      Opponent-process theory: The yin and yang of motivation
      Cognitive theory
      Maslow's hierarchy: Ordering motivational needs
      A final word about the theories of motivation
   ▪ **Recap and Review I**

    Human Needs and Motivation: Eat, Drink, and Be Daring
      Thirst
      Hunger
          Biological factors in eating
          The weight set point, metabolism and obesity
          Social factors in eating
          Eating disorders
  Psychology at Work Treating Eating Disorders
  The Informed Consumer of Psychology Dieting and Losing Weight Successfully
  Human Needs and Motivation: Sex and the Needs for Achievement
          The facts of life: Human sexual motivation
          Masturbation: Solitary sex
          Heterosexuality
            Premarital sex
            Marital sex
          Homosexuality and bisexuality
     The need for achievement: Striving for success
          Measuring achievement motivation
          Learning to achieve: The development of achievement motivation
          Training achievement motivation in adults
     The need for affiliation: Striving for friendship
     The need for power: Striving for impact on others
   ▪ **Recap and Review II**

    Understanding Emotional Experiences

The functions of emotions
Deciphering Our Own Emotions
The James-Lange theory: Do gut reactions equal emotions?
The Cannon-Bard theory: Physiological reactions as the result of emotions
The Schachter-Singer theory: Emotions as labels
Summing up the theories of emotion
The Cutting Edge Are Nonverbal Expressions of Emotion Universal Across Cultures?
▪ **Recap and Review III**

Looking Back
Key Terms and Concepts

Now that you have surveyed the chapter, read **Looking Ahead**, pages 294-295.
Question: _____
Read: _____

Focus on the questions on page 295.

<u>**CONCEPTS AND LEARNING OBJECTIVES**</u>   *Survey:* _____

These are the concepts and the learning objects for Chapter 9.   Read them carefully as part of your preliminary survey of the chapter.

Concept 1: The theories of motivation examine basic instincts, drives, levels of arousal, expectations, and self-realization as possible motive sources. Many approaches may actually be complementary, and each explaining an aspect of the forces that direct and energize behavior.

  1. Define motivation and emotions, and discuss the role of each in behavior. (pp. 294-295)

  2. Describe and distinguish the instinct, drive reduction, and arousal theories of motivation. (pp. 295-298)

  3. Describe incentive theory and opponent process theory of motivation. (pp. 298-301)

  4. Describe how cognitive theory accounts for motivation, and discuss Maslow's hierarchy of motivation. (pp. 301-303)

Concept 2: Thirst and hunger are two motives that have a physiological basis, and the needs for achievement, affiliation, and power are learned motives.

  5. Outline and describe the processes involved in the physiological motivations of thirst and hunger. (pp. 304-310)

  6. Describe and distinguish achievement, affiliation, and power motivation. (pp. 316-318)

Concept 3: The variety of sexual behavior includes masturbation; premarital, and marital activity; and homosexual and bisexual activity.

7. Describe how sexual normality is understood and defined by society, and discuss whether masturbation is normal. (pp. 310-312)

8. Describe the heterosexual patterns of sexual behavior, including premarital sex, marital sex (pp. 312-313)

9. Describe the similarities and differences between normal sexuality and homosexual and bisexual behavior. (pp. 314-315)

Concept 4: Emotions are highly complex experiences that combine physiological arousal, situational conditions, and cognitive understanding. In addition, Emotions serve a number of functions related to preparing for action, shaping behavior, and regulating interaction. The three major theories of emotion are the James-Lange theory, the Cannon-Bard theory, and the Schachter-Singer theory.

10. Describe the functions of emotions and the range of emotional expression. (pp. 320-322)

11. Identify the key points of each theory of emotions - the James-Lange theory, the Cannon Bard theory, and the Schachter-Singer theory - and distinguish each theory from the others. (pp. 323-328)

CHAPTER SUMMARY

There are several ways you can use this summary as part of your systematic study plan. You may read each concept summary and then read the corresponding pages in the text, or you may read the entire summary and then read the entire chapter in the text. As you finish each section, complete the **Recap and Review** questions that are supplied in the text.

Concept 1: Prologue and Looking Ahead
         Explanations of Motivation

Survey: _____
Read: _____

Pages 294-303

The story of Peter Potterfield in the Prologue describes the importance and necessity of simple biological needs like fluid, and the ways in which individuals can be affected by those basic needs. These factors that energize and direct behavior comprise the major focus of the study of **motivation. Motives** are the desired goals that underlie behavior. Psychologists who study motivation seek to understand why people do the things they do. The study of **emotions** includes the internal experience at any given moment.
    There are a number of approaches to understanding motivation. An early approach focused on instincts as inborn, biologically determined patterns of behavior. The instinct theories argue that there exist preprogrammed patterns of behavior. The problems with these theories include the difficulty in determining a set of instincts, and the fact that instinct theories do not explain why a behavior occurs. Also, they are unable to account for the variety of behavior.
    Drive-reduction theories focus on behavior as an attempt to remedy the shortage of some basic biological requirement. In this view, a **drive** is a

motivational arousal that energizes a behavior to fulfill a need. **Primary drives** meet biological requirements, while **secondary drives** have no obvious biological basis. The need to achieve, for instance, is not a biological need. Primary drives are resolved by reducing the need that underlies them. Primary drives are also governed by a basic motivational phenomenon of known as **homeostasis**, the goal of maintaining optimal biological functioning. Drive reduction theories have difficulty explaining behavior that is not directed at reducing a need, but may be directed instead at maintaining or increasing arousal. Also, behavior appears to be motivated occasionally by curiosity as well.

The theory that explains motivation as being directed toward maintaining or increasing excitement is the **arousal theory**. If the levels of stimulation are too low, arousal theory says that we will try to increase the levels. **The Yerkes-Dodson** law suggests that each kind of task has an optimum level of arousal. Performance on simple tasks benefits from higher levels of arousal than the optimum level for complex tasks. However, if arousal is too high, both complex and simple tasks suffer. Arousal theory has been applied in many fields. If students are highly aroused, their performance on tests may be hampered.

In motivational terms the reward is the **incentive**. Incentive theory explains why behavior may be motivated by external stimuli. The properties of the incentive direct and energize behavior. External incentives can be powerful enough to overcome the lack of internal stimuli drives. This view is compatible with the drive reduction theory, as incentives work to ''pull'' and drives to ''push'' behavior.

According to another theory, the **opponent-process theory of motivation**, the stimuli that produce arousal also cause a later, opposite response as the body tries to calm down. Also, each time the stimuli recur, the second, opponent response gets stronger. This theory explains drug addiction: each time the second response strengthens, more of the drug must be taken in order to increase the initial response. When the initial response is negative, like the terror of sky-diving, the opponent process will be positive, and it will strengthen even if the initial fright weakens.

Cognitive theories of motivation focus on our thoughts, expectations, and understandings of the world. For instance, **expectancy-value theory** combines our expectations of reaching a goal with the value we place on it to account for the degree of motivation. **Intrinsic motivation** refers to the value an activity has in the enjoyment of participating in it, and extrinsic motivation refers to behavior that is done for a tangible reward. We work harder for a task that has intrinsic motivation. Also, as tangible rewards become available, intrinsic motivation declines and extrinsic motivation increases.

Abraham Maslow conceptualized motivational needs as fitting in a hierarchy from basic to higher-order. The first level of needs is that of the basic physiological needs of water, food, sleep, and sex. The second level is that of safety, having a secure and safe environment. The third level, the first of the higher-order needs, is that of love and belongingness. The fourth level is self-esteem, and the final level is of self-actualization. **Self-actualization** is a state of fulfillment where people realize their potential.

Concept 2:   Human Needs and Motivation: Eat,   *Survey:* ____
             Drink, and Be Daring   *Read:* ____

                                                                  Pages 304-310

Thirst signals one of the most important of human needs. Without water we will die in a few days. Three mechanisms produce thirst. The first is the variation of the salt concentration in the body. When it reaches certain levels, it triggers the hypothalamus. The second is the total volume of fluid in the circulatory system. The third is a rise in body temperature or an increase in energy use. The mouth and the stomach apparently work together to indicate when enough fluid has been taken in to restore the proper balance.

One-quarter of Americans are considered more than 20 percent overweight and thus suffering from **obesity**. Most nonhumans will regulate their intake of food even when it is abundant. Animals will also seek specific kinds of foods of which they have been deprived. Hunger is apparently quite complex, consisting of a number of mechanisms that signal changes in the body. One is the level of the sugar glucose in the blood. The higher the level of glucose, the less hunger is experienced. The **hypothalamus** monitors the blood chemistry. A rat with a damaged lateral **hypothalamus** will starve itself to death, and one with the **ventromedial hypothalamus** damaged will experience extreme overeating. One theory suggests that the body maintains a **weight set point**. This set point controls whether the hypothalamus calls for more or less food intake.

Internal biological factors do not explain our eating behavior fully. For instance, we eat meals on a customary schedule and thus feel hungry on that schedule. We eat about the same amount even if our exercise has changed, and we prefer certain types of food. Oversensitivity to external cues and insensitivity to internal cues are related to obesity. Also, reports of hunger in obese people do not correspond with the period of time deprived of food.

Weight set point has been implicated as a cause for obesity. Overweight people may have higher set points than normal weight people. The size and number of fat cells may account for the high set points. Differences in people's metabolism may also account for being overweight. **Metabolism** is the rate at which energy is produced and expended. People with high metabolic rates can eat as much food as they want and not gain weight. People with low metabolism eat little and still gain. There is evidence that people may be born to be fat, that weight is controlled genetically. Children may learn that food is a form of consolation if they are given food after being upset; thus, food becomes a treatment for emotional difficulties.

Anorexia nervosa is a disease that afflicts primarily females. Sufferers refuse to eat and may actually starve themselves to death. **Bulimia** is a condition in which individuals will binge on large quantities of food and then purge themselves with vomiting or laxatives. People suffering from bulimia are treated by being taught to eat foods they enjoy and to have control over their eating. Anorexia is treated by reinforcing weight gain, that is, giving privileges for success. The causes of these eating disorders are thought by some to be a chemical imbalance and by others to be the societal expectations placed on the sufferers of the disorders.

The Informed Consumer of Psychology addresses techniques for effective dieting. The recommendations include remembering that there is no easy way to lose weight, that reasonable goals must be set, that exercise must be included, that attention must be given to internal cues, that fad diets should be avoided, and that to maintain the weight level when it is reached one must establish appropriate habits.

Concept 3: Human Needs and Motivation: Sex   *Survey:* ____
and the Needs for Achievement   *Read:* ____

Pages 310-318

Sexual behavior in humans is filled with meaning, values, and feelings. The basic biology of the sexual response helps us understand the importance of sexual behavior. Human sexual behavior is not governed by the genetic control that other animals experience. In males, the **testes**, part of the male genitals, secrete androgen beginning at puberty. Androgen increases the sex drive and produces secondary sex characteristics like body hair and voice change. When women reach puberty, the **ovaries**, the female reproductive organs produce estrogen, the female sex hormone. Estrogen reaches it highest levels during **ovulation**, the release of eggs from the ovaries. In many animals, the period of ovulation is the only time females are receptive to sex. Women remain receptive throughout their cycles. Though biological factors are important, humans are also conditioned to respond to a wide range of stimuli that lead to arousal.

Sexual behavior is influenced by expectations, attitudes, beliefs, and the state of medical and biological knowledge. Normal sexual behavior is described by the range of behaviors from traditional marital sexual intercourse to bizarre behaviors. Defining what is normal can be approached by determining the deviation for an average or typical behavior, though there are many behaviors that are unusual statistically but not abnormal. Another approach is to compare behavior against a standard or ideal form. However, the selection of a standard is difficult, since it must be universally acceptable. A reasonable approach to defining sexual normality is to consider the psychological consequences of the behavior. If it produces a sense of distress, anxiety, or guilt or is harmful to a person, then it should be considered abnormal. Until Albert Kinsey undertook his study of sexual behavior, little was known about sexual behavior of typical Americans. Kinsey collected a large number of sexual histories. One criticism of his approach is with regard to his sampling techniques which led him to interview a large section of college students and well-educated individuals. Also, since the surveys were based on volunteers, it is uncertain whether the attitudes of individuals willing to share sensitive information are different from those who did not volunteer. Kinsey's work has led to a number of other national surveys.

Masturbation is sexual self-stimulation, and its practice is quite common. Males masturbate more often than females, with males beginning in early teens, though females start later and reach a maximum frequency later. Though thought of as an activity to be done when other sexual partners are unavailable, almost three-quarters of married men masturbate. Negative attitudes about masturbation continue, though it is perfectly healthy and harmless.

Heterosexuality refers to sexual behavior between men and women. It includes all aspects of sexual contact - kissing, caressing, sex play, and intercourse. Premarital sex continues to be viewed through a double standard, as something acceptable for males but unacceptable for females. However, sexual activity among unmarried women is high according to several surveys. When younger and older females are compared, there appears to be an increase in premarital sexual activity. Males have shown a similar increase in activity, though it is not as dramatic.

The average married couple has intercourse six times a month, and the longer a couple is married, the less frequently intercourse occurs. The frequency of sexual intercourse has increased with the availability of contraceptives and of abortion. The fact that sex is more openly discussed and displayed in the media and the notion that female sexuality is acceptable has contributed to the increase in activity.

Humans are not born with an innate attraction to the opposite sex. **Homosexuality** refers to sexual attraction for members of the same sex, while bisexuality refers to sexual attraction for both sexes. At least 20 to 25 percent of males and about 15 percent of females have had an adulthood homosexual experience and between 5 and 10 percent of both males and females are exclusively homosexual. Though people view homosexuality and heterosexuality as distinct orientations, Kinsey places the two orientations on a scale. There are a number of theories accounting for sexual orientation, with some focusing on biological factors and others on social factors. Recent evidence suggests that there may be a physical difference in the anterior hypothalamus of heterosexual and homosexual males. Other theories focus on childhood and family background. Some psychoanalysts suggest male homosexuals have overprotective and dominant mothers and passive fathers. Learning theory suggests that sexual orientation is learned through rewards and punishments. Experiences with unpleasant outcomes would lead to linking the unpleasant experience with the opposite sex. Rewarding experiences would be incorporated into sexual fantasies. These fantasies are then positively reinforced by the pleasure of orgasm. The problem with learning theory is that the expected punishments of homosexuality from society should outweigh the rewards and prevent the learning. Most researchers believe that a combination of factors must be at work.

The **need for achievement** is a learned characteristic involving the sustained striving for and attainment of a level of excellence. People with high needs for achievement seek out opportunities to compete and succeed. People with low needs for achievement are motivated by the desire to avoid failure.

The **Thematic Apperception Test (TAT)** is used to test achievement motivation. It requires that the person look at a series of ambiguous pictures and then write a story that tells what is going on and what will happen next. Stories are then scored for the amount of achievement imagery used in the story - the amount of striving to win or working hard images that suggest an achievement orientation. The achievement levels of societies have been analyzed by examining the achievement imagery in children's stories.

It is believed that people learn the need for achievement through high standards set by parents, who also praise success and encourage their children warmly. The question of whether achievement can be trained in adults has been explored by McClelland and Winter in a village in India. They asked the experimental group to imagine themselves as more successful and then to make concrete step-by-step plans for achievement. The experiment was a success, as the experimental group increased their business activity and created new jobs.

The **need for affiliation** refers to the needs we have of establishing and maintaining relationships with others. People high in affiliation needs tend to be more concerned with relationships and to be with their friends more. The need for power is a tendency to seek impact, control, or influence over others.

Concept 4:   Understanding Emotional Experiences   *Survey:* ____
             Deciphering Our Own Emotions   *Read:* ____

Pages 319-328

Though difficult to define, **emotions** are understood to be the feelings that have both physiological and cognitive aspects and influence behavior. Physical changes occur whenever we experience an emotion, and we identify these changes as emotions. Some psychologists argue that separate systems account for the cognitive responses and the emotional responses. A current controversy involves whether emotions take precedence over cognitions. Finally, some argue that we first have cognitions and then emotional responses follow. A number of important functions of emotions have been identified. They include preparing us for action by preparing effective responses to a variety of situations. They shape our future behavior by promoting learning that will influence making appropriate responses in the future by leading to the repetition of responses that lead to satisfying emotional feelings. They also help regulate interactions with others.

We have many ways to describe the experiences of emotion that we have. The physiological reactions that accompany fear are associated with the activation of the autonomic nervous system. They include: an increase in breathing rate, an increase in heart rate, a widening of the pupils, a cessation of the functions of the digestive system, and a contraction of the muscles below the surface of the skin. Though these changes occur without awareness, the emotional experience of fear can be felt intensely. Whether these physiological responses are the cause of the experience or the result of the experience of emotion remains unclear.

The **James-Lange theory of emotion** states that emotions are the perceived physiological reactions that occur in the internal organs. They called this **visceral experience**. One of the problems with this view is that in order for this theory to be valid, the visceral changes would have to be fairly rapid, whereas emotional experiences often occur before visceral changes can take place. Another problem is that physiological arousal does not invariably produce emotional experience. Finally, internal organs produce limited sensations.

The **Cannon-Bard theory of emotion** rejects the view that physiological arousal alone leads to the perception of emotion. In their theory, the emotion producing stimuli is first perceived, then the thalamus activates the viscera and at the same time a message is sent to the cortex. The difference between emotional experiences depends upon the message received by the cortex.

The **Schachter-Singer theory of emotion** emphasizes that the emotion experienced depends on the environment and on comparing ourselves with others. Schachter and Singer conducted a classic experiment in which subjects were injected with epinephrine to cause physiological arousal. One group was informed about the effects and another was kept uninformed. These two groups were then exposed to either a situation in which a confederate of the experimenter was acting angry and hostile or in which the confederate was acting euphoric. The informed subjects were not affected by the situation because they accounted for their arousal as the effects of the drug, but the uninformed subjects accounted for their physiological arousal according to the situation. The experiment then supports the cognitive view of emotions, that emotions depend on general arousal that is labeled according to cues in the environment. The Schachter-Singer theory of emotions has been applied to other circumstances, one of which involved an attractive female as subject who asked males a series of questions and then gave them her telephone number so they could get the results of the survey. Two groups of men were involved. One group had just crossed a 450-foot suspension bridge over a deep canyon and the other crossed a stable bridge over a shallow stream. Those who crossed the canyon reported a stronger attraction to the woman, accounting for their arousal by the presence of the female rather than the fear of the canyon.

For each of the three major theories, there is some contradictory evidence. Emotions are complex phenomena that no single theory can yet explain adequately.

♦ Now that you have surveyed, questioned, and read the chapter and completed the **Recap and Review** questions, review **Looking Back**, pages 328-329. *Review:* ____

♦ For additional practice through recitation and review, test your knowledge of the chapter material by answering the questions in the **Key Word Drill**, the **Practice Questions**, and the **Essay Questions**.

KEY WORD DRILL   *Recite:* ____

The following **Fill in the Blank** and **Matching Questions** test key words from the text. Check your answers with the Answer Key in the back of the *Study Guide*.

FILL IN THE BLANK

1. _____ includes all the factors that direct and energize behavior.

2. An organism tries to maintain an internal biological balance, or ''steady state,'' through _____.

3. The _____ is an external stimulus that directs and energizes behavior by being anticipated as a reward.

4. _____ is defined as being more than _____ percent above the average weight for a person of a particular height.

5. The body strives to maintain weight at the _____ _____ _____.

6. The eating disorder with symptoms that include various degrees of self-starvation in an attempt to avoid obesity is called _____, and the eating disorder characterized by vast intake of food that may be followed by self-induced vomiting is called _____.

7. _____ is the term for sexual self-stimulation.

8. _____ is an attraction to a member of one's own sex.

9. The _____ _____ consists of a series of ambiguous pictures about which a person is asked to write a story.

10. Feelings such as happiness, despair, and sorrow that generally have both physiological and cognitive elements and that influence behavior are called _____.

MATCHING QUESTIONS

___C_ 11. motives

___d_ 12. emotions

___g_ 13. drive

___e_ 14. primary drives

___f_ 15. secondary drives

___a_ 16. intrinsic motivation

___b_ 17. instinct

a. Motivation causing people to participate in an activity for a tangible reward.

b. An inborn pattern of behavior that is biologically determined.

c. Desired goals that prompt behavior.

d. The internal feelings experienced at any given moment.

e. Biological needs such as hunger, thirst, fatigue, and sex.

f. Drives in which no biological need is fulfilled.

g. A motivational tension or arousal that energizes behavior in order to fulfill a need.

_b_ 18. drive-reduction theory

_d_ 19. arousal theory

_f_ 20. Yerkes-Dodson law

_e_ 21. incentive theory

_c_ 22. opponent-process theory
of motivation

_a_ 23. cognitive theories of
motivation

a. Theories explaining motivation by focusing
on the role of an individual's thoughts,
expectations, and understanding of the
world.

b. The theory which claims that drives are
produced to obtain our basic biological
requirements.

c. The theory which postulates that increases
in arousal ultimately produce a calming
reaction in the nervous system, and vice
versa.

d. The belief that we try to maintain certain
levels of stimulation and activity,
increasing or reducing them as necessary.

e. The theory explaining motivation in terms
of external stimuli.

f. The theory that a particular level of
motivational arousal produces optimal
performance of a task.

_____

_g_ 24. expectancy-value theory

_c_ 25. heterosexuality

_f_ 26. homosexuality

_e_ 27. self-actualization

_d_ 28. need for achievement

_b_ 29. need for affiliation

_a_ 30. need for power

a. A tendency to want to seek impact,
control, or influence on others in order to
be seen as a powerful individual.

b. A need to establish and maintain
relationships with other people.

c. Sexual behavior between a man and a woman.

d. A stable, learned characteristic in which
satisfaction comes from striving for and
achieving a level of excellence.

e. A state of self-fulfillment in which people
realize their highest potential.

f. A sexual attraction to a member of one's
own sex.

g. A view that suggests that people are
motivated by expectations that certain
behaviors will accomplish a goal and their
understanding of the importance of the
goal.

_d_ 31. hypothalamus

_a_ 32. lateral hypothalamus

_c_ 33. ventromedial hypothalamus

_e_ 34. metabolism

_b_ 35. visceral experience

a. The part of the brain which, when damaged, results in an organism's starving to death.

b. The ''gut'' reaction experienced internally, triggering an emotion.

c. The part of the brain which, when injured, results in extreme overeating.

d. The structure in the brain that is primarily responsible for regulating food intake.

e. The rate at which energy is produced and expended by the body.

_____   _____

_b_ 36. James-Lange theory of emotion

_c_ 37. Cannon-Bard theory of emotion

_a_ 38. Schachter-Singer theory of emotion

a. The belief that emotions are determined jointly by a nonspecific kind of physiological arousal and its interpretation, based on environmental cues.

b. The belief that emotional experience is a reaction to bodily events occurring as a result of an external situation.

c. The belief that both physiological and emotional arousal are produced simultaneously by the same nerve impulse.

PRACTICE QUESTIONS   *Recite and Review:* ____

Test your knowledge of the chapter material by answering these **True-False** and **Multiple Choice** Questions. Check your answers with the Answer Key in the back of the *Study Guide.*

TRUE-FALSE QUESTIONS

T   (F)   1. Motivation is studied only in humans, since it is rarely observed in lower animals.

(T)   F   2. Curiosity has been demonstrated in both humans and animals.

T   (F)   3. Drive-reduction theories are adequate to explain behaviors in which the goal is to maintain a particular level of excitement.

T   (F)   4. Maslow's theory of self-actualization applies only to people who have exceptional accomplishments and distinctions.

T (F)   5. Self-actualization can be attained more readily if no attention
            is paid to lower motivational states.

T (F)   6. Bulimia, an eating disorder, affects men and women in equal
            numbers.

T (F)   7. There are rather clear classes of behavior which experts agree
            constitute normal and abnormal sexual behavior.

(T) F   8. Homosexuals and bisexuals are as well adjusted as heterosexuals.

(T) F   9. People with low achievement motivation tend mainly to be
            motivated by the desire to avoid failure.

(T) F 10. Emotions prepare us for action, shape our future, and help us
            regulate our behavior.

MULTIPLE CHOICE QUESTIONS

1. The study of motivation seeks ways of:
    (a) identifying why people behave the way they do.
    b. discussing the relationship between peoples' emotions and their
        past experiences.
    c. understanding genetic inheritance.
    d. identifying social pressures affecting an individual's emotions.

2. According to the text, the main function of motivation is to:
    a. create tension.
    b. provide feeling.
    c. promote learning of survival behaviors.
    (d) provide direction to behavior.

3. The story of Peter Potterfield, who survived on a narrow crest of Chimney
    Rock, illustrates how:
    a. physical training required for mountain climbing was responsible for
        his survival.
    b. preparation before the accident provided Potterfield with the minimal
        nutrition he needed to survive.
    (c) survival was the complex result of biological and other factors.
    d. prudent actions saved his life, but the accident ended his mountain
        climbing career.

4. Primary drives are motives that:
    a. people rate as being most important to them.
    b. seem to motivate an organism the most.
    c. are least likely to be satisfied before self-actualization can occur.
    (d) have a biological basis and are universal.

5. Which of the following is the best example of a drive that is common to both
    humans and animals?
    a. power   c. cognition
    (b) hunger   d. achievement

6. The process by which an organism tries to maintain an optimal level of internal biological functioning is called:
   a. primary drive equilibrium.   c. drive reduction.
   b. homeostasis.   d. opponent-process theory.

7. The compensatory activity of the autonomic nervous system, which returns the body to normal levels of functioning after a trauma, is called:
   a. homeostasis.   c. biofeedback.
   b. biorhythmicity.   d. transference.

8. According to the text, a motivation behind behavior in which no obvious biological need is being fulfilled is the definition of:
   a. a primary drive.   c. a secondary drive.
   b. an achievement.   d. instinct.

9. Which of the following would be considered a secondary drive?
   a. power   c. thirst
   b. hunger   d. sleep

10. The basic premise of the Yerkes-Dodson law is that:
    a. instincts are the primary motivational force for behavior.
    b. there is an optimal level of arousal for task performance.
    c. secondary drives are brought about by experience and learning.
    d. homeostatic balance is maintained by compensation for deviations.

11. According to the Yerkes-Dodson law, the effect of a high level of arousal on performance of a complex task would be:
    a. enhancement of performance.   c. irrelevant to performance.
    b. impairment of performance.   d. to accelerate performance.

12. The major prediction from the Yerkes-Dodson law is that:
    a. performance of simple tasks will be enhanced by greater levels of arousal; performance of complex tasks will be enhanced by lower levels of arousal.
    b. increasing levels of arousal result in decreased task performance.
    c. different people have different curves at different times.
    d. the particular level of arousal that leads to optimal performance of a task is determined by the combined strengths of other drives (such as hunger and fatigue).

13. The incentive theory of motivation focuses on:
    a. instincts.
    b. the characteristics of external stimuli.
    c. drive reduction.
    d. the rewarding quality of various behaviors which are motivated by arousal.

14. According to the text, some psychologists feel that the incentive theory of motivation is strengthened when combined with complementary concepts drawn from:
    a. instinct theory.   c. arousal theory.
    b. drive-reduction theory.   d. opponent-process theory.

15. Which of the following theories of motivation specifically seeks to explain both drug addiction and the physiological and emotional reactions that occur in situations involving extreme danger?
    a. arousal
    b. drive-reduction
    c. cognitive
    d. opponent-process

16. According to the text, which motivation theory attempts to explain motivation in terms of the external stimuli which direct and energize behavior?
    a. incentive
    b. opponent-process
    c. arousal
    d. cognitive

17. Our hopes that a behavior will cause us to reach a certain goal and our understanding that the goal will be meaningful or important to us are combined in:
    a. the expectancy-value theory of motivation.
    b. the drive-reduction theory of motivation.
    c. Maslow's hierarchy of motivation.
    d. theory of extrinsic motivation.

18. Advertisements for a job boast that it offers $4 more than minimum wage, a guaranteed cash bonus after thirty days, and a paid vacation. This advertisement emphasizes the concept of:
    a. opponent-process motivation.
    b. arousal motivation.
    c. drive-reduction motivation.
    d. extrinsic motivation.

19. Motivation that causes a person to behave in a particular manner for a reward is called:
    a. intrinsic motivation.
    b. extrinsic motivation.
    c. achievement motivation.
    d. instinctual motivation.

20. Which theory is least tied to biological mechanisms?
    a. instinct theory
    b. cognitive theory
    c. drive-reduction theory
    d. arousal theory

21. According to Maslow, which of the following must be met before people can fulfill any higher-order motivations?
    a. extrinsic needs
    b. intrinsic needs
    c. primary drives
    d. secondary drives

22. According to Maslow, which of the following is the highest state of self-fulfillment?
    a. self-esteem
    b. self-actualization
    c. self-satisfaction
    d. self-centeredness

23. Which alternative below is not associated with thirst?
    a. changes in the salt concentration in the cells of the body
    b. changes in total volume of fluid in the circulatory system
    c. a significant decrease in body weight
    d. an increase in body temperature

24. According to the text, which of the following is thought to be primarily involved in the physiological regulation of eating behavior?
    a. cortex
    b. amygdala
    c. hypothalamus
    d. hippocampus

25. For the American public, which factor appears to play the least significant role in hunger?
    a. blood chemistry
    b. stomach contractions
    c. number and size of fat cells
    d. weight set point

26. Which alternative below is correct about nonobese versus obese individuals?
    a. Small tumors in the hypothalamus account for about 60 percent of all cases of obesity.
    b. Obese individuals will work harder than nonobese individuals so that they can consume food.
    c. Obese individuals seem less responsive to internal hunger cues than nonobese individuals.
    d. Nonobese individuals are more critical and rejecting of unpleasant tasting food than are obese individuals.

27. At which of the following ages does the amount of fat cells in the body usually stop declining?
    a. 24 years of age
    b. 20 years of age
    c. 12 years of age
    d. 2 years of age

28. Which of the following mechanisms may underlie obesity?
    a. The fat cells may be too small.
    b. The weight set point may be too high.
    c. The metabolic rate may be too high.
    d. The number of fat cells may have been increased after puberty.

29. Which of the following is an eating disorder usually affecting attractive, successful females between the ages of 12 and 20 who refuse to eat and sometimes literally starve themselves to death?
    a. metabolic malfunction
    b. bulimia
    c. anorexia nervosa
    d. obesity

30. Sonya developed a cycle of binge eating, during which she consumed a variety of gourmet foods and wines and then induced vomiting afterward. Her doctor told Sonya that she could do permanent damage to her health if she continued the behavior and that if she continued she could become:
    a. ischemic.
    b. depressed.
    c. volumetric.
    d. bulimic.

31. According to the text, which alternative below is not good advice for a person trying to lose weight?
    a. Exercise regularly.
    b. Reduce the influence of external cues and social behavior on your eating.
    c. Choose a diet program that gives rather rapid weight losses so that you will stay motivated.
    d. Remember, when you reach your desired goal, you're not finished!

32. Which alternative below is not a criterion for sexual abnormality?
    a. a standard or ideal
    b. frequency of the behavior
    c. deviation from the average
    d. psychological consequences

33. Which of the following statements about masturbation is true?
    a. Most of society views masturbation as a healthy, normal activity.
    b. The majority of people surveyed have masturbated at least once.
    c. Males and females begin masturbation at puberty.
    d. Psychologists view people who masturbate as poorly adjusted.

34. Masturbation is:
    a. usually viewed as inappropriate behavior.
    b. practiced more by men than women.
    c. more common in older men than younger men.
    d. commonly regarded by experts as counterproductive to learning about one's sexuality.

35. Which of the following trends was most pronounced between the mid-1960s and mid-1980s in America?
    a. An increased percentage of females engaged in premarital sex.
    b. An increased percentage of males engaged in extramarital sex.
    c. A decreased percentage of males engaged in premarital sex.
    d. A decreased percentage of females engaged in extramarital sex.

36. Which statement about marital sexual intercourse is correct?
    a. There are few differences in the frequency of marital sex for younger and older couples.
    b. The average frequency of marital sex is 1.3 times per week.
    c. The frequency of marital sex is closely related to happiness in the marriage.
    d. The frequency of marital sex today is higher than ever before.

37. Which alternative below is correct about homosexuality?
    a. Homosexuality appears to result entirely from environmental factors.
    b. Genetic and hormonal factors seem to be the predictors of who will become homosexual.
    c. Hormonal differences in people cause them to be attracted to individuals of their own sex.
    d. Homosexuals are as well-adjusted as heterosexuals.

38. Jane finished her college degree with honors and received a variety of excellent job offers. Instead, she decided to enter graduate school to acquire more advanced skills and get even better job offers. Jane is demonstrating her:
    a. need for affiliation.   c. fear of failure.
    b. need for achievement.   d. need for power.

39. Which alternative below is not true of the need for achievement?
    a. Individuals with a high need for achievement choose situations in which they are likely to succeed easily.
    b. It is a learned motive.
    c. Satisfaction is obtained by striving for and attaining a level of excellence.
    d. High need for achievement is related to economic and occupational success.

40. Which of the following statements is true of people with high achievement motivation?
    a. They choose tasks which they can do easily.
    b. They choose difficult tasks for the challenge.
    c. They choose tasks at which they can compete against a standard.
    d. They choose friends who have low achievement motivation.

41. The _____ is used to measure an individual's need for achievement.
     a. Scholastic Aptitude Test
     b. Intelligence Quotient Test
     c. Yerkes-Dodson Achievement Analysis
     d. Thematic Apperception Test

42. According to the text, women, as opposed to men, tend to channel their need
     for power through:
     a. socially responsible ways
     b. questionable means
     c. quietly aggressive ways
     d. uncharted, high-risk opportunities

43. According to the text, emotions play an important role in all of the
     following except:
     a. making life interesting.
     b. helping us to regulate social interaction.
     c. informing us of internal bodily needs.
     d. preparing us for action in response to the external environment.

44. According to the text, which of the following functions of emotion involves
     the activation of the sympathetic nervous system in order to make our
     response to situations more effective?
     a. preparation for action
     b. regulation of social interactions
     c. labeling feelings
     d. making us feel sad

45. William James and Walter Lange suggested that major emotions correlate with
     particular ''gut reactions'' of internal organs. They called this internal
     response:
     a. a physiological pattern.   c. an autonomic response.
     b. a psychological experience.   d. a visceral experience.

46. According to the James-Lange theory of emotion, _____ determines the
     emotional experience.
     a. physiological change   c. an instinctive process
     b. a cognitive process   d. the environment

47. Which theory postulates that emotions are identified by observing the
     environment and comparing ourselves with others?
     a. Schachter-Singer theory   c. James-Lange theory
     b. Cannon-Bard theory   d. Plutchik's theory

ESSAY QUESTIONS   *Recite and Review:* ____

Essay Question 9.1: Theories of Motivation

Describe each of the main theories of motivation and attempt to explain a single behavior from the point of view of each theory.

_____

_____

_____

_____

_____

_____

_____

_____

_____

_____

_____

_____

_____

_____

_____

_____

_____

_____

_____

_____

Essay Question 9.2:   The Changing Sexual Attitudes

What factors have led to the changes in sexual attitudes recently? How have they changed since the sexual revolution began in the late 1960s?

_____

_____

_____

_____

_____

_____

_____

_____

_____

_____

_____

_____

_____

_____

_____

_____

_____

_____

_____

_____

_____

_____

ACTIVITIES AND PROJECTS

1. The next time you experience an emotion that is clear enough for you to
    give it a label, take time afterward to analyze which theory of emotion
    best applies to your particular emotional experience. As an example,
    would the James-Lange theory apply? Did your experience follow from
    physiological cues? Or did these processes happen simultaneously as
    suggested by the Cannon-Bard theory? Or did cognitive processes and
    labeling on the basis of context play a major role in your experience of
    the emotion?

2. Determine where you believe that you fit on Maslow's hierarchy of needs.
    How do you know that you are at that particular level? What types of
    thought patterns and behaviors might you engage in during your striving
    to the next level in the hierarchy? You may also identify your specific
    concerns and behaviors as they fit each of the levels of Maslow's
    hierarchy. What behaviors would you identify with your eventual
    self-actualization?

C H A P T E R
10
DEVELOPMENT

Detailed Outline   *Survey:* ____

This detailed outline contains all the headings in Chapter 10: Development. If you are using the SQ3R method, then an examination of the outline is the best way to begin your survey of the chapter.

Prologue: The Twin Connection
Looking Ahead

Nature and Nurture: A Fundamental Developmental Issue
The Cutting Edge Born to Be Shy?: Inhibited and Uninhibited Children
   Addressing the nature-nurture question
   Studying development
   The start of life: Conception and beyond
      Genetic influences on the fetus
      Prenatal environmental influences
- **Recap and Review I**

How We Develop Physically and Socially
   Growth after birth
   Development of perception: Taking in the world
   Development of social behavior
      Measuring attachment
      The father's role
Social relationships with peers
Psychology at Work Who's Caring for the Children?: Determining the
      Effects of Day Care
   Erikson's theory of psychosocial development
- **Recap and Review II**

Cognitive Development
   Piaget's theory of cognitive development
      Sensorimotor stage: From birth to 2 years
      Preoperational stage: From 2 to 7 years
      Concrete operational stage: From 7 to 12 years
      Formal operational stage: From 12 years to adulthood
      Stages versus continuous development: Is Piaget right?
   Information-processing approaches
The Informed Consumer of Psychology Maximizing Cognitive Development
- **Recap and Review III**

Adolescence: Becoming an Adult
   Physical development: The changing adolescent
   Moral and cognitive development: Distinguishing right from wrong
      Moral development in women

Psychosocial development: The search for identity
Stormy adolescence: Myth or reality?
Early and Middle Adulthood: The Middle Years of Life
Physical development: The peak of health
Social development: Working at life
The Later Years of Life: Growing Old
Physical changes in the elderly: The old body
Cognitive changes: Thinking about - and during - old age
Memory changes in old age: Are the elderly forgetful?
The social world of the elderly: Old but not alone
The Informed Consumer of Psychology Adjusting to Death
▪ **Recap and Review IV**

Looking Back
Key Terms and Concepts

Now that you have surveyed the chapter, read **Looking Ahead**, pages 332-333.
Question: _____
Read: _____

Focus on the questions on page 333.

CONCEPTS AND LEARNING OBJECTIVES   Survey: _____

These are the concepts and the learning objects for Chapter 10. Read them
carefully as part of your preliminary survey of the chapter.

Concept 1: The fundamental issue for developmental psychology is the interaction
between nature and nurture in human development. Psychologists are interested
in finding ways to maximize genetic potential by enriching the environment.
Development from conception to birth illustrates the interaction of nature
and nurture.

1. Define developmental psychology and the phenomena that it studies,
especially the issues related to the roles of nature and nurture in
development. (pp. 332-337)

2. Describe the events that occur from conception to birth. (pp. 338-341)

Concept 2: Physical and social development are marked by dramatic changes during
childhood, from birth to about 12 years of age. Both physical and perceptual
skills grow rapidly in the early months and years, and attachment is one of
the most important social developments in the first years of life. Cognitive
development refers to the changes in the understanding of the world, and the
period of childhood shows dramatic stages in the process of development.

3. Describe the progress of physical growth from birth to the end of
childhood. (pp. 341-346)

4. Describe the social influences on development. (pp. 346-349)

5. Outline and describe the psychosocial stages identified by Erik Erikson.
(pp. 349-350)

6. Outline and describe the cognitive developmental stages identified by
Jean Piaget. (pp. 351-357)

Concept 3: Adolescence begins with the growth spurt and puberty, and continues until the end of the teenage years. Social and moral development occur, with the adolescent focusing on problems of identity.

  7. Define adolescence and the physical changes that mark its beginning. (pp. 357-359)

  8. Describe the moral and cognitive developments that occur during adolescence. (pp. 360-363)

  9. List and describe Erikson's psychosocial stages relevant to adolescence and adulthood. (pp. 363-365)

Concept 4: Early and middle adulthood are marked by the formation of a family, the establishment and success (or failure) in work, and the gradual progress toward old age. Some people experience a midlife crisis, but most are able to pass through middle age easily.

  10. Define adulthood and describe the physical changes that accompany it. (pp. 365-366)

  11. Discuss the concerns of adulthood that result from demands of society and the pressures of work. (pp. 366-368)

Concept 5: Old age does not conform to our myths about it, and the elderly often lead active, happy lives. One of the more difficult transitions is that of facing the prospects of death.

  12. Define old age, the physical changes that accompany it, and the theories that attempt to account for it. (pp. 368-369)

  13. Identify the changes that occur in cognitive ability, intelligence, and memory during old age. (pp. 369-372)

  14. Describe the challenges and changes that the elderly face in their social worlds as they age. (pp. 372-373)

CHAPTER SUMMARY

There are several ways you can use this summary as part of your systematic study plan. You may read each concept summary and then read the corresponding pages in the text, or you may read the entire summary and then read the entire chapter in the text. As you finish each section, complete the **Recap and Review** questions that are supplied in the text.

Concept 1:   **Prologue and Looking Ahead**   *Survey:* ____
                   Nature and Nurture: A Fundamental   *Read:* ____
                   Developmental Issue

                                                                        Pages 332-341

The Prologue describes two sets of twins separated at birth. One set, Gerald Levey and Mark Newman, have greatly similar characteristics. The other set, Joan Gardiner and Jean Nelson, have quite different interests. Though there exists quite a bit of evidence supporting the role of genetics in development, the genetic inheritance does not explain everything.

Developmental psychology is the branch of psychology focused on explaining the similarities and differences among people that result from the growth and change of individuals throughout life. Developmental psychologists look to both the genetic background that provides built-in biological programming and the environmental influences.

Developmental psychologists are interested in a fundamental question of distinguishing the causes of behavior that are **environmental** from the causes that result from **heredity**. This question is identified as the **nature-nurture issue**. The issue can be traced back to John Locke's view that the infant is born with a mind that is like a blank sheet (tabula rasa) as opposed to the French philosopher Jean Jacques Rousseau's suggestion that people have natural characteristics that govern their behavior. However, both nature and nurture are involved, and it is not a question of nature or nurture. Both **genetic makeup** (the biological inheritance) and the environment have influence, and the debate is over the extent to which each affects behavior. Some theories focus on learning and the role of the environment and other theories focus on the role of growth and **maturation**, or the development of biologically predetermined patterns, in causing developmental change. The theories agree on some points. Genetics provides for some behaviors and sets limits on some traits and behaviors. Heredity sets limits on intelligence and limits on physical abilities. (Table 10-1 lists characteristics with strong genetic components.) Environment plays a role in enabling individuals to reach the potential allowed by their genetic background. Developmental psychologists take an **interactionist** position arguing that behavior and development are determined by genetic and environmental influences. An example of this interactionist position is presented in *The Cutting Edge*. Jerome Kagan's study of inhibited and uninhibited children suggests that inhibited children have an inborn characteristic of greater physiological reactivity. However, the stress experienced through childhood is a major factor in the appearance of shyness later.

One major difficulty faced by developmental psychologists is that of being able to find ways to separate the influences of genetics and environment in order to study them. One way is to observe animals with similar genetic backgrounds in different environments. The difficulty presented by this approach is generalizing the results to humans. Another approach is the use of **identical twins**. Different behaviors displayed by identical twins must have some environmental component. Many studies seek to find identical twins who were separated at birth by adoption. Nontwin siblings who are raised apart also make contributions to these kinds of studies. The opposite approach takes people of different genetic backgrounds and examines their development and behavior in similar environments. Animals with different genetic backgrounds can be placed in situations where the environments can be experimentally manipulated.

Two categories of research are used by developmental psychologists. **Cross-sectional research** refers to the use of a sample of subjects that is based on a selection of groups that represent different ages at the same point in time. The problem with this approach is that different age groups may have had significantly different environmental influences. **Longitudinal research** refers to the selection of a sample from the population and following the sample's development through an extended period of time. The problem with this approach is that many individuals may drop out or they may become familiar with the tests being used to measure their development. An alternative method is called **cross-sequential research**. It combines the selection of different age groups with the following of the groups through time. However, the amount of time is less than in longitudinal research since different age groups are represented. In this approach age changes can be observed in different age groups without the lengthy longitudinal approach.

Development begins at the point of **conception** when the male's sperm penetrates the female's egg. The fertilized egg is at this point called a

zygote. (The zygote contains twenty-three pairs of **chromosomes**, one-half from the father the other half from the mother.) Each chromosome contains thousands of **genes**, the individual units that carry genetic information.   Genes are responsible for the development of the systems of the body, heart, circulatory, brain, lungs, and so on. And many genes control specific unique characteristics. Sex is determined by a set of chromosomes that combines an X chromosome from the mother and a Y or an X from the father. Girls have an XX combination and boys have an XY combination. At four weeks, the zygote becomes a structure called the **embryo**. (The embryo has a rudimentary heart, brain, intestinal tract, and other organs. By the eighth week, the embryo has arms and legs. Beginning with the eighth week, the embryo faces a **critical period** of development - a period during which specific growth must occur if the individual is to develop normally. Eyes and ears must form, and environmental influences can have significant effects. At the ninth week the individual is called a **fetus**. At sixteen to eighteen weeks the movement of the fetus can be felt by the mother. At the twenty-fourth week, the fetus has the characteristics of a newborn, though it cannot survive outside the mother if born prematurely. At twenty-eight weeks, the fetus can survive if born prematurely, and this is called the **age of viability**. At twenty-eight weeks the fetus will weigh about three pounds.

In 2 to 5 percent of all cases, children have serious birth defects. Common genetic defects include **phenylketonuria (PKU)**, a metabolic disorder that can be treated; **sickle-cell anemia**, a disease afflicting African-Americans, and children with the disease rarely live beyond childhood; **Tay-Sachs disease**, a disease that results in the inability to break down fat, causing death by age 3 or 4; and **Down syndrome**, a problem where an extra chromosome causes an unusual physical appearance and retardation.

Prenatal environmental influences include: the mother's nutritional and emotional state - emotionally anxious mothers tend to have babies that are irritable and who sleep and eat poorly; illness of the mother - diseases like **rubella** (German measles) can cause serious defects in the unborn child and AIDS can be passed from mother to child; drug use by the mother can have serious effects on the child, including **fetal alcohol syndrome**, and some babies can be born with their mother's addiction to drugs like cocaine.   Sometimes complications of delivery can cause serious problems, like entanglement of the umbilical cord leading to a loss of oxygen.

| Concept 2: | How We Develop Physically and Socially | *Survey:* ____ |
| | Cognitive Development | *Read:* ____ |

Pages 341-357

At birth, the newborn baby is called a **neonate**. The neonate looks strange because the journey through the birth canal squeezes and shapes the skull. The neonate is covered with **vernix**, a white greasy material that protects the skin prior to birth, and a soft hair called **lanugo**. The neonate is born with a number of **reflexes**, unlearned, involuntary responses. Most are necessary for survival and maturation. The **rooting reflex** causes neonates to turn their head toward anything that touches their cheeks. The **sucking reflex** makes the neonate suck on anything that touches its lips. The **gag reflex** clears the throat, and the **startle reflex** causes a number of movements when a loud noise is sounded. The **Babinski reflex** fans out the toes when the edge of the foot is touched. These reflexes are lost within several months and are replaced by more complex behaviors. Through the first year of life, major changes in physical ability occur, including learning to stand and walk.

In the first year of life, children triple their birth weight and their height increases by 50 percent. From 3 to 13 years of age, the child adds an average of 5 pounds and 3 inches per year. The proportion of body and body parts changes through the time period as well.

At birth the neonate has a limited capacity to focus vision and can focus only on objects within about 8 to 9 inches. They are also able to follow objects moving in their field of vision. Techniques have been developed to determine the perceptual abilities of neonates that depend upon changes in basic responses and reflexes. Heart rate is closely associated with the reaction to an object being perceived. Changes in heart rate signal **habituation**, or the decrease in responding to the same stimulus. A novel stimulus causes an increase in heart rate. Using this technique, developmental psychologists are able to tell when a baby can detect a stimulus. Other methods include the use of a nipple attached to a computer that measures the rate and force of sucking. Changes in stimuli correlate to changes in sucking. The perceptual abilities of infants have been found to be quite sophisticated. They show preference for certain patterns with contours and edges. They have a sense of size constancy. Neonates can discriminate facial expressions, and they respond to the emotion and mood of care givers. At the end of the first month, infants can distinguish some colors. By four and five months they can distinguish two- and three-dimensional objects. At the age of three days, newborns can distinguish their mothers' voices. By six months they can discriminate virtually any sound.

In addition to physical and perceptual growth, infants grow socially as well. **Attachment** refers to the positive emotional bond between a child and a particular individual. Harry Harlow demonstrated the importance of attachment by showing that baby monkeys preferred a terry cloth ''mother'' to a wire ''mother'' even though the wire version provided food and the terry cloth one did not. Others have since suggested that attachment develops from the responsiveness of the care giver to the signals given by the infant. Full attachment is achieved through a complex sequence of events described by the Attachment Behavioral System. Infants play an active role in the development of the bond. According to Klaus and Kennell, a critical period just after birth that is based on skin-to-skin contact is crucial to the mother and child bond. There appears to be little support for the hypothesis. Though early contact does make the mothers more responsive to the children, the effect lasts only three days and no long-term consequence has been found.

Erik Erikson has proposed an eight-stage theory of social development. Each stage of **psychosocial development** involves a basic crisis or conflict. Though each crisis is resolved as we pass through the stages, the basic conflict remains throughout life. First is the **trust-versus-mistrust stage** (birth to 1 year) in which feelings of trust are built on basic physiological and psychological needs, especially attachment. The **autonomy-versus-shame-and-doubt stage** (1 to 3 years) is marked by the development of independence if exploration and freedom are encouraged or shame if they are not. The **initiative-versus-guilt stage** (3 to 6 years) is marked by the conflict between the desire to initiate independent activities and the guilt that arises from the consequences. The final stage of childhood is the **industry-versus-inferiority stage** (6 to 12 years). However, on the positive side, development proceeds with the increase in competency while the opposite is failure and inadequacy.

Cognitive development refers to the developmental changes in the understanding of the world. Theories of cognitive development attempt to explain the intellectual changes that occur throughout life. Jean Piaget proposed that children passed through four distinct stages of cognitive development and that these stages differed in both the quantity of information acquired and the quality of knowledge and understanding. Maturation and relevant experiences are needed for children to pass through the stages.

Piaget's first stage is called the **sensorimotor stage,** and it is from birth to 2 years. This stage is marked by the child's lack of ability to use images, language, and symbols. Things not immediately present are not within the child's awareness until the development of **object permanence**, the awareness that objects continue to exist when they are out of sight.

The **preoperational stage** is from 2 to 7 years of age. Children gain the ability to represent objects internally and can use symbols for objects. Children's thinking has improved over the sensorimotor stage, but it is still inferior to adult thought. This stage is marked by **egocentric thought** in which the world is viewed from the child's perspective. The **principle of conservation**, which states that quantity is unrelated to appearance, is not understood during this period.

The **concrete operational stage** is from 7 to 12 years of age. Its beginning is marked by the mastery of the principle of conservation. Children develop the ability to think in a logical manner. They learn to understand reversibility, or the capacity of things to be reverted to a previous state. They are, however, bound to the concrete, physical world rather than abstract thoughts.

The **formal operational stage**, from 12 years to adulthood, is marked by the use of abstract, formal, and logical thought. Though it emerges at this time, it is used infrequently. Studies show that only 40 to 60 percent of college students reach this stage and only 25 percent of the general population do so.

Research has shown that Piaget underestimated the abilities of infants and children. Some psychologists suggest that cognitive development is more continuous than Piaget suggested. In this alternative view, the cognitive development is one of quantitative changes. Piaget has had significant influence on educational theory and curricula, even if some of his theory and research has been challenged.

An alternative to Piaget's theory is that of **information processing**, which examines how people take in, use, and store information. According to this theory, development requires the development of mental programs for approaching problems. The changes that occur relate to speed of processing, attention span, and improvement of memory. The size of chunks increases with age. Information processing also points to the changes in metacognition as a sign of development. **Metacognition** refers to the awareness and understanding of one's own cognitive processes.

Concept 3:   Adolescence: Becoming an Adult   *Survey:* _____
                                                                     Read: _____

Pages 357-365

Development continues throughout life, from adolescence to adulthood and old age. Western society has few rituals that help define the end of childhood, as do the Awa tribe of New Guinea and other tribal societies. The major biological changes that begin with the attainment of physical and sexual maturity and the changes in social, emotional, and cognitive function that lead to adulthood mark the period called **adolescence**.

The dramatic physical changes of adolescence include a growth in height, the development of breasts in females, the deepening of the male voice, the development of body hair, and intense sexual feelings. The growth spurt begins around age 10 for girls and age 12 for boys. **Puberty**, or the development of the sexual organs begins about a year later. There are wide individual variations, however. Better nutrition and medical care in western cultures is probably the cause of the decreasing age of onset of puberty. Early-maturing boys have an advantage over later-maturing boys, doing better in athletics and being more popular, though they do have more difficulties in school. Early-maturing girls are more popular and have higher self-concepts than those who mature late, but the obvious changes in breasts can cause separation from peers and ridicule. Late-maturers suffer because of the delay, with boys being ridiculed for their lack of coordination and girls holding lower social status in junior and high school.

Lawrence Kohlberg has identified a series of stages that people pass through in their moral development. Preadolescent children make moral judgments based on concrete, inflexible rules. Adolescents are able to reason more abstractly and comprehend moral principles. Kohlberg argues that everyone passes through a fixed series of six stages (though not all reach the final stages) that are divided into three levels. Kohlberg's ideas are considered to be generally valid, with some criticisms that suggest there is a difference between judgments and actual behavior.

Carol Gilligan has argued that Kohlberg's system is flawed in its application to the moral judgment of women. Different socialization experiences bring about a difference between the moral views of men and women. Men view morality in terms of justice and fairness, and women view morality in terms of responsibility toward individuals. Compassion is a more important factor for women. Since Kohlberg's views are based on justice, his system cannot adequately describe the moral development of women. Gilligan defines three stages for the moral development of women: The first stage is termed ''orientation toward individual survival.'' The second is ''goodness as self-sacrifice.'' The third is ''morality of nonviolence.'' Some have argued that she rejected Kohlberg's views too completely.

Erikson's theory of psychosocial development identifies the beginning of adolescence with his fifth stage, called the **identity-versus-role confusion stage**. During this stage individuals seek to discover their abilities, skills, limits, and **identity**. If one resolves this stage with confusion, then a stable identity will not be formed and the individual may become a social deviant or have trouble with close personal relationships later. The stage is marked by a shift from dependence on adults for information and the turn toward the peer group for support. During college, the **intimacy-versus-isolation stage** describes the basic conflict. This stage focuses on developing relationships with others. Middle adulthood finds people in the **generativity-versus-stagnation stage**. The contribution to family, community, work, and society make up generativity, and feelings of triviality about one's activities indicate the difficulties of the stage and lead to stagnation. The final stage is the **ego-integrity-versus-despair stage**, and it is marked by a sense of accomplishment if successful in life or a sense of despair if one regrets what might have been.

**Concept 4:   Early and Middle Adulthood: The Middle   *Survey:* ____
                Years of Life   *Read:* ____**

Pages 365-368

Early adulthood is generally considered to begin at about 20 years of age and last until about 40 to 45 years, and middle adulthood lasts to 40 to 45 to about 65 years of age. These ages have been studied less than any other. Fewer significant physical changes occur, and the social changes are diverse.

The peak of physical health is reached in early adulthood, and quantitative changes begin at about 25 years as the body becomes less efficient and more prone to disease through time. The major physical development is the female experience of **menopause**, the cessation of menstruation and the end of fertility. The loss of estrogen may lead to hot flashes, a condition which is successfully treated with artificial estrogen. Problems that were once blamed on menopause are now seen as resulting from the perceptions of coming old age and society's view of it. Though men remain fertile, the gradual decline of physical abilities has similar effects of menopause, causing the man to focus on the social expectations of youthfulness.

Daniel Levinson's model of adult development identifies six stages from beginning adulthood through the end of middle adulthood. At the beginning, the individual formulates a ''dream'' that guides career choices and the vision the person has of the future. At about 40 or 45, people enter a period called the **midlife transition** during which past accomplishments are assessed, and in some cases, the assessment leads to a **midlife crisis** in which the signs of physical aging and a sense that the career will not progress combine to force a reevaluation of and an effort to remedy their dissatisfaction. Most people go through the midlife transition without any difficulties. During the fifties, people become more accepting of others and their own lives. They realize that death is inevitable and seek to understand their accomplishment in terms of how they understand life. Since Levinson's research was based on males, the difference in roles and socialization has raised questions about whether women go through the same stages.

Concept 5:   The Later Years of Life: Growing Old   *Survey:* ____
                                                                           Read: ____

Pages 368-373

Gerontologists study development and the aging process beginning around the age of 65. Gerontologists are reexamining our understanding of aging, suggesting that the stereotype of aging is inaccurate. Napping, eating, walking, and conversing are the typical activities of both the elderly and college students. The obvious physical changes that appear in old age include thinning and graying hair, wrinkling and folding skin, and a loss of height. Vision and hearing become less sharp, smell and taste are less sensitive, reaction time slows, and oxygen intake and heart-pumping abilities decrease. Two types of theories have been offered to account for these changes. One group includes the **genetic preprogramming theories of aging** which suggest that here are preset time limits on the reproduction of human cells governed by genetics. The other group includes the **wear-and-tear theories of aging** which suggest that the body simply stops working efficiently. By-products of energy production accumulate, and cells make mistakes in their reproduction. Old age is not a disease, but is instead a natural biological process. Many functions, like sexual behavior, remain pleasurable long into old age. Neither of these theories explains why women live longer than men. At birth there are more males than females; by 65 years of age, 84 percent of women are still alive and 70 percent of men. A consequence of increased health awareness is that the gap is not increasing.
     The view that the elderly are forgetful and confused is no longer considered an accurate assessment. IQ tests usually include a physical performance component that measures the reaction time of the elderly even though the reaction time has nothing to do with intelligence. The elderly are often in ill health, and the comparison is usually healthy young adults with groups of less healthy elderly people. When healthy elderly are used for comparison, differences are less significant. Also, since more young people attend college, the elderly groups are often less educated. Tests show declines in **fluid intelligence** in old age but **crystallized intelligence** actually increases. Fluid intelligence may be more sensitive to changes in the nervous system than crystallized intelligence. Recent studies suggest that cognitive declines may be remedied by increasing the blood flow to the brain. The drug Nimodipine was given to elderly rabbits who could then be classically conditioned faster than rabbits not on the drug. When elderly were given special spatial training sessions, their performance on spatial skills tasks was better than for elderly who were not given the special training.
     One assumption about the elderly is that they are more forgetful. Evidence suggests that forgetfulness is not inevitable. Memory declines tend to be in

long-term memory and, specifically, with episodic memories. Life changes may cause a decline in motivation rather than actual memory impairment. Impairments can be compensated by mnemonic strategies. The decline in cognitive function associated with old age is called senility, but this is now viewed as a symptom caused by other factors, like **Alzheimer's disease**, anxiety, depression, or even overmedication.

Loneliness is a problem for only a small portion of the elderly, though social patterns do change in old age. Two theories account for how people approach old age. The **disengagement theory of aging** views aging as a gradual withdrawal from the world on physical, psychological, and social levels. Energy is lower and interaction lessens. This view sees aging as an automatic process. The **activity theory of aging** suggests that people are happiest who remain active and that people should attempt to maintain the activities and interests they develop during middle age. The nature of the activity is the most important factor, and not the quantity.

Death requires major adjustments, as the death of those near you causes changes in life and makes you consider the possibility of your own death. Elisabeth Kübler-Ross outlined five stages of the death process. The first is denial of the fact that one is dying. The second is anger at death. The third is bargaining with death, looking for ways to postpone it. The fourth is depression when the bargaining does not work. The fifth and final stage is acceptance.

♦ Now that you have surveyed, questioned, and read the chapter and completed the **Recap and Review** questions, review **Looking Back**, pages 374-376. *Review:*____

♦ For additional practice through recitation and review, test your knowledge of the chapter material by answering the questions in the **Key Word Drill**, the **Practice Questions**, and the **Essay Questions**.

KEY WORD DRILL   *Recite:* ____

The following **Fill in the Blank** and **Matching Questions** test key words from the text. Check your answers with the Answer Key in the back of the *Study Guide*.

FILL IN THE BLANK

1. _____ psychology studies patterns of growth and change occurring throughout life.

2. Individuals with identical genetic makeup are most likely _____ _____.

3. The point at which a fetus can survive if born prematurely is known as the _____ of _____.

4. Developmental psychologists refer to the positive emotional bond that develops between a child and a particular individual as _____.

5. The way in which people take in, use, and store information is often called _____ _____.

6. The developmental stage called _____ marks the transition from childhood to adulthood.

7. The distinguishing character of each individual is called _____,
    and is comprised of our roles and capabilities as well as our sense of self.

8. Beginning around the age of 40 _____
    can occur, and during this period we come to the realization that life is
    not indefinite.

9. The term _____ refers to specialists who study aging.

10. The ability to deal with new problems and situations is called _____
    intelligence, and intelligence based on the store of specific information,
    skills, and strategies that people have acquired through experience is
    called _____ intelligence.

MATCHING QUESTIONS

_C_ 11. environment

_F_ 12. heredity

_E_ 13. genetic makeup

_a_ 14. maturation

_g_ 15. interactionist

_h_ 16. cross-sectional
        research

_b_ 17. longitudinal research

_d_ 18. cross-sequential
        research

a. The unfolding of biologically predetermined
   behavior patterns.

b. A research method which investigates
   behavior through time as subjects age.

c. Influences on behavior that occur in the
   world around us - in family, friends,
   school, nutrition, and many other factors.

d. A research method which combines cross-
   sectional and longitudinal research.

e. The inherited biological factors that
   transmit hereditary information.

f. Influences on behavior that are transmitted
   biologically from parents to a child.

g. Someone who believes that a combination of
   genetic predisposition and environmental
   influences determines the course of
   development.

h. A research method in which people of
   different ages are compared at the same
   point in time.

_d_ 19. phenylketonuria (PKU)

_a_ 20. sickle-cell anemia

_e_ 21. Tay-Sachs disease

_c_ 22. Down syndrome

_b_ 23. rubella

_f_ 24. fetal alcohol syndrome

a. A disease of the blood that affects about 10 percent of America's African-American population.

b. German measles.

c. A disorder caused by the presence of an extra chromosome, resulting in mental retardation.

d. An inherited disease that prevents its victims from being able to produce an enzyme that resists certain poisons, resulting in profound mental retardation.

e. A genetic defect preventing the body from breaking down fat and typically causing death by the age of 4.

f. An ailment producing mental and physical retardation in a baby as a result of the mother's behavior.

_____   _____

_e_ 25. neonate

_a_ 26. vernix

_h_ 27. lanugo

_b_ 28. reflexes

_g_ 29. rooting reflex

_f_ 30. sucking reflex

_i_ 31. gag reflex

_c_ 32. startle reflex

_d_ 33. Babinski reflex

a. A white lubricant that covers a fetus, protecting it during birth.

b. Unlearned involuntary responses to certain stimuli.

c. The reflex in response to a sudden noise where the infant flings its arms, arches its back, and spreads its fingers.

d. The reflex where an infant's toes fan out in response to a stroke on the outside of its foot.

e. A newborn child.

f. A reflex that prompts an infant to suck at things that touch its lips.

g. A neonate's tendency to turn its head toward things that touch its cheek.

h. A soft fuzz covering the body of a newborn.

i. An infant's reflex to clear its throat.

b 34. trust-versus-mistrust stage

a 35. autonomy-versus-shame-and-doubt stage

d 36. initiative-versus-guilt stage

c 37. industry-versus-inferiority stage

a. The stage of psychosocial development where children can experience self-doubt if they are restricted and overprotected.

b. The first stage of psychosocial development occurring from birth to 18 months of age.

c. The period during which children may develop positive social interactions with others or may feel inadequate and become less sociable.

d. The period during which children experience conflict between independence of action and the sometimes negative results of that action.

---

b 38. sensorimotor stage

f 39. object permanence

c 40. preoperational stage

e 41. principle of conservation

d 42. concrete operational stage

a 43. formal operational stage

a. Characterized by abstract thought.

b. Little competence in representing the environment.

c. Characterized by language development.

d. Characterized by logical thought.

e. Quantity is unrelated to physical appearance.

f. Objects do not cease to exist when they are out of sight.

---

d 44. identity-versus-role-confusion stage

c 45. Intimacy-versus-isolation stage

b 46. generativity-versus-stagnation stage

a 47. ego-integrity-versus-despair stage

a. A period from late adulthood until death during which we review life's accomplishments and failures.

b. A period in middle adulthood during which we take stock of our contributions to family and society.

c. A period during early adulthood that focuses on developing close relationships with others.

d. A time in adolescence of testing to determine one's own unique qualities.

_c_ 48. genetic preprogramming theories of aging

_a_ 49. wear-and-tear theories of aging

_d_ 50. disengagement theory of aging

_b_ 51. activity theory of aging

a. Theories that suggest that the body's mechanical functions cease efficient activity and, in effect, wear out.

b. A theory that suggests that the elderly who age most successfully are those who maintain the interests and activities they had during middle age.

c. Theories that suggest a built-in time limit to the reproduction of human cells.

d. A theory that suggests that aging is a gradual withdrawal from the world on physical, psychological, and social levels.

_b_ 52. adolescence

_f_ 53. puberty

_d_ 54. identity

_a_ 55. menopause

_e_ 56. midlife transition

_c_ 57. midlife crisis

a. The point at which women stop menstruating, generally at around age 45.

b. The stage between childhood and adulthood.

c. The negative feelings that accompany the realization that we have not accomplished in life all that we had hoped.

d. The distinguishing character of the individual: who each of us is, what our roles are, and what we are capable of.

e. Beginning around the age of 40, a period during which we come to the realization that life is finite.

f. The period during which maturation of the sexual organs occurs.

PRACTICE QUESTIONS   *Recite and Review:* _____

Test your knowledge of the chapter material by answering these **True-False** and **Multiple Choice Questions**. Check your answers with the Answer Key in the back of the *Study Guide.*

TRUE-FALSE QUESTIONS

T   **F**   1.   Characteristics such as memory and height are entirely determined by heredity.

T   **F**   2.   The developing embryo is most vulnerable to drugs, toxic chemicals, and x-rays a few weeks before critical periods of development.

T   **F**   3.   The Babinski reflex is an involuntary response enabling an infant to clear his or her throat.

T   F   4.   The amount of time an adult spends with a child is less important than how the adult and child spend the time.

T   F   5.   Children who spend their days in day care are more likely to be socially cooperative.

T   F   6.   For a male, undergoing puberty late may have detrimental effects that persist for ten to fifteen years.

T   F   7.   Puberty dramatically changes how adolescents see themselves and how others see them.

T   F   8.   According to Kohlberg, only a small percentage of people reach stage 5 of his mode of moral reasoning.

T   **F**   9.   There is a great transition for women at age 40, whereas men go through a disruption and reorientation at about age 30.

T   **F**   10. Pleasure derived from sex usually decreases with age, as does frequency of sexual activity.

MULTIPLE CHOICE QUESTIONS

1.   When theories stress the role of heredity in their explanations of change in individual development, the focus of their accounts would be on:
   a.   maturation.   c.   environmental factors.
   b.   nurture.   d.   social growth.

2.   The philosophical view that infants are born with a blank slate favors which of the following as a dominant influence upon development?
   a.   interactionism   c.   nurture
   b.   nature   d.   dualism

3. The view of developmental psychologists today is that:
   a. environmental stimulation is necessary to achieve full genetic potential.
   b. genetic factors are most important in individual development.
   c. environmental influences are most important in individual development.
   d. different factors are important for different individuals.

4. The belief that a combination of genetic and environmental factors determines the course of development is the central point of view for:
   a. all psychologists.
   b. neuropsychologists.
   c. interactionists.
   d. social psychologists.

5. The units that produce particular characteristics in an individual are called:
   a. chromosomes.
   b. genes.
   c. spores.
   d. somes.

6. Which chromosome combination will result in a male child?
   a. XX
   b. YY
   c. XY
   d. XXX

7. At conception a zygote is formed. What is the next stage the organism progresses through after the zygote has developed?
   a. embryo
   b. neonate
   c. fetus
   d. fertilization

8. Certain events must take place in a specific time frame; otherwise, the entire sequence of fetal growth is thrown off and the result will be either no development or abnormal development. This time frame is called:
   a. longitudinal development.
   b. cross-section maturation.
   c. the resolution phase.
   d. the critical period.

9. Of the organs listed below, which is not yet formed at the embryonic stage?
   a. heart
   b. brain
   c. intestinal tract
   d. eyes

10. In prenatal development, the age of viability is a developmental stage in which:
    a. the eyes and other sense organs are functional.
    b. the fetus can survive if born prematurely.
    c. development has advanced sufficiently that the fetus is capable of learning from environmental cues.
    d. the sexual organs of the fetus are differentiated.

11. The unborn fetus has many of the features and characteristics of a newborn as early as:
    a. 8 weeks.
    b. 12 weeks.
    c. 16 weeks.
    d. 24 weeks.

12. At birth, the neonate is covered with a white, greasy substance which protects the skin prior to birth, called:
    a. veridical.
    b. vernix.
    c. fornix.
    d. lanugo.

13. A neonate is:
    a. a prenatal infant in its thirtieth to thirty-eighth week of development.
    b. a newborn infant.
    c. an infant born with deformities because of chromosomal abnormalities.
    d. a premature baby, up to the time at which the normal due date passes.

14. Which reflex below helps the newborn infant position its mouth onto its mother's breast when it feeds?
    a. rooting reflex   c. gag reflex
    b. startle reflex   d. surprise reflex

15. The most dramatic changes that occur during the first year after birth have to do with:
    a. speech development.
    b. overall growth.
    c. increase in head size relative to the rest of the body.
    d. the disappearance of reflexes.

16. According to research findings reported in the text, what is the earliest stage at which a child can imitate adult facial expressions?
    a. neonates   c. toddlers
    b. infants   d. preschoolers

17. Why are there generally differences in the form of attachment between the baby and its mother and father?
    a. Mothers spend more time directly nurturing their children, whereas fathers spend more time playing with them.
    b. Mothers spend more time playing with their children, whereas fathers spend more time nurturing them.
    c. Mothers generally are the primary caregivers so the attachment is stronger.
    d. Fathers spend more time doing things with their children than mothers.

18. According to the text, which statement best represents the father's typical attachment to his children?
    a. It is superior to the mother's attachment in most situations.
    b. It is aloof and detached.
    c. It is generous with affection, especially during verbal interaction.
    d. It is qualitatively different, but comparable to the mother's attachment.

19. Attending day care improves intellectual performance in children from _____, but does not significantly influence children from _____.
    a. middle-class families; poor and upper-class homes
    b. poor and middle-class homes; upper-class families
    c. poor families; middle- and upper-class homes
    d. upper-class families; middle-class and poor families

20. Erikson's theory of development:
    a. was based on experiences of psychotic women.
    b. covers an entire lifetime.
    c. takes a behaviorist approach.
    d. was derived from Piaget's cognitive approach to development.

21. According to Erikson, inconsistent care can lead a youngster to find it
    difficult to:
    a. trust another person.   c. compete in the real world.
    b. have feelings of accomplishment. d. pick appropriate role models.

22. Piaget's theory is one of:
    a. psychosocial development.   c. maturation.
    b. sensorimotor development.   d. cognitive development.

23. Jess and Luisa were playing with two balls of clay. Luisa was molding a
    cake and Jess was making a bowl. Jess then suggested they get new balls of
    clay so that they could make something different. Luisa informed him that
    no new clay was necessary; the clay could be remolded to make different
    objects. What principle was Luisa teaching to Jess?
    a. the principle of conservation
    b. the principle of reversibility
    c. the principle of egocentric thought
    d. the principle of logic

24. According to Piaget, a child who exhibits logical and abstract thought has
    achieved the:
    a. sensorimotor stage.   c. concrete operational stage.
    b. preoperational stage.   d. formal operational stage.

25. The last time Sara used her personal computer she observed that several
    files were not copied onto the floppy disk as she had expected. She
    carefully checked her sequence of operations and considered the
    characteristics of the software. After evaluating alternative explanations
    for what had happened, she correctly deduced why the files were not copied.
    Sara is in Piaget's:
    a. concrete operational stage of cognitive development.
    b. preoperational stage of cognitive development.
    c. sensorimotor stage of cognitive development.
    d. formal operational stage of cognitive development.

26. The period during development which is marked by dramatic physical and
    psychological change and attainment of sexual maturity is called:
    a. adulthood.   c. puberty.
    b. adolescence.   d. childhood.

27. Physical changes at the start of adolescence are largely a result of:
    a. secretion of hormones.
    b. the cessation of the secretion of certain hormones.
    c. growth of the brain.
    d. psychological turmoil.

28. How many stages does Kohlberg's model of moral reasoning have?
    a. two   c. six
    b. four   d. eight

29. A child thinks, ''If I steal a cookie, I will get spanked.'' In which level
    of moral development is this child functioning?
    a. amorality   c. conventional morality
    b. preconventional morality   d. postconventional morality

30.   Which of the following is not one of Kohlberg's stages of moral reasoning?
      a. preconventional   c. postconventional
      b. conventional   d. nonconventional

31.   According to Erikson, role confusion is most likely to occur during:
      a. early adulthood.   c. adolescence.
      b. early childhood.   d. middle adulthood.

32.   According to Erikson, college-age people typically contend with the
      conflicts found in the:
      a. intimacy-versus-isolation stage.
      b. generativity-versus-stagnation stage.
      c. ego-integrity-versus-despair stage.
      d. identity-versus-role-confusion stage.

33.   Being active in civic groups, assisting in recreational programs, and having
      a stable career are indications that one is in the _____ stage of
      development.
      a. intimacy versus isolation   c. generativity versus stagnation
      b. identity versus role confusion   d. ego-integrity versus despair

34.   According to the text, the most noteworthy feature of Erikson's theory of
      psychosocial development is that:
      a. both men and women are included in its descriptions of developmental
          changes.
      b. it accurately describes developmental changes that people in other
          cultures also experience.
      c. it has greatly increased understanding of infant development.
      d. it suggests that development is a lifelong process.

35.   Frank and his wife, who are both in their early thirties, want many
      children. Frank does not know when he will be incapable of fathering
      children, and he is getting worried that there might not be enough time.
      What would you say to Frank?
      a. Men lose their ability to father children in their late forties, just
          like women.
      b. Men lose their fertility in their late fifties, so his wife will lose
          her fertility first.
      c. Both men and women remain fertile into their sixties, so there is plenty
          of time left for them to have children.
      d. Men don't lose their ability to father children until well into old
          age.

36.   For most people, adulthood marks the peak of:
      a. physical health.   c. maturation.
      b. cognitive development.   d. accomplishment.

37.   Which of the following represents a major biological change in the life of
      a female during middle adulthood.
      a. puberty   c. menarche
      b. menopause   d. tumescence

38.   At what stage are individuals considered to be full-fledged adult members
      of society.
      a. adolescence   c. middle adulthood
      b. early adulthood   d. not until late adulthood

39. When a male in his early forties assesses his life and finds this a
     negative, demoralizing experience, he is going through:
     a. a sense of peace.   c. menopause.
     b. a midlife crisis.   d. menarche.

40. According to Levinson, which stage of development seems to show important
     differences between men and women?
     a. culmination   c. dream
     b. challenge   d. reality

41. According to the text, one way that the developmental stages of adult women
     differ from those of men is that:
     a. women have more difficulties developing a vision of what their future
         life will include.
     b. women's midlife crises are more likely to occur later in their lives.
     c. women's midlife crises are usually precipitated by their children
         leaving home, causing the ''empty nest syndrome.''
     d. women's developmental stages are more influenced by hormonal and
         physical changes.

42. Which theory suggests that some cells may become harmful to the body after
     a certain amount of time?
     a. opponent-process   c. wear-and-tear
     b. genetic preprogramming   d. gerontological

43. The theory of aging that is based on the notion that mechanical functions
     of the body stop working efficiently is called:
     a. genetic preprogramming.   c. wear-and-tear.
     b. genetic breakdown.   d. failure of function.

44. Doris, who is 75 years old, finds that she has a more difficult time hearing
     than when she was younger. Which theory best supports the conclusion that
     Doris' poor hearing is due to the fact that mechanical bodily functions stop
     working efficiently as an individual ages?
     a. genetic preprogramming theory   c. decreased consumption theory
     b. wear-and-tear theory   d. disengagement theory of aging

45. What natural condition, to date, is explained by neither the genetic
     preprogramming theory nor the wear-and-tear theory, according to
     developmental psychologists?
     a. deterioration of the circulatory system
     b. confusion and forgetting
     c. women living longer than men
     d. reduced visual acuity

46. Which type of intelligence actually increases with age?
     a. fluid intelligence   c. basic intelligence
     b. verbal intelligence   d. crystallized intelligence

47. Dr. Beegood is an authority on Egyptian mummies and has been retired for
     thirteen years. He was recently asked to speak at a monthly faculty
     luncheon. If he gives one of his ''canned'' presentations on mummies to the
     faculty, he will be drawing heavily from his:
     a. crystallized intelligence.   c. fluid intelligence.
     b. common sense.   d. practical intelligence.

48. One difference between crystallized and fluid intelligence is that, generally:
    a. fluid intelligence is useful only in certain situations.
    b. fluid intelligence declines with age.
    c. crystallized intelligence declines with age.
    d. crystallized intelligence is better in women.

49. A study done at Pennsylvania State University involved a program in which elderly individuals were taught strategies for dealing with problems. The results indicated that:
    a. declines in cognitive functioning in old age can, in part, be avoided.
    b. elderly people can be taught new skills.
    c. senility is usually unavoidable in old age.
    d. when elderly people exercise, they have less energy for intellectual performance.

50. A pattern of reduced social and physical activity as well as a shift toward the self rather than a focus on others characterizes the:
    a. deactivation theory of aging.   c. withdrawal theory of aging.
    b. activity theory of aging.   d. disengagement theory of aging.

ESSAY QUESTIONS   *Recite and Review:* ____

Essay Question 10.1: Stimulation of Children

One of the main points of the chapter is that developmental psychologists are interested in finding ways that individual potential can be maximized. Children can be stimulated through contact with parents, through play, while at day care, and they can be encouraged to explore by having the appropriate attachments. What would the world of a perfectly ''enriched'' child look like? Is it possible to overstimulate?

_____

_____

_____

_____

_____

_____

_____

_____

_____

_____

_____

_____

_____

_____

_____

_____

_____

_____

_____

Essay Question 10.2: Aging and Retirement

Apply the disengagement and the activity theories of aging to the question of mandatory retirement. Should there be a mandatory retirement age and, if either yes or no, what are the exceptions and who shall judge?

_____

_____

_____

_____

_____

_____

_____

_____

_____

_____

_____

_____

_____

_____

_____

_____

_____

_____

_____

_____

_____

_____

_____

ACTIVITIES AND PROJECTS

1. If you have the opportunity, observe a child under one year of age on
    several occasions for at least five minutes. Prior to the observation, list
    the activities and abilities you expect to be demonstrated. Include smile,
    vocalizations, ability to hold and grasp, interaction with others, etc.
    After making this list, create a tally of the behaviors you actually see in
    the observation (your list should include a number of specific actions).
    When your observation is complete, reflect on the types of actions that
    occurred but which you had not expected. What do your observations suggest
    concerning the theories described in the chapter?

2. Interview one or more people in the middle years of life and find out their
    views on life-span development. Do they view themselves as continuing
    through a developmental process physically, socially, cognitively, or in any
    other way? What are the major issues to be faced during the middle years,
    and how do these issues differ from earlier years that had to be faced?

C H A P T E R

11

PERSONALITY

DETAILED OUTLINE

Survey: ____

This detailed outline contains all the headings in Chapter 11: Personality. If you are using the SQ3R method, then an examination of the outline is the best way to begin your survey of the chapter.

Prologue: John Gotti
Looking Ahead

Psychoanalytic Theories of Personality
  Freud's psychoanalytic theory
      Structuring personality: Id, ego, and superego
      Developing personality: A stage approach
      Defense mechanisms
      Evaluating Freudian theory
  The neo-Freudian psychoanalysts
▪ **Recap and Review I**

Trait, Learning, and Humanistic Approaches: In Search of Personality
  Trait theories: Labeling personality
      Allport's trait theory: Identifying the basics
      The theories of Cattell and Eysenck: Factoring out personality
      Evaluating trait theories of personality
      Is personality a myth?: Personality versus situational factors
  Learning theories of personality
      Social learning theories of personality
      Evaluating learning theories of personality
  Humanistic theories of personality
      Evaluating humanistic theories
  Comparing approaches to personality
▪ **Recap and Review II**

Assessing Personality: Determining What Makes Us Special
  Reliability and validity
Psychology at Work ''Race Norming'': Where Psychology and Politics Meet
  Self-report measures of personality
  Projective methods
  Behavioral assessment
The Informed Consumer of Psychology Assessing Personality Assessments
The Cutting Edge To Tell the Truth: Can Integrity Tests Identify Honest People?
▪ **Recap and Review III**

Looking Back
Key Terms and Concepts

Now that you have surveyed the chapter, read **Looking Ahead**, pages 380-381.
> *Question:* ____
> *Read:* ____

Focus on the questions on page 381.

CONCEPTS AND LEARNING OBJECTIVES   *Survey:* ____

These are the concepts and the learning objects for Chapter 11. Read them carefully as part of your preliminary survey of the chapter.

Concept 1: Personality is the sum of the characteristics that define individuals and the consistency of behavior across situations and time. Psychoanalysis understands personality in terms of how a person manages the unconscious that seeks to dominate behavior.

1. Define personality and describe the basic structure of personality according to Sigmund Freud. (pp. 380-383)

2. Describe the psychosexual stages of development according to Freud. (pp. 383-385)

3. Define and describe the defense mechanisms and their role in psychoanalytic theory. (pp. 385-387)

4. Discuss the criticisms of the psychoanalytic theory of personality and the contributions made by the neo-Freudians. (pp. 387-388)

Concept 2: Three alternatives to psychoanalytic personality theory are: trait theory, which focuses on basic traits describing universal characteristics; learning theory, especially social learning theory, focusing on personality as a set of learned behaviors; and humanistic theory, which focuses on the uniqueness of the individual and the striving toward self-actualization.

5. Define trait and discuss how trait theories have been criticized based on the person-situation debate. (pp. 389-395)

6. Describe the approach to personality taken by the learning theorists. (pp. 395-397)

7. State and define the basic tenets of humanistic personality theory. (pp. 397-399)

Concept 3: Personality can be measured several ways. Tests must prove reliable and valid, and they must have standardized norms. The most frequently given assessments include the MMPI, the Rorschach test, and the TAT.

8. Discuss personality assessment and define the concepts of validity, reliability, and norms. (pp. 400-402)

9. Describe and distinguish tests based on self-report and projective techniques. (pp. 402-405)

10. Describe how behavioral assessment works, and discuss the general criticisms of assessment methods. (pp. 405-407)

CHAPTER SUMMARY

There are several ways you can use this summary as part of your systematic study plan. You may read each concept summary and then read the corresponding pages in the text, or you may read the entire summary and then read the entire chapter in the text. As you finish each section, complete the **Recap and Review** questions that are supplied in the text.

Concept 1: Prologue and Looking Ahead   *Survey:* ____
            Psychoanalytic Theories of Personality   *Read:* ____

Pages 380-388

The Prologue describes John Gotti and illustrates how a person can behave very differently from one situation to another. The field of psychology known as **personality** studies the characteristics that make a person unique and attempts to explain what makes a person act the same in different situations and through time.

   Psychoanalysts are concerned with understanding the hidden forces that govern people's behavior and remain outside of awareness. These forces have their roots in childhood experiences. This theory, called **psychoanalytic theory**, was developed by Sigmund Freud. Slips of the tongue are examples of how thoughts and emotions are held in the **unconscious**, the part of the personality that remains beyond the person's awareness. Slips reflect these hidden concerns. The unconscious also contains **instinctual drives**, which include infantile wishes, desires, demands, and needs that remain hidden because of the conflicts they can cause. Freud described conscious experience as the top of an iceberg, suggesting that the larger part of our personality was unconscious. In order to understand personality, these unconscious elements must be illuminated. The contents of the unconscious are disguised, thus requiring that slips of the tongue, fantasies, and dreams be interpreted in order to understand how unconscious processes direct behavior. Though his ideas were originally rejected, today we accept the notion that some part of our personality is beyond our awareness.

   Freud described a general model of the personality that contains three interacting structures: the id, ego, and superego. The **id** is the raw, unorganized, inherited part of the personality aimed at reducing the tension caused by basic drives of hunger, sex, aggression, and irrational impulses. The drives are powered by **libido**, or ''psychic energy,'' and the id operates according to the **pleasure principle**, or the desire for immediate gratification of all needs. Reality limits the expression of these id impulses. The **ego** is responsible for constraining the id. It serves as a buffer between reality and the pleasure-seeking demands of the id. The ego operates on the **reality principle**, in which restraint is based on the safety of the individual and an effort to integrate into society. The ego is the seat of the higher cognitive functions. The **superego** represents the rights and wrongs of society as represented by the parents. The superego is composed of two parts, the **conscience** and the **ego-ideal**. The conscience prevents us from behaving immorally and the ego-ideal motivates us to do the morally correct thing. Both the superego and the id make unrealistic demands. The ego must compromise between the moral perfectionist demands of the superego and the pleasure-seeking gratification sought by the id.

   Freud proposed a theory of development that accounted for how the adult personality comes into existence. Difficulties and experiences from a childhood stage may predict adult behaviors and each stage focuses on a biological function. The first period of development is the **oral stage** during which the baby's mouth is the focus of pleasure. This suggested to Freud that the mouth is the primary sight of sexual pleasure and if infants are overindulged or frustrated, then they can become fixated. **Fixated** means that an adult shows personality characteristics that are related to the stage. At about 12 to 18 months until the age of 3, the child is in the **anal stage**. The major source of pleasure moves to the anal region, and the child derives pleasure from the retention and expulsion of feces. If toilet training is particularly demanding, fixation can occur. Fixation can lead to unusual rigidity and orderliness or the extreme opposite of disorder or sloppiness. At the age of 3, the **phallic stage** begins and the source of pleasure moves to the genitals. The **Oedipal conflict** develops at this time. The differences between males and females becomes a concern, and the male begins to see his father as a rival for his mother, thus developing fantasies that parallel the Greek tragedy about Oedipus. The fear of retaliation causes the development of a ''castration anxiety.'' In the end, the child represses his desires for his mother and chooses an **identification** with father. For girls , the pattern is different. Girls develop desires for father and develop **penis envy**, a wish that they had the anatomical part, the penis, that is clearly missing. According to Freud, they blame their mothers for their ''castration.'' In the end girls identify with their mothers and repress these feelings. The next period is called the **latency period**, beginning around 5 or 6 and lasting to puberty. Sexual concerns become latent. The final period, the **genital stage**, begins at puberty. Mature adult sexuality emerges during this period.

Anxiety, an intense, negative emotional experience, arises as a signal of danger to the ego. Though anxiety may arise from realistic fears, the **neurotic anxiety** arises because of the irrational impulses from the id that threaten to break into consciousness. The ego has developed unconscious strategies to control the impulses called <u>**defense mechanisms**</u>. The primary defense mechanism is **repression**. In repression, unacceptable or unpleasant id impulses are pushed back into the unconscious. In repression, the anxiety-producing impulse is ignored, but it finds ways to be revealed, either through slips of the tongue or dreams or other symbolic ways. When repression does not work, other mechanisms are used. <u>**Regression**</u> involves using behavior from earlier stages of development to deal with the anxiety. <u>**Displacement**</u> is the process of redirecting the unwanted feeling onto a less threatening person. <u>**Rationalization**</u> occurs when reality is distorted by justifying events with explanations that protect our self-esteem. **Denial** occurs when a person simply refuses to acknowledge the existence of an anxiety-producing piece of information. **Projection** involves protecting oneself by attributing unwanted impulses and feelings to someone else. <u>**Sublimation**</u> is the diversion of unwanted impulses to socially acceptable behaviors. According to Freud, these mechanisms are used to some degree by everyone, though some people devote a large amount of energy to dealing with unacceptable impulses to the extent that daily life becomes hampered. He identified this tendency as neurosis.

Freud's theory is an elaborate and complex set of propositions. However, Freud is criticized for the lack of scientific support for his theory. Freud's theory is employed in after-the-fact explanations rather than predictive statements. Also, his observations were made with a limited population of upper-middle-class Austrian women living in the puritanical era of the early 1900s. Freud's theory has had major impact on psychology and many other fields. Freud's emphasis on the unconscious has been partially supported by current research by cognitive psychologists. Experimental techniques have been developed that allow the study of the unconscious in a more sophisticated manner.

The followers of Freud are known as **neo-Freudian psychoanalysts**. They tend to place greater emphasis on the role of the ego. Carl Jung rejected the primary importance of unconscious sexual urges in favor of viewing the primitive urges of the unconscious more positively. He suggested that people have a **collective unconscious**, a set of influences that are inherited from our ancestors. The collective unconscious is shared by everyone and appears in behavior across cultures. Jung also proposed the idea of **archetypes**, or universal symbolic representations of particular persons, objects, or experiences. Alfred Adler focused on the human motivation for striving for superiority as a quest for self-improvement and perfection. His concept of **inferiority complex** describes situations in which an adult attempts to overcome feelings of inferiority that have persisted since childhood. Other neo-Freudians include Erik Erikson (discussed in Chapter 10) and Karen Horney. Horney focused on the social and cultural factors in personality, particularly the relationship between parents and the child and how well the child's needs are met.

Concept 2: Trait, Learning, and Humanistic   *Survey:* _____
Approaches: In Search of Personality   *Read:* _____

Pages 389-399

A number of theories take a different approach than that of psychoanalysis. These include **trait theory**, which assumes that individuals respond to different situations in a fairly consistent manner. **Traits** are the enduring dimensions of personality characteristics along which people differ. Trait theories assume that all people have certain traits, and the degree to which a trait applies to a specific person varies. The approach taken has been to determine the basic traits necessary to describe personality.

Gordon Allport identified 18,000 separate terms that could be used to describe personality which he then reduced to 4500 descriptors. In order to make sense of this number, he defined three basic categories of traits. A **cardinal trait** is a single characteristic that directs most of a person's activities. Most people do not have cardinal traits, instead they have five to ten **central traits** that define major characteristics. **Secondary traits** are characteristics that affect fewer situations and are less influential than cardinal or central traits. Preferences would be secondary traits.

The statistical technique called **factor analysis**, in which relationships among a large number of variables are summarized into smaller, more general patterns, has been used to identify fundamental patterns or combinations of traits. Raymond Cattell suggested that there are forty-six **surface traits** or clusters of related behaviors. Cattell then reduced this number to sixteen source traits that represent the basic dimensions of personality. He then developed the Sixteen Personality Factor Questionnaire (16 PF). Hans Eysenck used factor analysis to identify two major dimensions. **Introversion-extroversion** is the dimension that is marked by be quiet and restrained individuals on one end and outgoing and sociable on the other. **Neuroticism-stability** is the dimension marked by moody and sensitive (neurotic) on the one hand and calm, reliable, and even-tempered (stability) on the other. Recent research has suggested that there are five traits: surgency, neuroticism, intellect, agreeableness, and conscientiousness.

Trait theories have an advantage of being straightforward and easy to apply to practical situations. However, a determination of which traits are fundamental is difficult to make. The traits offer little more than a basic description of the person, and they do not explain behavior.

Another objection that has arisen from trait theories but applies to all is the question of whether behavior is consistent over different situations. Walter Mischel has argued that the broad traits can explain only a minor portion of behavior. Most behavior can be explained by the situation in which it occurs. This has produced an ongoing controversy about the degree to which behavior is caused by personality factors or by situational factors. According to the traditional views, it is necessary to consider behavior over time to see the extent of consistency. Mischel has responded by arguing that consistency over time is not consistency over situations. One result of this controversy has been the realization that trait raters are more accurate if they do not know the subject, when multiple ratings and raters are used, and when the behavior observed is relevant to the trait being rated. Personality psychologists also look more to the characteristics of the situation that influence behavior of individuals with specific traits. The debate has also increased the focus on searching for the factors that produce specific traits. A study of 350 pairs of twins has determined that some traits are influenced more by heredity than others. Social potency and traditionalism have stronger genetic components, and achievement and social closeness have weaker genetic components. Other studies suggest that altruism, aggression, sexuality, political attitudes, and religious values may be influenced by heredity.

According to Skinner, personality is a collection of learned behavior patterns. Similarities across situations are caused by a similarity of reinforcements. Strict learning theorists are less interested in the consistency issue than they are in finding ways to modify behavior. In their view, humans are quite changeable.

Social learning theory emphasizes the role of a person's cognitions in determining personality. According to Bandura, people are able to foresee the outcomes of behaviors prior to carrying them out by using the mechanism of **observational learning**. We observe a model that displays a behavior and then relate the consequences of the behavior to determining whether or not to attempt the behavior. Bandura considers **self-efficacy**, the expectations of success, to be an important factor in determining the behaviors a person will display. Social learning theory places an emphasis on the reciprocity between individuals and the environment, viewing the interaction as one in which a feedback flows both ways. The key to understanding behavior, **reciprocal determinism,** refers to the interaction between environment, behavior, and the individual.

Traditional learning theories have been criticized for ignoring internal processes and reducing behavior to stimuli and responses. Traditional theories and social learning theory have been criticized for their highly **deterministic** view that maintains that behavior is controlled by forces outside the control of the person. The positive contribution has been to make the study of personality an objective and scientific venture.

Humanistic theory emphasizes the basic goodness of people and their tendency to grow to higher levels of functioning. Carl Rogers is a major representative of this approach. The positive regard others have for us makes us see and judge ourselves through the eyes of other people. The views others have of us may not match our own self-concept. If the difference is great, we may have problems with daily functioning. The discrepancy is overcome by support from another person in the form of **unconditional positive regard**, defined as an attitude of acceptance and respect no matter what the person says or does. Rogers and Maslow (Chapter 9) see the ultimate goal of personality growth to be **self-actualization**.

The criticisms of humanistic theory are centered on the difficulty of verifying the basic assumptions of the theory. The assumption that all people are basically ''good'' is unverifiable and injects nonscientific values into scientific theories.

Each theory looks to different aspects of the personality, and personality is most reasonably viewed from several perspectives. Personality theories can be compared on the following major issues: the unconscious versus conscious, nature versus nurture, freedom versus determinism, stability versus modifiability of characteristics, and nomothetic versus ideographic approaches. **Nomothetic approaches to personality** focus on broad uniformities in behavior. **Ideographic approaches to personality** focus on individual uniqueness.

Concept 3:   Assessing Personality: Determining What   *Survey:* ____
Makes Us Special   *Read:* ____

Pages 400-408

The intentionally vague statements that introduce the topic of assessment suggest that measuring different aspects of personality may require great care and precision. The assessment of personality requires discriminating the behavior of one person from that of another. **Psychological tests** are standard measures that measure aspects of behavior objectively.

Psychological tests must have **reliability**, that is, they must measure something consistently from time to time. A reliable test will produce similar outcomes in similar conditions. The question of whether or not a test measures the characteristic it is supposed to measure is called **validity**. If a test is reliable, that does not mean that it is valid. However, if a test is unreliable, it cannot be valid. All types of tests in psychology, including intelligence tests, assessments of psychological disorders, and the measurement of attitudes must meet tests of validity and reliability. If tests are both valid and reliable, then they can be used to establish norms to allow the results of a test to be interpreted. **Norms** are the standards of test performance that allow comparison of the scores of one test-taker to others who have taken it. The norm for a test is determined by calculating the average score for a particular group of people for whom the test is designed. Then, the extent to which each person's score differs from the others can be calculated. The selection of the subjects who will be used to establish a norm for a test are critical. A contemporary problem faces test creators in the development of a different set of norms for minorities. Critics of such an approach suggest that this is both unfair and contributes to bigotry. Supporters argue it is an affirmative-action tool that helps minorities.

Instead of conducting a comprehensive interview to determine aspects of childhood, social relationships, and success and failure, the use of **self-report measures** allows individuals to respond to a small sample questions. The most frequently used self-report measure is the **Minnesota Multiphasic Personality Inventory-2 (MMPI-2)**. Originally developed to distinguish people with psychological disturbances from people without, the MMPI scores have been shown to be good predictors of such things as whether college students will marry within ten years and whether they will get an advanced degree. The test has 567 true-false items covering items like mood, opinions, and physical and psychological health. The interpretation of the responses is important; there are no right or wrong answers. The test is scored on ten scales and includes a lie scale for people trying to falsify their answers. The MMPI has undergone a procedure called **test standardization** by which the test authors have determined which items best differentiate among groups of people, like differentiating those suffering depression, from normal subjects. This procedure has produced a number of subscales helpful in diagnosis. When the MMPI is used for proper reasons, it does a good job. However, some employers have used it as a screening tool and have applied the test improperly. Other tests are more appropriate for screening job applicants.

Projective personality tests require the subject to describe an ambiguous stimulus. The responses are considered to be projections of what the person is like. The best known is the Rorschach test which consists of symmetrical stimuli. The **Thematic Apperception Test (TAT)** consists of a series of pictures about which the person is asked to write a story. Inferences about the subject are then based on these stories. These tests are criticized because too much inference depends upon the scorer.

In order to obtain an objective test based on observable behavior, a **behavioral assessment** may be conducted either in a natural setting or in a laboratory under controlled conditions. The behavioral assessment requires quantifying behavior as much as possible. For instance, recording the number of social contacts or the number of aggressive acts would quantify the assessment. Behavioral assessment is appropriate for observing and remedying behavioral difficulties and psychological difficulties.

To find people with the right characteristics for a job, many companies are using personality tests for both hiring and advancement. One concern is for the use of these tests to determine if someone is honest. Career counseling has also utilized personality tests. When personality tests are being used, one must keep in mind the purpose of the test and remember that no decision should be made solely on the basis of the test and that tests are not infallible.

♦ Now that you have surveyed, questioned, and read the chapter and completed the **Recap and Review** questions, review **Looking Back**, pages 408-409. *Review:*____

♦ For additional practice through recitation and review, test your knowledge of the chapter material by answering the questions in the **Key Word Drill**, the **Practice Questions**, and the **Essay Questions**.

KEY WORD DRILL   *Recite:* ____

The following **Fill in the Blank** and **Matching Questions** test key words from the text. Check your answers with the Answer Key in the back of the *Study Guide*.

FILL IN THE BLANK

1. _____ is defined as the sum total of characteristics that differentiate people, or the stability in a person's behavior across different situations.

2. Physicians or psychologists with specialized training in Freudian psychology are known as _____.

3. A child's _____ with his or her opposite-sex parent is typically resolved through identification with the same-sex parent.

4. Theorists who place greater emphasis than Freud did on the functions of the ego and its influence on our daily activities have been given the name _____-_____.

5. _____ are characteristics that differentiate people from one another.

6. _____ _____ is used to combine traits into broader, more general patterns of consistency.

7. _____ suggests that people's behavior is shaped primarily by factors outside their control.

8. _____ approaches study personality by accentuating the uniformities across behavior while _____ approaches study personality by emphasizing what makes one person different from others and unique.

9. Consistency in the measurements made by a test is described as _____

_____, and the ability of a test to measure what it is supposed to measure is described as _____.

10. The standards of test performance are called _____.

11. _____ refers to the use of direct measures of an individual's behavior to describe characteristics indicative of personality.

MATCHING QUESTIONS

_C_ 12. unconscious

_b_ 13. instinctual drives

_d_ 14. id

_e_ 15. libido

_a_ 16. fixation

    a. Behavior reflecting an earlier stage of development.

    b. Infantile wishes, desires, demands, and needs hidden from conscious awareness.

    c. A person is unaware of this determinant of behavior.

    d. The raw, unorganized, inherited part of personality created by biological drives and irrational impulses.

    e. The sexual energy underlying biological urges.

_f_ 17. pleasure principle

_a_ 18. ego

_e_ 19. reality principle

_d_ 20. superego

_C_ 21. conscience

_b_ 22. ego-ideal

    a. Provides a buffer between the id and the outside world.

    b. Motivates us to do what is morally proper.

    c. Prevents us from doing what is morally wrong.

    d. Represents the morality of society as presented by parents, teachers, and others.

    e. The principle by which the ego operates.

    f. The principle by which the id operates.

_b_ 23. oral stage

_f_ 24. anal stage

_e_ 25. phallic stage

_a_ 26. identification

_g_ 27. penis envy

_c_ 28. latency period

_d_ 29. genital stage

a. A child's attempt to be similar to the same-sex parent.

b. An infant's center of pleasure is the mouth.

c. Children's sexual concerns are temporarily put aside.

d. Marked by mature sexual behavior.

e. A child's interest focuses on the genitals.

f. A child's pleasure is centered on the anus.

g. A girl's wish that she had a penis.

_d_ 30. anxiety

_b_ 31. neurotic anxiety

_f_ 32. defense mechanisms

_a_ 33. collective unconscious

_c_ 34. archetypes

_e_ 35. inferiority complex

a. The concept that we inherit certain personality characteristics from our ancestors and the human race as a whole.

b. Anxiety caused when irrational impulses from the id threaten to become uncontrollable.

c. Universal, symbolic representations of a particular person, object, or experience.

d. A feeling of apprehension or tension.

e. A phenomenon whereby adults have continuing feelings of weakness and insecurity.

f. Unconscious strategies used to reduce anxiety by concealing its source from themselves and others.

36. repression

37. regression

38. displacement

39. rationalization

40. denial

41. projection

42. sublimation

a. An unwanted feeling or thought directed toward a weaker person instead of a more powerful one.

b. Justify a negative situation to protect self-esteem.

c. Unacceptable or unpleasant id impulses are pushed back into the unconscious.

d. Attribute inadequacies or faults to someone else.

e. Behavior reminiscent of an earlier stage of development.

f. The refusal to accept anxiety-producing information.

g. The diversion of unwanted impulses into socially acceptable thoughts, feelings, or behaviors.

_____   _____

43. observational learning

44. self-efficacy

45. reciprocal determinism

46. self-concept

47. unconditional positive regard

48. self-actualization

a. The realization of one's highest potential.

b. The impression one holds of oneself.

c. Learned expectations about success determine behavior.

d. Supportive behavior for another individual.

e. The interaction of environment, behavior, and the individual causes people to behave the way that they do.

f. Learning by viewing the actions of others.

_____   _____

_a_ 49. cardinal trait

_g_ 50. central traits

_d_ 51. secondary traits

_c_ 52. surface traits

_f_ 53. source traits

_b_ 54. introversion-extroversion

_e_ 55. neuroticism-stability

a. A single trait that directs most of a person's activities.

b. The dimension encompassing shyness to sociability.

c. Clusters of a person's related behaviors that can be observed in a given situation.

d. Traits less important than central and cardinal traits.

e. Encompasses moodiness to even-temperedness.

f. The sixteen basic dimensions of personality.

g. A set of major characteristics that composes the core of a person's personality.

_f_ 56. psychological tests

_d_ 57. self-report measures

_a_ 58. Minnesota Multiphasic Personality Inventory-2 (MMPI-2)

_e_ 59. test standardization

_g_ 60. projective personality test

_c_ 61. Rorschach test

_b_ 62. Thematic Apperception Test (TAT)

a. Used to identify people with psychological difficulties.

b. Consists of a series of ambiguous pictures about which a person is asked to write a story.

c. Uses inkblots of indefinite shapes.

d. Gathering data by asking people about their behavior.

e. Validates questions in personality tests by studying the responses of people with known diagnoses.

f. Standard measures devised to objectively assess behavior.

g. Uses ambiguous stimuli to determine personality.

_d_ 63. psychoanalytic theory

_b_ 64. trait theory

_a_ 65. social learning theory

_c_ 66. humanistic theory

a. The theory that suggests that personality develops through observational learning.

b. A model that seeks to identify the basic traits necessary to describe personality.

c. The theory that emphasizes people's basic goodness and their natural tendency to rise to higher levels of functioning.

d. Freud's theory that unconscious forces act as determinants of personality.

PRACTICE QUESTIONS

Recite and Review: ____

Test your knowledge of the chapter material by answering these **True-False** and **Multiple Choice Questions**. Check your answers with the Answer Key in the back of the *Study Guide*.

TRUE-FALSE QUESTIONS

(T)   F   1. Children who are in Freud's latency stage are also typically in Erikson's industry versus inferiority stage.

(T)   F   2. According to psychoanalytic theory, the phallic stage runs from about ages 3 to 5.

T   (F)   3. A child who begins to wet the bed at night, when he or she never did so before, is probably displaying repression.

(T)   F   4. The neo-Freudians, Freud's successors, often disagree with Freud, especially with his emphasis on sex as an influence and motivator of human behavior.

(T)   F   5. A shortcoming of the trait approach to personality is that it yields a description of behavior, as opposed to an explanation.

(T)   F   6. Recent studies of personality show that heredity plays a larger role in a person's development and personality traits than was thought previously.

(T)   F   7. Clinicians use stories based on ambiguous pictures to draw inferences about the writer's personality characteristics.

T   (F)   8. Behavioral assessment and naturalistic observation provide a means for analyzing the results of projective personality tests.

MULTIPLE CHOICE QUESTIONS

1. According to Sigmund Freud, the _____ harbors repressed emotions and thoughts as well as instinctual drives.
   a. unconscious
   b. collective unconscious
   c. conscience
   d. conscious

2. Which of the following theories suggests that behavior is triggered largely by powerful forces found in the unconscious?
   a. humanistic theory
   b. learning theory
   c. psychoanalytic theory
   d. trait theory

3. According to psychoanalytic theorists, what is the most important factor in determining our everyday behavior?
   a. whom we come in contact with
   b. how we have learned to behave in the past
   c. our thinking patterns
   d. the unconscious

4. Freud's structure of personality has three major parts. Which alternative below is not one of them?
   a. libido
   b. id
   c. superego
   d. ego

5. Which of the following is least likely to involve making unrealistic demands on the person?
   a. the id
   b. the ego
   c. the superego
   d. the pleasure principle

6. Which of the following controls thought, solves problems, and makes decisions?
   a. id
   b. ego
   c. superego
   d. conscience

7. Listed below are four alternatives. Three of the four give pairs of items that are related. Which alternative below contains items that are not related?
   a. ego; reality principle
   b. Sigmund Freud; Viennese physician
   c. superego; ''executive'' of personality
   d. id; pleasure principle

8. From the psychoanalytic perspective, a rapist would be considered to have:
   a. unconditioned positive regard for his victim.
   b. a well-developed ego-ideal.
   c. a deficient superego.
   d. brain damage.

9. According to the text, Freud's concept of the ego-ideal refers to:
   a. infantile wishes, desires, demands, and needs hidden from conscious awareness.
   b. the part of the superego that motivates us to do what is morally proper.
   c. the part of personality that provides a buffer between the id and the outside world.
   d. the part of the superego that prevents us from doing what is morally wrong.

10. According to Freud's theory of psychosexual development, a child who is constantly putting things in its mouth is most likely at the:
    a.   genital stage.   c.   phallic stage.
    b.   anal stage.   d.   oral stage.

11. Of the following, a psychoanalyst most likely would view a thumbsucking 7-year-old as:
    a.   a normal youngster.
    b.   fixated at the oral stage of development.
    c.   having been breastfed as an infant.
    d.   ready to enter the phallic stage of development.

12. Tim kept his clothes hung up and neatly pressed, while his roommate Jack rarely laundered or hung up his clothes. Freud might have suggested that both men were fixated at the:
    a.   anal stage.   c.   phallic stage.
    b.   oral stage.   d.   genital stage.

13. A child who is in the midst of toilet training is probably in the:
    a.   genital psychosexual stage.   c.   phallic psychosexual stage.
    b.   anal psychosexual stage.   d.   oral psychosexual stage.

14. According to the text, mature sexual relationships begin to occur at which psychosexual stage?
    a.   phallic   c.   genital
    b.   oral   d.   anal

15. Defense mechanisms are developed to:
    a.   help the superego gain control of the id.
    b.   advance the collective unconscious.
    c.   protect the ego.
    d.   reveal latent content from dreams.

16. According to Sigmund Freud, defense mechanisms are:
    a.   unconscious.   c.   learned.
    b.   instinctive.   d.   reflexive.

17. A female college student accepts a date from a young man she greatly admires. At the time of the date, however, the man doesn't show up. In response she exclaims, ''I didn't want to go out with him anyway!'' This illustrates:
    a.   rationalization.   c.   regression.
    b.   denial.   d.   repression.

18. Which of the following defense mechanisms did Freud find most socially acceptable?
    a.   repression   c.   rationalization
    b.   sublimation   d.   projection

19. Generalizing from the text, what aspect of Freudian theory makes the theory most difficult to validate?
    a.   The developmental stages are all sexual.
    b.   It is difficult to study children.
    c.   The early childhood stages are still apparent in the adult.
    d.   The parts of the personality are unobservable.

20. Freud's ideas and theories have created an understanding of many phenomena in psychology and psychiatry. Which of the following is not one of them?
    a.   defense mechanisms
    b.   the unconscious
    c.   neural disorders as a cause of behavioral problems
    d.   childhood causes of adult psychological difficulties

21. According to the text, which of the following statements would not be a valid criticism of psychoanalytic theory?
    a.   Freud's theory is built on observations of patients who were a highly select and special group of women in Vienna.
    b.   It is difficult to make predictions about personality development and behavior from Freud's theory.
    c.   Freud used only that data from his cases that supported the ideas of his theory.
    d.   Research data do not strongly support Freud's theory.

22. Listed below are four alternatives. Three of the four list pairs of items that are related. Which alternative below contains items that are not related?
    a.   Jung; collective unconscious
    b.   Horney; women do not have penis envy
    c.   Adler; inferiority complex
    d.   Cattell; striving for superiority

23. Which of the following statements is most likely to be made by a trait theorist?
    a.   He really hurt her feelings, but he's rationalizing it away.
    b.   He really could have gone a long way, but his inferiority complex destroyed any confidence.
    c.   These are five stages in the process of his development toward fulfilling his highest potential.
    d.   He is a sensitive, warm, and considerate person.

24. According to trait theorists:
    a.   everyone has the same traits, but in different amounts.
    b.   everyone has different traits that do not change with time.
    c.   everyone has different traits, and they change with time.
    d.   everyone has different traits, but they cannot be measured.

25. For Gordon Allport, _____ traits were so distinct that having only one of these traits will define a person's personality.
    a.   general   c.   central
    b.   secondary   d.   cardinal

26. Which of the psychologists listed below is not a trait theorist?
    a.   Albert Bandura   c.   Raymond B. Cattell
    b.   Gordon Allport   d.   Hans Eysenck

27. What are the three important categories of personality dimensions, according to Gordon Allport?
    a.   primary, secondary, and tertiary
    b.   factors, traits, and features
    c.   source, surface, and circumscript
    d.   cardinal, central, and secondary

28. Factor analysis is:
    a. a method of recording data that requires sophisticated equipment.
    b. a method of understanding how the unconscious works.
    c. a statistical method of finding common traits.
    d. a sociometric method of determining personality traits in a group.

29. Which of the following statements about trait theories is true?
    a. They agree on a certain number of basic personality dimensions.
    b. They allow a comparison between individuals on the same scale.
    c. They explain the basis for a behavior as well as provide a label.
    d. They help explain how and why the defense mechanisms work.

30. Learning theorists are most interested in the:
    a. heritability of behavior.   c. randomness of behavior.
    b. stability of behavior.   d. modifiability of behavior.

31. According to Bandura, we can modify our own personalities through the use
    of:
    a. defense mechanisms.   c. psychoanalysis.
    b. drive reduction.   d. self-reinforcement.

32. Humanistic theories of personality assume that:
    a. man's basic goodness is contrasted with an evil unconscious.
    b. man is self-sufficient and the society corrupts the individual.
    c. man is basically good and desires to improve.
    d. man's fundamental depravity may be offset through education.

33. Which of the following theoretical points of view emphasizes to the greatest
    extent the individual's freedom of choice as a determinant of personality?
    a. psychoanalysis   c. social learning theory
    b. humanistic theory   d. trait theory

34. Three of the four alternatives below list pairs of items that are related.
    Which one contains items that are not related?
    a. Maslow; self-actualization
    b. Rogers; imitation
    c. Bandura; observational learning
    d. Skinner; learning theory

35. Stephanie loves art and wants to study it in college. Her parents want her
    to be a nurse and criticize her for her love of art. According to Carl
    Rogers, this conflict will lead to:
    a. Stephanie learning to love being a nurse.
    b. anxiety on the part of Stephanie.
    c. Stephanie becoming a fully functioning person.
    d. unconditional positive regard.

36. Various approaches to personality have names and concepts uniquely
    associated with them. Three of the four alternatives below list pairs of
    items that are related. Which alternative below contains items that are **not**
    related?
    a. trait theory; assessment of traits that make up personality
    b. learning theory; experiences with situations in the environment
    c. learning theory; Skinner
    d. psychoanalytic theory; consistency of behavior across situations

37. Which of the following theories are most closely associated with the nomothetic approaches to understanding personality?
   a. psychoanalytic and trait
   b. trait and social learning
   c. social learning and strict learning
   d. social learning and humanistic

38. If a test provides a consistent score for a particular individual over repeated administrations, the test is said to be:
   a. accurate.   c. reliable.
   b. valid.   d. statistical.

39. Which of the following situations best illustrates reliability as a quality of psychological tests?
   a. A prospective Air Force pilot takes a test, passes it, and becomes an excellent pilot.
   b. A college student studies diligently for an important exam and makes an A on it.
   c. A psychiatric patient takes a psychological test which yields the diagnosis the patient had suspected.
   d. A mentally retarded patient takes an intelligence test on Monday and again on Tuesday, getting the same result on each administration.

40. If an individual's test scores vary greatly from one session to the next, it is likely that the test itself is:
   a. unreliable and invalid.   c. nomothetic.
   b. unreliable only.   d. ideographic.

41. The MMPI was originally developed to:
   a. identify personality disorders.   c. locate traits.
   b. uncover unconscious thoughts.   d. test behavior

42. Which one of the following tests is most appropriately used in the employment setting?
   a. TAT
   b. Edwards Personal Preference Schedule
   c. MMPI
   d. Rorschach

43. Which one of the following tests is designed to uncover unconscious content?
   a. MMPI
   b. TAT
   c. California Psychological Inventory
   d. Edwards Personal Preference Schedule

44. Test stimuli are the most ambiguous on the:
   a. TAT.
   b. California Psychological Inventory.
   c. Rorschach.
   d. MMPI.

45. Which of the following tests are considered projective instruments?
   a. MMPI and TAT   c. Rorschach and MMPI
   b. TAT and 16 PF   d. Rorschach and TAT

46. When personality assessments are evaluated, it is important to keep in mind
    that:
    a. tests are infallible.
    b. decisions should not be based solely on the results of any one test.
    c. projective measures are more valid than other measures because they
        delve beneath the surface.
    d. most people lie on self-report measures.

ESSAY QUESTIONS   *Recite and Review:* ____

Essay Question 11.1: *Freud and Female Psychology*

Given that Sigmund Freud's theory appears to be primarily focused on male development, and thus on a male personality, identify the areas of Freud's theory that are the weakest with regard to psychological issues of women. Defend your response with other points of view presented in the text.

_____

_____

_____

_____

_____

_____

_____

_____

_____

_____

_____

_____

_____

_____

_____

_____

_____

_____

_____

_____

Essay Question 11.2: *Personality Placement Tests*

A major issue that will affect virtually everyone is the use of personality tests for job placement and promotion. Discuss the hazards, as well as some possible benefits, of using tests like the MMPI, behavioral assessments, the TAT, and other tests for employment purposes.

_____

_____

_____

_____

_____

_____

_____

_____

_____

_____

_____

_____

_____

_____

_____

_____

_____

_____

_____

_____

_____

_____

_____

ACTIVITIES AND PROJECTS

1. Write four descriptions of someone's personality, each based on a different
    theory of personality: (a) trait theory, (b) psychoanalytic theory, (c)
    learning theory, and (d) humanistic theory. You may opt to choose a friend,
    a family member, or a fictional character. With friends and family members,
    it is not a good idea to share the information with the subjects described.
    In your trait description, make a list of central and secondary traits, and
    include situational variables if you like. In your description, be sure to
    include hypotheses about unconscious conflicts and motivations and the use
    of defense mechanisms. With the learning theory, include the role of early
    experiences and reinforcement. Your humanistic description may include the
    person's strivings, level of self-actualization obtained, and self-concept.
    Which theoretical framework did you find the most useful to work with?
    Explain.

C H A P T E R

12

ABNORMAL BEHAVIOR

<u>**DETAILED OUTLINE**</u>   *Survey:* ____

This detailed outline contains all the headings in Chapter 12: Abnormal Behavior. If you are using the SQ3R method, then an examination of the outline is the best way to begin your survey of the chapter.

> **Prologue: Judy Smith**
> **Looking Ahead**
>
> **Normal Versus Abnormal: Making the Distinction**
>   Approaches to abnormality
>   Deviation from the average
>   Deviation from the ideal: Striving for perfection
>   Abnormality as a sense of subjective discomfort
>   Abnormality as the inability to function effectively
>   The continuum of abnormal and normal behavior: Drawing the line on
>   abnormality
> *The Cutting Edge* Homelessness
>   The prevalence of mental disorders: The mental state of the union
> ▪ **Recap and Review I**
>
> **Models of Abnormality: From Superstition to Science**
>   The medical model
>   The psychoanalytic model
>   The behavioral model
>   The cognitive model
>   The humanistic model
>   The sociocultural model
>   Applying the models: The case of Judy Smith
> *The Informed Consumer of Psychology* Do You Feel Abnormal?
> ▪ **Recap and Review II**
>
> **Classifying Abnormal Behavior: The ABCs of DSM**
>
> **The Major Disorders**
>   Anxiety disorders
>   Generalized anxiety disorder
>   Panic disorder
>   Phobic disorder
>   Obsessive-compulsive disorder
>   The causes of anxiety disorders
>   Somatoform disorders: When the psychological leads to the physical
>   Dissociative disorders
> ▪ **Recap and Review III**

    Mood disorders: The feeling is wrong
        Major depression
        Mania and bipolar disorders: Ups and downs
        Causes of mood disorders
    Schizophrenia: When reality is lost
        Solving the puzzle of schizophrenia
            Biological components
            Psychological components
        The multiple causes of schizophrenia
    Personality disorders: Lacking distress
    Beyond the major disorders
    Psychology at Work DSM and Culture - and the Culture of DSM
    The Informed Consumer of Psychology Deciding When You Need Help
    ▪ **Recap and Review IV**

    Looking Back
    Key Terms and Concepts

Now that you have surveyed the chapter, read **Looking Ahead**, page 413.
    Question: ____
        Read: ____

    Focus on the questions on page 413.

CONCEPTS AND LEARNING OBJECTIVES   *Survey:* ____

These are the concepts and the learning objects for Chapter 12. Read them
carefully as part of your preliminary survey of the chapter.

Concept 1: Abnormality is difficult to define, and it is best to consider
    behavior as on a continuum from normal to abnormal. Disorders are common in
    America, with as much as 20 percent of the population suffering some kind of
    abnormality.

    1. Define abnormal behavior and discuss the prevalence of mental disorders.
       (pp. 412-417)

Concept 2: The contemporary models that attempt to explain abnormal behavior are
    the medical model, the psychoanalytic model, the behavioral model, the
    cognitive model, the humanistic model, and the sociocultural model.

    2. Describe and distinguish the models of abnormality presented in the text,
       including the medical model, the psychoanalytic model, the behavioral
       model, the cognitive model, the humanistic model, and the sociocultural
       model. (pp. 418-423)

    3. Apply the models of abnormal behavior to specific instances.
       (pp. 423-424)

Concept 3: The DSM-IV-R is the system used by most professionals to classify
    mental disorders. Anxiety disorders, somatoform disorders, and conversion
    disorders are three major classes of disorders.

    4. Describe the classification system, the DSM-IV-R, used in the diagnosis
       and description of mental disorders. (pp. 425-428)

5. Describe the anxiety disorders and their causes. (pp. 428-432)

6. Describe the somatoform disorders and their causes. (pp. 432-434)

7. Describe the dissociative disorders and their causes. (pp. 434-435)

Concept 4: Mood disorders, schizophrenia, and personality disorders are three major disorders in the DSM-IV-R.

8. Describe the mood disorders and their causes. (pp. 436-439)

9. Describe the types of schizophrenia, its main symptoms, and the theories that account for its causes. (pp. 439-445)

10. Describe the personality disorders and their causes. (pp. 445-447)

11. Discuss the other forms of abnormal behavior described in the DSM-IV-R and issues related to seeking help. (pp. 447-449)

CHAPTER SUMMARY

There are several ways you can use this summary as part of your systematic study plan. You may read each concept summary and then read the corresponding pages in the text, or you may read the entire summary and then read the entire chapter in the text. As you finish each section, complete the **Recap and Review** questions that are supplied in the text.

Concept 1: Prologue and Looking Ahead   *Survey:* ____
          Normal Versus Abnormal: Making the Distinction   *Read:* ____

Pages 412-417

The Prologue illustrates that the development of mental illness can progress over years. The concerns that psychologists have about people like Judy Smith include concerns about why she would live on the street, whether early intervention would have helped, and others. Her case also shows the difficulty in distinguishing normal from abnormal behavior.

A passage from James Joyce's classic *Ulysses* suggests that madness cannot be determined by a small sample of a person's behavior. Four approaches are to the definition of abnormal behavior are examined in the text. They are: (1) *Deviation from the average*. This definition uses the statistical definition of behavior to define ''abnormal'' as behavior that is statistically unusual or rare. The problem with this approach is that simply being unusual or rare does not define abnormal: individuals with high IQs are quite rare, but they are not considered abnormal. (2) *Deviation from the ideal*. This definition classifies behavior as abnormal if it deviates from the ideal or standard behavior. However, society has very few standards on which everyone agrees. (3) *Abnormality as a sense of subjective discomfort*. This approach focuses on the consequences of behavior that make a person experience discomfort. However, some people who engage in what others would consider abnormal behavior do not experience discomfort. (4) *Abnormality as the inability to function effectively*. People who are unable to adjust to the demands of society and unable to function in daily life are considered abnormal in this view. Judy Smith would be classified as abnormal in this view even if the choice to live on the streets was her own.

None of the four approaches is broad enough to include all possibilities of abnormal behavior, and the line between normal and abnormal remains unclear. The best way to solve the problem is to consider normal and abnormal as on a continuum, or scale, of behavior rather than to consider them absolute states. The point at which society should intervene is also ambiguous. The criteria for intervention in most states require that a person be: (1) dangerous to self, (2) incapable of providing for basic needs, (3) unable to make reasonable decisions about treatment, (4) in need of treatment. *The Cutting Edge* takes up the issue of homelessness and abnormal behavior, and the complexities of intervention.

Determining the number of people with signs of abnormal behavior is a difficult task. A survey of 18,000 Americans found that 20 percent currently had a mental disorder and a total of one-third had experienced a disorder at some time in their lives. Projecting these figures onto the entire population suggests that 29 million people have one or more mental disorders, with 13 million taking a drug to treat anxiety, 10 million abusing alcohol or some other drug, and 11 million having irrational fears. Only about one in five ask for help. Other surveys suggest that 20 percent of the children have a developmental, emotional, or learning problem.

Concept 2:   Models of Abnormality: From Superstition   *Survey:* ____
**   to Science**   *Read:* ____

                                                                    Pages 418-424

In the past, abnormal behavior has been attributed to the bite of a tarantula, to witchcraft, or to demonic possession. The contemporary approach includes six major perspectives on abnormal behavior:

- The **medical model of abnormality** views the cause of abnormal behavior to have a physical origin such as a hormone or chemical imbalance or a physical injury. Many abnormal behaviors have been linked to physical causes, though this view has been criticized because there are many instances in which no physical cause is known.
- The **psychoanalytic model of abnormality** maintains that abnormal behavior comes from childhood. The conflicts of childhood that remain unresolved can cause abnormal behavior in adulthood. One problem with this approach is the difficulty of linking childhood problems with adult behaviors. On the other hand, this approach does suggest that individuals have a rich inner life and that prior experiences do have a profound effect on the present.
- The **behavioral model of abnormality** views the behavior itself as the problem; understanding that behavior is a response to stimuli that one finds in one's environment. In order to understand the behavior one must examine the circumstances in which it occurs. The strength of this approach is its emphasis on the present and on dealing with the observable problems.
- The **cognitive model of abnormality** assumes that cognitions are central to a person's abnormal behavior which can then be changed by learning new cognitions. This model is derived from the behavioral model and sometimes is called the cognitive behavioral approach.
- The **humanistic model of abnormality** emphasizes the control and responsibility people have for their own behavior. This model considers people to be basically rational, oriented to the social world, and motivated to get along with others. Abnormal behaviors are signs of the person's inability to fulfill basic human needs. This model has been criticized for its reliance on unscientific and unverifiable information.
- The **sociocultural model of abnormality** assumes that behavior is shaped by the

family group, society, and culture. The stresses and conflicts people experience promote and maintain abnormal behavior. An extreme position suggests that there is no abnormal behavior and that, instead, society is intolerant of deviant behavior. The evidence for the view comes from the link between sociocultural factors and abnormal behavior.

These models can be applied to the case of Judy Smith. A proponent of the medical model would want to have her examined for physical problems. A psychoanalyst would seek to find out about her past. A behavioral theorist would concentrate on the rewards and punishments she received for behaving as she does. Proponents of the cognitive model would focus on her cognitions about the world and try to understand how she developed her misguided cognitions. The humanistic and sociocultural approaches would concentrate on her view of herself in relation to others. The humanistic theorist would suggest that she has made a series of choices about how to live, and the sociocultural theorist would focus on how society has contributed to her problems. Any single approach may be inadequate in dealing with her problems.

One phenomenon that may afflict psychology students is the **medical student's disease**. Often, as medical students learn about a disease or symptom, they begin to believe that they are experiencing the symptom. Psychology students are also likely to interpret their behaviors as reflecting one of the abnormal conditions.

Concept 3:   Classifying Abnormal Behavior: The ABCs of DSM   *Survey:* ____
The Major Disorders   *Read:* ____

Pages 425-435

One standard classification system has been accepted by most professionals for classifying mental disorders. Devised by the American Psychiatric Association, the system is known as the *Diagnostic and Statistical Manual of Mental Disorders,* **Fourth Edition - Revised (*DSM-IV-R*)**. The manual has more than 200 diagnostic categories. It evaluates behavior according to five dimensions called axes. The first three axes address the maladaptive behaviors exhibited, the nature of any personality disorders or developmental problems, and any physical disorders. The fourth and fifth axes address the severity of stressors and the general level of functioning. The *DSM-IV-R* attempts to be descriptive and to avoid suggestions of cause. Revised periodically, the objective of the manual is to provide precise description and classification. Criticisms include the fact that it reflects categories that assume a physiological view of causes (arising from the fact that it was developed by physicians) and that the categories are inflexible. In other views, the labeling of an individual as deviant is seen as a lifelong, dehumanizing stigma. Often, the diagnosis is seen as the explanation of the problem. A classic study by Rosenhan illustrated how the stigma of being labeled mentally ill can linger. Eight people, including Rosenhan, presented themselves to mental hospitals complaining of only one symptom, hearing voices. Though they did not complain of the symptom again, they stayed for an average of nineteen days and were released with labels like ''schizophrenia in remission.'' None of the impostors was detected by the staff. Despite its drawbacks, the *DSM-IV-R* does provide a reliable and valid way to classify psychological disorders.

Everyone experiences **anxiety**, a feeling of apprehension or tension, at some time. When anxiety occurs without external reason and interferes with daily functioning, the problem is known as **anxiety disorder**. The types of anxiety disorder are:

- **Generalized anxiety disorder** refers to the disorder in which an individual experiences long-term consistent anxiety without knowing why. The anxiety makes the person unable to concentrate, and life becomes centered on the anxiety.

- **Panic disorder** is distinguished by panic attacks that may last a few seconds or several hours. In a panic attack, the individual feels anxiety rise to a peak and gets a sense of impending doom. Physical symptoms of increased heart rate, shortness of breath, sweating, faintness, and dizziness may be experienced.
- **Phobic disorder** has as its primary symptom a **phobia**, an irrational fear of specific objects or situations. Exposure to a specific stimulus may cause a full-blown panic attack. (A list of common phobias is given in Table 12-2.) Phobias may be minor, or they may cause extreme suffering.
- **Obsessive-compulsive disorder** is characterized by unwanted thoughts and the impulse to carry out a certain action. **Obsessions** are thoughts or ideas that keep recurring. Though everyone has some obsessions, when they continue for days and months and include bizarre images, they make it difficult for the individual to function. **Compulsions** are urges to repeat behaviors that seem strange and unreasonable even to the person who feels compelled to act. If they cannot carry out the action, extreme anxiety can be experienced. The cleaning ritual, as described in the text, is a good example of a compulsion. Carrying out the action usually does not reduce the anxiety.

The causes of anxiety disorders are not fully understood. A tendency for both identical twins to have an anxiety disorder if one of them has the disorder suggests that there may be a biological cause. Some chemical deficiencies in the brain have also been linked to the disorder. The behavioral approach suggests that anxiety is a learned response to stress and that the anxiety is reinforced by subsequent encounters with the stressor. The cognitive approach suggests that anxiety grows out of inappropriate and inaccurate cognitions.

Hypochondriasis involves a constant fear of illness, and physical sensations are misinterpreted as disease symptoms. The symptoms are not faked, hypochondriacs actually experience the symptoms. Hypochondriasis belongs to a class of disease known as **somatoform disorders**, which are psychological difficulties that take physical form. There are no underlying physical problems to account for the symptoms, or if there does exist a physical problem, the person's reaction exaggerates it. A major somatoform disorder is **conversion disorder**, a disorder in which actual physical symptoms are caused by psychological problems. Conversion disorders usually have a rapid onset; a person may awaken one morning totally blind or with a numb hand (called ''glove anesthesia''). One characteristic is that individuals with conversion disorders seem relatively unconcerned with the symptoms. Conversion disorders have occurred on a large scale. One example is the inexplicable symptoms experienced by student aviators who, rather than quit, developed problems that would otherwise require them to quit, thus allowing a face-saving way to leave the program. Generally, conversion disorders occur when an emotional stress can be reduced by having a physical symptom.

Dissociative disorders have been the most dramatized, including the multiple personality stories of *The Three Faces of Eve* and *Sybil*. The central factor is the dissociation, or splitting apart, of critical parts of the personality. The three major dissociative disorders are:

- **Multiple personality** occurs when two or more distinct personalities are present in the same individual. Each personality is a separate person with desires and reactions to situations. Even vision can change when the personality changes. Since they reside in only one body, they must take turns, causing what appears to be quite inconsistent behavior.
- **Dissociative amnesia** is a failure or inability to remember past experiences. In psychogenic amnesia, information has not been forgotten; it simply cannot

be recalled. In some cases memory loss can be quite total, as illustrated in the case of Jane Doe, who had to go on television to have her identity discovered.

- **Dissociative fugue** is a state in which people take an impulsive, sudden trip and assume a new identity. After a period of time, they realize that they are in a strange place, often cannot recall what they did while wandering.

Concept 4: The Major Disorders (Continued)

Survey: ____
Read: ____

Pages 436-449

Changes in mood are a part of everyday life. However, mood changes can be extreme enough to cause life-threatening problems and to cause an individual to lose touch with reality. These situations result from **mood disorders**, disturbances in mood severe enough to interfere with daily life. **Major depression** is one of the more common mood disorders. As many as 14 million people are experiencing major depression at any time. Twice as many women as men experience major depression, and one in four females will encounter it at some time. Depression is not merely sadness, but involves feelings of uselessness, worthlessness, loneliness, and despair. Major depression is distinguished by the severity of the symptoms.

Mania refers to an extended state of intense euphoria and elation. Also, people experience a sense of happiness, power, invulnerability, and energy. They may be involved with wild schemes. When mania is paired with bouts of depression, it is called a **bipolar disorder**. The swings between highs and lows can occur every several days or can be over a period of years. Typically, the depression lasts longer than the mania.

The psychoanalytic view holds that depression is anger at oneself. Major depression and bipolar disorder may have a biological cause, and heredity may play a role in bipolar disorder. The cognitive approach draws on the experience of **learned helplessness**, a state in which people perceive that they cannot escape from or cope with stress. According to this view, depression is a response brought on by helplessness. Aaron Beck has suggested that depression involves faulty cognitions held by the sufferers about themselves. Theories about the cause of depression have not explained why twice as many women get it as men. One theory suggests that the stress for women is higher at certain times of life. Women are also more subject to physical and sexual abuse, earn less money than men, and report greater unhappiness with marriage.

Schizophrenia refers to the class of disorders in which severe distortion of reality occurs. Thinking, perception, and emotion deteriorate; there is a withdrawal from social interaction; and there may be bizarre behavior. (Classes of schizophrenia are listed in Table 12-4.) The characteristics of schizophrenia include:

- A decline from a previous level of functioning.
- Disturbances of thought and language in which logic is peculiar, thoughts do not make sense, and linguistic rules are not followed.
- **Delusions** are unshakable beliefs that have no basis in reality, involving thoughts of control by others, persecution, or the belief that thoughts are being broadcast to others.
- Perceptual disorders occur in which schizophrenics do not perceive the world as everyone else does, and they may have hallucinations, the experience of perceiving things that do not actually exist.
- Emotional disturbances include a lack of emotion or highly inappropriate emotional responses.

- Schizophrenics tend to withdraw from contact with others.

The symptoms follow two courses: **process schizophrenia** develops symptoms early in life, with a gradual withdrawal from the world; and **reactive schizophrenia**, which has a sudden and conspicuous onset of symptoms. Reactive schizophrenia responds well to treatment; process schizophrenia is more difficult to treat. Another distinction has been drawn between positive-symptom and negative-symptom schizophrenia. Negative symptom refers to symptoms like withdrawal or loss of ability to function, and positive symptom refers to disordered behavior like hallucinations, delusions, and extremes of emotionality.

Schizophrenia is recognized to have both biological and psychological components at its root. The biological components are suggested by the fact that schizophrenia is more common in some families than others. This suggests a genetic link to the disease. Another biological explanation suggests the presence of a chemical imbalance or a structural defect. The **dopamine hypothesis** suggests that schizophrenia occurs when there is an excess activity in the areas of the brain that use dopamine to transmit signals across nerve cells. Drugs that block dopamine action are effective in reducing symptoms. These drugs take effect immediately, but the symptoms linger for several weeks, suggesting that there must be other factors at work. Structural differences in the brains of schizophrenics have also been found.

Psychological factors include the immediate environment of the schizophrenic person. Psychoanalysis suggests that schizophrenia is a form of regression to earlier stages. The families of schizophrenics display abnormal communication patterns. The faulty communication patterns support the behavioral view of the **learned-inattention theory** of schizophrenia. According to this view, schizophrenia is a learned set of responses to social stimuli. Schizophrenics have learned to ignore the appropriate stimuli. Others then respond to them in a negative way, reinforcing the behavior until the person tunes out completely.

The predominant approach to explaining schizophrenia that combines both biological and psychological factors is the **predisposition model of schizophrenia**. This model says that individuals inherit a predisposition to schizophrenia that makes them vulnerable to stress, and the effect of the stressors occurs when they are coupled with the genetic predisposition.

Personality disorders are characterized by inflexible, maladaptive personality traits. People with personality disorders tend not to be distressed by them. The best known personality disorder is the **antisocial or sociopathic personality disorder**. People with this disorder have no regard for moral or ethical rules or for the rights of others. The characteristics of the disorder include: a lack of conscience, guilt, or anxiety over transgressions, impulsive behavior and inability to withstand frustration, and manipulation of others. Explanations include a neglecting or rejecting family, coming from a social group where the societal rules have broken down, and severe socioeconomic deprivation. The **narcissistic personality disorder** is characterized by an exaggerated sense of self-importance in which the person with the disorder expects special treatment and disregards the feelings of others.

Other forms of abnormal behavior described by the *DSM-IV-R* include **psychoactive substance-use disorder**, **sexual disorders**, and **organic mental disorders**. The *Psychology at Work* section discusses the differences between cultures in the nature of abnormal behavior.

The decision concerning if and when to seek help for psychological disorders is difficult, but several guidelines should help. If the following signals are present, help should be considered: long-term feelings of distress that interfere with functioning, occasions when stress is overwhelming, prolonged depression, withdrawal from others, chronic physical problems, a fear or phobia that prevents normal functioning, feelings that other people are talking about the person or are out to get the person, or the inability to interact effectively with others.

♦ Now that you have surveyed, questioned, and read the chapter and completed the **Recap and Review** questions, review **Looking Back**, pages 450-451.   *Review:* _____

♦ For additional practice through recitation and review, test your knowledge of the chapter material by answering the questions in the **Key Word Drill**, the **Practice Questions**, and the **Essay Questions**.

KEY WORD DRILL   *Recite:* _____

The following **Fill in the Blank** and **Matching Questions** test key words from the text. Check your answers with the Answer Key in the back of the *Study Guide*.

FILL IN THE BLANK

1. The approach that focuses on unlearning faulty cognitions about the world is called the _____-_____ approach.

2. The feeling that symptoms and illnesses one studies are characteristic of oneself has been named the _____ _____ disease.

3. The abbreviation ____ ____ ____-__-____ refers to the manual that presents comprehensive diagnostic categories for identifying problems and behaviors.

4. _____ disorder refers to the occurrence of feelings of apprehension and fear without obvious external cause that may hinder normal function.

5. _____ are thoughts or ideas that keep recurring, and the term _____ refers to the urge to carry out an act repeatedly that even the sufferer realizes is unreasonable.

6. Intense, irrational fears of specific objects or situations are called _____-_____ .

7. People who suffer from _____ experience severe distortions of reality that may lead to antisocial behavior, silly or obscene behavior, hallucinations, and disturbances in movement.

8. _____ are firmly held beliefs with no basis in reality.

9. _____ are perceptions of things that do not actually exist.

10. The severe form of depression that interferes with concentration, decision making, and sociability is called _____ depression.

MATCHING QUESTIONS

___d___ 11. medical model

___a___ 12. psychoanalytic model

___e___ 13. behavioral model

___c___ 14. cognitive model

___f___ 15. humanistic model

___b___ 16. sociocultural model

a. Suggests that abnormality stems from childhood conflicts over opposing desires regarding sex and aggression.

b. Suggests that people's behavior, both normal and abnormal, is shaped by familial, societal, and cultural influences.

c. Suggests that people's thoughts and beliefs are a central component to abnormal behavior.

d. Suggests that when an individual displays symptoms of abnormal behavior, the cause is physiological.

e. Suggests that abnormal behavior itself is the problem to be treated, rather than viewing behavior as a symptom of some underlying medical or psychological problem.

f. Suggests that abnormal behavior results from an inability to fulfill human needs and capabilities.

___c___ 17. generalized anxiety disorder

___e___ 18. panic disorder

___b___ 19. panic attack

___d___ 20. phobic disorder

___a___ 21. dissociative disorder

a. Characterized by the splitting apart of critical personality facets that are normally integrated.

b. Sudden anxiety characterized by heart palpitations, shortness of breath, sweating, faintness, and great fear.

c. The experience of long-term anxiety with no explanation.

d. Characterized by unrealistic fears that may keep people from carrying out routine daily behaviors.

e. Anxiety that manifests itself in the form of panic attacks.

___d___ 22. hypochondriasis

___e___ 23. somatoform disorder

___a___ 24. conversion disorder

___c___ 25. multiple personality

___f___ 26. dissociative amnesia

___b___ 27. dissociative fugue

a. Characterized by actual physical disturbances.

b. A condition in which people take sudden, impulsive trips, sometimes assuming a new identity.

c. Characteristics of two or more distinct personalities.

d. A misinterpretation of normal aches and pains.

e. Psychological difficulties that take on physical form.

f. A failure to remember past experience.

_____   _____

___e___ 28. anxiety

___b___ 29. mood disorder

___d___ 30. mania

___a___ 31. bipolar disorder

___c___ 32. learned helplessness

a. A disorder in which a person alternates between euphoric feelings of mania and bouts of depression.

b. Affective disturbance severe enough to interfere with normal living.

c. A state in which people give up fighting stress, believing it to be inescapable, leading to depression.

d. An extended state of intense euphoria and elation.

e. A feeling of apprehension or tension.

_____   _____

___d___ 33. process schizophrenia

___c___ 34. reactive schizophrenia

___e___ 35. dopamine hypothesis

___b___ 36. learned-inattention theory of schizophrenia

___a___ 37. predisposition model of schizophrenia

a. Suggests that individuals may inherit tendencies that make them particularly vulnerable to stressful factors in the environment.

b. Suggests that schizophrenia is a learned behavior consisting of a set of inappropriate responses to social stimuli.

c. Onset of symptoms is quick and conspicuous.

d. Symptoms begin early in life and develop slowly.

e. Suggests that schizophrenia occurs when there is excess activity in certain areas of the brain.

_a_ 38. personality disorder

_f_ 39. antisocial or sociopathic personality disorder

_e_ 40. narcissistic personality disorder

_c_ 41. psychoactive substance use disorder

_b_ 42. sexual disorders

_d_ 43. organic mental disorders

a. Characterized by a set of inflexible, maladaptive traits that keep a person from functioning properly in society.

b. A form of abnormal behavior in which one's sexual activity is unsatisfactory.

c. Disordered behavior involving drug abuse.

d. Problems having a purely biological basis.

e. Characterized by an exaggerated sense of self and an inability to experience empathy for others.

f. Individuals display no regard for moral and ethical rules or for the rights of others

---

PRACTICE QUESTIONS

Recite and Review: ____

Test your knowledge of the chapter material by answering these **True-False** and **Multiple Choice Questions**. Check your answers with the Answer Key in the back of the *Study Guide*.

TRUE-FALSE QUESTIONS

T (F) 1. Premarital sex, and other behaviors discouraged by religious groups, are considered abnormal because they deviate from average.

(T) F 2. Normal and abnormal behavior are best thought of conceptually as being on the separate ends of a continuum, rather than distinct categories.

T (F) 3. Abnormal behavior is a certain symptom of an underlying problem, according to the behavioral model of abnormality.

(T) F 4. The psychoanalytic theory of abnormality has difficulty proving that a person's childhood experiences are related to his or her subsequent abnormal behavior.

T (F) 5. *The Diagnostic and Statistical Manual of Mental Disorders*, 4th Edition, Revised (*DSM-IV-R*) was written by clinical psychologists.

T (F) 6. The *DSM-IV-R* is used mainly as a guide to treat mental disorders.

(T) F 7. What all dissociative disorders have in common is that they allow people to escape from some anxiety-producing situation.

T (F) 8. Today cases of multiple personality are about as common as cases of bipolar disorder.

T (F) 9. Major depression is more common in men than in women.

T   F   10. The classification of undifferentiated schizophrenia is given to
              patients who cannot be typed into any of the other categories.

MULTIPLE CHOICE QUESTIONS

1.   The prologue about Judy Smith in the chapter on abnormal psychology
     illustrates that:
     a.   new programs are helping rehabilitate ''street people'' with mental
          disorders.
     b.   women living in the street are subjected to many more hardships than
          men.
     c.   individuals with a behavioral disorder are not always aware of their
          own abnormal behavior.
     d.   when people are denied medication for their mental disorders, they are
          likely to have serious relapses.

2.   Which of the following is **not** an approach to defining abnormality?
     a.   the sense of subjective discomfort
     b.   behavior that deviates from religious values
     c.   inability to function effectively
     d.   behavior that deviates from an ideal standard

3.   In most states, which one of the following is **not a criterion for**
     abnormality?
     a.   The person requires treatment.
     b.   The person is dangerous to him- or herself.
     c.   The person suffers subjective discomfort.
     d.   The person is not capable of providing for basic physical needs.

4.   All of the following are required in order for society to intervene legally
     and provide mental health treatment **except**:
     a.   The person must be dangerous to himself or herself.
     b.   The person must be chemically dependent.
     c.   The person must be incapable of providing for basic needs.
     d.   The person must require treatment.

5.   According to community surveys, approximately what percentage of American
     adults suffer from a mental disorder?
     a.   5   c.   20
     b.   10   d.   30

6.   If someone's abnormal behavior is related to an endocrine system
     malfunction, their problem best fits the:
     a.   medical model of abnormality.
     b.   psychoanalytic model of abnormality.
     c.   behavioral model of abnormality.
     d.   sociocultural model of abnormality.

7.   Which of the following models of abnormality is likely to hold most strongly
     to the concept that the patient has little control over his or her actions?
     a.   the medical model   c.   the behavioral model
     b.   the sociocultural model   d.   the humanistic model

8. The _____ model of abnormality suggests that when an individual displays the symptoms of abnormal behavior, the diagnosed causes are physiological.
   a. humanistic   c. psychoanalytic
   b. medical   d. sociocultural

9. The psychoanalytic model of abnormality suggests that abnormal behavior derives from:
   a. failure to develop logical thought processes.
   b. physiological malfunctions.
   c. unresolved childhood conflicts.
   d. confusion in the collective unconscious.

10. Which of the following models of abnormality most emphasizes factors such as sex and aggression as being causes of abnormal behavior?
    a. the medical model   c. the behavioral model
    b. the psychoanalytic model   d. the humanistic model

11. According to the text, which of the following models of abnormality has recently been broadened to include cognitive learning factors?
    a. the medical model   c. the behavioral model
    b. the psychoanalytic model   d. the humanistic model

12. Which of the following models of abnormality is most likely to emphasize the patient's responsibility and participation in the treatment?
    a. the medical model   c. the behavioral model
    b. the psychoanalytic model   d. the humanistic model

13. Which of the following models of abnormality is least likely to see the therapist as the expert who cures the patient?
    a. the behavioral model   c. the medical model
    b. the humanistic model   d. the psychoanalytic model

14. Which statement below is **not** consistent with the sociocultural model of abnormality?
    a. Behavior is shaped by our family, by society, and by the culture in which we live.
    b. There is something wrong with a society that is unwilling to tolerate deviant behavior.
    c. Competing psychic forces within the troubled person erode values and personal standards.
    d. Abnormal behaviors are more prevalent among some social classes than others.

15. ''The kinds of stresses and conflicts that people experience in their daily interactions with others can promote and maintain abnormal behavior.'' This statement is consistent with the _____ model of abnormality.
    a. sociocultural   c. humanistic
    b. behavioral   d. psychoanalytic

16. According to the text, proponents of which model are most likely to take the position that there is no such thing as abnormal behavior?
    a. the sociocultural model   c. the behavioral model
    b. the psychoanalytic model   d. the medical model

17. Many people with psychological disorders come from broken homes and low-income backgrounds. To understand the effects of these and similar

conditions on abnormal behavior, a comprehensive diagnosis must include
insights from the:
    a.   behavioral model.   c.   humanistic model.
    b.   psychoanalytic model.   d.   sociocultural model.

18. Deciding that you suffer from the same sorts of problems you read about is
called the:
    a.   medical student's disease.   c.   self-fulfilling prophecy.
    b.   halo effect.   d.   self-delusional approach.

19. The purpose of the *DSM-IV-R* is to:
    a.   diagnose physical disorders.
    b.   provide a description of an individual's disorder.
    c.   define the treatments for particular types of disorders.
    d.   reveal the cause of behavior disorders.

20. In the *DSM-IV-R* there are approximately _____ different diagnostic
categories.
    a.   50   c.   200
    b.   100   d.   500

21. Which of the following pieces of information is not included in the
DSM-IV-R?
    a.   classification   c.   prognosis
    b.   description   d.   cause

22. Which classification would be found in the *DSM-IV-R*?
    a.   neurosis   c.   psychosis
    b.   mood disorders   d.   insanity

23. According to the text, which of the following is **not** a reasonable criticism
of the *DSM-IV-R*?
    a.   Mental disorders are classified into a ''category'' rather than along
        a continuum.
    b.   The *DSM-IV-R* materials usually do not reflect changing views in
        society about mental disorders, since the manual is updated only every
        fifteen years.
    c.   The *DSM-IV-R*'s system of classification may be too heavily influenced
        by the medical model.
    d.   A diagnosis may become an explanation for a problem.

24. The term used to describe nervousness and fear that has no apparent
justification and impairs normal daily functioning is:
    a.   psychosomatic disorder.   c.   anxiety disorder.
    b.   personality disorder.   d.   neurotic disorder.

25. When someone experiences long-term chronic worry without knowing why, the
diagnosis is usually:
    a.   generalized anxiety disorder.   c.   panic attack.
    b.   insomnia.   d.   microphobia.

26. Feelings of impending doom or even death paired with sudden and overwhelming
bodily reactions are typical symptoms of:
    a.   obsessive-compulsive disorder.   c.   personality disorder.
    b.   panic attack.   d.   generalized anxiety disorder.

27. Sue was having a disagreement with her fiance when she suddenly became extremely anxious and felt a sense of impending, unavoidable doom. Her heart beat rapidly, she was short of breath, became faint and dizzy, and felt as if she might die. Sue was experiencing:
    a. obsessive-compulsive disorder.   c. generalized anxiety disorder.
    b. panic disorder.   d. phobic disorder.

28. The psychiatrist listened patiently as his client revealed a series of episodes involving irrational fears of water. The psychiatrist probably labeled the client's symptoms as:
    a. obsessive-compulsive disorder.   c. organic reactions.
    b. phobic reactions.   d. schizophrenic reactions.

29. Sarah is terrified to ride in an elevator in any building. She is especially bothered by the small, confined space and the fact that she is ''trapped'' until the elevator doors open. Usually, she avoids this unpleasantness by refusing to ride in elevators. Sarah is experiencing:
    a. phobic disorder.   c. tension disorder.
    b. panic disorder.   d. freeform disorder.

30. Sandra has been having a difficult time at college, since she has been very tense and anxious during her professors' lectures. She has been much better lately because she distracts herself by counting the number of times her professors say ''the'' during their lectures. Sandra's ''counting'' suggests she is experiencing:
    a. obsessive-compulsive disorder.   c. panic disorder.
    b. phobic disorder.   d. generalized anxiety disorder.

31. Psychological difficulties that take on a physical form but have no actual physical or physiological abnormality are called:
    a. somatoform disorders.   c. psychophysical disorders.
    b. psychological disorders.   d. freeform disorders.

32. The lead singer for a heavy metal group finds that, two or three hours before an important concert, he cannot talk or sing. The group's doctor cannot find any medical reason for the singer's problem. The doctor is also surprised that the singer seems unconcerned. If the singer's symptoms are the result of a psychological disorder, it would most likely be diagnosed as:
    a. obsessive-compulsive disorder.   c. panic disorder.
    b. conversion disorder.   d. somatoform disorder.

33. A woman seeks treatment for her behavioral disorder. A clinical psychologist evaluates her and tells her that she has multiple personalities. This woman is experiencing:
    a. schizophrenic disorder.   c. dissociative disorder.
    b. conversion disorder.   d. somatoform disorder.

34. The main character in the book *Sybil* suffered from:
    a. schizophrenia.   c. disordered personality.
    b. dissociative personality.   d. multiple personality.

35. Together, multiple personality, amnesia, and dissociative fugue are called:
    a. depressive disorders.   c. somatoform disorders.
    b. schizophrenic disorders.   d. dissociative disorders.

36. Unable to account for the past three weeks, Portland native Tony X could recall memories prior to his amnesia, but could not relate how he arrived in Tucson. The above description exemplifies:
    a. multiple personality.   c. hypochondriasis.
    b. dissociative fugue.   d. panic attack.

37. What is one difference between dissociative fugue and dissociative amnesia?
    a. In fugue, memory can be restored with drugs.
    b. In amnesia, the memory loss is temporary.
    c. In fugue, past memory is eventually regained.
    d. In amnesia, the memories are physically lost.

38. The most common problem experienced in outpatient clinics is:
    a. depression.   c. personality disorders.
    b. anxiety disorders.   d. dissociative disorders.

39. A bipolar disorder is one in which an individual has:
    a. opposing phobias.
    b. alternation of mania and depression.
    c. a split personality.
    d. alternation of phobia and panic.

40. According to the text, which mental disorder below is generally the most severe and debilitating to the afflicted person?
    a. panic disorder   c. schizophrenic disorder
    b. hypochondriasis   d. obsessive-compulsive disorder

41. According to the text, the most overwhelming characteristic of schizophrenia is:
    a. loss of touch with reality.   c. severe mood swings.
    b. repetitive ritualistic behavior. d. split personality.

42. When minor symptoms of schizophrenia follow a severe case or episode, the disorder is called:
    a. disorganized schizophrenia.   c. paranoid schizophrenia.
    b. catatonic schizophrenia.   d. residual schizophrenia.

43. Which mental disturbance below is most likely to result in the afflicted person's using language in ways that do not follow conventional linguistic rules?
    a. schizophrenia   c. dissociative fugue
    b. multiple personality   d. depressive disorder

44. According to your text, process schizophrenia is different from reactive schizophrenia, because with reactive schizophrenia, the patient:
    a. experiences a sudden and conspicuous onset of symptoms.
    b. is less withdrawn.
    c. may be dangerously aggressive and abusive to others.
    d. is less likely to have a hereditary basis for the disorder.

45. _____ schizophrenia is characterized by gradual onset, general withdrawal from the world, blunted emotions, and poor prognosis.
    a. Paranoid   c. Process
    b. Catatonic   d. Reactive

46. Schizophrenia produces many dramatic and debilitating changes in a person
    affected with this disorder. Which alternative below is not one of them?
    a.   delusions
    b.   multiple personality
    c.   decline from an earlier level of functioning
    d.   withdrawal

47. Which of the following accounts of schizophrenia assumes that inappropriate
    behavior is learned by attending to stimuli that are not related to normal
    social interaction?
    a.   learned helplessness hypothesis   c.   predisposition model
    b.   dopamine hypothesis   d.   learned-inattention theory

48. According to the text, personality disorder is best characterized by:
    a.   firmly held beliefs with little basis in reality.
    b.   a mixture of symptoms of schizophrenia.
    c.   a set of inflexible, maladaptive traits.
    d.   an extended sense of euphoria and elation.

ESSAY QUESTIONS   *Recite and Review:* _____

Essay Question 12.1: *Defining Mental Illness*

Discuss the implications of Rosenhan's study in which he and eight others faked mental illness in order to challenge the ability of mental hospitals to distinguish abnormal behavior from normal and the effects of labeling. What are the scientific issues related to his study? Are there any ethical issues?

_____

_____

_____

_____

_____

_____

_____

_____

_____

_____

_____

_____

_____

_____

_____

_____

_____

_____

_____

_____

_____

_____

Essay Question 12.2: *Schizophrenia*

Describe the types of schizophrenia, its symptoms, and its causes. Compare the differing theories concerning the cause of schizophrenia.

_____

_____

_____

_____

_____

_____

_____

_____

_____

_____

_____

_____

_____

_____

_____

_____

_____

_____

_____

_____

_____

ACTIVITIES AND PROJECTS

1. Review the models of abnormality described in the text: psychoanalytical, medical, behavioral, cognitive, humanistic, and sociocultural. Which of these models appeals to you the most? Which the least? Next, find the key issues in Chapter 1. Does the way in which these models answer these key issues affect their appeal or lack of appeal to you? What measure would you use to test the usefulness or value of each of these models? Can your measure be supported?

13

TREATMENT OF ABNORMAL BEHAVIOR

DETAILED OUTLINE

Survey: ____

This detailed outline contains all the headings in Chapter 13: The Treatment of Abnormal Behavior. If you are using the SQ3R method, then an examination of the outline is the best way to begin your survey of the chapter.

Prologue: Alice, Martha, and Sandy
Looking Ahead

Psychotherapy: Psychological Approaches to Treatment
  Psychodynamic treatment: Piercing the unconscious
      Psychoanalysis: Freud's therapy
      Contemporary alternatives to psychoanalysis
  Behavioral approaches to treatment
      Classical conditioning approaches
      Observational learning and modeling
      Operant conditioning approaches
      How does behavior therapy stack up?
  Cognitive approaches to therapy
▪ **Recap and Review I**

  Humanistic approaches to therapy
      Client-centered therapy
      Existential therapy
      Gestalt therapy
      Humanistic approaches in perspective
  Group therapy
      Family therapy
  Comparing psychotherapeutic approaches
  Evaluating psychotherapy
  Which kind of therapy works best?
Psychology at Work Racial and Ethnic Factors in Treatment: Should
  Therapists Be Color-Blind?
▪ **Recap and Review II**

Biological Treatment Approaches: The Medical Model at Work
  Drug therapy
      Antipsychotic drugs
      Antidepressant drugs
The Cutting Edge Prozac: Miracle Drug or Media Madness?
      Antidepressant drugs (continued)
      Antianxiety drugs
  Electroconvulsive therapy (ECT)
  Psychosurgery
  Biological treatment in perspective: Can abnormal behavior be cured?

Community psychology: Focus on prevention
The Informed Consumer of Psychology Choosing the Right Therapist
- **Recap and Review III**

Looking Back
Key Terms and Concepts

Now that you have surveyed the chapter, read **Looking Ahead**, pages 454–455.
> *Question:* ____
>   *Read:* ____

Focus on the questions on page 455.

CONCEPTS AND LEARNING OBJECTIVES   *Survey:* ____

These are the concepts and the learning objects for Chapter 13. Read them
carefully as part of your preliminary survey of the chapter.

Concept 1: Psychotherapy seeks to remedy psychological difficulties.
    Psychodynamic approaches attempt to resolve unconscious conflicts and
    behavioral approaches apply learning theory to therapy.

1. Define psychotherapy and distinguish its main types. (pp. 454–456)

2. Describe how psychodynamic therapy approaches treatment of abnormal
   behavior, and discuss the major techniques and concepts employed by
   psychodynamic therapists. (pp. 457–459)

3. Describe the behavioral approaches to therapy, including aversive
   conditioning and systematic desensitization, observational learning, and
   the use of operant conditioning principles. (pp. 459–463)

4. Discuss and distinguish the cognitive behavioral therapy approaches of
   rational emotive therapy and cognitive therapy. (pp. 463–465)

Concept 2: Humanistic psychotherapy focuses on issues related to the person's
    taking responsibility for his or her own actions and solving issues regarding
    the meaning of life. Psychotherapy is considered to be effective, but some
    therapies are more appropriate for certain disorders than are others.

5. Describe the three kinds of humanistic therapy included in the text:
   Rogers's client-centered therapy, existential therapy, and gestalt
   therapy; and describe group therapy. (pp. 466–470)

6. Outline the dimensions used to compare psychotherapy, the methods used
   to evaluate psychotherapy, and arguments that support the interpretation
   of the success or failure of psychotherapies. (pp. 470–475)

Concept 3: Drug therapy has made psychotic patients calmer, alleviated
    depression, and calmed anxiety. Electroconvulsive therapy and psychosurgery
    are controversial treatments of last resort. The community health movement
    now must cope with deinstitutionalized patients and has also led to the
    development of hot lines and campus crisis centers.

7. Name and describe drugs used in the treatment of abnormal behavior and

discuss the problems and controversies surrounding their use. (pp. 476-479)

8. Describe the medical techniques of electroconvulsive therapy and psychosurgery, and discuss the effectiveness of drug and medical therapies. (pp. 479-480)

9. Describe possible approaches to the prevention of abnormal behavior through the use of the community approach and deinstitutionalization; also discuss suggestions one may follow in selecting a psychotherapist. (pp. 480-483)

CHAPTER SUMMARY

There are several ways you can use this summary as part of your systematic study plan. You may read each concept summary and then read the corresponding pages in the text, or you may read the entire summary and then read the entire chapter in the text. As you finish each section, complete the **Recap and Review** questions that are supplied in the text.

Concept 1: **Prologue and Looking Ahead**   *Survey:* ____
              Psychotherapy: Psychological Approaches   *Read:* ____
              to Treatment

                                                                 Pages 454-465

The Prologue introduces three different approaches to therapy to illustrate that therapy is not a uniform process. There are today over 250 different kinds of treatment. The common goal of therapy is relief of the psychological disorder and enabling individuals to achieve richer, more meaningful lives. Psychologically based therapy is called **psychotherapy**, a process in which a patient (client) and a professional work together to deal with psychological difficulties. **Biologically based therapy** depends on drugs and other medical procedures. Many therapists today draw upon the large number of therapies for the approach most suited to the client, and is considered an **eclectic approach to therapy**.

   Psychodynamic therapy assumes that the primary causes of abnormal behavior are unresolved conflicts from the past and anxiety over unconscious impulses. The **defense mechanisms** that individuals use to guard against anxiety do not bury these anxieties completely, and they emerge in the form of **neurotic symptoms**. Freud said that the way to deal with the unwanted desires and past conflicts was to confront them, to make them conscious. The role of the psychodynamic therapist is then to explore the unconscious conflicts and help the patient understand them.

   Freudian therapy is called **psychoanalysis**, and it tends to be lengthy and expensive. Patients meet with their therapists four to six times a week for several years. The technique often used is called **free association**, during which the patient will say anything that comes to mind, no matter how insignificant. The ramblings are assumed to be clues from the unconscious, and the therapist looks for connections in the patient's words. Another method is **dream interpretation**; again the therapist looks for clues to the unconscious in the dream. People censor thoughts when they dream, so there is a distinction between the **manifest content of dreams**, or the description of the dream, and the **latent content of dreams**, or the message of the dreams. Sometimes the patient will unconsciously resist the probing. **Resistance** refers to an inability to discuss or reveal particular memories or thoughts. The patient finds it difficult to talk about these particular issues. **Transference** is a phenomenon in which the relationship between the analyst and the patient becomes emotionally charged, and the analyst symbolically takes on the role of significant others from the patient's past. Transference is used to help the patient re-create the past and work through it more positively.

Today psychodynamic psychotherapy is shorter, and the therapist takes a more active role, controlling the course of therapy and emphasizing the present more than the past. It is still criticized for being time-consuming and expensive, and only certain kinds of patients are well-suited for this kind of therapy. It is difficult to prove that psychodynamic therapies are successful, and some critics challenge the entire theoretical basis for the approach.

The principles of reinforcement are central to **behavioral treatment approaches** which suggest that both abnormal and normal behavior is learned. To modify abnormal behavior, new behaviors must be learned. Behavioral psychologists are not interested in the past history of the individual, focusing instead on the current behavior. Classical conditioning principles are applied to behaviors like alcoholism, smoking, and drug abuse, with a technique known as aversive conditioning. In **aversive conditioning**, the unwanted behavior is linked with a stimulus that produces an unpleasant response, like a drug that produces vomiting when mixed with alcohol. The long-term effectiveness of the approach is questionable. The most successful classical conditioning technique is known as **systematic desensitization** in which a person is taught to relax and is then gradually exposed to an anxiety-provoking stimulus. One approach involves the development of a **hierarchy of fears** that the patient can use to become exposed to less threatening stimuli at first. The patient relaxes and then imagines the first stimulus on the list for as long as he or she can remain relaxed. The patient then progresses through the hierarchy, eventually actually being placed in the situation or exposed to the stimuli that cause anxiety. Systematic desensitization has been used successfully with phobias, anxiety disorders, and impotence.

Observational learning is used in therapy by **modeling** appropriate behaviors. People can be taught skills and ways of handling anxiety by observing a model cope with the same situation. The ''Fearless Peer'' approach helps children overcome their fear of dogs by having another child pet and play with a dog.

Operant conditioning techniques are used in settings where rewards and punishments can be controlled. One example is that of the **token economy** in which individuals are rewarded with tokens that can be exchanged for desired objects or opportunities. **Contingency contracting** is a variant of token economy, and it requires a written agreement between the therapist and the client. The contract sets behavioral goals to be reached and specifies the consequences of reaching the goals. Depending on the problem addressed, behavior therapy claims success rates between 50 and 90 percent.

Cognitive approaches to therapy attempt to change faulty cognitions held by patients about themselves and the world. The therapies are typically based on learning principles and thus are often called **cognitive-behavioral approaches**. **Rational-emotive therapy** is one of the best examples of the cognitive approach. The therapist attempts to restructure the person's belief system into a more realistic, rational, and logical set of views. Therapists take an active and directive role in therapy, directly challenging patterns of thought that appear to be irrational. Another form of therapy is Aaron Beck's **cognitive therapy**. He is less confrontive and more like a teacher. Clients are given assignments to help them uncover information that will lead them to think more appropriately.

Concept 2:   Psychotherapy: Psychological Approaches
          to Treatment (Continued)

Survey: ____
Read: ____

Pages 466-475

Humanistic psychotherapy depends upon the perspective of self-responsibility as the basis for treatment. The view is that we control our own behavior, make choices about how to live, and it is up to us to solve our problems. Humanistic therapists see themselves as guides or facilitators.

Nondirective counseling refers to approaches that do not offer interpretations or answers to problems. First practiced by Carl Rogers, **client-centered** therapy was founded on the nondirective approach. Rogers attempted to establish a warm and accepting environment in order to enable the client to make realistic and constructive choices about life. The therapist must provide a sense of **unconditional positive regard,** an acceptance of the individual without conditions no matter what attitude is expressed by the client. It is rare to find client-centered therapy practiced in its pure form because therapies usually now include some directive aspects.

Concern with the meaning and uniqueness of life has given rise to **existential therapy**, an approach based on the problem of dealing with personal freedom and the anguish, fear, and concern that accompanies such fear. The goal of existential therapy is to help the client come to grips with freedom, to find his or her place in the world, and to develop a system of values that gives meaning to life. The therapist is more directive, and probes and challenges the client's views.

Gestalt therapy has the goal of integrating the client's thoughts and feelings into a whole, or gestalt. The approach was developed by Fritz Perls. He asked the client to go back and work on unfinished business, playing the part of the angry father and taking other roles of a conflict. This leads the client to increase perspectives on a situation. Humanistic approaches lack specificity, and the form of treatment is most appropriate for the same type of person treated by psychoanalysis. However, the emphasis on human responsibility and uniqueness and on creating an environment that is supportive can help clients find solutions to psychological difficulties.

Group therapy is a form of treatment that has several people meet with a therapist at the same time. Problems, usually one held in common with all group members, are discussed with the group. Members of the group provide social support and share how they may have dealt with similar situations. Groups vary according to therapeutic approach and degree of guidance offered by the therapist. Groups are economical, but critics argue that they do not replace the one-on-one aspect of individual therapy.

Family therapy is a specialized form of group therapy that involves two or more members of a family. Therapists focus on the entire family system rather than only on the family member with the problem, and each family member is expected to contribute to the solution. Family therapists assume that family members engage in set patterns of behavior, and the goal of therapy is to get the family to adopt more constructive behaviors.

Psychotherapy can be classified using several dimensions. They are: directive versus nondirective approaches, inner control of behavior versus external control of behavior, long-term versus short-term therapy, historical versus here-and-now focus, and cognitive change versus behavior change. These dimensions are more on a continuum rather than either/or distinctions.

Deciding which therapy is appropriate for which kind of problem is a difficult task, but a more critical question is whether any psychotherapy is effective. Hans Eysenck published an article in 1952 that challenged whether psychodynamic therapy was effective. He compared a group receiving treatment with one composed of people on a waiting list for treatment. The group that received no therapy had done just as well as the group that received therapy. The symptoms went away due to **spontaneous remission**, or recovery without treatment. Eysenck's study was challenged on the basis of the data he used. One main problem with studies of the effectiveness of psychotherapy is that the data is primarily self-reported data from the client and the therapist. Since there are no agreed-upon criteria for mental health, even independent judgment is difficult. Eysenck's early work resulted in a number of studies, most of which conclude that therapy does work.

The question of which therapy is the best still remains. The methodological issues include questioning the nature of cure. Reducing depression-related anxiety using psychodynamic treatment may not be equivalent to reducing phobia-related anxiety using behavior therapy. One solution is to compare the cure rates for treatment groups and for nontreated control groups. Another treatment can be compared similarly. Then the two treatments can be compared on their cure rates relative to their control groups. In a study based on this method, therapies were 70 to 85 percent more successful than nontreated controls. Other studies have supported this data. The National Institute of Mental Health is currently conducting a large study that compares cognitive therapy, interpersonal therapy, drug therapy, and placebos in depressed patients. In a pilot study, the three therapies had success rates of about 40 percent and the placebo had a success rate of about 20 percent. Evidence suggests that there is only a minor difference between therapies, and that, for most people, therapy is better than no therapy. In a small number of cases, people are actually harmed by therapy. It is also clear that particular kinds of therapy are also more appropriate for some than for others. Psychodynamic and humanistic therapies work well with problems that require insight; behavioral therapy works well with problems that arise because of circumstances like a phobia or lack of specific skills. Some therapies may be more appropriate to specific types of people. Therapists must take into account how the factors of race, ethnicity, cultural heritage, and social class affect the nature of psychological problems and the course of treatment. The number of eclectic approaches to therapy is increasing, and therapists have a number of treatment techniques from which to select.

Concept 3:   Biological Treatment Approaches: *Survey:* ____
The Medical Model at Work   *Read:* ____

Pages 476-483

Biologically based treatments that treat brain chemical imbalances and other neurological factors directly are regularly used for some problems. In **drug therapy**, drugs are given that alleviate symptoms for a number of psychological disturbances. In the mid-1950s, **antipsychotic drugs** were introduced, causing a major change in the treatment of patients in mental hospitals. These drugs alleviate symptoms related to the patient's loss of touch with reality, agitation, and overactivity. Antipsychotic drugs greatly improved the atmosphere in the hospital by calming patients. The drug introduced was **chlorpromazine**, and it proved successful in treating the symptoms of schizophrenia. Drug therapy is now used for more than 90 percent of the hospitalized patients. Antipsychotic drugs work by blocking dopamine production at sites where the electrical impulses travel across nerve receptors. The drugs do not cure, and they have severe side effects, including dryness of mouth, dizziness, and tremors. They also have a numbing effect on the emotional responses of patients. **Antidepressant drugs** are used to improve the moods of severely depressed patients. Antidepressant drugs work by increasing the concentration of certain neurotransmitters. Tricyclic drugs increase the concentration of norepinephrine and serotonin; bupropion drugs increase dopamine. Antidepressant drugs can produce long-term recoveries from depression. One antidepressant, **fluxetine** - also known as **Prozac** - has been the center of recent controversy. Prozac blocks the reabsorption of the neurotransmitter serotonin. Though it has few side effects, some have claimed that it made them suicidal and a few have claimed that it drove them to homicidal behavior (the ''Prozac defense''). One fear is that because of its popularity, people with minor depression will seek prescriptions of the drug rather than seek more suitable treatment. **Lithium**, a form of simple mineral salt, has been used to treat bipolar disorders. It ends manic episodes 70 percent of the time; though its success with depression is not as good. Unlike other treatments, lithium is seen as a preventive medication. People who have had manic-depressive episodes in the past take small doses as a means of preventing the return of the symptoms.

Antianxiety drugs - Valium, Miltown, Librium - are the drugs most prescribed by physicians. Antianxiety drugs reduce the anxiety level experienced by reducing excitability and increasing drowsiness. They have side effects that include fatigue and dependence. When combined with alcohol, some are lethal. The drugs also mask the source of the anxiety and allow the person simply to ignore the cause of the problem.

On the mistaken notion that epileptics - who experience convulsions - do not have schizophrenia, physicians in the 1930s found a way to induce convulsions using electric shocks. **Electroconvulsive therapy** (ECT) is administered by passing an electric current of 70 to 150 volts through the head of a patient for about one-twenty-fifth of a second. The patient is usually sedated and given muscle relaxants to prevent violent contractions. ECT is controversial because of its side effects, which include disorientation, confusion, and memory loss. Many patients fear ECT, and some people believe that it may cause permanent neurological damage. It continues to be used because it does help severely depressed patients when other treatments are ineffective.

Psychosurgery is brain surgery used to alleviate psychological symptoms. An early procedure was prefrontal lobotomy in which parts of the frontal lobes are removed or destroyed. The patients are then less subject to emotional impulses. Patients also suffered personality changes, becoming bland and unemotional. Patients can also die from the treatment. Drug therapies ended the frequent use of psychosurgery, and today it is used to alleviate problems like severe and uncontrollable pain. More precise surgical procedures are used with only very small areas of the brain being destroyed.

Psychotherapy and medical therapy are intended to restore the patient to a previous state of health; **community psychology** is intended to help prevent or minimize psychological disorders. In the 1960s, plans were made for a nationwide network of community mental-health centers that could provide inexpensive mental-health services, short-term therapy, and educational programs. Former mental patients were returning to the community in a process known as **deinstitutionalization**. The community centers were expected to ensure that the deinstitutionalized patients continued to get proper treatment and that their civil rights were maintained. The original goals were not met; mental disorders have not declined. Many people who need treatment do not get it. Positive results include the development of ''hot lines'' where people can call for help and talk to a trained person immediately. The college crisis center also grew out of this movement. The volunteers on hot lines receive careful training for telephone counseling and are prepared to respond to a variety of situations and to make referrals for additional treatment.

Whether one has chosen the right therapist can be determined by considering the following: the relationship between client and therapist should be comfortable, the therapist should have appropriate credentials and training, clients should feel that they are making progress, and clients should be aware that they must contribute effort to the therapy.

♦ Now that you have surveyed, questioned, and read the chapter and completed the **Recap and Review** questions, review **Looking Back**, page 484.   *Review:* ____

♦ For additional practice through recitation and review, test your knowledge of the chapter material by answering the questions in the **Key Word Drill**, the **Practice Questions**, and the **Essay Questions**.

KEY WORD DRILL   *Recite:* ____

The following **Fill in the Blank** and **Matching Questions** test key words from the text. Check your answers with the Answer Key in the back of the *Study Guide*.

FILL IN THE BLANK

1. _____ is the process in which a client and a professional attempt to remedy the client's psychological difficulties.

2. _____ learning occurs by watching others' behavior and the consequences of that behavior and then _____, or imitating the behavior.

3. The examination of a patient's dreams to find clues to the unconscious conflicts and problems being experienced is called _____ _____.

4. Recovery without treatment is called _____ _____.

5. _____ _____ is a therapeutic technique in which the therapist creates a warm, supportive environment to allow the client to understand and work out problems.

6. In most therapies, the therapist tries to establish a sense of _____ _____, an attitude that is supportive of the client regardless of his or her words or actions.

7. The medical technique of _____ attempts to control psychological problems through drugs, and the technique called _____ involves brain surgery.

8. According to Freud, _____ symptoms are abnormal behavior brought about by anxiety associated with unwanted conflicts and impulses.

9. _____ refers to the approach to therapy that uses a variety of treatment methods rather than just one.

10. _____ required the transfer of former mental patients from institutions into the community.

11. Treatment involving the administration of an electric current to a patient's head is known as _____ _____.

12. _____ _____ refers to the surgical destruction of a patient's frontal lobes to improve the control of emotionality.

MATCHING QUESTIONS

_____13. biologically based
therapy

_____14. psychodynamic
therapy

_____15. psychoanalysis

_____16. behavioral treatment
approaches

_____17. cognitive approaches
to therapy

_____18. rational-emotive
therapy

_____19. cognitive therapy

a. Basic sources of abnormal behavior are
unresolved past conflicts and anxiety.

b. Attempts to restructure one's belief into a
more realistic, rational, and logical
system.

c. Appropriate treatment consists of learning
new behavior or unlearning maladaptive
behavior.

d. A form of psychodynamic therapy that often
lasts for many years.

e. Uses drugs and other medical procedures to
improve psychological functioning.

f. People's faulty cognitions about themselves
and the world are changed to more accurate
ones.

g. People are taught to change illogical
thoughts about themselves and the world.

_____20. free association

_____21. manifest content

_____22. latent content

_____23. resistance

_____24. transference

a. A patient's transfer of certain strong
feelings for others to the analyst.

b. The ''true'' message hidden within dreams.

c. The patient says everything that comes to
mind, providing insights into the patient's
unconscious.

d. An inability or unwillingness to discuss or
reveal particular memories, thoughts, or
motivations.

e. The surface description and interpretation
of dreams.

_____25. aversive conditioning

_____26. systematic
desensitization

_____27. token system

_____28. contingency
contracting

a. A person is rewarded for performing desired
behaviors.

b. Breaks unwanted habits by associating the
habits with very unpleasant stimuli.

c. Requires a written contract between a
therapist and a client that sets behavioral
goals and rewards.

d. A stimulus that evokes pleasant feelings is
repeatedly paired with a stimulus that
evokes anxiety.

_____ 29. client-centered therapy

_____ 30. humanistic therapy

_____ 31. existential therapy

_____ 32. gestalt therapy

_____ 33. group therapy

_____ 34. family therapy

_____ 35. community psychology

a. People discuss problems with others who have similar problems.

b. The therapist reflects back the patient's statements in a way that helps the patient to find solutions.

c. People have control of their behavior, can make choices about their lives, and are essentially responsible for solving their own problems.

d. A movement aimed toward preventing psychological disorders.

e. Addresses the meaning of life, allowing a client to devise a system of values that gives purpose to his or her life.

f. Attempts to integrate a client's thoughts, feelings, and behavior into a whole.

g. Family as a unit to which each member contributes.

_____ 36. antipsychotic drugs

_____ 37. antidepressant drugs

_____ 38. antianxiety drugs

_____ 39. chlorpromazine

_____ 40. lithium

_____ 41. fluxetine

a. Prozac, a widely used antidepressant drug.

b. Used in the treatment of schizophrenia.

c. Improves a patient's mood and feeling of well-being.

d. Used in the treatment of bipolar disorders.

e. Alleviate stress and feelings of apprehension.

f. Temporarily alleviate symptoms such as agitation and overactivity.

PRACTICE QUESTIONS   *Recite and Review:* _____

Test your knowledge of the chapter material by answering these **True-False** and **Multiple Choice Questions**. Check your answers with the Answer Key in the back of the *Study Guide*.

TRUE-FALSE QUESTIONS

T   F   1. If a patient fails to meet an appointment or is reluctant to discuss a particular topic, a psychoanalyst might interpret this as transference.

T   F   2.   A psychoanalyst would be more concerned with your recollection
                 of a dream than the meaning you place on what happened last
                 week.

T   F   3.   Behaviorists and psychoanalysts alike are concerned with the
                 causes of abnormal behavior.

T   F   4.   Dr. Morgan uses modeling, role play and a token system in order
                 to teach children adaptive social skills. Dr. Morgan is more
                 than likely a behaviorist.

T   F   5.   Rational-emotive therapy is an example of the cognitive
                 behavioral approach to therapy.

T   F   6.   Humanistic therapists view the doctor as the expert, having
                 primary responsibility for treatment.

T   F   7.   Unconditional positive regard is expressed by the therapist
                 toward the client in the client-centered approach to
                 psychotherapy.

T   F   8.   Eysenck, investigating different psychotherapies in a 1952
                 study, found that such treatments were approximately 50-70
                 percent more effective than expected.

T   F   9.   The primary use of antianxiety drugs is to overcome depression.

T   F   10.   More than half of all Americans have a family member who has
                 taken an antianxiety drug at one time or another.

MULTIPLE CHOICE QUESTIONS

1. According to the text, what is the common goal of all types of therapy?
    a.   integrating the individual into society
    b.   relieving psychological disorders
    c.   relieving fears and anxiety
    d.   reassembling the parts of the personality

2. According to the text, there are over _____ different kinds of
    treatment.
    a.   50   c.   175
    b.   100   d.   250

3. According to the text, the category of therapy in which change is brought
    about through discussions and interactions between client and professional
    is called:
    a.   eclectic therapy.   c.   psychotherapy.
    b.   semantic therapy   d.   interpersonal therapy.

4. An eclectic approach to therapy is one that:
    a.   uses a combination of different methods.
    b.   uses an unorthodox method.
    c.   uses techniques based on hidden motives.
    d.   uses institutionalization along with therapy.

5. Clients requiring some form of medical treatment are typically treated by a:
   a. psychiatric nurse.   c. psychiatrist.
   b. counseling psychologist.   d. clinical psychologist.

6. Based on the descriptions in the text, if you were having trouble adjusting to the death of a friend, who would you be most likely to see?
   a. psychiatrist   c. psychiatric social worker
   b. psychoanalyst   d. counseling psychologist

7. Charles is the director of guidance at a student mental health clinic. He holds a degree appropriate to his position, so he must hold a doctorate or master's degree in:
   a. psychiatric social work.   c. clinical psychology.
   b. counseling psychology.   d. educational psychology.

8. The basic premise of psychodynamic therapy is the notion that abnormal behavior is:
   a. repressing normal behaviors that need to be uncovered.
   b. the result of the ego repressing the superego.
   c. rooted in unresolved past conflicts, buried in the unconscious.
   d. the result of the ego failing to gain access to consciousness.

9. According to Freud, in order to protect our egos from the unwanted entry of unacceptable unconscious thoughts and desires, we all use:
   a. transference.   c. systematic desensitization.
   b. aversive conditioning.   d. defense mechanisms.

10. According to Freud, neurotic symptoms are caused by:
    a. defense mechanisms.   c. inappropriate choices.
    b. anxiety.   d. contingency contracting.

11. Listed below are terms associated with psychodynamic therapy. Which alternative below does not belong?
    a. hierarchy of fears   c. defense mechanisms
    b. neurotic symptoms   d. transference

12. What technique is used in psychoanalysis to help the patient remember the experiences of a past relationship?
    a. transcendence   c. translation
    b. transference   d. transrotation

13. According to the text, most psychodynamic psychotherapists prefer:
    a. minority patients.   c. YAVIS patients.
    b. white patients.   d. schizophrenic patients.

14. Which of the following approaches to therapy would be **least** concerned with the underlying causes of abnormal behavior?
    a. psychoanalytic   c. eclectic
    b. behavioral   d. humanistic

15. Which problem below is least likely to be treated with aversive conditioning?
    a. substance (drug) abuse   c. smoking
    b. depression   d. alcoholism

16. What happens to the reaction to alcohol following aversive conditioning for alcoholism?
    a.   The reaction takes on that response associated with the aversion.
    b.   There is no longer a craving for the alcohol.
    c.   There is a fear of the alcohol.
    d.   The alcohol becomes a source of anxiety.

17. A technique used to reduce anxiety or eliminate phobias, which is based on classical conditioning, is called:
    a.   biofeedback.   c.   systematic desensitization.
    b.   behavior modification.   d.   aversive conditioning.

18. Which of the following is **not** a component of systematic desensitization?
    a.   operant conditioning   c.   hierarchy of fears
    b.   relaxation   d.   imagery

19. There is a saying, ''Monkey see, monkey do!'' This saying illustrates:
    a.   observational learning.   c.   systematic desensitization.
    b.   gestalt therapy.   d.   aversive conditioning.

20. The behavioral-treatment approach uses all of the following techniques **except:**
    a.   aversive conditioning.   c.   modeling.
    b.   systematic desensitization.   d.   symptom substitution.

21. According to the text, in rational-emotive therapy, the therapist challenges the client's:
    a.   irrational views of the world.   c.   paranoid views of the world.
    b.   egotistical views of the world. d.   defensive views of the world.

22. Peggy, a 17-year-old client of Dr. Ertle, explains, ''I answered a question wrong in history class and made a perfect fool of myself.'' In response Dr. Ertle says, ''Is it important for you to be perfectly competent in every area of your life?'' Dr. Ertle is using:
    a.   behavioral therapy.   c.   humanistic therapy.
    b.   rational-emotive therapy.   d.   existential therapy.

23. Which therapy assumes people experience unhappiness and psychologically disordered lives because of unrealistic and inappropriate ideas that they hold about themselves and the world?
    a.   rational-emotive therapy   c.   psychoanalytic therapy
    b.   gestalt therapy   d.   behavioral therapy

24. Which of the following approaches to treatment takes the view that it is primarily the responsibility of the client to make needed changes?
    a.   behavioral therapy   c.   humanistic therapy
    b.   rational-emotive therapy   d.   psychoanalytic therapy

25. The approach that is the best known of the humanistic therapies and assumes at the outset that a person's troubles reflect unfulfilled potential is called:
    a.   rational-emotive therapy.   c.   systematic desensitization.
    b.   gestalt therapy.   d.   client-centered therapy.

26. In humanistic therapy, unconditional positive regard is provided to the client:
    a.   as a reinforcement when goals have been met.
    b.   as part of the contingency contract.
    c.   no matter what the client says or does.
    d.   to help resolve inner conflicts.

27. According to the text, the goal of client-centered therapy is to enable people to reach the potential for:
    a.   getting in touch with reality.
    b.   understanding the unconscious.
    c.   taking control of their thoughts.
    d.   self-actualization.

28. According to the text, which of the following therapies is most closely associated with the concepts of freedom, values, and the meaning of human existence?
    a.   behavioral therapy   c.   humanistic therapy
    b.   rational-emotive therapy   d.   existential therapy

29. If a therapist asks you to act out some past conflict or difficulty in order to complete unfinished business, he or she most likely is using:
    a.   behavior therapy.   c.   rational-emotive therapy.
    b.   existential therapy.   d.   gestalt therapy.

30. Helen is in therapy with a psychotherapist to work through her feelings about her recent broken engagement. She is telling her therapist that she really didn't love her fiance, and that she realized how different she and her fiance are. Suddenly, her therapist says, ''Helen, I heard the words that you just said, but they don't tell the same message that your facial expression and other nonverbal cues do. See if you can sense the differences.'' Helen's therapist is most likely:
    a.   a gestalt therapist.   c.   a client-centered therapist.
    b.   a psychoanalytic therapist.   d.   a behavioral therapist.

31. According to the text, which therapies emphasize establishing inner rather than outer control of behavior?
    a.   psychodynamic and humanistic   c.   psychodynamic and behavioral
    b.   rational-emotive and behavioral   d.   behavioral and humanistic

32. According to the text, psychotherapies are often compared and evaluated in many ways. Which alternative below is **not** one of them?
    a.   cognitive change versus behavioral change
    b.   long-term therapy versus short-term therapy
    c.   personal characteristics versus situational factors
    d.   historical focus versus here-and-now focus

33. Which of the following is **not** used to describe the behavioral approach to therapy?
    a.   directive   c.   environmentalistic
    b.   learned behavior   d.   biological

34. One study showed that cognitive therapy and ''interpersonal'' therapy were
    _____ effective in treating depression compared with drug therapy.
    a.   much more   c.   at least as
    b.   more   d.   less

35. Spontaneous remission refers to:
    a. recovery without treatment.
    b. spontaneous recovery in classical conditioning-based therapies.
    c. return to a state of illness after a period of recovery.
    d. sudden withdrawal from the world into a catatonic state.

36. Generalizing from the discussion in the text, both humanistic and psychoanalytic approaches to therapy are more appropriate for clients who are:
    a. highly verbal.
    b. severely disordered.
    c. experiencing sexually related disorders.
    d. reluctant to converse with someone else.

37. According to the text, chlorpromazine is most commonly used in the treatment of:
    a. mood disorders.   c. schizophrenia.
    b. anxiety disorders.   d. bipolar disorder.

38. According to the text, antipsychotic drugs alleviate psychotic symptoms by:
    a. increasing neurotransmitter function.
    b. blocking the production of dopamine.
    c. slowing down the autonomic nervous system.
    d. sedating the patients.

39. Antidepressant drugs modify the concentrations of some neurotransmitters in the brain. According to the text, which brain chemical below is **not** associated with various antidepressant medications for the treatment of depression?
    a. serotonin   c. acetylcholine
    b. dopamine   d. norepinephrine

40. According to the text, which drug is used to help prevent future occurrences of the behavioral disorder that it is used to treat?
    a. Valium   c. chlorpromazine
    b. Lithium   d. Librium

41. According to the text, which medication would most likely be given to someone experiencing a manic episode?
    a. Lithium   c. chlorpromazine
    b. Valium   d. Librium

42. Antidepressant drugs improve the mood of depressed patients by:
    a. increasing the activity of the autonomic nervous system.
    b. suppressing the function of certain neurotransmitters.
    c. increasing the speed of neural transmission.
    d. increasing the concentration of certain neurotransmitters.

43. Which of the following types of treatment appears actually to cure the disorder, so that when the treatment is discontinued the symptoms tend not to recur?
    a. antipsychotic drugs   c. antianxiety drugs
    b. antidepressant drugs   d. chlorpromazine

44. Which of the following statements about antianxiety drugs is true?
     a.   They are relatively free of side effects.
     b.   They are used primarily in cases of serious anxiety disorder.
     c.   They are the most common drugs prescribed by physicians.
     d.   They eliminate the anxiety as well as its source.

45. Today, electroconvulsive shock treatment (ECT) is usually reserved for severe cases of:
     a.   mania.   c. depression.
     b.   schizophrenia.   d. panic attack.

46. According to the text, which of the following types of treatment is rarely if ever still used?
     a.   electroconvulsive shock therapy   c. psychotherapy
     b.   antipsychotic drugs   d. psychosurgery

47. A procedure by which areas of the brain are removed or destroyed in order to control severe abnormal behaviors is called:
     a.   psychosurgery.   c. electroconvulsive therapy.
     b.   shock therapy.   d. personality therapy.

48. According to the text, which of the following would suggest that you had chosen a good therapist or style of therapy?
     a.   You feel somewhat afraid of the therapist.
     b.   You don't need to put effort into the therapy.
     c.   You feel no particular sense of progress.
     d.   You are involved in the therapy.

ESSAY QUESTIONS   *Recite and Review:* ____

Essay Question 13.1: *The Effectiveness of Psychotherapy*

Describe the reasons why you think that psychotherapy works. Draw upon the principles of psychology that have been discussed in previous chapters, such as learning principles, theories of personality, and theories of development to explain why you think it is effective.

_____

_____

_____

_____

_____

_____

_____

_____

_____

_____

_____

_____

_____

_____

_____

_____

_____

_____

_____

_____

_____

_____

_____

Essay Question 13.2: *Should Electroconvulsive Therapy Be Banned?*

Describe the advantages and disadvantages of electroconvulsive therapy. Do you think that it should be banned from use? Explain your answer.

_____

_____

_____

_____

_____

_____

_____

_____

_____

_____

_____

_____

_____

_____

_____

_____

_____

_____

_____

_____

_____

_____

_____

14

SOCIAL PSYCHOLOGY

DETAILED OUTLINE   *Survey:* ____

This detailed outline contains all the headings in Chapter 14: Social Psychology. If you are using the SQ3R method, then an examination of the outline is the best way to begin your survey of the chapter.

Prologue: David Koresh
Looking Ahead

Attitudes, Behavior, and Persuasion
    Forming and maintaining attitudes
        Classical conditioning and attitudes
        Operant conditioning approaches to attitude acquisition
    Persuasion: Changing attitudes
        Message source
        Characteristics of the message
        Characteristics of the recipient or target
    The link between attitudes and behavior
▪ **Recap and Review I**

Social Cognition: Understanding Others
    Understanding what others are like
        Impression formation
    Attribution processes: Understanding the causes of Behavior
    Biases in attribution: To err is human
        The fundamental attribution bias
        The halo effect
        Assumed-similarity bias
    Self-perception theory: Understanding our own behavior
▪ **Recap and Review II**

Social Influence
    Conformity: Following what others do
        Gender differences in conformity: Fact or fiction?
    Compliance: Submitting to direct social pressure
        The foot in the door: When a small request leads to a larger one
        The door-in-the-face technique: Where a large request leads to a
           smaller one
    Obedience: Obeying direct orders
Psychology at Work The Price Is Right?: The Practice of Social Influence

The Informed Consumer of Psychology Strategies for Maintaining Your Own
  Position
  ▪ **Recap and Review III**

  **Liking and Loving: Interpersonal Attraction and the Development of
  Relationships**
  How do I like thee? Let me count the ways
The Cutting Edge Is Beauty in the Eye of the Baby?
  How do I love thee? Let me count the ways
  Tracing the course of relationships: The rise and fall of liking and
    loving
  The decline of a relationship
  ▪ **Recap and Review IV**

  Aggression and Prosocial Behavior: Hurting and Helping Others
  Hurting others: Aggression
      Instinct approaches: Aggression as a release
      Frustration-aggression approaches: Aggression as a reaction to
        frustration
      Observational learning approaches: Learning to hurt others
      Media aggression: Does it hurt to watch TV?
      The link between aggressive pornography and violence toward women
  Reducing and preventing aggression
  Helping others: The brighter side of human nature
  ▪ **Recap and Review V**

  Looking Back
  Key Terms and Concepts

Now that you have surveyed the chapter, read **Looking Ahead**, pages 488-489.
    Question: ____
        Read: ____

    Focus on the questions on page 489.

CONCEPTS AND LEARNING OBJECTIVES   *Survey:* ____

These are the concepts and the learning objects for Chapter 14. Read them
carefully as part of your preliminary survey of the chapter.

Concept 1: Attitudes are composed of affective, behavioral, and cognitive
    components. People attempt to maintain a consistency between their attitudes
    and behavior.

    1. Define and distinguish the components of attitude; and discuss the
       relationship of attitude and behavior. (pp. 488-490)

    2. Describe the roles of classical and operant conditioning in the formation
       and maintenance of attitudes. (pp. 490-491)

    3. Discuss the means by which attitudes can be changed. (pp. 491-493)

    4. Describe cognitive dissonance theory and self-perception theory and how
       each accounts for the relationship between attitudes and behavior. (pp.
       493-496)

Concept 2: We form schemas to help us categorize people and events in the world around us and to help predict the actions of others. Schemas help us form impressions about people. Attributions are the efforts to assign causes and otherwise explain behavior.

   5. Define social cognition, schemas, and impression formation. (pp. 497-498)

   6. Outline the basic premises of attribution theory and the biases that arise due to attributions. (pp. 499-501)

Concept 3: Social influence includes behaviors that result from the actions of others, as found in conformity, compliance, and obedience.

   7. Define social influence and conformity and describe the factors that influence conformity. (pp. 503-505)

   8. Define compliance and describe how the foot-in-the-door and the door-in-the-face techniques lead to compliance. (pp. 505-506)

   9. Describe the factors that influence the extent of obedience and the strategies that one can use to hold a position. (pp. 506-509)

Concept 4:   The study of liking has revealed a number of factors that influence the degree of friendship between people. Loving is more than intense liking, being qualitatively different. Sternberg has identified companionship, passion, and commitment as three components of love.

   10. Define interpersonal attraction and describe the factors that contribute to friendship and liking. (pp. 510-512)

   11. Describe the efforts that have been made to understand love, and outline the components of Sternberg's theory of love. (pp. 512-514)

   12. Outline the course of relationships from beginning to end. (pp. 514 -517)

Concept 5: Aggression involves the intention to hurt another. Observational learning theory suggests that violence depends in part on seeing others commit and be rewarded for violent acts. Prosocial behavior involves helping others.

   13. Define aggression and compare the instinctual, frustration-aggression, and observational learning theories of aggression. (pp. 519-523)

   14. Discuss the relationship of the media to aggression and pornography. (pp. 523-525)

   15. Define prosocial behavior, altruism, and empathy, and discuss their role in leading individuals to help other. (pp. 525-526)

CHAPTER SUMMARY

There are several ways you can use this summary as part of your systematic study plan. You may read each concept summary and then read the corresponding pages in the text, or you may read the entire summary and then read the entire chapter in the text. As you finish each section, complete the **Recap and Review** questions that are supplied in the text.

Concept 1:   Prologue and Looking Ahead   *Survey:* ____
Attitudes, Behavior, and Persuasion   *Read:* ____

Pages 488-496

The Prologue's description of David Koresh places the incident in the context of **social psychology**. Social psychology is the study of how peoples' thoughts, feelings, and actions are affected by others. Attempts to persuade people to purchase specific products involve principles derived from the study of attitudes. **Attitudes** are learned predispositions to respond in a favorable or unfavorable manner to a particular person or object. According to the **ABC model**, attitudes have three components. The **affective component** includes emotions about something, the **behavior component** consists of a predisposition or intention to act in a certain way, and the **cognitive component** refers to the beliefs and thoughts we have about a person or object.

The formation of attitudes follows classical and operant learning principles. Attitudes can be formed by association, as soldiers who had been stationed in the Persian Gulf may develop negative attitudes about sand.   Advertisers link products with a positive feeling or event so that the product will evoke the positive feeling in consumers.   Attitudes can be reinforced positively or punished by the responses others may have to them, and a person may develop an attitude through **vicarious learning**. Vicarious learning occurs when a person learns something through observation of others.   Children learn prejudices through others by hearing or seeing others express prejudicial attitudes. Television, films, and other media also are means by which we develop attitudes vicariously.

Celebrity endorsements are meant to match the product with a particular type of person, and the celebrity must be believable and trustworthy and must represent qualities that the advertisers want to project. Changing attitudes depend on these factors in persuasion. The source of the message can have major impact when the communicator is attractive and believable, has the appropriate expertise, and does not appear to have an ulterior motive. The character of the message is also important, and when an unpopular message is presented, it will be more effective if both sides are presented. Fear-producing messages are also effective unless the fear is too strong and the message is ignored as a defense mechanism.

Another important component consists of the characteristics of the recipient. The intelligence of the recipient influences the ability to remember and recall the message, yet intelligent people are more certain of their opinions. Highly intelligent people tend to be more difficult to persuade. A small difference in persuadability exists between men and women, with women being slightly easier to persuade. The means by which the information is processed also has influence on the persuasion. **Central route processing** occurs when the recipient considers the arguments involved. **Peripheral route processing** occurs when the recipient uses information that requires less thought. Central route processing produces more long-lasting change. In some cases, a celebrity may detract from a central route message by causing the recipient to focus on information other than the message.

Attitudes influence behavior, but the strength of the relationship varies. People do try to keep behavior and attitudes consistent. Sometimes, in order to maintain the consistency, behavior can influence attitudes. **Cognitive dissonance** occurs when a person holds two **cognitions** (attitudes or thoughts) that are contradictory.   The individual is motivated to reduce the dissonance by (1) modifying one or both of the cognitions, (2) changing the perceived importance of one cognition, (3) adding cognitions, or (4) denying that the two cognitions are related.   In cases where dissonance is aroused, the prediction is that behavior or attitudes will change in order to reduce the dissonance. In a classic experiment, subjects were offered $1 to convince others that a boring task was interesting. Others were paid $20. Those paid a small amount actually changed their attitudes about the task because the small amount caused dissonance where the large amount did not. After collecting information about a decision, people often engage in **selective exposure** to reduce the dissonance caused by making a choice. In this process, people select only information that supports their choice. Darryl Bem's **self-perception theory** is one alternative to dissonance theory. Bem suggests that people form their attitudes by observing their behavior, and sometimes attitudes are not clear until behavior makes them so.

Concept 2:   Social Cognition: Understanding Others   *Survey:* ____
              Attribution Processes: Understanding the   *Read:* ____
              Causes of Behavior

                                                                   Pages 497-501

The area of social psychology called **social cognition** is focused on understanding how we develop our understanding of others and how we explain the behavior of others. Social cognition refers to the processes that underlie our understanding of the world. Individuals have highly developed **schemas**, or sets of cognitions, about people and experiences. Schemas are important because they organize how we recall, recognize, and categorize information about others. They also help us make predictions about others.

Impression formation refers to the process by which an individual organizes information about another, forming an overall impression. Information given to people prior to meeting them can have dramatic effects on how the person is perceived. Research has focused on how people pay attention to unusually important traits called **central traits** as they form impressions of others. Information-processing approaches have been used to develop mathematical models of how personality traits are combined to form impressions. Research suggests that we form a psychological average of the individual traits. As we experience people, our impressions become more complex. Schemas are susceptible to a variety of factors - like mood - that can influence the accuracy of our impressions.

Attribution theory attempts to explain how we take specific instances of behavior and decide the specific causes of a person's behavior. The first determination is whether the cause is situational or dispositional. **Situational causes** result from the environment. A dispositional cause is the person's internal traits or personality characteristics.

Since people do not always possess knowledge sufficient to make logical attributions, there are several biases in the way they are made. People tend to attribute other people's behavior to dispositional causes and their own behavior to situational causes. This bias is known as the **fundamental attribution bias**. This bias is common because people tend to focus on the behaving person rather than the more stable situation, and when they consider their own behavior, the changes in the environment are more noticeable. The **halo effect** refers to our tendency to assume that if a person has some positive characteristics, then other positive traits are present, and if there are negative traits, other negative traits are present. The halo effect reflects **implicit personality theories**, theories that indicate how we think traits are grouped together in individuals. The **assumed-similarity bias** is the assumption that other people think just like you.

People make attributions of others, and they can act as observers of their own behavior. Bem's theory of self-perception suggests that people monitor their own behavior and make judgments about themselves based on what they see.

According to the theory, you use your own behavior to understand underlying motivation, acting like an outside observer of your behavior. Racial, ethnic, and social class factors influence attributions. For instance, African-Americans are less likely to attribute success to internal factors. In contrast, white children are more likely to attribute success to ability and effort. When attributions are based on internal factors, the perception is that increased effort will result in success. Japanese and Chinese students attribute their success to internal effort, which may explain the high achievement of Asian students.

Concept 3:   Social Influence

Survey: ____
Read: ____

Pages 503-509

The area called **social influence** is concerned with how the actions of an individual affect the behavior of others.

In uncertain situations, we tend to look to the behavior of others to guide our own behavior. **Conformity** is the change in behavior or attitudes that results from a desire to follow the beliefs or standards of other people. An experiment by Solomon Asch demonstrated the power of the judgments of others on the perceptual judgments of an individual subject. The subject would hear the judgments about which one of three lines was identical to a fourth ''standard'' line, and even though the judgments were quite visibly wrong, the subject would conform to the judgments of the group (which were always uniformly the same). About 75 percent of the subjects conformed to the group judgment at least once. Research since the time of Asch's experiment has found several variables that produce conformity:

- The characteristics of the group influence the judgment more if the group is attractive to the group members. Individuals that have a low social rank - **status** - in the group are more likely to conform to the group.
- The individual's response conforms more when it must be made publicly.
- The nature of the task influences conformity. The more ambiguous the task, the higher the conformity. If the individual is less competent, conformity is also higher.
- If the group is unanimous, pressures to conform are greatest. If people with dissenting views have a supporter, called a **social supporter**, then conformity is reduced.

For a long time the prevalent view was that women are more easily influenced than men. Research in the 1970s showed that the tasks and topics used in earlier research were more familiar to men, thus biasing the outcomes. However, more recent research has now reconfirmed the view that women are more likely to conform, possibly because of the tendency to want to get along with others.

The behavior that occurs in response to direct, explicit pressure to endorse a particular view or to behave in a certain way is called **compliance**. Several techniques are used by salespersons to get customers to comply with purchase requests. One technique is called the **foot-in-the-door technique** in which a person agrees to a small request and is then asked to comply with bigger request. Compliance increases when the person first agrees to the smaller request. The technique works because compliance to the small request increases interest. Another explanation suggests that self-perceptions are formed based on compliance to the initial request, and compliance to the larger request is a result of a desire to be consistent.

The **door-in-the-face technique** is the opposite of the foot-in-the-door technique. The door-in-the-face technique follows a large request with a smaller one, making the second request appear more reasonable. In a study, half the subjects were willing to take on small obligation after being asked to make a major commitment where only 17 percent of the control group agreed. One reason why the technique works is because of **reciprocal concessions**, a process in which the requesters are seen to make a compromise and a second refusal would make the person being asked appear unreasonable. Another reason is that people desire to present themselves well to others. Other techniques include **low-balling** where an agreement is reached and then additional costs are revealed, and we tend to stick to the original virtues of the decision. The that's-not-all technique presents a deal at an inflated price; then a number of incentives are added. The not-so-free sample is another method that creates a psychic cost by giving ''free'' samples. These samples instigate a norm of reciprocity, leading people to buy as a matter of reciprocation.

Compliance follows a request, but obedience follows direct orders. **Obedience** is defined as a change in behavior due to the commands of others. Obedience occurs in situations involving a boss, teacher, parent, or someone who has power over us. The classic study by Stanley Milgram involved subjects administering shocks to people they thought to be other subjects, supposedly testing to see if shocks would improve memory. The other subjects were actually confederates of the experimenter. Psychiatrists predicted that no more than 2 percent of the subjects would administer the strongest shocks, but almost two-thirds of the subjects gave the highest level of shock. Subjects reported their reasons for giving the level of shock to be their belief that the experimenter was responsible for the ill effects of the shocks. The experiment has been criticized for establishing extreme conditions and for methodological reasons.

There are several strategies available that will help a person avoid the pressures of compliance and obedience. One method is called **inoculation** in which individuals become resistant to persuasion by being exposed to information that refutes opposing arguments. When people learned that a persuasive message was about to be given, a process called **forewarning**, then they were less likely to be persuaded. With an awareness of the forthcoming argument counter to their own beliefs, individuals tend to prepare arguments that support their own position. **Consistency** is not only effective at reducing persuadability but can also change the attitude of the persuader. Apparently the unyielding repetition of one's own position can cause others to rethink their position. Another strategy requires that individuals initially go along with the group, establish their competence, and then behave more independently.

Concept 4: **Liking and Loving: Interpersonal Attraction and the Development of Relationships**   *Survey:* ____
                                                                                                        Read: ____

Pages 510-517

Another area of social influence is called **interpersonal attraction** which encompasses the factors that lead to positive feelings about others. Research on liking has identified the following factors as important in the development of attraction between people:

- **Proximity** refers to the physical nearness or geographical closeness as a factor in development of friendship. Proximity leads to liking.
- Mere exposure also leads to liking. The more often one is exposed to any stimulus, the more the stimulus is liked. Familiarity with a stimulus can evoke positive feelings.
- Similarity influences attraction because we assume that people with similar backgrounds will evaluate us positively. This is called the **reciprocity-of-**

liking effect. We also assume that when we like someone, that person likes us in return.

- Need complimentarity refers to attraction that is based on the needs that the partner can fulfill. We may then be attracted to the person that fulfills the greatest number of needs. The **need-complimentarity hypothesis** was first proposed in the 1950s, and the evidence to support it has been inconsistent. It does appear that people with complimentary abilities are attracted to one another.

- Physical attractiveness is a key factor if all other factors are equal. More attractive people tend to be more popular. Physical attractiveness may be the single most important factor in college dating. There is also a great deal of consensus about what constitutes attractiveness, including the dimensions of facial configurations that make faces attractive. Emphasis on facial dimensions discounts the effects of personality. Attractiveness has an influence on the levels of attention in infants, and leads them to be more socially responsive; infants played longer with a doll with an attractive face. The downside to physical attractiveness is in areas like work, where attractive women are hampered by stereotypes, which view women as having risen to a position as a consequence of attractiveness rather than skill. Physical attractiveness is also an asset in social situations.

For a long time social psychologists considered research into love too difficult to conduct scientifically. Love is not merely a more intense liking, but differs from liking on qualitative grounds. An early effort by Rick Zubin involved a scale that was able to distinguish those who scored high on love from those who did not. High scorers were found to gaze at each other more and to have intact relationships six months after the test. Physiological arousal was hypothesized to characterize loving, and arousal for whatever reason was found to be attributed as a feeling of love for a person present during arousal. This theory does explain that when someone is rejected or hurt by another, they may still feel themselves in love as a consequence of arousal. Several kinds of love have been hypothesized, one being **passionate** (or **romantic**) **love**, which is an intense state of absorption in another person. Another is **companionate love**, which is strong affection that we have for someone with whom our lives are deeply involved. Robert Sternberg has proposed that love is made of three components. The **intimacy component** includes feelings of closeness and connectedness; the **passion component** is made of the motivational drives related to sex, physical closeness, and romance; and the **decision/commitment component** encompasses the initial cognition that one loves someone and the long-term feelings of commitment to maintain love.

More than one out of two marriages ends in divorce. The behavior of couples in developing relationships changes in predictable ways. The pattern, in order, is: people interact more often, they seek each other's company, they open up more to each other, they begin to understand each other's points of view, they make investments in the relationship, they begin to feel a psychological well-being associated with the relationship, and then they start behaving like a couple. As the relationship develops, the individuals themselves may experience growth and change. Goals for the relationship may differ. Even if both want marriage, they may want different kinds of mates. Preferences differ according to both culture and sex. Successful relationships can be distinguished by the rate at which the individual components evolve. In strong loving relationships, commitment peaks and then remains stable while intimacy grows over the course of the relationship. Passion shows a marked decline through time.

Relationships deteriorate for a number of reasons. One factor is the change in the judgments about the partner's behavior. Forgetfulness that is initially charming may become ''boorish indifference.'' Communication may become disrupted. Decline follows a common pattern. The first phase occurs when a person decides that the relationship cannot be tolerated. In the second phase, the person confronts the partner and tries to determine if repair is possible. The next phase is marked by a public acknowledgment that the relationship is being dissolved and an accounting is made to others. The fourth and last phase is ''grave dressing,'' which is the major activity of ending the physical and psychological relationship. The degree of distress experienced depends upon what the relationship was like prior to the breakup. The number of activities that were mutually shared and the expectation of the difficulty entering a new relationship influence the amount of distress experienced.

Concept 5: Aggression and Prosocial Behavior: Hurting   *Survey:* ____
**   and Helping Others**   *Read:* ____

Pages 519-526

The Kitty Genovese story (Chapter 1) initiated the study of aggression and prosocial behavior. These kinds of incidents give a negative and pessimistic impression of human behavior. The helping behavior of many, however, counteracts the impression. Social psychology seeks to explain these extremes.

Aggression occurs at societal and individual levels, and the basic questions concern whether aggression is inevitable or whether it results from particular circumstances. **Aggression** is defined as the intentional injury of or harm to another person. Instinct theories explain aggression as the result of innate urges. Konrad Lorenz suggested that aggressive energy is built up through the instinct of aggression and that its release is necessary. The discharge of this energy is called **catharsis**. Lorenz suggested that society should provide an acceptable means of achieving catharsis, like sports. There is no way to test this theory experimentally.

The frustration-aggression theory says that the frustration of a goal always leads to aggression. **Frustration** is defined as the thwarting of a goal-directed behavior. More recently the theory has been modified to suggest that frustration creates a readiness to act aggressively. Actual aggression depends upon the presence of **aggressive cues**, stimuli that have been associated in the past with aggression. In one experiment, the presence of a rifle and a revolver increased the amount of aggression. Subjects who had viewed a violent movie were also more aggressive.

The observational learning view suggests that we learn to act aggressively by observing others. Aggression is not inevitable and can be seen in terms of the rewards and punishments it involves. In the example of a girl hitting a younger brother for damaging her toy, the instinct theory would suggest that the act results from pent-up aggression, the frustration-aggression theory would say that the frustration of not being able to play with the toy led to aggression, and the observational theory would say that aggression had been previously reinforced. Observational learning theory also suggests that the rewards and punishments received by a model are important in the learning of aggression. This formulation has wide support.

Observational theory suggests that if children observe violence that is in some way rewarded, they will be more likely to act violently. Studies have shown that children who watched a lot of television as third-graders became more aggressive adults than those who did not watch as much television. Watching media violence can lead to an increased readiness to act violently and an insensitivity to the suffering of victims. Violence seems to lower inhibitions against aggression, and viewing violence may cause us to interpret even nonaggressive acts as aggressive. Also, continued exposure may desensitize us to violence.

Recent evidence suggests that there may be a link between certain kinds of erotic material and aggression. In an experiment, angered males who viewed an erotic movie that contained violence later showed more aggression toward a female than subjects who had not viewed the film. Viewing violence toward women desensitizes emotional and physiological reactions about violence directed at women. The issue is made more complicated by the First Amendment rights to free speech. Actually, hard-core pornography contains less violence toward women than do R-rated movies.

Prosocial behavior refers to helping behavior. The prosocial behavior studied most by psychologists is bystander intervention. When more than one person witnesses an emergency, **diffusion of responsibility**, the tendency for people to feel that responsibility is shared among those present, increases. Latané and Darley developed a four-step model describing the process of helping others: The first step is the awareness that someone requires help. In the second step, the individual may look to the behavior of others and interpret their inaction as an indication that help is not needed. The third step involves assuming responsibility for taking action. If people with life-saving training are present, then those that have no training are less likely to help because they do not have expertise. The fourth step is deciding and implementing some form of help. Helping may be indirect, in the form of calling the police, or direct in the form of giving first aid or driving the person to the hospital. A **rewards-cost approach** helps predict the nature of help given. The rewards of helping must outweigh the costs. Once the decision to help has been made, one actual step remains, that of giving help. In some cases people act altruistically. **Altruism** is helping behavior that is beneficial to others but may require self-sacrifice. Some people who intervene in situations and offer help may have personality characteristics that differentiate them from others. People high in **empathy** may be more likely to respond than others. Situational factors and mood may also affect helping behavior. Both good and bad moods appear to increase helping behavior.

♦ Now that you have surveyed, questioned, and read the chapter and completed the **Recap and Review** questions, review **Looking Back**, pages 527-528. *Review:* ____

♦ For additional practice through recitation and review, test your knowledge of the chapter material by answering the questions in the **Key Word Drill**, the **Practice Questions**, and the **Essay Questions**.

KEY WORD DRILL   *Recite:* ____

The following **Fill in the Blank** and **Matching Questions** test key words from the text. Check your answers with the Answer Key in the back of the *Study Guide*.

FILL IN THE BLANK

1. _____ psychology is concerned with how people's thoughts, feelings, and actions are affected by others.

2. The ABC model suggests that an attitude has three components: _____ _____, and _____.

3. _____ learning occurs by observing others.

4. Sets of cognitions about people and social experiences are called _____.

5. The causes of behavior that are based on environmental factors are called _____ causes, and the causes of behavior that are based on internal traits or personality factors are called _____ causes.

6. When a person changes behavior or an attitude as a result of a desire to follow the beliefs or standards of other people, that person is involved in _____.

7. _____ occurs in response to direct, explicit pressure to endorse a particular point of view or to behave in a certain way.

8. _____ depends upon the notion that aggression is built up and must be discharged through violent acts.

9. Stimuli that have been associated with aggression in the past are considered to be _____ _____.

10. The general term that describes the positive feelings for others, including both liking and loving, is _____ _____.

MATCHING QUESTIONS

_____ 11. attitudes

_____ 12. affect component

_____ 13. behavior component

_____ 14. cognition component

a. A predisposition to act in a way that is relevant to one's attitude.

b. Learned predispositions to respond in a favorable or unfavorable manner to a particular object.

c. That part of an attitude encompassing how one feels about the object of one's attitude.

d. The beliefs and thoughts held about the object of one's attitude.

_____ 15. central route processing

_____ 16. peripheral route processing

_____ 17. cognitive dissonance

_____ 18. selective exposure

_____ 19. self-perception theory

a. Characterized by thoughtful consideration of the issues.

b. An attempt to minimize dissonance by exposing oneself only to information that supports one's choice.

c. Characterized by consideration of the source and related general information rather than of the message itself.

d. Attitudes are formed by observing one's own behavior.

e. The conflict resulting from contrasting cognitions.

_____20. impression formation

_____21. central traits

_____22. fundamental attribution bias

_____23. halo effect

_____24. assumed-similarity bias

a. Major traits considered in forming impressions of others.

b. Organizing information about another individual to form an overall impression of that person.

c. Tendency to think of people as being similar to oneself.

d. A tendency to attribute others' behavior to dispositional causes but to attribute one's own behavior to situational causes.

e. An initial understanding that a person has positive traits is used to infer other uniformly positive characteristics.

_____   _____

_____25. foot-in-the-door technique

_____26. door-in-the-face technique

_____27. reciprocal concessions

_____28. low-balling

a. After an agreement is reached, the seller reveals additional costs and the buyer complies.

b. Compliance with an important request is more likely if it follows compliance with a smaller previous request.

c. Requesters appear to compromise their initial request, thereby inviting a compromise in return.

d. A large request, refusal of which is expected, is followed by a smaller request.

_____   _____

_____29. obedience

_____30. inoculation

_____31. forewarning

_____32. consistency

a. Exposure to arguments opposing one's beliefs, making the subject more resistant to later attempts to change those beliefs

b. A subject is told in advance that a persuasive message is coming in order to reduce the effect of social influence.

c. A change in behavior due to the commands of others.

d. The persistence of those holding an unpopular view that eventually brings about a change in the majority.

_____   _____

_____33. passionate (or romantic) love

_____34. companionate love

_____35. intimacy component

_____36. passion component

_____37. decision/commitment component

a. The motivational drives relating to sex, physical closeness, and romance.

b. Feelings of closeness and connectedness.

c. The initial cognition that one loves someone, and the longer-term feelings of commitment.

d. The strong affection we have for those with whom our lives are deeply involved.

e. A state of intense absorption in someone that is characterized by physiological arousal, psychological interest, and caring for another's needs.

_____   _____

_____38. proximity

_____39. reciprocity-of-liking effect

_____40. need-complementarity hypothesis

_____41. prosocial behavior

_____42. diffusion of responsibility

_____43. rewards-costs approach

_____44. altruism

_____45. empathy

a. Helping behavior that is beneficial to others while requiring sacrifice on the part of the helper.

b. The hypothesis that people are attracted to others who fulfill their needs.

c. One person's experiencing of another's emotions, in turn increasing the likelihood of responding to the other's needs.

d. The tendency to like those who like us.

e. The tendency for people to feel that responsibility for helping is shared among those present.

f. Any helping behavior.

g. Nearness to another, one cause for liking.

h. The notion that, in a situation requiring help, a bystander's perceived rewards must outweigh the costs if helping is to occur.

_____   _____

PRACTICE QUESTIONS   *Recite and Review:* _____

Test your knowledge of the chapter material by answering these **True-False** and **Multiple Choice Questions**. Check your answers with the Answer Key in the back of the *Study Guide*.

TRUE-FALSE QUESTIONS

T   F   1. Classical conditioning has rarely been effective when used in advertising.

T   F   2. Presenting a viewpoint that is counter to that held by a group of intelligent people is unlikely to be effective in persuading them to change their view.

T   F   3. People generally try to strive for consistency between their attitudes and their behavior.

T   F   4. A person usually observes many of another person's traits before fitting the other person into a particular schema.

T   F   5. When we view a person in either a negative or positive manner at first impression, the halo effect may lead us to infer the existence of additional, similar traits which we have not observed.

T   F   6. Conformity is a social pressure which is not in the form of a direct order.

T   F   7. Compliance to a request will often increase if the requester makes what appears to be a compromise after the first refusal, thus inviting the refuser to offer a compromise in return.

T   F   8. Unless the initial interactions are negative, repeated exposure to any stimulus makes people enjoy it more.

T   F   9. In Sternberg's conceptualization, passionate love is a kind of love resulting from a combination of components that are the basic elements of love.

T   F   10. Due to the proportion of sexual behavior being higher in X-rated movies than in R-rated movies, the effect X-rated movies have on violence toward women is higher.

T   F   11. Altruism is very aggressive, injurious behavior that is enacted without remorse.

MULTIPLE CHOICE QUESTIONS

1. Social psychologists study learned predispositions to respond in a favorable or unfavorable way to a particular person or object. These learned predispositions are called:
   a. impressions.
   b. values.
   c. attitudes.
   d. opinions.

2. Negative and positive feelings about other people, objects, and concepts
    reveal which component of our attitude?
    a. cognitive   c. affective
    b. intentional   d. behavioral

3. Which of the following statements represents a positive cognitive component
    of an attitude about green beans?
    a. I like green beans better than any other vegetable.
    b. Green beans are a tasty source of vitamins.
    c. Green beans grow on vines.
    d. I eat green beans regularly.

4. The component of an attitude which refers to the beliefs and thoughts we
    hold about a particular object is called:
    a. affect component.   c. behavioral component.
    b. manner component.   d. cognitive component.

5. One of the basic processes that underlie the formation and development of
    attitudes relates to learning principles. Which of the following learning
    methods best explains how attitudes are acquired?
    a. peripheral route processing   c. central route processing
    b. classical and operant conditioning d. punishment

6. Many corporations link their products with beautiful women or strong,
    handsome men. Which of the following suggests that classical conditioning
    is being used to sell the product?
    a. They feel that the product will ''sell itself'' with this method.
    b. Companies believe that individuals will buy their product since only
        beautiful people will buy such good quality.
    c. The positive feelings associated with good-looking people will be
        paired with their products.
    d. They feel that beautiful men and women usually make the best
        salespeople.

7. Advertisers often try to link a product they want consumers to buy to a:
    a. positive feeling or event.   c. peripheral route.
    b. cognition.   d. dissonant stimulus.

8. A 5-year-old boy who overhears his father tell his mother that ''Southerners
    are ignorant'' may grow up to believe this opinion and adopt it as an
    attitude as a result of the process of:
    a. direct reinforcement.   c. cognitive dissonance.
    b. vicarious learning.   d. persuasive communication.

9. According to the text, a message that presents only the communicator's side
    of an issue is called:
    a. a two-sided argument.   c. a one-sided argument.
    b. a fear-producing message.   d. a message source.

10. For a message that presents an unpopular viewpoint, if it presents both the communicator's point of view and an opponent's point of view, it is most likely to be:
    a. dangerous because it may cause people to disagree with the communicator.
    b. a slanted message, because the communicator cannot possibly be fair.
    c. difficult for most audiences to understand due to the need to present simple messages.
    d. more effective for the communicator because it appears to be more precise and thoughtful.

11. Many variables influence the effectiveness of a communication to create attitude change. In which of the following situations will the impact be the greatest?
    a. The recipient appraises the message with central route processing.
    b. The recipient of the message is male.
    c. The recipient appraises the message by peripheral route processing.
    d. The recipient is very intelligent.

12. An individual who holds two contradictory attitudes or thoughts is likely to experience a kind of psychological tension known as:
    a. attribution theory.   c. stereotypes.
    b. reverse bias.   d. cognitive dissonance.

13. According to Festinger's theory of cognitive dissonance, if a smoker holds the cognitions ''I smoke'' and ''Smoking causes cancer,'' he or she should be motivated to do all of the following except:
    a. modify one or both cognitions.
    b. enter a stop-smoking program.
    c. make the attitudes consistent.
    d. change the importance of one cognition.

14. Of the following, the best example of cognitive dissonance is:
    a. stating that women should earn less money than men for doing the same job.
    b. exaggerating the merits of a product in order to promote sales.
    c. knowing that cigarette smoking is harmful, but doing it anyway.
    d. thinking that handicapped people cannot hold good jobs and therefore not recommending them.

15. An attempt to minimize dissonance by exposing oneself only to information that supports one's choice is known as:
    a. dissonance reduction.   c. cognitive dissonance.
    b. cognitive reduction.   d. selective exposure.

16. Sets of cognitions about people and social experiences are known as:
    a. impression formations.   c. prophecies.
    b. biases.   d. schemas.

17. Impression formation is the process by which:
    a. an individual exaggerates the good personality traits of a stranger.
    b. drastic differences in people are determined by contrasting certain important traits.
    c. experiences create an overall picture of an individual and place him or her in a stereotypical ingroup.
    d. an individual organizes information about another individual to form an overall impression of that person.

18. According to the text, when forming an impression of another person, people rely heavily on:
    a. central tendencies.   c. primary traits.
    b. central traits.   d. schematic tendencies.

19. Warm and cold are considered:
    a. attributions that have little impact on first impressions.
    b. central traits.
    c. stereotyped descriptions of men and women.
    d. the basis for ingroup-outgroup bias.

20. The theory that seeks to explain, on the basis of samples of an individual's behavior, what the specific causes of that behavior are is known as:
    a. situation theory.   c. attribution theory.
    b. consensus theory.   d. disposition theory.

21. Which one of the following statements is the best example of dispositional attribution bias?
    a. John is being good because the teacher is watching.
    b. Even though I am not feeling sociable, I will go to the party if you do.
    c. I become very anxious when criticized.
    d. Sue is staying up all night to study because she is a conscientious student.

22. Which of the situations below best describes a situational cause for the described behavior?
    a. Barbara straightens the guest room, which is normally a messy sewing room, because relatives will be staying at her house for a week.
    b. Chris helps an old lady across the street because he is always thoughtful.
    c. John, who is sometimes grumpy, frowns about an exam as he walks down the hall.
    d. Mindy is a punctual person who is on time for school every morning.

23. According to the text, information that is high in consensus, low in consistency, and low in distinctiveness leads to attributions which are:
    a. dispositional.   c. situational.
    b. fundamental.   d. mixed.

24. The tendency for people to attribute others' behavior to dispositional causes and their own behavior to situational causes is what type of bias?
    a. ingroup versus outgroup   c. dispositional attribution
    b. fundamental attribution   d. stereotypic attribution

25. One important concept that the fundamental-attribution bias illustrates about attributional processes is that:
    a. people make explanations about others that tend to be less flattering than the explanations they make about themselves.
    b. people sometimes observe their own behavior and make judgments about others on the basis of their own behavior.
    c. people tend to overrate the effect of situation on others.
    d. people tend to underrate the effect of situation on themselves.

26. Conformity is a change in behavior or attitude brought about by:
    a.   an increase of knowledge.
    b.   a desire to follow the beliefs or standards of others.
    c.   intense pressure to be a distinct individual.
    d.   an insecure self-image.

27. Considering that Asch's experiment involved a perceptual judgment that was fairly obvious, what variable related to conformity does the experiment appear to contradict?
    a.   The task variable - if an individual feels competent in a task, conformity is less likely.
    b.   The characteristics of the group - the group members were completely unknown to the subjects because the experiment was done blindly.
    c.   The nature of the response - since the subjects were allowed to write down an answer, there should have been little pressure.
    d.   The nature of the group - since the group could not agree, the subject should have be freer to respond without pressure.

28. What measure may be most effective for reducing the tendency of people to conform in a group situation?
    a.   Make sure all members value the group highly.
    b.   Include lots of members in the group.
    c.   Use a show of hands when voting.
    d.   Use a secret ballot when voting.

29. According to the text, which of the following has been shown to affect the amount of conformity displayed by members of a group?
    a.   obedience of each member of the group to the legal authority
    b.   the kind of task the group is assigned
    c.   the amount of individuality expressed by each person in the group, as measured by how each is dressed
    d.   the consistency of the group's leader

30. People working on tasks and questions that are ambiguous are more susceptible to:
    a.   inoculation.   c.   forewarning.
    b.   obedience.   d.   social pressure.

31. The sales technique by which someone first asks you to comply with a small request and later makes a larger request is called:
    a.   door-in-the-face.   c.   foot-in-the-mouth.
    b.   foot-in-the-door.   d.   fly-in-the-face.

32. What is the correct term for the technique in which a large request is asked, followed by expected refusal and later a smaller request?
    a.   obedience   c.   door-in-the-face technique
    b.   social compliance   d.   foot-in-the-door technique

33. The classic experiment demonstrating the power of authority to produce obedience was performed by:
    a.   Albert Bandura.   c.   Stanley Milgram.
    b.   Solomon Asch.   d.   B. F. Skinner.

34. The Milgram study on obedience showed that:
   a. very few subjects were willing to ''electrocute'' the learner.
   b. about one-third of the subjects were willing to ''electrocute'' the learner.
   c. the majority were willing to ''electrocute'' the learner.
   d. all of the subjects were willing to ''electrocute'' the learner.

35. In the Milgram study on obedience, those who were willing to ''electrocute'' the learner did so because:
   a. they thought the learner would not be hurt.
   b. they thought they would not be held responsible for injury.
   c. they thought the learner deserved the shocks.
   d. they thought they would be punished for noncompliance.

36. The procedure in which subjects are warned in advance that a persuasive message is coming is known as:
   a. consistency.
   b. forewarning.
   c. inoculation.
   d. compliance.

37. The unyielding persistence of a minority group in advocating its platform may reduce persuasibility and even change attitudes of many members of the majority. According to the text, this technique is called:
   a. conformity.
   b. consistency.
   c. compliance.
   d. obedience.

38. Proximity is defined as:
   a. nearness to another person.
   b. a tendency to like those who like us.
   c. a tendency of those whom we like to like us.
   d. distance from another.

39. Of the following, which factor is the best predictor of whether two people will be initially attracted to each other?
   a. similarity
   b. mere exposure
   c. proximity
   d. complementarity

40. Physical attractiveness is usually advantageous to a beautiful person. Which vocation below sometimes makes physical attractiveness a personal liability?
   a. a male high school teacher
   b. a female nurse
   c. a male defense attorney
   d. a female manager in a major corporation

41. According to many social psychologists, love represents:
   a. a greater quantity than liking.
   b. a different physiological state than liking.
   c. an emotion, unlike liking.
   d. essentially the same state as liking.

42. The text describes a popular questionnaire used by some social psychologists which contains items such as ''I would do almost anything for (person's name to whom the individual completing the questionnaire is attracted).'' ''I think that (person's name) is unusually well adjusted.'' The questionnaire is designed to measure:
   a. proximity.
   b. companionate love.
   c. love and liking.
   d. need complementarity.

43. According to Sternberg's theory of love, each of the following is a
    component of love except:
    a.   intimacy.   c.   decision/commitment.
    b.   passion.   d.   individuation/separation.

44. According to Levinger, which of the following events seems to be an
    important reason for the decline of a relationship?
    a.   a change in judgments about the meaning of the partner's behavior
    b.   an increase in punishment of the partner
    c.   turning to others for the needs that the partner used to fulfill
    d.   an increase in discussions that are critical of the partner

45. When a loving relationship deteriorates, there are several indications.
    Which of the following is not mentioned in your text as an indicator?
    a.   A partner may begin to invite and agree with criticism of the other
         partner from people outside the relationship.
    b.   Communications may become disrupted in the relationship.
    c.   There is an increase in criticism about the partner's behavior.
    d.   A partner engages in an extramarital affair.

46. During _____ of a relationship on the decline, more and more friends
    and acquaintances of the affected couple are made aware of the demise of the
    relationship and the reasons for it.
    a.   Phase 1   c.   Phase 3
    b.   Phase 2   d.   Phase 4

47. According to Duck, the phase of the decline of a relationship in which a
    person confronts the partner in order to determine whether the relationship
    should be terminated or repaired is:
    a.   Phase 1.   c.   Phase 3.
    b.   Phase 2.   d.   Phase 4.

48. The phase of a relationship on the decline, in which each partner copes with
    the demise of the relationship so that events associated with it appear
    reasonable and acceptable, is called:
    a.   dyadic.   c.   grave dressing.
    b.   ambivalent.   d.   social.

49. The most recent formulation of the frustration-aggression theory states that
    frustration:
    a.   always leads to aggression.
    b.   arouses an innate need for catharsis.
    c.   leads to aggression only when others are present.
    d.   produces anger, leading to a readiness to act.

50. Frustration is most likely to lead to aggression:
    a.   in the presence of aggressive cues.
    b.   immediately after being frustrated.
    c.   during late adolescence.
    d.   several hours after being frustrated.

51. Prosocial is a more formal way of describing behavior that is:
    a.   helping.   c.   innate.
    b.   cathartic.   d.   aggressive.

52. Diffusion of responsibility can occur when:
     a.   aggressive cues are present.
     b.   the catharsis hypothesis is in effect.
     c.   there is more than one bystander to an incident.
     d.   innate behaviors are operative.

ESSAY QUESTIONS   *Recite and Review:* _____

Essay Question 14.1:   *The Consistency between Attitudes and Behavior*

Much has been made of attitudes and behavior and how they may or may not be consistent. Describe a situation in which your attitudes and behavior may not have been consistent. Then compare the cognitive dissonance explanation and the self-perception explanation of the situation.

_____

_____

_____

_____

_____

_____

_____

_____

_____

_____

_____

_____

_____

_____

_____

_____

_____

_____

_____

_____

_____

Essay Question 14.2: *Should Pornography Be Banned?*

Discuss how the current evidence of the relationship between pornography and violence against women should be used. Should pornography be banned? Try to defend your answer with evidence from the text and with reasoned arguments.

_____

_____

_____

_____

_____

_____

_____

_____

_____

_____

_____

_____

_____

_____

_____

_____

_____

_____

_____

_____

_____

_____

_____

ACTIVITIES AND PROJECTS

1. Think about how you became friends or acquaintances with those you currently
    know. What roles were played by the following factors in the formation and
    maintenance of your relationships: proximity, mere exposure, similarity,
    physical attraction, the reciprocity-of-liking effect?

2. Watch some prime-time television and keep a log of violent incidents. How
    many violent incidents can you count in one hour? What is the nature of the
    violence? Do you believe that television violence leads to real violence?
    Explain.

LIVING WITH OTHERS IN A DIVERSE WORLD

DETAILED OUTLINE   *Survey:* _____

This detailed outline contains all the headings in Chapter 15: Living With Others in a Diverse World. If you are using the SQ3R method, then an examination of the outline is the best way to begin your survey of the chapter.

Prologue: Rodney King
Looking Ahead

Stress and Coping
    The high cost of stress
    The general adaptation syndrome model: The course of stress
    The nature of stressors: My stress is your pleasure
        Categorizing stressors
Psychology at Work Posttraumatic Stress Disorder: Reliving Catastrophe
    Coping with stress
        Coping style: The hardy personality
        Social support: Turning to others
The Informed Consumer of Psychology Coping Strategies That Work
        Turning threat into challenge
        Making a threatening situation less threatening
        Changing one's goals
        Taking physical action
        Preparing for stress before it happens
▪ **Recap and Review I**

Stereotypes, Prejudice, and Discrimination
    Racial stereotypes
    Gender and sex stereotypes
The Cutting Edge Sexual Harassment
    Gender and sex differences: More similar than different
▪ **Recap and Review II**

Psychology in a Global Perspective
    Individualism and collectivism: The individual versus the group
    War, peace, and terrorism
    Psychology and the promotion of peace
▪ **Recap and Review III**

Looking Back

Key Terms and Concepts

Now that you have surveyed the chapter, read **Looking Ahead**, pages 532-533.
   Question: ____
      Read: ____

Focus on the questions on page 533.

CONCEPTS AND LEARNING OBJECTIVES   *Survey:* ____

These are the concepts and the learning objects for Chapter 15. Read them carefully as part of your preliminary survey of the chapter.

Concept 1: Health psychology focuses on the prevention, diagnosis, and treatment of medical problems. A key factor that health psychologists must understand is that of stress.

   1. Describe and illustrate Selye's general adaptation syndrome to stress. (pp. 532-536)

   2. Identify major stressors and their consequences, especially posttraumatic stress disorder. (pp. 536-540)

   3. Describe the coping strategies, including defense mechanisms, types of coping, hardiness, and related strategies. (pp. 540-543)

Concept 2: Gender differences are primarily a result of social expectations and cultural patterns. Minor differences have been described in personality and cognitive skills. Schemas can lead to stereotypes, which can also be detrimental in the form of prejudice and discrimination.

   4. Describe how stereotypes are formed and the aspects of stereotypes that lead to discrimination. (pp. 544-546)

   5. Describe the bases of sexuality and gender, and discuss the sources of our typical attitudes toward them. (pp. 546-548)

   6. Discuss the roles of personality and cognition in the development and perception of gender and sexuality. (pp. 548-551)

   7. Identify the biological and environmental sources of gender and sexual schemas. (pp. 551-553)

Concept 3: The culture in which people are raised profoundly affects their values and world views. Cross-cultural psychologists are interested in identifying how an individual's behavior is affected by the culture in which he or she lives, and in promoting peaceful co-existence among all cultures.

   8. Distinguish individualism from collectivism and describe how these two types of culture differ from one another. (pp. 553-556)

   9. Describe how misperceptions of another culture can lead to unnecessary animosity between countries. (pp. 556-557)

   10. Describe the average American's view of the threat of nuclear war. (pp. 557-559)

   11. Discuss how psychologists are trying to prevent international conflicts
       by changing both governmental policy and the views of individuals.
       (pp. 559-560)

CHAPTER SUMMARY

There are a number of ways you can use this summary as part of your systematic
study plan. You may read each concept summary and then read the corresponding
pages in the text, or you may read the entire summary and then read the entire
chapter in the text. As you finish each section, complete the **Recap and Review**
questions that are supplied in the text.

Concept 1: Prologue and Looking Ahead   *Survey:* ____
**   Stress and Coping**   *Read:* ____

                                                                    Pages 532-543

The response to events that threaten or challenge a person is called **stress**, and
the events themselves are called stressors. **Stressors** can be both pleasant and
unpleasant events, though the negative events can be more detrimental. Some view
life as a sequence of stresses, with our responses being minor adaptations.
Sometimes, though, adaptation requires a major effort and may have responses that
result in health problems.
     The most immediate reaction to stress is a physiological response, including
an increase in adrenal hormones, an increase in heart rate and blood pressure,
and changes in how the skin conducts electrical charges. This change initially
helps the body respond to the stress. Continued stress can result in a decline
of the body's ability to cope biologically. Body tissues can actually
deteriorate. Minor problems can be made worse. The class of medical problems
called psychosomatic disorders, disorders caused by the interaction of
psychological, emotional, and physiological problems, are also related to stress.
Ulcers, asthma, arthritis, blood pressure, and eczema are common **psychosomatic
disorders**. High levels of stress interfere with people's ability to cope with
current and new stressors.
     Hans Selye proposed that everyone goes through the same set of physiological
responses no matter what the cause is, and he called this the **general adaptation
syndrome (GAS)**. The first stage of the GAS is the **alarm and mobilization stage**,
during which the presence of a stressor is detected and the sympathetic nervous
system is energized. The second stage is the **resistance stage**, during which the
person attempts to cope with the stressor. If coping is inadequate, the person
enters the **exhaustion stage**. The person's ability to cope with stress declines
and the negative consequences appear. These include illness, psychological
symptoms like the inability to concentrate, and possibly disorientation and
losing touch with reality. People wear out in this stage. In order to escape
the problems of this stage, people must often avoid the stressor - essentially,
get some rest from the problem. The GAS has provided a model that explains how
stress leads to illness. The primary criticism has focused on the fact that the
model suggests that every stress response is physiologically the same. There is
little room for psychological factors in the model also.
     If people are to consider an event stressful, they must perceived the event
to be threatening and must lack the ability to cope with it adequately. The same
event may not be stressful for everyone. The perception of stress may depend
upon how one attributes the causes for events.
     There are three classes of events that are considered stressors. The first
is **cataclysmic events**, strong stressors that affect many people at the same time.
Most people deal with the stress of these event rather well because they tend to

experience the event and share the problem. Some people experience prolonged problems due to catastrophic events, and this is called posttraumatic stress disorder. People may experience flashbacks or dreams during which they reexperience the event. The symptoms can include a numbing of emotional experience, sleep difficulties, problems relating to others, and drug problems, among others. The second class of stressor is **personal stressors**, which include life events that are of a personal or individual nature, like the death of a parent or spouse, the loss of a job, or a major illness. Typically, personal stressors cause an immediate major reaction that tapers off. Sometimes, though, the effects can last for a long time, such as the effects of being raped. The third class of stressors is called **background stressors**, and they include standing in long lines, traffic jams, and other daily hassles. **Daily hassles** can add up, causing unpleasant emotions and moods. A critical factor is the degree of control people have over the daily hassles. When they have control, the stress reactions are less. On the other side of daily hassles are **uplifts**, positive events that lead to a pleasant feelings.

We cannot escape stress; it is a normal part of living. Our many efforts to control, reduce, or learn to tolerate stress are known as **coping**. Many of our responses are habitual. The **defense mechanisms** are reactions that help control stress by distorting or denying the actual nature of the situations. Denying the significance of a nearby geological fault is an example. Emotional insulation is another example in which a person does not feel emotions at all. A more positive means of dealing with stress is the use of one of three types of strategies. They are: (1) problem solving, (2) avoidance, or (3) seeking social support. Problem solving involves setting goals to deal with the situation. Avoidance techniques involve doing something other than dwelling on the stressor. Social support involves seeking help from others or confiding in a relative. Another classification of methods distinguishes **emotion-focused coping**, the conscious regulation of emotions, from **problem-focused coping**, the management of the stressful stimulus. People use both strategies, but they are more likely to use the emotion-focused strategy when they perceive the problem as unchangeable.

People can be described as having coping styles. The style of **hardiness** refers to the style that is associated with a low rate of stress-induced illness. Hardiness consists of three components: commitment, challenge, and control. Commitment is a tendency to be involved in whatever we are doing with a sense that it is important and meaningful. Challenge refers to the view that change is the standard condition of life. Control refers to the sense of being able to influence events. The hardy person is optimistic and approaches the problem directly.

Relationships with others can help people cope with stress. The knowledge of a mutual network of concerned, interested people helping individuals experience lower levels of stress is called **social support**. Social support demonstrates the value of a person to others and provides a network of information and advice. Also, actual goods and services can be provided through social support networks. Even pets can contribute to this support.

Stress can be dealt with through several steps: Turn stress into a challenge, make the threatening situation less threatening by changing attitudes about it, change goals in order to remove oneself from an uncontrollable situation, and take physical action. The most successful approach requires that the person be prepared for stress. One method of is called inoculation. With **inoculation**, stress is dealt with through preparation for both the nature of the possible stressors and developing or learning clear strategies for coping.

Concept 2:   Stereotypes, Prejudice, and Discrimination

Survey: _____
Read: _____

Pages 544-553

The negative side of schemas is the development of stereotypes. **Stereotypes** are the beliefs and expectations about members of groups held simply as the result of membership in the group. Common stereotypes are maintained concerning racial, religious, and ethnic categories. Though people are unwilling to express the prejudices they feel because these views violate social norms, a recent study has demonstrated that these attitudes persist. Stereotypes apply to more than race, religion, and ethnicity. Any group is subject to stereotyping, a bias known as the **ingroup-outgroup bias**. Less favorable views are held of groups of which we are not members, called **outgroups**, and more favorable opinions about members of groups to which we belong, or **ingroups**. When negative stereotypes lead to negative action against a group or members of a group, the behavior is called **discrimination**. Stereotypes can actually cause members of stereotyped groups to behave according to the stereotype, a phenomenon known as **self-fulfilling prophecy**. Expectations about a future event increase the likelihood that the event will occur. People are also primed to interpret behaviors according to stereotypes. If you are striving to make a positive impression, you may behave according to the stereotyped expectations people have of you.

From the very beginning of life the child is exposed to societal expectations that lead to the formation of a **gender role**, defined as the set of expectations that indicate appropriate behavior for men and women. The expectations differ significantly, and the result is that one sex stereotypes the other. **Stereotyping** is the process of forming beliefs and expectations about members of a group based on membership in the group. Stereotypes based on gender roles result in **sexism**, which consists of negative attitudes and behavior toward a person based on that person's sex. In our society, the stereotype of the male is that he must be competent, and the stereotype of the female is that she must be warm and expressive. We also hold competence in higher esteem than warmth and expressiveness, creating a bias based on sex. However attitudes have changed little since this topic was first studied by Broverman twenty years ago. Women continue to be discriminated against in occupations, and the attitudes in the workplace contribute to the occurrence of sexual harassment, which is defined by unwanted sexual advances, coercion forcing an employee to participate in a relationship, physical conduct where the employee is touched or the recipient of threatening gestures, or visual harassment in which pornographic materials are displayed. Women continue to select careers that are traditionally female-dominated.

The actual differences between men's and women's behavior is quite small. Also, what differences do exist are based on the difference between the average group differences, not the differences between individuals. Though males as a group may be more aggressive than females, there are many males less aggressive than many females.

In addition to expressing less aggression, women tend to feel greater anxiety and guilt when they are aggressive. Women tend to have lower levels of self-esteem, and they tend to have lower confidence levels concerning how they will do on future tasks. The lower self-esteem and lower aggressiveness may explain why women are reluctant to enter high-prestige professions. Contrary to the stereotype, men apparently talk more than women, though women have more precise speech. Female speech is less assertive and more tentative. Men and women also differ in their nonverbal behavior. Males communicate power and dominance, and females communicate less power. Men are also more likely to touch others, while women are more likely to be touched.

The major cognitive difference that has been identified is that of boys having better quantitative and spatial abilities than girls. Recent studies have shown that the major difference has resulted in slightly better performance on high school mathematics problem solving. Recent studies have also shown that the difference on verbal skills is insignificant. Even though the difference on mathematics performance is insignificant, the high scorers on the mathematics sections of the Scholastic Aptitude Test are predominantly male.

Both biological and environmental factors contribute to gender and sex differences. Hormones may play a role in the differences between male and female brains. Prenatal exposure to **androgens**, the male sex hormones, may slow the growth of the left hemisphere. The right hemisphere, responsible for mathematical problem solving, may then be strengthened. When **estrogen**, the female sex hormone, levels are high, women perform better on tasks requiring verbal skill and muscle coordination.

Environmental causes of gender differences include the amount and kind of interaction between parents and their children. Fathers play more roughly with their infant sons than daughters, and middle class mothers talk more to their daughters. These differences lead to different experiences of the socialization process. **Socialization** is the way individuals learn the rules and norms of socially appropriate behavior. The socialization process includes information gained from television and the educational system. Boys are more likely to receive attention from teachers. Sandra Bem has suggested that socialization produces **gender schema**, cognitive frameworks that organize and guide a child's understanding of gender-relevant information. In order to get around gender schemas, society must encourage **androgynous** activity, in which the gender roles include both male and female characteristics.

Concept 3: Psychology in a Global Perspective

Survey: ____
Read: ____

Pages 553-560

The customs and habits of individuals in different cultures can be quite different. Some of these differences are quite obvious to visitors: for example, styles of clothing, interpersonal spacing, and diet. Other differences are less obvious yet, more fundamental; such as beliefs, values and world views. For psychologists, the potential influence of culture on people's behavior raises important questions. Recently, the discipline of **cross-cultural psychology** has emerged to investigate such questions.

One of the main concerns of cross-cultural psychologists is in grouping different cultures on the basis of some characteristic or quality. Along this line, the distinction between cultures that stress the importance of individual concerns over the concerns of groups (**individualism**), and cultures that stress group concern over individual concerns (**collectivism**) has been extremely important in understanding the psychology of a given culture. For example, compared to individualistic cultures, collectivisitic cultures, which are common in Asia, tend to be less industrial, believe that intelligence is malleable as opposed to fixed, and tend to distribute rewards more equally among its citizenry.

Another concern of cross-cultural psychologists is in promoting peace in the world community. Approaches to achieve this goal are many and diverse. Some psychologists have taken to understanding how individuals of one culture perceive (and misperceive) other cultures. Others have focused on specific threats to international peace, such as the threat of nuclear war. Psychologists have identified two basic alternatives: nuclear freeze and deterrence. Some experts suggest the implementation of a **nuclear arms freeze**, in which the world's nuclear powers pledge to build no new nuclear weapons (which already exist in sufficient quantities to destroy the world many times over). The notion of a weapons freeze runs counter to the strategy of deterrence that the superpowers have traditionally employed. **Deterrence** is the notion that threats of large-scale retaliation against an enemy attack are the most effective means of preventing the attack in the first place.

These psychologists have attempted to outline strategies both for individuals (e.g., how can people be made to take responsibility for reducing the threat of nuclear war?), and for governments (e.g., what is the best strategy for dealing with hostage situations, or how effective has deterrence theory been in preventing war?)

The goal of promoting world peace has lead psychologists to step up their efforts to understand the thorny issues involved. Although few of the ideas developed by psychologists to promote peace have been implemented, many remain optimistic about the changing of the unsuccessful tactics that governments have traditionally employed when dealing with international issues.

♦ Now that you have surveyed, questioned, and read the chapter and completed the **Recap and Review** questions, review **Looking Back**, pages 561-562. *Review:* ____

♦ For additional practice through recitation and review, test your knowledge of the chapter material by answering the questions in the **Key Word Drill**, the **Practice Questions**, and the **Essay Questions**.

KEY WORD DRILL   *Recite:* ____

The following Fill in the Blank and Matching Questions test key words from the text. Check your answers with the Answer Key in the back of the Study Guide.

FILL IN THE BLANK

1. _____ refers to our response to events that are threatening or challenging.

2. Medical problems caused by an interaction of psychological, emotional, and physical difficulties are usually called _____ _____.

3. Many war veterans experience _____ disorder, a phenomenon in which the victims of major catastrophes reexperience aspects of the original stress event through dreams and flashbacks.

4. People often use _____ which are unconscious strategies that help to reduce anxiety by concealing its source from themselves and others.

5. When we have certain expectations about the occurrence of an event or behavior, these expectations can become _____-_____ and actually increase the likelihood that the event or behavior will happen.

6. When negative stereotypes lead to negative action against a group or members of a group, the behavior is called _____.

7. _____ are male sex hormones, and _____ is the female sex hormone.

8. Individuals learn what society deems appropriate behavior, including gender roles, through the process called _____.

9. _____ is the idea that a group's well-being is more important than that of the individual.

10. Some experts suggest the implementation of a _____ _____ _____ in which the world's nuclear powers pledge to build no new nuclear weapons as an alternative to reducing the threat of war.

MATCHING QUESTIONS

_____11. stressors

_____12. psychosomatic disorders

_____13. alarm and mobilization

_____14. resistance

_____15. exhaustion

a. Circumstances that produce threats to our well-being.

b. A person's initial awareness of the presence of a stressor.

c. The stage of failure to adapt to a stressor, leading to physical, psychological, and emotional problems.

d. The stage of coping with the stressor.

e. Medical problems caused by an interaction of psychological, emotional, and physical difficulties.

_____   _____

_____16. cataclysmic events

_____17. personal stressors

_____18. background stressors

_____19. daily hassles

_____20. uplifts

a. The same as background stressors.

b. Strong stressors that occur suddenly, affecting many people at once (e.g., natural disasters).

c. Events, such as the death of a family member, that have immediate negative consequences which generally fade with time.

d. Minor positive events that make one feel good.

e. Events such as being stuck in traffic that cause minor irritations but have no long term ill effects, unless they continue or are compounded by other stressful events.

_____   _____

_____ 21. coping

_____ 22. defense mechanisms

_____ 23. social support

_____ 24. inoculation

_____ 25. emotion-focused coping

_____ 26. problem-focused coping

_____ 27. hardiness

a. Preparation for stress before it is encountered.

b. The efforts to control, reduce, or learn to tolerate the threats that lead to stress.

c. Unconscious strategies people use to reduce anxiety by concealing its source from themselves and others.

d. Knowledge of being part of a mutual network of caring, interested others.

e. The conscious regulation of emotion as a means of dealing with stress.

f. Characterized by commitment, challenge, and control.

g. The management of a stressful stimulus as a way of dealing with stress.

_____ 28. stereotype

_____ 29. ingroup-outgroup bias

_____ 30. discrimination

_____ 31. outgroups

_____ 32. ingroups

a. Groups to which an individual belongs.

b. Negative behavior toward members of a particular group.

c. Beliefs and expectations about members of a group are held simply on the basis of membership in that group.

d. The tendency to hold less favorable opinions about groups to which we do not belong, while holding more favorable opinions about groups to which we do belong.

e. Groups to which an individual does not belong.

_____ 33. cross-cultural psychology   a. The idea that a group's well-being is more important than that of the individual.

_____ 34. collectivism

_____ 35. individualism   b. A situation in which the world's powers pledge to build no new nuclear weapons.

_____ 36. nuclear arms freeze   c. The notion that threats of large-scale retaliation against an enemy attack are the most effective means of preventing the attack in the first place.

_____ 37. deterrence

d. The branch of psychology that investigates the similarities and differences in psychological functioning in various cultures and ethnic groups.

e. The notion that personal identity, freedom, uniqueness, and worth of individuals is a central value.

_____   _____

PRACTICE QUESTIONS   *Recite and Review:* _____

Test your knowledge of the chapter material by answering these **True-False** and **Multiple Choice Questions**. Check your answers with the Answer Key in the back of the *Study Guide*.

TRUE-FALSE QUESTIONS

T   F   1. The resistance stage of Selye's general adaptation syndrome is characterized by the failure to adapt to a stressor that may then lead to serious physical and psychological problems.

T   F   2. Situations that are stressful are very similar for different people.

T   F   3. Even daily hassles usually require a lot of coping energy from people.

T   F   4. The result of loss of control and the ensuing stress is poorer health.

T   F   5. Stereotyping is applied only to racial, ethnic and gender groups.

T   F   6. With the large increase in women entering the work force, career stereotypes are changing dramatically.

T   F   7. Hyde and her colleagues note that the differences between men and women in terms of cognitive skills are negligible.

T   F   8. Male students receive more attention, help, and eye contact in a classroom than do female students.

T   F   9.   The approach of refusing to deal with terrorists under any
                  circumstances has proven to be a fail-safe solution.

T   F   10.   The most suitable means of defense is an arms buildup, according
                  to the strategy of deterrence.

MULTIPLE CHOICE QUESTIONS

1.   Which of the following individuals developed the general adaptation
     syndrome model?
     a.   Martin Seligman   c. B. F. Skinner
     b.   Hans Selye   d. Sigmund Freud

2.   Which alternative below is not a stage of Selye's general adaptation
     syndrome?
     a.   resistance   c. alarm and mobilization
     b.   challenge   d. exhaustion

3.   Selye's model, the general adaptation syndrome, assumes that _____
     occur regardless of the cause of the stress.
     a.   the same physiological reactions
     b.   stress-related illnesses
     c.   physical and psychological adaptations
     d.   the same psychological reactions

4.   The alarm and mobilization stage of Selye's general adaptation syndrome is
     characterized by:
     a.   preparing to react to the stressor.
     b.   increased resistance to disease.
     c.   emotional and physical collapse.
     d.   becoming aware of the presence of a stressor.

5.   It was the end of the year, and Max realized that he had failed to reach
     his sales goals, so he set new goals for the following year. Max's behavior
     is typical for a person at the _____ stage of the general adaptation
     syndrome.
     a.   resistance   c. alarm and mobilization
     b.   exhaustion   d. repression

6.   According to the general adaptation syndrome, the point at which the
     greatest negative consequences of stress appear is called the:
     a.   resistance stage.   c. alarm and mobilization stage.
     b.   acceptance stage.   d. exhaustion stage.

7.   Which event below is likely to cause the greatest general adaptation
     syndrome (GAS) changes in most people?
     a.   studying for an introductory psychology quiz
     b.   meeting the author of your psychology text
     c.   having a two-day bout with a common cold
     d.   learning and adjusting to the fact that your mother has terminal
          cancer

8. Which event below is likely to produce the greatest changes in various
    bodily systems activated by the general adaptation syndrome?
    a. getting a date with that ''awesome'' person in your English class
    b. learning you've just tested positive for HIV virus (AIDS)
    c. eating Sunday dinner with seconds for dessert
    d. going to your roommate's home to visit his or her parents

9. According to the text, events that are strong stressors and that occur
    suddenly and affect many people simultaneously are called:
    a. cataclysmic stressors.   c. uplifts.
    b. background stressors.   d. personal stressors.

10. Upon visiting the doctor's office and going through extensive testing,
    Michael finds out that he has a lung disease. Which type of stress is
    Michael likely to experience?
    a. cataclysmic stress   c. posttraumatic stress
    b. personal stress   d. background stress

11. Another term used to describe daily hassles such as a traffic jam, long
    lines, or a broken watch is:
    a. uplift.   c. natural stressors.
    b. personal stressors.   d. background stressors.

12. Whereas walking to work may be considered _____, walking in the
    woods may be considered _____.
    a. controlled activity; uncontrolled activity
    b. healthy; stressful
    c. personal stress; background stress
    d. a hassle; an uplift

13. Background stressors do not require much coping or response, but continued
    exposure to them may produce:
    a. an inability to use problem-focused techniques.
    b. as great a toll as a single, more stressful incident.
    c. as great a toll as a cataclysmic event.
    d. psychosomatic illness.

14. The textbook defines uplifts to be:
    a. minor irritations of life which are encountered daily.
    b. minor positive events that make a person feel good.
    c. exhilarating experiences which leave a person in a dazed state.
    d. major positive life events.

15. The ability to tolerate, control, or reduce threatening events is called:
    a. defense.   c. coping.
    b. arousal.   d. adaptation.

16. Someone who is classified as hardy:
    a. is unable to cope with stress at all.
    b. is unlikely to develop stress-related disease.
    c. is unlikely to view stress as a challenge.
    d. has conscious or unconscious coping strategies.

17. An individual is most likely to view groups to which he or she belongs as:
    a. outgroups.   c. ingroups.
    b. subgroups   d. central groups

18. When it was discovered that the new couple who moved into the neighborhood were Jews, conversations among the neighbors revealed the typical _____ picturing Jews as shrewd and self-centered people.
    a. cognition   c. central trait
    b. stereotype   d. stigma

19. According to the text, which of the following situations leads people to behave in ways that actually fulfill a stereotype?
    a. when they want to please someone who holds the stereotype
    b. when they want to prevent reverse discrimination
    c. when they think that someone has a self-fulfilling prophecy
    d. when they belong to an outgroup

20. Gender roles are based on:
    a. what men and women have the physical ability to do.
    b. biologically determined norms.
    c. learned abilities.
    d. culturally determined expectations.

21. Suzy's father always longed for a son. In fact, she had been expected to be her father's first son. As Suzy grew older, she was competitive and aggressive and liked playing sports, going fishing, mowing the lawn, and repairing automobiles. Suzy's behavior is consistent with her father's:
    a. stereotype for her.   c. sex role for her.
    b. sexism toward her.   d. gender role for her.

22. The negative stereotype about someone that is based on that individual's sex is called:
    a. gender role.   c. psychosexual bias.
    b. sexism.   d. gender schema.

23. Sexism produces:
    a. negative attitudes and behavior toward a group.
    b. positive attitudes and behavior toward a group.
    c. positive and negative attitudes and behavior toward a group.
    d. negative attitudes and positive behavior toward a group.

24. Which of the following is the best example of a culturally determined stereotype?
    a. Redheads have short tempers.
    b. Men are taller than women.
    c. Advanced education leads to greater income.
    d. Computers will be used more and more in the future.

25. According to Broverman's study of stereotypes, which of the following is more typically male than female?
    a. tactful   c. religious
    b. gentle   d. independent

26. Long-term research attempting to determine differences between males and females on measures of intelligence showed that males score higher than females in:
    a. high school mathematics.
    b. grammar and language arts.
    c. diction and pronunciation of words.
    d. music courses.

27. Which alternative below best summarizes current thinking on differences in verbal skills between men and women?
    a.   Men are superior to women in verbal skills.
    b.   Women are superior to men in verbal skills.
    c.   There are no differences in verbal skills between men and women.
    d.   Men are superior in verbal skills until adolescence, when women gain superiority for the rest of their lives.

28. Gender differences are determined by _____ forces.
    a.   societal   c.   biological sex
    b.   cultural   d.   biological and environmental

29. Socialization refers to the process by which an individual:
    a.   learns the rules and norms for appropriate behavior.
    b.   enters into relationships with other males and females.
    c.   learns the roles and behaviors that are appropriate for sexual encounters.
    d.   behaves in a cooperative and understanding manner to promote harmony in social situations.

30. According to Sandra Bem, the cognitive framework that organizes and guides a child's understanding of gender is called:
    a.   sex role.   c.   gender schema.
    b.   gender role.   d.   stereotyping.

31. According to Sandra Bem, androgyny is:
    a.   damaging to American youth.
    b.   restricting the flexibility with which men and women can behave.
    c.   behavior which includes both typical masculine and feminine roles.
    d.   an inherited predisposition.

32. Because he must show resolve and affection, assertiveness and love, a single male parent may develop:
    a.   bisexuality.   c.   sexism.
    b.   androgyny.   d.   gender schema.

33. The discipline of psychology that would be most concerned with how to promote a peaceful world community is:
    a.   cross-cultural psychology.   c.   community psychology.
    b.   peace psychology.   d.   international psychology.

34. The belief that workers in an organization should be rewarded to the extent that they have contributed to the organization's success is:
    a.   individualism.   c.   equality.
    b.   equity.   d.   capitalism.

35. In psychology the term ''collectivism'' refers to:
    a.   how rewards are distributed within a culture.
    b.   how economically developed a culture is.
    c.   the importance of individual goals in relation to group goals.
    d.   cultures in Eastern Asia.

36. One approach to dealing with terrorists is to refuse to deal with them. This approach is _____ in the short term and _____ in the long term.
    a.   effective, effective   c.   effective, ineffective
    b.   ineffective, effective   d.   ineffective, ineffective

37. When asked about the threat of nuclear war, the average American will report that:
    a. they are unable to think about a nuclear war.
    b. they do the best they can to reduce the specter of nuclear war.
    c. they would really miss their friends and families should such a war break out.
    d. there is a pretty good chance that they personally will die during such a war.

38. With regard to the effectiveness of deterrence theory, research has shown:
    a. strong evidence that it is not very effective.
    b. strong evidence that it is moderately effective.
    c. slight evidence that it is not very effective.
    d. slight evidence that it is moderately effective.

ESSAY QUESTIONS   *Recite and Review:* ____

Essay Question 15.1: *Stress and Its Effects*

Calculate the degree of stress in your life using Table 15-1. Interpret the results using the scoring information at the bottom of the table. What does this say about the cause of illness and the role of stress in your health?

_____

_____

_____

_____

_____

_____

_____

_____

_____

_____

_____

_____

_____

_____

_____

_____

_____

_____

_____

_____

_____

_____

Essay Question 15.2: *Values of an Industrialized Country*

In general, individualistic countries tend to be more industrially developed than collectivistic countries. Being correlational, it is not certain which causes which. Develop an explanation for why the industrialization of a country would affect its values as well as an explanation for why the values of a culture would influence its economy.

_____

_____

_____

_____

_____

_____

_____

_____

_____

_____

_____

_____

_____

_____

_____

_____

_____

_____

_____

_____

CHAPTER 1: Answer Key

FILL IN THE BLANK	MATCHING				TRUE-FALSE

FILL IN THE BLANK	MATCHING				TRUE-FALSE
1. psychology	15. b	23. b	32. d	38. d	1. F obj. 3 p. 6
2. social psychology	16. a	24. c	33. c	39. c	2. F obj. 3 p. 6
3. environmental	17. c	25. d	34. e	40. e	3. F obj. 3 p. 9
4. program evaluation	18. d	26. a	35. a	41. b	4. F obj. 5 p. 12
5. models			36. f	42. g	5. T obj. 5 p. 12
6. structuralism	19. a	27. c	37. b	43. a	6. T obj. 6 p. 12
7. introspection	20. c	28. d		44. f	7. T obj. 5 p. 13
8. functionalism	21. b	29. a			8. F obj. 7 p. 15
9. gestalt	22. d	30. b			9. T obj. 8 p. 17
10. free will; determinism		31. e			10. T obj. 8 p. 17
11. experimental bias					11. F obj. 12 p. 31
12. experimenter expectation					12. F obj. 12 p. 33
13. placebo					
14. scientific method					

MULTIPLE CHOICE

1. d obj. 1 p. 2	14. b obj. 3 p. 8	27. a obj. 5 p. 14	40. d obj. 10 p. 22
2. a obj. 1 p. 2	15. c obj. 3 p. 8	28. d obj. 7 p. 14	41. d obj. 10 p. 24
3. b obj. 1 p. 3	16. d obj. 3 p. 8	29. a obj. 6 p. 15	42. c obj. 11 p. 24
4. b obj. 1 p. 3	17. d obj. 4 p. 8	30. c obj. 6 p. 15	43. d obj. 11 p. 24
5. a obj. 2 p. 4	18. d obj. 4 p. 9	31. b obj. 6 p. 15	44. d obj. 12 p. 24
6. c obj. 2 p. 5	19. b obj. 5 p. 11	32. c obj. 7 p. 15	45. d obj. 13 p. 33
7. c obj. 3 p. 5	20. d obj. 5 p. 12	33. a obj. 7 p. 15	46. d obj. 13 p. 33
8. d obj. 2 p. 5	21. d obj. 5 p. 12	34. b obj. 8 p. 17	47. a obj. 13 p. 34
9. b obj. 2 p. 6	22. b obj. 5 p. 13	35. c obj. 7 p. 16	48. b obj. 14 p. 35
10. d obj. 4 p. 6	23. c obj. 5 p. 13	36. c obj. 6 p. 18	49. d obj. 14 p. 35
11. d obj. 4 p. 7	24. c obj. 5 p. 13	37. c obj. 6 p. 18	
12. a obj. 3 p. 7	25. c obj. 5 p. 13	38. a obj. 9 p. 21	
13. b obj. 3 p. 7	26. b obj. 5 p. 14	39. c obj. 9 p. 21	

Essay Question 1.1: Conceptual Models

■ Identify the key principle of the model you have chosen. For instance, in the psychodynamic model, one of the key principles is unconscious motivation. For the biological model, the focus is on the physiological and organic basis of behavior.

■ Offer a reason, perhaps an example, that illustrates why you like this model. Asserting that you just "liked it" or that "it makes the most sense" is not a sufficient answer.

■ Identify one or two models that you clearly reject. Again, your response must be reasoned rather than asserted.

Keep in mind that this was the introductory chapter and that you will learn much more about the unique contributions made by each model throughout the book.

Essay Question 1.2: Deceptive Practices

■ Try to imagine yourself in this kind of situation—if you have had a similar experience (where you were deceptively manipulated) an example of your reactions would be appropriate.

■ Psychologists are now expected to avoid harm, which can include undue stress, and to inform subjects to the extent possible. Also, informed consent suggests that a subject may discontinue at any point.

■ In some cases there do exist alternatives, but in others, the only alternative is naturalistic observation, and the desired qualities of experimental research, such as establishing cause and effect relationships, are likely to be lost.

CHAPTER 2: Answer Key

FILL IN THE BLANK	MATCHING				TRUE-FALSE
1. neuroscientists; biopsychologists	11. a	23. b	28. f	36. h	1. T obj. 3 p. 45
2. absolute refractory period	12. e	24. e	29. d	37. e	2. T obj. 5 p. 55
3. action potential	13. c	25. c	30. a	38. a	3. T obj. 5 p. 55
4. opiate receptor	14. b	26. d	31. e	39. f	4. F obj. 6 p. 71
5. paraplegia	15. d	27. a	32. g	40. b	5. T obj. 9 p. 73
6. homeostasis			33. c	41. g	6. F obj. 8 p. 69
7. magnetic resonance imaging (MRI) scan	16. e		34. h	42. c	7. F obj. 8 p. 66
8. electroencephalogram (EEG)	17. a		35. b	43. d	8. T obj. 10 p. 74
9. lateralization	18. d				9. T obj. 6 p. 58
10. brain modules	19. f				10. T obj. 3 p. 46
	20. g				11. F obj. 4 p. 50
	21. b				12. F obj. 1 p. 41
	22. c				

MULTIPLE CHOICE

1. b obj. 1 p. 41	14. b obj. 4 p. 50	27. c obj. 7 p. 61	40. b obj. 9 p. 69
2. d obj. 2 p. 42	15. c obj. 4 p. 51	28. b obj. 7 p. 61	41. d obj. 9 p. 69
3. d obj. 2 p. 42	16. b obj. 4 p. 51	29. a obj. 7 p. 61	42. a obj. 9 p. 70
4. b obj. 2 p. 44	17. b obj. 5 p. 53	30. d obj. 7 p. 61	43. c obj. 9 p. 70
5. d obj. 2 p. 44	18. b obj. 5 p. 53	31. a obj. 8 p. 63	44. c obj. 9 p. 70
6. d obj. 3 p. 45	19. d obj. 5 p. 53	32. a obj. 8 p. 64	45. c obj. 9 p. 70
7. d obj. 3 p. 46	20. a obj. 5 p. 55	33. b obj. 8 p. 67	46. b obj. 9 p. 71
8. c obj. 4 p. 47	21. c obj. 5 p. 55	34. a obj. 8 p. 67	47. b obj. 9 p. 72
9. c obj. 2 p. 45	22. c obj. 5 p. 55	35. d obj. 8 p. 68	48. a obj. 10 p. 74
10. d obj. 3 p. 46	23. a obj. 5 p. 55	36. d obj. 8 p. 68	49. a obj. 11 p. 76
11. d obj. 3 p. 48	24. a obj. 6 p. 59	37. b obj. 8 p. 68	50. a obj. 11 p. 76
12. a obj. 4 p. 48	25. b obj. 7 p. 59	38. c obj. 8 p. 69	
13. b obj. 4 p. 49	26. d obj. 7 p. 61	39. a obj. 8 p. 69	

Essay Question 2.1: The Benefits of Knowledge about the Brain

■   Knowledge about brain function should provide greater knowledge about behavior.

■   An understanding of neurotransmitter function can be applied to many phenomena, such as pain, drug abuse, healing processes, and thinking processes.

■   Knowledge of male and female differences will help us understand differences and similarities among individuals as well.

Essay Question 2.2: Ethics and Brain Research

■   Split brain research may actually create the phenomena observed, yet many people wish to use it to substantiate strong differences between left- and right-brain dominant individuals. Also, this research depends upon this operation.

■   The danger of transplanting tissue is not that it will create some monster, but that tissue needed may come from sources that raise questions, like fetal tissue.

■   You should identify moral and ethical reasons both for and against this research and related procedures.

CHAPTER 3: Answer Key

FILL IN THE BLANK	MATCHING				TRUE-FALSE
1. stimulus	11. c	21. b	29. b	35. b	1. T obj. 1 p. 85
2. signal detection	12. a	22. f	30. f	36. c	2. F obj. 2 p. 85
3. accommodation; adaptation	13. d	23. d	31. d	37. a	3. F obj. 4 p. 93
4. opponent-process	14. e	24. c	32. a	38. f	4. T obj. 6 p. 99
5. olfactory cells	15. b	25. g	33. c	39. e	5. F obj. 7 p. 104
6. perception		26. h	34. e	40. d	6. F obj. 9 p. 108
7. gestalt laws	16. d	27. a			7. T obj. 10 p. 114
8. top-down; bottom-up	17. c	28. e			8. F obj. 10 p. 114
9. constructive	18. a				9. T obj. 11 p. 117
10. Müller-Lyer	19. b				10. T obj. 12 p. 120

MULTIPLE CHOICE

1. b obj. 1 p. 84	14. b obj. 4 p. 93	27. d obj. 7 p. 104	40. c obj. 10 p. 114
2. c obj. 1 p. 85	15. d obj. 4 p. 93	28. a obj. 7 p. 104	41. c obj. 11 p. 116
3. d obj. 2 p. 85	16. d obj. 4 p. 94	29. b obj. 7 p. 104	42. b obj. 11 p. 117
4. c obj. 2 p. 85	17. a obj. 5 p. 96	30. b obj. 7 p. 105	43. a obj. 11 p. 117
5. a obj. 2 p. 85	18. a obj. 5 p. 96	31. b obj. 7 p. 105	44. d obj. 11 p. 117
6. a obj. 2 p. 85	19. c obj. 6 p. 99	32. d obj. 8 p. 106	45. d obj. 11 p. 117
7. b obj. 2 p. 85	20. a obj. 6 p. 100	33. a obj. 8 p. 106	46. d obj. 11 p. 118
8. a obj. 3 p. 87	21. b obj. 6 p. 101	34. c obj. 8 p. 107	47. b obj. 12 p. 120
9. a obj. 3 p. 87	22. b obj. 6 p. 101	35. d obj. 9 p. 108	48. b obj. 12 p. 120
10. a obj. 3 p. 87	23. a obj. 6 p. 101	36. b obj. 9 p. 108	49. a obj. 12 p. 120
11. c obj. 4 p. 91	24. a obj. 6 p. 102	37. d obj. 10 p. 113	50. a obj. 12 p. 122
12. b obj. 4 p. 92	25. c obj. 6 p. 103	38. b obj. 10 p. 114	
13. c obj. 4 p. 92	26. c obj. 7 p. 104	39. b obj. 10 p. 114	

Essay Question 3.1: The Problem of Extra Senses

The major points that should be included in your answer:

- Discuss the importance of sensory selectivity—of sense organs being sensitive to limited ranges of physical stimuli.

- Though we would probably adjust to the differences, additional information might create duplications.

- Describe the things we would be able to hear, smell, taste, and feel if our sensory ranges were broader.

- Reflect on the possibility that our ability for sensory adaptation might have to increase.

Essay Question 3.2: The Importance of Perceptual Constancy

The major points that should be included in your answer:

- A definition of perceptual constancy.

- Examples of perceptual constancy—perhaps the shrinking of objects as they become more distant, the consistency of shapes in our environment like doors, tables, etc., and the predictability of colors based on color constancy.

- Perceptual constancy aids distance and form perception, so our abilities at depth, movement, and object perception would be greatly limited.

CHAPTER 4: Answer Key

FILL IN THE BLANK	MATCHING				TRUE-FALSE
1. consciousness	11. d	21. e	29. e	35. b	1. T obj. 2 p. 131
2. altered states of consciousness	12. c	22. c	30. a	36. h	2. F obj. 2 p. 132
3. circadian rhythms	13. e	23. f	31. c	37. a	3. F obj. 3 p. 133
4. unconscious wish fulfillment	14. a	24. g	32. b	38. d	4. T obj. 2 p. 134
5. hypnosis	15. b	25. a	33. d	39. f	5. F obj. 4 p. 134
6. meditation; mantra		26. h	34. f	40. g	6. T obj. 3 p. 139
7. psychoactive	16. a	27. b		41. e	7. F obj. 3 p. 140
8. addictive	17. e	28. d		42. c	8. T obj. 7 p. 150
9. stimulants; depressants	18. c				9. T obj. 7 p. 154
10. narcotics	19. d				10. T obj. 8 p. 157
	20. b				

MULTIPLE CHOICE			
1. d obj. 1 p. 129	14. c obj. 2 p. 135	27. b obj. 4 p. 141	40. b obj. 7 p. 154
2. a obj. 1 p. 130	15. c obj. 3 p. 137	28. b obj. 4 p. 141	41. b obj. 7 p. 154
3. a obj. 2 p. 131	16. c obj. 3 p. 137	29. d obj. 4 p. 141	42. b obj. 7 p. 157
4. a obj. 2 p. 132	17. a obj. 3 p. 137	30. a obj. 4 p. 142	43. d obj. 8 p. 157
5. a obj. 2 p. 132	18. d obj. 3 p. 138	31. d obj. 4 p. 143	44. c obj. 8 p. 157
6. b obj. 2 p. 132	19. b obj. 3 p. 138	32. b obj. 5 p. 145	45. c obj. 8 p. 158
7. d obj. 2 p. 132	20. b obj. 3 p. 139	33. d obj. 6 p. 147	
8. d obj. 2 p. 132	21. b obj. 3 p. 140	34. a obj. 6 p. 147	
9. c obj. 2 p. 133	22. d obj. 3 p. 140	35. a obj. 6 p. 147	
10. d obj. 2 p. 133	23. a obj. 3 p. 140	36. d obj. 7 p. 149	
11. d obj. 2 p. 133	24. a obj. 3 p. 141	37. c obj. 7 p. 149	
12. b obj. 2 p. 134	25. c obj. 4 p. 141	38. b obj. 7 p. 150	
13. d obj. 2 p. 135	26. a obj. 4 p. 141	39. b obj. 7 p. 153	

Essay Question 4.1: Hypnotism

The major points that should be included in your answer:

■   One view argues that the phenomenon is real (that of Hilgard), another that the phenomenon is not distinct enough to be considered a separate state of consciousness, and yet another suggests that people pretend to be hypnotized.

■   Whether the state is real or not (you must select and defend one of the points of view), you should make reference to the positive consequences for pain control, behavior change, and other uses.

Essay Question 4.2: Decriminalizing Psychoactive Drugs

The major points that should be included in your answer:

■   Identify the drugs that have been involved in this issue lately. This would include marijuana., But also some have argued that drug use should be completely legalized and viewed as a medical or psychological problem.

■   State your view, identifying which drug(s) should be decriminalized and which should not. Many people suggest that the medical benefits of some drugs cannot be explored and used because of their status. Other reasons should be offered as well. For instance, the use of some drugs can be considered victimless, though the drug trade has many victims.

■   If you believe that all drugs should remain illegal, then support your reasoning. Harm to society and to individuals is a common argument. Examples could be given.

CHAPTER 5: Answer Key

FILL IN THE BLANK	MATCHING				TRUE-FALSE
1. learning	11. c	23. a	35. b	42. c	1. T obj. 1 p. 165
2. maturation	12. e	24. f	36. e	43. e	2. F obj. 1 p. 168
3. blocking	13. g	25. b	37. c	44. f	3. T obj. 2 p. 170
4. law of effect	14. f	26. d	38. g	45. d	4. F obj. 2 p. 171
5. superstitious behavior	15. a	27. e	39. a	46. b	5. F obj. 3 p. 174
6. shaping	16. d	28. c	40. f	47. a	6. T obj. 4 p. 177
7. programmed instruction	17. b		41. d		7. T obj. 5 p. 178
8. biological constraints		29. c			8. F obj. 5 p. 179
9. cognitive map	18. b	30. e			9. F obj. 6 p. 182
10. learned helplessness	19. a	31. d			10. T obj. 6 p. 182
	20. e	32. f			
	21. c	33. a			
	22. d	34. b			

MULTIPLE CHOICE

1. d obj. 1 p. 164	14. b obj. 2 p. 170	27. c obj. 4 p. 176	40. b obj. 6 p. 187
2. a obj. 1 p. 165	15. d obj. 2 p. 170	28. a obj. 5 p. 177	41. d obj. 7 p. 187
3. d obj. 1 p. 165	16. d obj. 2 p. 170	29. c obj. 5 p. 177	42. a obj. 7 p. 188
4. c obj. 1 p. 165	17. b obj. 2 p. 170	30. b obj. 5 p. 177	43. b obj. 7 p. 189
5. c obj. 1 p. 168	18. c obj. 2 p. 171	31. b obj. 5 p. 177	44. d obj. 8 p. 190
6. a obj. 1 p. 168	19. a obj. 2 p. 171	32. c obj. 5 p. 179	45. c obj. 9 p. 192
7. a obj. 1 p. 168	20. a obj. 2 p. 171	33. d obj. 5 p. 180	46. c obj. 9 p. 195
8. a obj. 1 p. 168	21. a obj. 3 p. 172	34. d obj. 6 p. 182	47. b obj. 10 p. 196
9. b obj. 1 p. 168	22. b obj. 3 p. 174	35. d obj. 6 p. 183	
10. a obj. 1 p. 168	23. a obj. 4 p. 175	36. a obj. 6 p. 183	
11. d obj. 2 p. 168	24. d obj. 4 p. 176	37. d obj. 6 p. 183	
12. d obj. 2 p. 169	25. d obj. 4 p. 176	38. a obj. 6 p. 184	
13. d obj. 2 p. 170	26. c obj. 4 p. 176	39. d obj. 6 p. 186	

Essay Question 5.1: Using Physical Punishment

■   Cite examples of the use of physical punishment. Describe alternatives for each use.

■   Identify the conditions under which physical punishment may be necessary. These could include the need for swift and attention-getting action to prevent physical harm. Some parents use corporal punishment when children hit one another; some do so to establish control when alternatives have failed.

■   Indicate your views and explain them.

Essay Question 5.2: Which Approach Is Correct?

■   Describe each of the three approaches in such a way that they are clearly distinguished.

■   Identify points of contradiction among the views. In classical conditioning, the stimuli must precede the responses; in operant conditioning, the reinforcing stimuli comes after the response; in observational learning, the behavior does not need to be practiced. Mental processes are also involved in observational learning.

■   Observational learning may actually be reconciled with the other two once mental processes and reinforcement of the model (rather than the learner) are allowed.

CHAPTER 6: Answer Key

FILL IN THE BLANK	MATCHING				TRUE-FALSE
1. memory	11. d	22. f	29. b	36. c	1. T obj. 3 p. 209
2. chunk	12. f	23. a	30. g	37. g	2. T obj. 4 p. 211
3. mnemonics	13. a	24. e	31. c	38. a	3. F obj. 4 p. 211
4. explicit; implicit	14. c	25. d	32. a	39. d	4. T obj. 6 p. 217
5. levels-of-processing theory	15. e	26. b	33. e	40. b	5. F obj. 7 p. 219
6. tip-of-the-tongue phenomenon	16. b	27. g	34. f	41. e	6. F obj. 7 p. 219
7. constructive processes		28. c	35. d	42. f	7. F obj. 9 p. 225
8. schemas	17. e				8. F obj. 9 p. 225
9. decay	18. d			43. a	9. F obj. 9 p. 225
10. interference	19. b			44. c	10. F obj. 11 p. 229
	20. c			45. e	
	21. a			46. d	
				47. b	

MULTIPLE CHOICE

1. a obj. 1 p. 205	14. b obj. 4 p. 211	27. c obj. 6 p. 219	40. b obj. 11 p. 229
2. b obj. 1 p. 205	15. c obj. 4 p. 211	28. d obj. 7 p. 219	41. a obj. 11 p. 229
3. b obj. 1 p. 205	16. a obj. 4 p. 211	29. b obj. 6 p. 219	42. d obj. 11 p. 229
4. a obj. 2 p. 206	17. b obj. 4 p. 214	30. b obj. 9 p. 225	43. b obj. 12 p. 230
5. b obj. 2 p. 206	18. a obj. 4 p. 214	31. c obj. 9 p. 226	44. a obj. 12 p. 230
6. b obj. 2 p. 207	19. c obj. 4 p. 214	32. d obj. 9 p. 226	45. a obj. 12 p. 231
7. b obj. 2 p. 207	20. d obj. 4 p. 214	33. b obj. 9 p. 226	
8. a obj. 3 p. 208	21. c obj. 4 p. 214	34. a obj. 9 p. 226	
9. b obj. 3 p. 208	22. d obj. 5 p. 215	35. c obj. 9 p. 227	
10. c obj. 3 p. 208	23. a obj. 5 p. 215	36. b obj. 10 p. 228	
11. b obj. 3 p. 209	24. a obj. 6 p. 217	37. d obj. 11 p. 229	
12. b obj. 3 p. 210	25. d obj. 6 p. 217	38. c obj. 11 p. 229	
13. b obj. 4 p. 211	26. d obj. 6 p. 218	39. b obj. 9 p. 226	

Essay Question 6.1: Writing about Eyewitness Testimony

- State the evidence supporting the fallibility of witnesses and describe the potential problems that can arise from mistaken witnesses.

- Some of the problems come from questions that are designed to mislead. Psychologists can support efforts to reform this process and to design techniques that will help witnesses improve their memories.

- One might argue that psychologists would interfere with and compound the problem further by making contributions that are intended to improve witness memory.

Essay Question 6.2: Comparing the Laboratory and Real Life

- Give several examples of laboratory research. The advantages include control over the experiment and the ability to document that prior memories do not influence the outcome.

- Identify experiences that are best examined in an everyday context. Much case study and archival research is based on reports that are made when an event occurs or on reports from several points of view and are thus a form of everyday memory research. Other examples should be given.

- As stated in the text, both of these techniques are needed to understand memory fully.

CHAPTER 7: Answer Key

FILL IN THE BLANK	MATCHING						TRUE-FALSE
1. cognition	11. e	21. b	27. a	32. b			1. F obj. 3 p. 241
2. thought	12. b	22. a	28. d	33. c			2. T obj. 3 p. 241
3. concepts	13. d	23. e	29. e	34. e			3. T obj. 3 p. 242
4. deductive; inductive	14. a	24. f	30. c	35. d			4. T obj. 4 p. 248
5. well-defined; ill-defined	15. c	25. d	31. b	36. a			5. T obj. 5 p. 250
6. functional fixedness		26. c					6. T obj. 5 p. 250
7. language	16. d			37. d			7. T obj. 6 p. 251
8. learning-theory	17. c			38. b			8. F obj. 6 p. 252
9. linguistic-relativity hypothesis	18. a			39. a			9. F obj. 7 p. 253
10. cognitive complexity	19. e			40. c			10. T obj. 7 p. 254
	20. b						11. F obj. 9 p. 258
							12. F obj. 9 p. 258

MULTIPLE CHOICE

1. d obj. 1 p. 237	14. d obj. 4 p. 245	27. c obj. 7 p. 253	40. b obj. 9 p. 259
2. b obj. 1 p. 237	15. a obj. 5 p. 246	28. c obj. 8 p. 256	41. c obj. 10 p. 259
3. a obj. 1 p. 237	16. d obj. 4 p. 248	29. b obj. 8 p. 256	42. b obj. 10 p. 259
4. c obj. 1 p. 238	17. d obj. 4 p. 248	30. d obj. 8 p. 257	43. b obj. 10 p. 260
5. c obj. 1 p. 238	18. d obj. 4 p. 248	31. b obj. 9 p. 257	44. a obj. 10 p. 260
6. b obj. 1 p. 238	19. b obj. 5 p. 249	32. b obj. 9 p. 257	45. c obj. 10 p. 261
7. d obj. 2 p. 239	20. a obj. 5 p. 249	33. b obj. 9 p. 258	46. d obj. 10 p. 261
8. c obj. 2 p. 239	21. c obj. 5 p. 249	34. c obj. 9 p. 258	47. d obj. 10 p. 261
9. a obj. 2 p. 241	22. d obj. 6 p. 251	35. c obj. 9 p. 258	
10. d obj. 3 p. 242	23. a obj. 6 p. 251	36. d' obj. 9 p. 258	
11. b obj. 3 p. 242	24. a obj. 6 p. 251	37. d obj. 9 p. 259	
12. c obj. 5 p. 244	25. b obj. 7 p. 253	38. b obj. 9 p. 259	
13. b obj. 4 p. 245	26. b obj. 7 p. 253	39. a obj. 9 p. 259	

Essay Question 7.1: Problem Solving

■ Describe your problem or challenge. It would be best to identify both the positive and the negative aspects of the challenge. What is gained and what is given up?

■ Define the problem in terms of the steps that must be taken to achieve the solution.

■ State several possible solution strategies as they apply to your problem.

■ State how you will know when you have effectively solved the problem. Remember, if the problem is long-term, selecting one solution strategy may preclude using another.

Essay Question 7.2: Is Language Uniquely Human?

■ Chimpanzees acquire an ability to speak comparable to that of a two-year-old child.

■ The physical ability in humans to produce language has the greatest production capability.

■ You may be familiar with research in dolphin and whale communication or work with other animals. Examples could be used to support your answer.

■ What is meant by "unique" must be defined to complete this answer. Indeed human language is unique, but other animals do communicate.

CHAPTER 8: Answer Key

FILL IN THE BLANK	MATCHING				TRUE-FALSE
1. intelligence	11. c	15. f	22. d		1. T obj. 1 p. 271
2. deviation IQ score	12. b	16. g	23. f		2. T obj. 1 p. 272
3. achievement; aptitude	13. a	17. a	24. b		3. F obj. 2 p. 273
4. g-factor	14. d	18. e	25. e		4. F obj. 2 p. 273
5. triarchic		19. d	26. c		5. F obj. 2 p. 273
6. mental retardation		20. b	27. a		6. T obj. 3 p. 274
7. least-restrictive environment		21. c			7. T obj. 4 p. 276
8. mainstreaming					8. F obj. 3 p. 278
9. culture-fair					9. F obj. 6 p. 283
10. heritability					10. T obj. 8 p. 287

MULTIPLE CHOICE			
1. d obj. 1 p. 268	14. c obj. 2 p. 272	27. c obj. 3 p. 275	40. b obj. 6 p. 283
2. d obj. 1 p. 270	15. c obj. 2 p. 272	28. d obj. 4 p. 276	41. a obj. 6 p. 283
3. c obj. 1 p. 270	16. a obj. 2 p. 272	29. a obj. 4 p. 277	42. a obj. 7 p. 283
4. a obj. 1 p. 270	17. d obj. 2 p. 272	30. b obj. 4 p. 278	43. d obj. 7 p. 283
5. a obj. 2 p. 271	18. c obj. 2 p. 273	31. b obj. 4 p. 278	44. c obj. 8 p. 287
6. c obj. 2 p. 271	19. a obj. 2 p. 273	32. b obj. 6 p. 281	45. d obj. 8 p. 287
7. c obj. 2 p. 271	20. d obj. 2 p. 273	33. c obj. 6 p. 281	46. c obj. 8 p. 288
8. c obj. 2 p. 271	21. a obj. 2 p. 273	34. b obj. 6 p. 281	
9. b obj. 2 p. 271	22. c obj. 3 p. 274	35. d obj. 6 p. 282	
10. a obj. 2 p. 271	23. b obj. 3 p. 274	36. d obj. 6 p. 282	
11. a obj. 2 p. 271	24. d obj. 3 p. 274	37. b obj. 6 p. 282	
12. a obj. 1 p. 272	25. a obj. 3 p. 275	38. d obj. 6 p. 282	
13. a obj. 1 p. 272	26. a obj. 3 p. 275	39. b obj. 6 p. 283	

Essay Question 8.1: Defining Intelligence

■   Describe Binet's conception of intelligence, the g-factor view, Gardner's multiple intelligence, the triarchic theory, and the concepts of practical and emotional intelligence. (A good answer would not have to have all of these approaches.)

■   State which you find most acceptable and for what reason. For instance, the concept of practical intelligence may be appealing because it focuses on something other than educational ability.

■   The most important evidence is evidence that predicts, but if a definition appears to agree with commonly held views, then it too will have some validity because people do act upon these kinds of views.

Essay Question 8.2: The Heredity/Environment Question

■   Note that this returns to one of the major issues introduced in the beginning of the text and that there is no ready answer for the debate.

■   The most fundamental issue is that we have quite a bit of evidence supporting both the role of the environment and the role of genetic factors. Psychologists do not want to select one over the other.

■   Of particular relevance was the discussion of problem solving and creativity.

■   The extent to which intelligence is dependent upon the environment affects the possibility of developing a culture-fair test.

CHAPTER 9: Answer Key

FILL IN THE BLANK	MATCHING				TRUE-FALSE
1. motivation	11. c	18. b	24. g	31. d	1. F obj. 1 p. 294
2. homeostasis	12. d	19. d	25. c	32. a	2. T obj. 2 p. 297
3. incentive	13. g	20. f	26. f	33. c	3. F obj. 2 p. 297
4. obesity; twenty (20)	14. e	21. e	27. e	34. e	4. F obj. 4 p. 301
5. weight set point	15. f	22. c	28. d	35. b	5. F obj. 4 p. 302
6. anorexia nervosa; bulimia	16. a	23. a	29. b		6. F obj. 5 p. 308
7. masturbation)	17. b		30. a	36. b	7. F obj. 7 p. 311
8. homosexuality				37. c	8. T obj. 9 p. 314
9. Thematic Apperception Test (TAT)				38. a	9. T obj. 6 p. 365
10. emotions					10. T obj. 10 p. 322

MULTIPLE CHOICE			
1. a obj. 1 p. 294	14. b obj. 3 p. 298	27. d obj. 5 p. 307	40. c obj. 6 p. 316
2. d obj. 1 p. 294	15. d obj. 3 p. 300	28. b obj. 5 p. 307	41. d obj. 6 p. 316
3. c obj. 2 p. 295	16. a obj. 3 p. 300	29. c obj. 5 p. 308	42. a obj. 6 p. 318
4. d obj. 2 p. 296	17. a obj. 4 p. 301	30. d obj. 5 p. 309	43. c obj. 10 p. 321
5. b obj. 2 p. 296	18. d obj. 4 p. 301	31. c obj. 5 p. 309	44. a obj. 10 p. 321
6. b obj. 2 p. 296	19. b obj. 4 p. 301	32. b obj. 7 p. 311	45. d obj. 11 p. 323
7. a obj. 2 p. 296	20. b obj. 4 p. 301	33. b obj. 7 p. 312	46. a obj. 11 p. 323
8. c obj. 2 p. 296	21. c obj. 4 p. 301	34. b obj. 7 p. 312	47. a obj. 11 p. 324
9. a obj. 2 p. 296	22. b obj. 4 p. 302	35. a obj. 8 p. 312	
10. b obj. 2 p. 297	23. c obj. 5 p. 304	36. d obj. 8 p. 313	
11. b obj. 2 p. 297	24. c obj. 5 p. 306	37. d obj. 9 p. 314	
12. a obj. 2 p. 298	25. b obj. 5 p. 307	38. b obj. 6 p. 316	
13. b obj. 3 p. 299	26. c obj. 5 p. 307	39. a obj. 6 p. 316	

Essay Question 9.1: Theories of Motivation

■ Describe each of the main theories: instinct, drive reduction, arousal, incentive, opponent process, cognitive, and need theories.

■ Select an activity—it could be anything from watching television to playing a sport—and describe the behavior involved from the point of view of the motivation theories (no more than one sentence each).

■ Remember, some behaviors, like those satisfying basic needs, will be easier to describe from the points of view of some theories while others will be easier to describe from other theories.

Essay Question 9.2: The Changing Sexual Attitudes

■ Social acceptance of sexual activity and increased visibility of activity in the media have contributed to the increase in activity.

■ AIDS and campaigns for safer sex have caused some populations to reconsider risky sexual practices.

■ The double standard has changed slightly.

■ The sixties were marked by a sexual freedom that has been affected to some extent by AIDS and by the aging of the population.

CHAPTER 10: Answer Key

FILL IN THE BLANK	MATCHING				TRUE-FALSE
1. developmental psychology	11. c	25. e	38. b	48. c	1. F obj. 1 p. 335
2. identical twins	12. f	26. a	39. f	49. a	2. F obj. 2 p. 338
3. age of viability	13. e	27. h	40. c	50. d	3. F obj. 3 p. 342
4 attachment	14. a	28. b	41. e	51. b	4. T obj. 4 p. 346
5. information processing	15. g	29. g	42. d		5. T obj. 4 p. 348
6. adolescence	16. h	30. f	43. a	52. b	6. T obj. 8 p. 359
7. identity	17. b	31. i		53. f	7. T obj. 8 p. 359
8. midlife transition	18. d	32. c	44. d	54. d	8. T obj. 8 p. 362
9. gerontologists		33. d	45. c	55. a	9. F obj. 11 p. 366
10. fluid; crystallized	19. d		46. b	56. e	10. F obj. 12 p. 368
	20. a	34. b	47. a	57. c	
	21. e	35. a			
	22. c	36. d			
	23. b	37. c			
	24. f				

MULTIPLE CHOICE

1. a obj. 1 p. 334	14. a obj. 3 p. 342	27. a obj. 7 p. 358	40. c obj. 11 p. 367
2. c obj. 1 p. 334	15. b obj. 3 p. 343	28. c obj. 8 p. 360	41. b obj. 11 p. 368
3. a obj. 1 p. 334	16. a obj. 3 p. 345	29. b obj. 8 p. 361	42. b obj. 12 p. 369
4. c obj. 1 p. 335	17. a obj. 4 p. 347	30. d obj. 8 p. 361	43. c obj. 12 p. 369
5. b obj. 2 p. 338	18. a obj. 4 p. 347	31. c obj. 9 p. 363	44. b obj. 12 p. 369
6. c obj. 2 p. 338	19. c obj. 4 p. 348	32. a obj. 9 p. 363	45. c obj. 12 p. 369
7. a obj. 2 p. 338	20. b obj. 5 p. 350	33. c obj. 9 p. 363	46. d obj. 13 p. 370
8. d obj. 2 p. 338	21. a obj. 5 p. 350	34. d obj. 9 p. 364	47. a obj. 13 p. 370
9. d obj. 2 p. 338	22. d obj. 6 p. 352	35. d obj. 10 p. 365	48. b obj. 13 p. 370
10. b obj. 2 p. 339	23. b obj. 6 p. 353	36. a obj. 10 p. 365	49. b obj. 13 p. 371
11. d obj. 2 p. 339	24. d obj. 6 p. 354	37. b obj. 10 p. 365	50. d obj. 14 p.372
12. b obj. 3 p. 342	25. d obj. 6 p. 355	38. b obj. 11 p. 365	
13. b obj. 3 p. 342	26. b obj. 7 p. 358	39. b obj. 11 p. 367	

Essay Question 13.2: Stimulation of Children

- Describe the factors that you consider important for early exposure. Can a child's later learning be enhanced through early exposure to academic skills like spelling and math? Or should the focus be on processes like imagination and creative work?

- What criteria would you use to identify overstimulation? Keep in mind that the child must feel safe and have a secure attachment in order to explore the environment freely.

Essay Question 14.2: Aging and Retirement

- First, describe each of these two theories and offer an example of how they differ.

- The activity theory suggests that a successful retirement would require a level of activity that would allow continuity.

- Retirement serves as an important marker of age in the disengagement theory.

- Describe the benefits (such as making room for people entering the job market) or costs (loss of expertise) of mandatory retirement in order to support your yes or no answer.

CHAPTER 11: Answer Key

FILL IN THE BLANK	MATCHING					TRUE-FALSE
1. personality	12. c	23. b	36. c	49. a	56. f	1. T obj. 2 p. 384
2. psychoanalysts	13. b	24. f	37. e	50. g	57. d	2. T obj. 2 p. 384
3. Oedipal conflict	14. d	25. e	38. a	51. d	58. a	3. F obj. 3 p. 385
4. neo-Freudians	15. e	26. a	39. b	52. c	59. e	4. T obj. 4 p. 387
5. traits	16. a	27. g	40. f	53. f	60. g	5. T obj. 5 p. 392
6. factor analysis		28. c	41. d	54. b	61. c	6. T obj. 5 p. 394
7. determinism	17. f	29. d	42. g	55. e	62. b	7. T obj. 9 p. 405
8. nomothetic; idiographic	18. a					8. F obj. 9 p. 406
9. reliability; validity	19. e	30. d	43. f		63. d	
10. norms	20. d	31. b	44. c		64. b	
11. behavioral assessment	21. c	32. f	45. e		65. a	
	22. b	33. a	46. b		66. c	
		34. c	47. d			
		35. e	48. a			

MULTIPLE CHOICE

1. a obj. 1 p. 381	14. c obj. 2 p. 385	27. d obj. 5 p. 390	40. a obj. 8 p. 401
2. c obj. 1 p. 381	15. c obj. 3 p. 385	28. c obj. 5 p. 390	41. a obj. 9 p. 402
3. d obj. 1 p. 381	16. a obj. 3 p. 385	29. b obj. 5 p. 392	42. b obj. 9 p. 404
4. a obj. 1 p. 382	17. b obj. 3 p. 386	30. d obj. 6 p. 396	43. b obj. 9 p. 405
5. b obj. 1 p. 382	18. b obj. 3 p. 386	31. d obj. 6 p. 396	44. c obj. 9 p. 405
6. b obj. 1 p. 382	19. d obj. 4 p. 386	32. c obj. 7 p. 397	45. d obj. 9 p. 405
7. c obj. 1 p. 383	20. c obj. 4 p. 387	33. b obj. 7 p. 397	46. b obj. 10 p. 407
8. c obj. 1 p. 383	21. c obj. 4 p. 387	34. b obj. 7 p. 398	
9. b obj. 1 p. 383	22. d obj. 4 p. 388	35. b obj. 7 p. 398	
10. d obj. 2 p. 384	23. d obj. 5 p. 389	36. d obj. 6 p. 399	
11. b obj. 2 p. 384	24. a obj. 5 p. 390	37. a obj. 7 p. 399	
12. a obj. 2 p. 384	25. d obj. 5 p. 390	38. c obj. 8 p. 401	
13. b obj. 2 p. 384	26. a obj. 5 p. 390	39. d obj. 8 p. 401	

Essay Question 11.1: Freud and Female Psychology

■　The weakest area is Freud's developmental stages, particularly with the Oedipus complex. Freud's concept of penis envy is not well accepted by many.

■　Just as Gilligan contests Kohlberg's views of moral development, one could argue that Freud's concept of a genital stage rests on masculine norms.

Essay Question 11.2: Personality Placement Tests

■　According to the text, MMPI and the TAT were developed for specific purposes, and the extension of them to job placement depends upon their being validated for the application to placement.

■　One major problem is the use of norms or averages to prepare job "profiles." These are still average and composite pictures of the individual and may unfairly discriminate against those who do not fit the profile.

CHAPTER 12: Answer Key

FILL IN THE BLANK	MATCHING				TRUE-FALSE
1. cognitive-behavioral	11. d	22. d	33. d	38. a	1. F obj. 1 p. 414
2. medical student's	12. a	23. e	34. c	39. f	2. T obj. 1 p. 415
3. DSM-III-R	13. e	24. a	35. e	40. e	3. F obj. 2 p. 420
4. anxiety	14. c	25. c	36. b	41. c	4. T obj. 2 p. 420
5. obsessions; compulsion	15. f	26. f	37. a	42. b	5. F obj. 4 p. 425
6. phobias	16. b	27. b		43. d	6. F obj. 4 p. 425
7. schizophrenia					7. T obj. 7 p. 434
8. delusions	17. c	28. e			8. F obj. 7 p. 434
9. hallucinations	18. e	29. b			9. F obj. 8 p. 437
10. major	19. b	30. d			10. T obj. 9 p. 440
	20. d	31. a			
	21. a	32. c			

MULTIPLE CHOICE			
1. c obj. 1 p. 413	14. c obj. 2 p. 422	27. b obj. 5 p. 429	40. c obj. 9 p. 440
2. b obj. 1 p. 415	15. a obj. 2 p. 422	28. b obj. 5 p. 430	41. a obj. 9 p. 440
3. c obj. 1 p. 415	16. a obj. 2 p. 422	29. a obj. 5 p. 430	42. d obj. 9 p. 440
4. b obj. 1 p. 416	17. d obj. 2 p. 423	30. c obj. 6 p. 431	43. a obj. 9 p. 440
5. c obj. 1 p. 417	18. a obj. 3 p. 424	31. a obj. 6 p. 432	44. a obj. 9 p. 442
6. a obj. 2 p. 419	19. b obj. 4 p. 425	32. b obj. 6 p. 432	45. c obj. 9 p. 442
7. a obj. 2 p. 419	20. c obj. 4 p. 425	33. c obj. 7 p. 434	46. b obj. 9 p. 442
8. b obj. 2 p. 419	21. d obj. 4 p. 426	34. d obj. 7 p. 434	47. d obj. 9 p. 444
9. c obj. 2 p. 420	22. b obj. 4 p. 426	35. d obj. 7 p. 434	48. c obj. 10 p. 446
10. b obj. 2 p. 420	23. b obj. 4 p. 427	36. b obj. 7 p. 435	
11. c obj. 2 p. 421	24. c obj. 5 p. 428	37. c obj. 7 p. 435	
12. d obj. 2 p. 422	25. a obj. 5 p. 428	38. a obj. 8 p. 436	
13. b obj. 2 p. 422	26. b obj. 5 p. 429	39. b obj. 8 p. 438	

Essay Question 12.1: Defining Mental Illness

- The Rosenhan study suggests that mental health workers label their clients with rather unshakable labels. The labels also lead to interpretations of behavior that continue to confirm the diagnosis (note that some stayed for many weeks even though they only complained of the symptom once on admission to the hospital).

- The issues of deception and the use of subjects who had not given their consent are major issues.

- A brief examination of the study does not explain the contexts involved: few people voluntarily walk into a mental hospital and complain of a major symptom. The sudden disappearance of the symptom could be considered abnormal as well.

Essay Question 12.2: Schizophrenia

- Describe the major symptoms (see pages 440 and 441 in the text).

- Distinguish process and reactive, and examine the list of types on page 440 of the text.

- Discuss the biological and psychological components.

CHAPTER 13: Answer Key

FILL IN THE BLANK	MATCHING				TRUE-FALSE
1. psychotherapy	13. e	20. c	29. b	36. f	1. F obj. 2 p. 458
2. observational; modeling	14. a	21. e	30. c	37. c	2. T obj. 2 p. 458
3. dream interpretation	15. d	22. b	31. e	38. e	3. F obj. 3 p. 459
4. spontaneous remission	16. c	23. d	32. f	39. b	4. T obj. 3 p. 462
5. nondirective counseling	17. f	24. a	33. a	40. d	5. T obj. 4 p. 464
6. unconditional positive regard	18. b		34. g	41. a	6. F obj. 5 p. 466
7. drug therapy; psychosurgery	19. g	25. b	35. d		7. T obj. 5 p. 467
8. neurotic		26. d			8. F obj. 6 p. 471
9. eclectic		27. a			9. F obj. 7 p. 478
10. deinstitutionalization		28. c			10. T obj. 8 p. 478
11. electroconvulsive therapy					
12. prefrontal lobotomy					

MULTIPLE CHOICE

1. b obj. 1 p. 455	14. b obj. 3 p. 459	27. d obj. 5 p. 467	40. b obj. 7 p. 477
2. d obj. 1 p. 455	15. b obj. 3 p. 460	28. d obj. 5 p. 467	41. a obj. 7 p. 477
3. c obj. 1 p. 455	16. a obj. 3 p. 460	29. d obj. 5 p. 468	42. d obj. 7 p. 477
4. a obj. 1 p. 456	17. c obj. 3 p. 460	30. a obj. 5 p. 468	43. b obj. 7 p. 477
5. c obj. 1 p. 456	18. a obj. 3 p. 462	31. a obj. 6 p. 470	44. c obj. 7 p. 477
6. d obj. 1 p. 456	19. a obj. 3 p. 462	32. b obj. 6 p. 470	45. c obj. 8 p. 480
7. b obj. 1 p. 456	20. d obj. 3 p. 463	33. d obj. 6 p. 470	46. d obj. 8 p. 480
8. c obj. 2 p. 457	21. d obj. 4 p. 464	34. c obj. 6 p. 471	47. a obj. 8 p. 480
9. d obj. 2 p. 457	22. b obj. 4 p. 464	35. a obj. 6 p. 471	48. d obj. 9 p. 482
10. b obj. 2 p. 457	23. a obj. 4 p. 464	36. a obj. 6 p. 474	
11. a obj. 2 p. 458	24. c obj. 5 p. 466	37. c obj. 7 p. 476	
12. b obj. 2 p. 458	25. d obj. 5 p. 467	38. b obj. 7 p. 476	
13. c obj. 2 p. 459	26. c obj. 5 p. 467	39. c obj. 7 p. 477	

Essay Question 13.1: The Effectiveness of Psychotherapy

■   Identify the reasons you think psychotherapy works. These may include: psychotherapy offers a chance to reflect on life's problems in a safe environment, it offers a sense of control over one's problems, it provides new ways of coping with and understanding stress.

■   Select at least two of the previously discussed concepts and describe their roles in depth.

■   Remember, Esyenck's early study that suggested that psychotherapy was no more effective than being on a waiting list.

Essay Question 13.2: Should Electroconvulsive Therapy Be Banned?

■   Describe your response to the idea of electrical shock being passed through your brain as a means of therapy. Would you want this to be done?

■   What assumptions are made about the harm or benefit of using ECT? Do we assume that it must have some unseen long-term effect?

CHAPTER 14: Answer Key

FILL IN THE BLANK	MATCHING				TRUE-FALSE
1. social	11. b	20. b	29. c	38. g	1. F obj. 2 p. 490
2. affect; behavior; cognition	12. c	21. a	30. a	39. d	2. T obj. 3 p. 492
3. vicarious	13. a	22. d	31. b	40. b	3. T obj. 4 p. 494
4. schemas	14. d	23. e	32. d	41. f	4. F obj. 5 p. 497
5. situational; dispositional		24. c		42. e	5. T obj. 6 p. 500
6. conformity	15. a		33. e	43. h	6. T obj. 7 p. 503
7. compliance	16. c	25. b	34. d	44. a	7. T obj. 8 p. 504
8. catharsis	17. e	26. d	35. b	45. c	8. T obj. 10 p. 511
9. aggressive cues	18. b	27. c	36. a		9. F obj. 11 p. 514
10. interpersonal attraction	19. d	28. a	37. c		10. F obj. 14 p. 524
					11. F obj. 15 p. 526

MULTIPLE CHOICE

1. c obj. 1 p. 489	14. c obj. 4 p. 494	27. a obj. 7 p. 504	40. d obj. 10 p. 512
2. c obj. 1 p. 489	15. d obj. 4 p. 495	28. d obj. 7 p. 504	41. b obj. 11 p. 514
3. b obj. 1 p. 489	16. d obj. 5 p. 497	29. b obj. 7 p. 504	42. c obj. 11 p. 514
4. d obj. 1 p. 489	17. d obj. 5 p. 498	30. d obj. 7 p. 504	43. d obj. 11 p. 514
5. b obj. 2 p. 490	18. b obj. 5 p. 498	31. b obj. 8 p. 505	44. a obj. 12 p. 517
6. c obj. 2 p. 490	19. b obj. 5 p. 498	32. c obj. 8 p. 506	45. d obj. 12 p. 517
7. a obj. 2 p. 490	20. c obj. 6 p. 499	33. c obj. 9 p. 506	46. c obj. 12 p. 517
8. b obj. 2 p. 491	21. d obj. 6 p. 499	34. c obj. 9 p. 508	47. b obj. 12 p. 517
9. c obj. 3 p. 492	22. a obj. 6 p. 499	35. b obj. 9 p. 508	48. c obj. 12 p. 517
10. d obj. 3 p. 492	23. c obj. 6 p. 499	36. b obj. 9 p. 509	49. d obj. 13 p. 521
11. a obj. 3 p. 493	24. b obj. 6 p. 499	37. b obj. 9 p. 509	50. a obj. 13 p. 521
12. d obj. 4 p. 494	25. a obj. 6 p. 500	38. a obj. 10 p. 511	51. a obj. 15 p. 525
13. b obj. 4 p. 494	26. b obj. 7 p. 503	39. a obj. 10 p. 512	52. c obj. 15 p. 525

Essay Question 14.1: The Consistency Between Attitudes and Behavior

■   Situations that might be relevant are those in which you did something, like go on a date with someone, that you really were not that interested in doing. The mismatch between the attitude (lack of interest) and behavior (going out), while not that great does illustrate the problem.

■   Describe how you felt after the specific incident or act and whether you changed your attitudes (She/he is actually pleasant to be with). Or perhaps, you wait until after the behavior to form your attitude (consistent with the self-perception theory).

■   Be sure to make the difference between the two views clear.

Essay Question 14.2: Should Pornography Be Banned?

■   R-rated films have more violence against women, and X-rated movies are more explicitly sexual.

■   The evidence needs to be clear regarding whether the link is with pornography and actual violence or between media violence and actual violence.

■   Distinguish banning pornography for moral reasons and banning it for safety reasons.

CHAPTER 15: Answer Key

FILL IN THE BLANK	MATCHING	TRUE-FALSE

1. stress
2. psychosomataic disorders
3. posttraumatic stress
4. defense mechanisms
5. self-fulfilling prophecies
6. discrimination
7. androgens; estrogen
8. socialization
9. collectivism
10. nuclear arms freeze
	11. a 16. b 21. b 28. c
	12. e 17. c 22. c 29. d
	13. b 18. e 23. d 30. b
	14. d 19. a 24. a 31. e
	15. c 20. d 25. e 32. a
	                   26. g
	                   27. f 33. d
	                         34. a
	                         35. e
	                         36. b
	                         37. c
		1. F obj. 1 p. 534
		2. F obj. 2 p. 536
		3. F obj. 2 p. 538
		4. T obj. 3 p. 539
		5. F obj. 4 p. 544
		6. F obj. 5 p. 546
		7. T obj. 6 p. 550
		8. T obj. 7 p. 550
		9. F obj. 11 p. 558
		10. T obj. 10 p. 559

MULTIPLE CHOICE

1. b obj. 1 p. 534 2. b obj. 1 p. 536 3. a obj. 1 p. 534 4. d obj. 1 p. 534 5. c obj. 1 p. 534 6. d obj. 1 p. 535 7. d obj. 1 p. 536 8. b obj. 1 p. 536 9. a obj. 2 p. 537 10. b obj. 2 p. 537 11. d obj. 2 p. 538 12. d obj. 2 p. 538 13. b obj. 2 p. 538	14. b obj. 2 p. 540 15. c obj. 3 p. 540 16. b obj. 3 p. 541 17. c obj. 4 p. 545 18. b obj. 4 p. 544 19. a obj. 4 p. 544 20. d obj. 5 p. 546 21. d obj. 5 p. 546 22. b obj. 5 p. 546 23. a obj. 5 p. 546 24. a obj. 6 p. 546 25. d obj. 5 p. 547 26. a obj. 6 p. 550	27. c obj. 7 p. 549 28. d obj. 7 p. 551 29. a obj. 7 p. 552 30. c obj. 7 p. 552 31. c obj. 7 p. 552 32. b obj. 7 p. 552 33. a obj. 8 p. 554 34. b obj. 8 p. 555 35. c obj. 8 p. 555 36. b obj. 9 p. 558 37. d obj. 10 p. 557 38. c obj. 11 p. 559	

Essay Question 15.1: Stress and Its Effects

- Tabulate the stress score for yourself using Table 15-1.

- Determine whether you are at risk or normal. Do the events that contribute to your score seem part of the normal course of life, or have you experienced an unusual number of things recently?

- Identify any recent illnesses that would have been influenced by the stress.

Essay Question 15.2: Value of an Industrialized Country

- Determine the role played by a culture that is individualistic versus collectivistic relative to its economic status in the world.

- Examine how the general value orientation held by people living in a specific culture affects behavior.

- Compare cultures that stress the joint welfare of all its members with a culture that is more individualistic.